LETTERS
to a
WAR BRIDE

LETTERS *to a* WAR BRIDE

A Young Battalion Surgeon Comes of Age in War-Torn Europe

TIMOTHY MCKAY

Mill City Press, Minneapolis

To Linda

Timothy F. McKay

July, 2016

Mill City Press, Inc.
322 First Avenue N, 5th floor
Minneapolis, MN 55401
612.455.2293
www.millcitypublishing.com

ISBN-13: 978-1-63413-624-2
LCCN: 2015909691

Distributed by Itasca Books

Edited by Kristin Swan
Cover Design by Alan Pranke
Typeset by Colleen Rollins
Cover: Captain R. James McKay, Jr.

Printed in the United States of America

Contents

Preface

In 1999, not long after my mother's death, my brothers and I found a box of letters with a note on top in my mother's handwriting: "Letters to a War Bride." The box held a collection of nearly all the letters my father wrote to her during his 20 months in Europe during and after World War II, a period in our parents' lives that we knew little about. My mother came from a family with an extraordinary sense of history. They were prolific writers of letters and poetry, and I suspect there are few American families as well documented as hers. My mother must therefore have realized the importance of the history contained in these letters. Her impulse may have been to burn them, as so many war brides did; after all, they were very personal love letters intended for her eyes only. Instead, she censored them, leaving intact the bulk of each. The final paragraph of almost all the letters has been cut off; one can assume what those paragraphs contained.

As the youngest of four sons and the unofficial family historian, I was intrigued by the letters. I had wanted to know more about my father, and here was an opportunity to penetrate his reserve. In 2011 and 2012, I spent many days with him, reading aloud all the letters, which total several hundred. When a passage stimulated a memory from my father, I recorded whatever he had to say. Like most combat veterans, my father shared very little of his wartime experiences until the last few years of his life. He had a few amusing anecdotes he would tell occasionally, stories that gained embellishments with years and telling. The letters provided an ideal avenue to go back with him to a time he had put away in a tightly sealed compartment of his mind. As he sat and listened, I could see him transported back to that time, and he was almost eager to flesh out the history for me. The real origins of his embellished anecdotes were revealed in the letters, as he had written about the actual events in real time. One example is a story he always told as if it had happened to him personally. He described interrogating a German officer about the impending end of the war when a large flight of allied bombers came over. According to my father, the officer spat on the ground and said, with a snarl, "Propaganda." Then from one of the envelopes came a cartoon cut from *Stars and Stripes*, the military newspaper. The cartoon depicted the same anecdote. He had obviously enjoyed it, mailed it to my mother, and over the years transformed it into a personal memory. Letters strip away the tricks played by memory over several decades, which is what makes them so valuable to historians. What follows are excerpts from my father's letters (and a few of my mother's), with brief explanatory text added by me when I thought it would add to the reader's appreciation of the story. I have included a few letters my father wrote to his parents, particularly in the period between when he joined the army and when he shipped out. The letters were almost all handwritten. The excerpts preserve the writers' original wording and spelling, including return address and salutation. Where I have omitted passages, I have indicated this with ellipses. Anything I have added to the letters themselves for clarification is enclosed in brackets. My father's signature appears at the bottom of the letters that my mother left intact. In selecting from among the hundreds of pages of correspondence my mother saved, I have tried to include enough to give the reader a feel for the times, the war, the life of a battalion surgeon, and the personal emotions, impressions, and challenges faced by a husband and an army doctor stationed a long way from home for a protracted period. What emerges is a portrait of a man very much in love, driven to practice medicine, living through the most intense training possible as he dealt with all the medical challenges a war could throw at him.

My father died the morning after Thanksgiving, in 2012. I was with him, and the sense of the life he had lived was overpowering. His full lifetime of accomplishments and the family he left behind stand as testament to his remarkable ambition and ability. Four months after his death, I spent a day at the National Archives in Beltsville, Maryland, reading every surviving record of the 275th Engineer Combat Battalion, and searching all of the records of the 75th Division for clues about the 275th's activities. The Battalion records are amazingly scanty. The best references are the Monthly Action Reports, which were filed each month from January 1945 until the end of the war in May. The Archives contain only two photos attributed to the 275th, both of which appear in the book. I have used photos from other units where they illustrate activities similar to those of my father's battalion.

In the spring of 2014, I spent 25 days in Europe visiting all the sites that were important to my father during and after the war. I had prepared for months, making contacts via email, searching for individuals from the letters, and planning a route with all the places my father had been. The journey was magical. I found most of the specific places he mentioned, and talked with many people connected in some way to my father or the 75th Infantry Division. Now I can visualize where he was: the terrain, the villages and cities, the fields and forests. I have a feel for the people in all four countries he was stationed in—Belgium, France, Holland, and Germany—with a taste of their national and regional personalities. I have a handle on where the fighting occurred in relation to where my father was, and what the three companies of his battalion were doing at various times.

My own family joined me in Alsace and Champagne. Watching my daughters search for and find the foxholes where their grandfather and his battalion spent a frigid night dug into the snow and frozen soil of an Alsatian wood gave me an overwhelming sense of the continuity of history. If I didn't know before, I certainly knew then why I was writing this book.

Introduction

My father, Robert James McKay Jr., was born in New York City in 1917, just six months after the United States entered the "war to end all wars." He grew to adolescence in the prosperous 1920s, and was educated largely during the not-so-prosperous 30s. The 40s brought medical school, immediately followed by World War II.

Jim McKay was, above all else, a doctor. He knew when he was eight years old that he wanted to be a doctor. As Dr. R. J. McKay Jr. he was a legendary figure in American pediatrics. As plain old Jim McKay he was a great-grandfather, grandfather, father, brother, son, and husband. He grew up in rural New Jersey while his father worked in New York City for the International Nickel Company, commuting most days by train. The family's country home was in Basking Ridge and was known simply as "the farm." He went to private schools from the age of 8, and from the age of 12, Jim attended boarding school at Lawrenceville, about 40 miles south of Basking Ridge.

He was a precocious student and an enthusiastic participant in all the school had to offer, from sports of all kinds to cultural events and an active social life. In 1934, at age 16, Jim graduated from Lawrenceville. He took a year off before starting Princeton, spending time with his Montgomery grandparents in Indiana in the summer and fall. In January 1935, Jim sailed to Europe, spending a couple of weeks in England with a family friend, then four months living with a family in Frankfurt, Germany. His goal was to immerse himself in the culture and learn the language. It was two years into Hitler's regime, and Jim got his first exposure to this highly regulated society, and the already pervasive oppression.

At Princeton, Jim took a heavy course load his freshman and sophomore years in order to be able to spend his junior year abroad, this time in Munich. He soon bought a motorcycle despite being forbidden to do so, and proceeded to pursue his usual hectic lifestyle, socially, athletically, and academically. Elected president of the 25-member Junior Year group, Jim was stretching his wings at the age of 20. Jim reported that the Gestapo searched his apartment in preparation for a visit by Hitler. Jim did a lot of travelling, and with his extensive knowledge of the country from his previous stay there three years earlier, he was able to take full advantage of his time in Germany. He also visited France, improving his proficiency in a language he had studied for eight years. By the time he returned home, Jim had a unique perspective, both practical and political, on European culture. He knew the German people, language, and geography very well. He also knew that war was inevitable.

Jim graduated from Princeton in 1939 and went on to Harvard Medical School, just as Germany invaded Poland. At Harvard, Jim worked hard, but played even harder. In one letter home he describes a weekend:

> Dear Mom and Dad, . . . We had lab until 12:30, then took the afternoon off. Played two hours of tennis, put the windshield on the motorcycle, got my new suit fitted, went to three beer parties, ate supper, and took Hennie Adams out dancing. . . . Sunday morning I worked and played squash, then Dan [Jim's brother] and I went out to Blackfans for a very enjoyable lunch. There were a couple of doctors there. Took Dan back to Tech [MIT], played touch football afterward and got back to the med school at 4. Worked until 6:30, took Hennie to an early movie on the motorcycle, and was in bed at 10:30. That completes the news.

Jim was in the habit of dating nurses on weeknights, because they had to be back in quarters by 10 p.m., which gave him some time to study afterwards. At one point Jim was dating five different girls at the same time, each of whom thought she was the special one. They soon found each other out, however, and Jim found it hard to get a date for a while. One can't help but think of Hawkeye Pierce from the *M*A*S*H* television series (Jim's favorite TV show).

Medical school was accelerated beginning in 1940 in order to graduate as many doctors as possible for the military. Jim signed up as an officer in the Army Medical Corps Reserve in the fall of 1940, out of patriotism, his knowledge of Hitler's oppression, his expectation that all doctors would be taken into the military, and the hope that his early registration would help him.

Jim first met Liz Foote in the summer of 1941, when he needed a date at the last minute for a double date with his roommate, Brownie, and his fiancée, Ditty Wheeler. Ditty was an old friend of Liz's from her days at Buckingham School. Ditty suggested that Jim call Liz, and she accepted, mainly for the chance to see Ditty. Liz had a boyfriend at the time, so she wasn't interested in dating Jim again that fall. Jim and Liz then dated intermittently through the winter. In the summer of 1942, Jim was sitting around with Jack Wiley on a Saturday, with nothing particular to do. They decided to get dates for the evening, and Jim thought of Liz, whom he hadn't seen in a few months. Jim called Liz at her home in Belmont, and she and a classmate, who was living in the Foote house at the time, agreed to go out. The four of them went to a beach south of Boston, where they spent the afternoon walking and talking. Jim and Liz had a wonderful time, began dating regularly, and soon fell in love. In December, they got engaged. In March, Jim graduated from medical school and in April started his accelerated internship in pediatrics at Babies Hospital in NYC. On May 30, 1943, he and Liz were married at Kings Chapel in Boston by her father, Unitarian minister Henry Wilder Foote II. The couple lived at 128 Fort Washington Avenue, just east of 10th Avenue in the Washington Heights section of Manhattan, with a view of the Hudson River.

Fig. 1.1. Liz at Vassar in 1940.

Liz was educated at Vassar and received her masters degree in social work from Simmons College. Shortly after their honeymoon, she found a job as a medical social worker at Presbyterian Hospital in New York, the same hospital where Jim was a pediatric intern. She kept the job through the war, balancing her professional competence with the fear for her husband that permeated her being. In one letter to Jim she said it all: "Oh God, what will it be like to live without fear again?"

After the war their letters were full of plans for a family and speculation on where to settle down. As Jim dealt with the headaches of medical care for the occupying American troops, he dreamed of getting back to Liz and beginning his career.

Chapter One

Training: Spring and Summer 1944

Ten months after his wedding, Jim landed in the army in March of 1944. Commissioned as a First Lieutenant, he started with six weeks at the Army Field Service School at Camp Carlisle in Pennsylvania, where orientation for medical officers took place. They learned military tactics, the use of map and compass, navigation at night, and other skills. They had lectures of all sorts, including one on combat medicine from a major who had been at Guadalcanal. The lesson on army regulations ended up being the most useful for Jim. The major stressed the need to read regulations as they came through, because there are regulations for everything in the army, and no matter what a medical officer might need in the army, somewhere he could find a regulation permitting it. Aside from considerable experience in all aspects of medicine, the army taught Jim administration and how to deal with bureaucracy, skills he would use all his life.

Carlisle Barracks, PA
March 20, 1944

Dear Mom and Dad . . . We get up at 6:30 every morning and don't stop till midnight and are rushed every minute. Last Saturday night I spent two hours on the train & 7 hours yesterday doing the assigned work for today (It was assigned Sat. afternoon)!!! . . .

Outside of not having time to turn around, I like Carlisle fine & am getting a lot out of it. They really teach us a lot of good practical stuff, which will be useful outside as well as inside the army. There is not as much stress on physical conditioning as I would like, but you can't have everything. . . .

We are doing military tactical problems now. . . .

Liz spent two weekends with Jim while he was at Carlisle, staying at Jim's brother Dan and sister-in-law Alice's home in Philadelphia. Following Army Field Service School, doctors were sent for six weeks to an army hospital to learn army medicine. Jim was assigned in mid-April to LaGarde General

Hospital in New Orleans. Liz was able to take a leave of absence from her job at Presbyterian Hospital in New York to join him. They had six pleasant weeks there with a light workload.

La Garde General Hospital,
New Orleans, LA., April 17, 1944

Dear Mom & Dad:

As Liz probably wrote you, we had a not unpleasant trip down and were very fortunate in finding a nice room about 15-20 minutes from the hospital on the bus, including the walk at both ends. We did not have kitchen privileges at first but Liz talked the landlady (Mrs. Sere) into it, so we eat there over half the time. . . . The house is small and new in a new section which is much cooler than in town. We have a nice corner room facing north & west with a big modern bathroom right next to it. Mr. & Mrs. Sere are a 70 year old French couple (Canadian French) with no children. . . .

La Garde is a very pleasant place to work, partly because there isn't much work to do. . . . Since we only get about 1 patient a day . . . In the afternoon we have two hours of lectures and 1 hour of physical training. . . .

We have enjoyed eating downtown several times but it usually costs $4-$5. . . . we pay $15 a week for our room.

La Garde General Hospital,
New Orleans, LA., May 2, 1944

Dear Dad and Mom . . .

Last week I was assigned to the Neuro Psychiatric Service. It was very interesting. This week I am on Surgery & will stay here for another one. I'm on the G-U ward = kidney stones & related disorders. Both of these services are a lot busier than the contagious ward.

Last Wednesday we had a short road march in the afternoon. One Thursday we rode out in trucks about 40 miles to the infiltration course (where you crawl across a space of ground with barbed wire strung across in spots with machine gun fire over your head & land mines exploding around you. That was not bad at all, especially as it was a beautiful clear day . . .

The tennis is not so hot. I have played doubles twice at the New Orleans Country Club with my partner, Major Mathers.

Sunday we had dinner at the Soules', friends of Liz's father and mother, over near Tulane. It was most enjoyable. Liz is not working, since she could not get a half time job. She comes out to the hospital most of the day every Monday and does Red Cross work with the officers' wives.

In early June, Jim went from New Orleans to Camp Breckenridge in Henderson, Kentucky, where he was assigned as medical officer to the 275th Engineer Combat Battalion of the 75th Infantry Division, with which he served until the end of the war. The 75th division had three infantry regiments of 5,000 men each, and each regiment consisted of three battalions. Each battalion comprised three companies of 150 men each, plus a Headquarters and Supply Company (known as H & S), which might have 50 men. Known as the battalion surgeon, Jim was the only doctor for the 500 men of the battalion, assisted by medics in each company. The battalion surgeon provides all basic care as well as public health functions such as inspections of dining facilities and VD education for the troops. Camp Breckinridge served three divisions, or 45,000 men. Soldiers at Camp Breckenridge went through a mild form of boot camp, and received basic training. Jim and Liz lived in an apartment there. Jim was very busy for the first few weeks.

Jim at Camp Breckinridge in 1944.

Camp Breckinridge, KY.
June 8, 1944

Dear Dad and Mom: It was good to see Ma again. I was only sorry that her BOSS could not have been with her. We sure appreciate having the car, and also Ma's driving out with Liz. I am sorry to have so little time to spend visiting, but we're really in the Army here. Things have been even worse since Ma left. Last week I was only home 3 times, but this week it has only been once. . . .

All this week we have been working like beavers. We have been expecting a 2nd Army inspection the past two days. Everyone has been beating their brains out getting ready for it . . .

. . . The woman at the Red Cross in Henderson said she was terribly short of case workers for home relief—consisting mostly of family interviews, etc., but said she just didn't think Liz would be able to do the work since she had never worked for the Red Cross. . . . From the sound of it, Liz could do about twice what this woman does and do it better, but the woman is just too G-D dumb to see it or else is too scared of being shown up. It is just the same attitude that the doctors I have run into from the middle west have, as a general rule. Your vaunted middle-western educational institutions certainly fail far more than the eastern ones in teaching liberality. They are so convinced that their "down-to-earth" methods are better than any of that fancy eastern stuff that they stubbornly maintain their ignorance by refusing to learn from any one from the east. . . . At least they don't try to skin you alive like the New Orleanians did.

We are still on the fence about whether or not to join the country club in Henderson. . . .

Liz ended up working four hours a day in a nursery school. In July, Jim got leave, and he and Liz went home to the farm in Basking Ridge for several days. On their return, the 275th set up camp 26 miles from Henderson on the Green River for training in launching boats, river crossings, and engineering problems.

Somewhere near the Green River, Ky.
July 27, 1944

Dear Dad and Mom:

Our trip out was fine until we got to Terre Haute and had the Evansville train pull out while we were running for it. We then had to wait 5 hours to sit on our bags in the aisle to Evansville, arriving about 8 P.M. We went directly to our new apartment which is <u>very</u> nice—to my way of thinking just what we wanted, barring the rather slender kitchen.

The river training had already started on Sunday so I came out here Monday. . . . We are about 26 miles from Henderson. The Green River is about as wide as the Delaware up around Sussex County, but is 35–40 feet deep. The water is a bright deep green and clean, so that it is nice to swim in. For me the business is little more than a camping and fishing trip at Uncle Sam's expense. Fletcher, my driver, is here and sort of acts as guide. He fixes my bed up at night and clears everything up in the AM, catches bait, paddles the boat etc., etc. It is not only a fishing trip, but DE LUXE !!!" . . .

Jim's driver was an 18- or 19-year-old Kentuckian named W. S. Fletcher Jr., known as Fletch, who was a real country boy from the hills and hollers of Kentucky. The two men were an unlikely pair, but hit it off and worked well together all through the war.

275th Engineer Combat Battalion,
Camp Breckinridge, KY
August 8, 1944.

Dear Folks:

Welcome letters arrived from both of you Saturday. Both the fishing rod and the spinners and other artificial bait arrived yesterday. . . . Last night I caught a 2 1/2 pound catfish on the bucktail spinner casting!! He struck and felt just like a bass. . . .

Last week I spent mostly in garrison due to a terrific pile of routine and administrative work. This week I am again in the field but have to divide my time between two bivouac areas 20 miles apart. The result is that I spend 4–5 hours a day riding a truck and do not have nearly enough time for fishing or swimming.

We had the Colonel for dinner Saturday night. Sunday evening we had juleps with Mel and Maria Osborne. The Colonel wishes to be remembered to Ma and says that he wishes he had been able to see more of her here.

Weekend before last we bought a set of golf clubs and bag—used—at the Country Club for $30. They seem to be good clubs and are of such a size that Liz and I can both use them. I thought that she might have one more thing to occupy her if she had the clubs. I am trying to get her to take a few lessons. They are only $1 per half hour lesson.

Hope that Pop is feeling better and Ma is not overdoing it. Mike the Reb sounds fine. Who do you think he looks like now?

Love,

Jim.

"Mike the Reb" was Jim's nephew, Mike McKay, son of Jim's brother Dan and his wife, Alice. Dan became an engineer and during the war was in the Navy, stationed in shipyards in the US. At the time of Reb's birth, they were living on board a small boat moored in the Delaware River. Dan, Alice, and Reb spent a fair amount of time at the farm in Basking Ridge.

Camp Breckinridge, KY
September 12, 1944.

Dear Folks: . . .

The last two weeks of my three weeks in the field turned into a rat-race as I had to hold sick call both in camp and out at the river 30 miles away the first week of the last two, and the last week I had sick call at two bivouac areas about 20 miles apart. The "racing" back and forth all the time at 25 miles an hour (our speed limit) really got me down and I had one hell of a belly ache by the time we got back to camp. I slowed down, though, and started to take some care about my eating and it cleared up. We are eating with the companies now instead of in an officers mess, and the food is terribly greasy for my stomach's consumption. You know what greasy food has always done to me. Now I only eat the items without much grease and get along OK. If it wasn't possible to eat Liz's good food in addition, I'd starve, though. However, when we get in the field we'll eat a uniform pre-cooked canned ration a good deal of the time. While that is monotonous, it at least agrees with me so I'm not too worried.

Last week the Colonel started us in again having exercises at 5:45 AM, and that is driving every one nuts. He is on leave this week, so we aren't having them. . . .

Liz has been working in a nursery school, which keeps her occupied at least part of the time. She works about 4 hours a day. . . .

I am gaining a good deal of valuable experience in a lot of ways. For instance, I would not be scared to go into general practice now. My work here is very like it in a lot of ways. The past two weeks I have had the medical care of 3 battalions. . . .

Lots of love,
Jim

MEDICAL DETACHMENT
275th ENGINEER COMBAT BATTALION
Camp Breckinridge, Ky. APO #451

27 October, 1944.

Dear Dad: . . .

HAPPY BIRTHDAY!!!!!

On the occasion of your 57th birthday tomorrow, . . . thank you for the timely, pertinent, excellent advice which you have given, together with the admirable restraint with which you have dispensed it. . . .

As you have probably gathered by now, the last weeks have been hectic for Liz and me. The greatest part of the actual work involved is now over, but not the mental strain. I am more fortunate than many, because, if I have to be in the Army, my present job is about the best I could have. If one has to be in, I think the place to be is with troops. There is an amazing amount of independence and responsibility in my job, and the few people to whom I am responsible are all people whom I find it very easy to work for. While many of our officers leave much to be desired from a social and congenial point of view, I'm sure that would be true anywhere, and there are some with whom it is not bad at all to get along. I like the men in my detachment and the respect and liking appears to be mutual.

The same goes for the men in the battalion as a whole. The officers of the Medical Battalion, the big and entirely medical unit of the division, are a good bunch of guys whom I know pretty well and with whom I get along fine, with one or two exceptions. . . .

Liz and I have not done anything in particular lately except to try to have as much time together as possible. The longer we are married the more I love her and the better wife I am convinced she is. I hope that you and Ma feel the same way.

They are lining up for retreat now, so I will have to close this.

Much love to both you and Ma, and again, HAPPY BIRTHDAY!

Jim

The division received orders to ship out in early October, and Liz drove back east with other officers' wives. Twelve hours after they left, the orders were changed and the division remained at Camp Breckinridge, and Liz returned for another couple of weeks in Henderson before the division actually left.

When the 75th finally left Kentucky, they were staged at Camp Shanks on the Hudson River awaiting departure, and Jim saw Liz one more time in New York, arriving at his parents' apartment at five one afternoon, leaving at four the next morning to get back to camp.

Chapter Two

Off to War: November 1944

Jim's battalion shipped out on the *Aquitania*, which was a large, fast, British ship, the largest of the Cunard Line. The ship was part of a convoy that took nine days crossing. Convoys were routinely harassed by German submarines and so took random zig-zag routes across the North Atlantic. This convoy met no trouble. They landed at Greenock, Scotland, near Glasgow, about November 21, 1944. On the ship was a group of officers ostensibly there to prepare for a new army to come to Europe, but it turned out that the "new army" was a security ruse to scare the Germans.

14 Nov 44

Dearest Liz:

Today I spent a lazy day, mostly just sitting around and playing poker, at which, after many ups & downs, I finally lost my limit of $5.00 & quit. Had a few patients only, all with very minor ailments.

In spite of the fascination of those good and bad poker hands, sweetie, your husband still found time to miss his wife. It will sure be a relief when the war is over and we can be relatively certain of seeing each other regularly—at least every other night. This business certainly makes the hospital seem easy in that respect, doesn't it?

The food today relaxed a bit from the apex it hit yesterday, but was still good. Again, I'll sure be happy eating your meals when the time comes around, no matter how good these meals may be.

Liz, in case any of my letters have a big hole cut out of them, don't worry about what you miss, it won't be much, as I censor my own letters & am trying to be as strict with myself as with the men. The result will be that there won't be much there, even if it does turn out to be censorable. We are only supposed to write on one side of the paper, because if you write on both, when they cut one side they also cut out some innocent stuff on the other side.

Darling, I've stayed up too late—it's already midnight, so I better quit. Your husband misses you like hell and loves you a lot more, squizzle-puss.

Jim

This business of trying to write letters without saying anything is sure difficult. I'm sorry if they sound stilted & asinine. Perhaps I'll get onto it before too long. J.

Aboard ship
17 Nov 44

Dearest Liz:

Your two letters were received in good order & were very welcome. As you can see we are now on a ship, headed I cannot say where. It's a damn nice ship, and our set-up is very good. A bunch of us, eleven to be exact occupy a first class cabin with a private bath. The ex-first class lounge & library are open to the officers as club rooms, which makes it really very nice, tho somewhat crowded as one would expect on a ship during war time. One of the things I like are the restrictions on smoking—only on the open decks & in the lounge. I'm writing this in the library where it is not permitted. The lounge gets to where you not only need a knife but a strong, sharp one to cut the atmosphere. Our food is very good, with only two meals a day—Breakfast & supper. I get mine at 9:40 AM and 7:40 PM.

I've been playing a lot of bridge & poker. The bridge has come back very well & I've done O.K. in poker. Out of 8 times playing poker in November, I'm now $10.10 ahead. Today I was pretty woozy most of the day, but got up about 5:30 and played poker till now (10 PM) with time out for supper. I won $9.95 & quit in order to get this written before they close the library at 10:25.

Your set-up at Presbyterian sounds very good. I hope that it turns out to be as pleasant as it looks as if it would. Sweetie, I was glad to hear that you prefer your "wifely duties" to social work, in spite of the fact that it may interfere with an otherwise brilliant & satisfying career in the latter which the former could not possibly replace. . . .

Good night, Liz. I love you with all my heart.

Jim

18 Nov 44

Dearest Liz:

. . . today I have been MOD [Medical Officer of the Day]. . . . This is a great racket which I now wish I had oftener. I get midnight supper, and breakfast in bed if I want it. Also saw a movie tonight—"King's Row." . . . The tour of duty is from 11 AM to 11 AM the next morning. . . .

This afternoon I had a number of calls and took a nap. . . . Tonight I will sleep in the ship's hospital and stay here till I go off duty tomorrow morning. . . .

Reed is the battalion morale officer. He is sleeping in our room and spends all his time talking either about sex or how we are going to get sunk going over or killed when we get there, so we have now named him the "Sex and Morale Officer" and never let him forget it for a minute. . . .

This trip is really very pleasant . . . the only trouble with it is that I miss you and would enjoy it so much more if you were here to enjoy it with, and that we were just going on a honeymoon sightseeing tour together. . . .

20 Nov 44

Dearest Liz:

Yesterday I was woozier than usual, so I did not write. . . .

Today was the coldest day we have had since being on board and I've worn my sweater all day. . . .

My MOD stint wasn't bad. We had one negro come in about midnight on a stretcher, exhausted partly from seasickness & partly from putting on a good act. It kept us up a while giving him an infusion, etc.

You know, darling, in one way I miss you, but in another way I don't, because, along with the first, in spite of the separation our love is a strong, secure, & comforting thing which braces me rather than being a source of worry. I miss you like hell, but feel that your love is right here all the time, just as mine is with you all the time . . .

We don't have our footlockers with us & without thinking, like a damn fool, I left all your pictures in mine. Hell! We'll get them back when we reach our destination, however. . . .

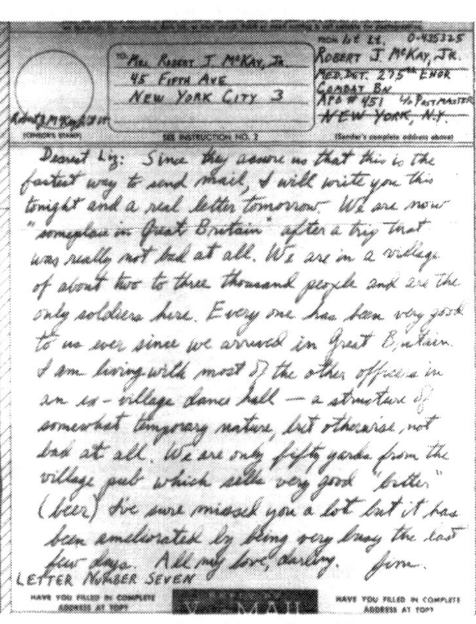

To: Mrs. Robert J. McKay, Jr.
45 Fifth Ave
New York City 3

From: 1st Lt. 0-435325
Robert J McKay, Jr.
Med. Det. 275th Engr
Combat Bn
APO # 451 c/o Postmaster
New York, N.Y.

Dearest Liz: Since they assure us that this is the fastest way to send mail, I will write you this tonight and a real letter tomorrow. We are now "someplace in Great Britain" after a trip that was really not bad at all. We are in a village of about two to three thousand people and are the only soldiers here. Every one has been very good to us ever since we arrived in Great Britain. I am living with most of the other officers in an ex-village dance hall — a structure of somewhat temporary nature, but otherwise, not bad at all. We are only fifty yards from the village pub which sells very good "bitter" (beer). I've sure missed you a lot but it has been ameliorated by being very busy the last few days. All my love, darling. Jim.

LETTER NUMBER SEVEN

HAVE YOU FILLED IN COMPLETE ADDRESS AT TOP?

V-MAIL

HAVE YOU FILLED IN COMPLETE ADDRESS AT TOP?

Jim's first V-mail to Liz.

After the *Aquitania* landed at Greenock, the men travelled by train to Wales. The 275th went to Velindre, a small village about 10 miles north of Swansea. They were billeted in houses in the village. The military developed their own mail system to handle the vast quantity of letters back and forth, in an attempt to save cargo space on the ships. V- (or Victory) mail, involved the writer using a special form that combined letter and envelope. The letter was then microfilmed down to a thumbnail-sized piece of film, shipped overseas, and blown back up, printed, and delivered. More than a billion letters were handled this way during the war, but most letters were still sent the old-fashioned way. During the war, the troops and their correspondents exchanged more than seven billion letters.

All letters from the troops abroad were censored to eliminate any mention of where they were or what the army was up to. From a letter Jim wrote after V-E Day, we were able to fill in where he had been. Those locations are shown in brackets. Jim was often the officer assigned to censor the troops' letters, including his own. He conscientiously stuck to the regulations.

[Velindre]
Letter Number Eight

Dearest Liz:

As I said in my V-Mail letter, we are now "somewhere in Great Britain" in a country village of two to three thousand people.

I can now tell you a little about our boat trip. We (the Engineers) were the first troops on the boat & acted as MPs and clean up men for the full trip. I didn't have any special duty except for being MOD one night. It was pretty soft except for a distinctly "motheaten" full colonel who pulled his rank on me and made me put him in the hospital with a cold & a 100 temperature. . . . We were on a good boat with good food & had no extremes of weather either way, though I did get a little woozy several times—but then your husband is no sailor.

The harbour where we landed was beautiful. The interplay of clouds, mist & sunlight against the green of the land running down to the water was just like the sort of painting you would like to paint. . . .

We got off the boat in the late afternoon and were taken to an officers club mess (Enlisted men to an enlisted mess) where we had supper, beer and one shot of whiskey. Afterwards we started our trip here. The countryside here is very pretty—green grass, hedgerows, holly, etc. There are a number of streams in which the fishing is said to be very good. Unfortunately the season is February to September.

The town inn is about Fifty yards from our quarters and I just interrupted this letter to go over there in order to get a couple of beers before closing time (ten P.M.) The beer (bitter) is very good and costs about twenty one cents a pint (1 shilling, tuppence). We can also get chips (French fried potatoes) to eat with the beers. Most of the boys like the dark (stout) better, but, as usual, I am drinking light (bitter).

Tonight we were drinking our bitter in front of the fire in the inn parlor with a bunch of townspeople. When Brianes & I left to go home about five minutes of ten, two girls there asked us to walk home with them as they live right near our quarters. Mine was a cute blonde "pie-face" whose husband is a doctor in the British Navy. However, from her talk about how long her husband had been away, how lonely she was, how she hoped she'd see me, how nice it would be to take a walk in the moonlight if it weren't so cold; I suspect I'd better steer clear of her or run into some embarrassing situations. I'm afraid that your husband wouldn't be much use to her because all he could think of while walking her home was how much he'd like to be walking you home, pooh-poohing the beautiful moonlight, of course. Apparently the rumors we'd heard about the women in Britain going wild as monkeys was no exaggeration. I thought I could just talk to a doctor's wife & keep it platonic, but apparently not. . . .

The men & the administrative offices are about five minutes walk from our quarters which are just on the edge of the village. The walk is along a pretty little path down a little alley between stone walls which look to be hundreds of years old, across & along a brook, through a farmyard, over a little hill, & thru a turnstile gate with a holly bush right by it. The dispensary is in the annex of one of the town churches about 75 yards from here (our quarters). Our quarters are in what used to be where the town held their dances. It is easiest to describe by saying it is just like a youth hostel in a small town. . . . I have no kick, tho, because it's probably the best we'll see for a long time. Our food is plentiful and very good. The people are all very friendly and hospitable. The overall impression is that the people are glad to see us and ready to go out of their way to be friendly and treat us right.

Up until tonight I've been so busy that there has hardly been time to miss you but I have. Every time there are five free minutes I get just as lonely as hell for you, sweetie. Our quarters are cold as hell at night and, though I have enough covers, I can't help wishing my automatic Belmont Bedwarmer was there. The war news makes me hopeful that it won't be too long till she'll be keeping me warm at night again. The scarf and sweater she made are helping a lot in the meantime. Sweetie, will you make me a pair of mittens as heavy as possible? It looks as if they may come in handy before the winter is over.

I hope you are enjoying your job & that things aren't going too badly. Have you found a place to live yet? DON'T WORK TOO HARD, especially if you are giving blood every now and then. I hope that living with my folks is not too hard on you. Have you seen D. & Alice and how does Mary June look & act pregnant? Does your job continue OK?

Goodnight, Liz, and your husband sure loves you and misses you & wishes like hell he was with his wife.

Jim

P.S. This letter and letter number seven (V-mail) are being mailed at the same time. Will you send me some air-mail stamps? J.

V-Mail
1st Lt Robert J. McKay, Jr. D-435325
Med Det 275th Eng Bat
APO #451 0/1 PM
New York, N.Y.
26 Nov., 1944

Dear Mom and Dad:

Today was so darn busy I don't know which way to turn tonight, so I'll just relax, write a couple of letters and have a beer. From my letters to Liz you undoubtedly know that I'm in Great Britain and in very pretty country. The Colonel and I drove over to a nearby town for some medical supplies today and saw some of the countryside. . . . Ma, will you please give Liz the pin with the green stone for Christmas and also a subscription to the New Yorker? I'll send a money order home to cover it and anything else I ask you to get as soon as I'm able to. Will sure miss Christmas at home. Will you please send me some air mail stamps and some stationery? The latter is almost impossible to get here. Don't either of you go overdoing now, and keep Liz from doing so. Let me hear from you. No letters yet. Love, Jim

Please send Griff's address.

Somewhere in Great Britain [Velindre]
26 Nov. 1944
Letter Number Nine

Dearest Liz:

As yet we have received no mail but the battalion mail clerk is out someplace looking for it & I'm hoping he'll find at least one letter from you. Your husband sure wants to hear from you, darling, 'cause he loves you so much.

Today was Sunday, the day of rest. I got up at five o'clock, had breakfast & censored some mail. Then had an inspection of the men's individual equipment, held sick call, had lunch, wrote out the medical & sanitation orders for this camp, drove with the Col. to a nearby town to pick up some medical supplies & arrange for entertainment for the men & dry cleaning for the officers. We had a sixteen mile drive thru beautiful country, which was very pleasant. The

Red Cross Worker in charge of the canteen where we went was an ex Montana schoolteacher with no social service experience. Incidentally, when we were on our trip here, a couple of very pretty American Red Cross girls served doughnuts & coffee. Wetendorf kept trying to get one of them to give him a kiss & I thought of the possibility of you in the same situation & shuddered. You'd better stay out of the ARC.

Will you send me a leather stationery case & lots of stationery & air mail stamps? The latter two are very difficult to come by. That is why I'm writing so small today—have no idea how long I'll have to use the same paper. . . .

Tonight at supper a couple of the boys interrupted a reverie on my part by saying "Lt McKay looks as if he were sick or something—homesick." They were right. I was thinking about you & wishing I were with you. John Green just walked by and said "Doc, you look like a manic-depressive at his lowest point." Again I was thinking of you while writing & feeling very low because you aren't here, twiddle pom.

Sweetie, I love you and miss you and all your little wifely idiosyncrasies, and I hope like hell I'll hear from you soon.

Goodnight, darling.

Jim

Let me know how long it takes to get my letters. J.

[Velindre]
V-Mail
1st Lt. Robert J. McKay, JR
0-435325 MED DET 275th ENGR COMBAT BN
c/o Postmaster, APO #451
New York, N.Y.
27 Nov. 1944

DARLING: Your letter written Nov. 19 and mailed Nov. 20 arrived this morning (AIR MAIL). It was the first mail to catch up with us and it was just like Christmas around the battalion when it came. That is the first letter I've received since leaving the US. . . . Was terribly busy today. Had sick call, made out requisitions, inspected, drove quite a ways to a station hospital, ferreted out the red cross, the MP's and the Pro Station in the same town in preparation for the men going there on pass, and talked various people out of extra supplies for our dispensary. Got back at six, ate, and then worked all evening in the PX we have set up for the enlisted men. I helped out because there was a crowd and the boys were slow figuring out the British money. Tomorrow I'm going to be away all day at a mess sanitation school. Sweetie, It was so good to hear from you and I hope it will be often now. I, too feel that nothing can phase me as long as we're together. That is why I can take the war fairly well—because to a certain extent we are even now.

All my love, Jim

Letter number ten

[Velindre]
V-Mail
1st Lt. Robert J. McKay, JR
0-435325 MED DET 275th ENGR COMBAT BN
APO #451 c/o PM
New York, N.Y
Tuesday, 28 Nov. 1944

Dearest Liz:

This is just a hurried note before I hit the hay. It is quarter of one and I just got in from the trip to the mess inspection school. It was a long trip to a city I hadn't seen before and was very interesting. Besides seeing the city we also had lunch in an old castle (completely renovated) where some troops are now staying. The Colonel has had another brainwave. He had a ten mile march this morning which only those who were busy as the dickens missed. He has now said everyone who didn't take it today will take it tomorrow. I don't mind the march much, but I am tired and have more work deadlined for tomorrow than I can do anyway. He sure knows how to pick the minus psychological moment! Darling, all the way home tonight, during a beautiful drive in the moonlight, I was thinking of you and wondered if possibly you might not be doing the same on the other end. Your husband sure misses you. Good night and I love you.

Jim

[Velindre, Wales]
Letter number eleven
29 Nov 44

Dearest Liz:

. . . Yesterday a bunch of us went to mess inspectors school . . . saw my first thatched roofs . . . The drive was really something. It was a long way to start with, and what with the combination of British roads, all narrow and running every which way, lack of specific directions, fog, and a big truck on a little road, we had quite a time, but really enjoyed it, too, as it served to show us some of the country and break the monotony. We had supper in the city we went to. . . . With the dinner we had a drink of scotch & a couple of good beers, and a barmaid whose line alone was worth the price of admission (it set us back $2.50). . . .

Hagie told me tonight that the Colonel was recommending me for promotion. I only hope that we stay put long enough for it to go through. I became eligible the twenty fifth. . . .

Jim

Somewhere in Great Britain [Velindre, Wales]
30 November, 1944

Dearest Liz:

Disappointment is rampant around here tonight, but especially in your husband's breast—I mean chest. The mail failed to materialize! . . .

Today we went on a short march which was really a lot of fun, though I had sort of sore feet to start with. . . . This afternoon I went over to the hospital in a nearby town with several men. While visiting one of my men on one of the wards I saw the first good looking nurse discovered so far. Frankly, sweetie, she didn't compare with you in looks, and even less in temperament. — One of that unpleasant type that plays up like the dickens to all the unmarried doctors and is nasty as hell to everyone else.

The Colonel told me before supper that he was going to sign my promotion papers tonight. . . .

We have our quarters in pretty good shape now. They are nice and warm (comparatively) every night and we have hot water for showers almost every day. We have plugged up a lot of crannies and done a lot of repair work. There was a negro unit here before us, we discovered, and they sure left things in a hell of a mess. It wasn't so much dirt as just letting things get run down and making no attempt to keep them in repair.

Tonight there is a dance here, but without you I have no heart to go, and with you I wouldn't want to go, probably. Darling, I was glad, too, that we got some time together other than those last days at the Officer's Club at Camp. In a way, I have a lot in common with the people here. They wall themselves up in their homes behind reserve, fences, hedges, and small windows, but at least their home life can be private. Most of the Americans don't seem to want that. . . . What the heck is a home for? — Your husband will never make a communist for that reason alone, I'm afraid, sweetie.

Tomorrow there is a formal ball being given in a nearby town by the local military gentry. I may go, as it should be a chance to meet and talk to some nice people on a somewhat higher intellectual level than is possible around here, though there are a number of nice big homes hereabouts. . . .

By the way, get Dad to take an indoor picture of you in your black evening dress sometime when you're out at the farm, will you? I don't have any pictures of my wife as a glamour girl. . . .

Jim

P.S. Wamble just came in and said the footlockers arrived tonight.

By the end of November, Allied forces were steadily pushing the German army back into Germany. Belgium was completely liberated on November 2, and southern Holland was now in Allied hands. In late November, Metz and Strasbourg, France, were liberated.

Somewhere in Great Britain [Velindre, Wales]
2 December, 1944

Dearest Liz:

. . . The dance last night turned out to be a lot of fun. It was the Home Guard Regimental Ball for that town. . . . The men were all either in uniform or evening clothes and the ladies in evening gowns. I met a number of nice people, young and old. . . . They had a lot of Paul Jones dances to start with in order to get everyone acquainted and dancing. There were a number of pretty girls and good dancers who dance in a style I could get along with. . . . We left at one-thirty, and got home about two-thirty. Most of the boys were somewhat disappointed from the lack of something beyond social intercourse, but it was fine for me and I had a lot of fun, especially as I met two sisters, who were a lot of fun. . . . We had a lot of fun dancing the "Hokey-Pokey" which is sort of an up-to-date British "Big Apple." . . .

One consolation I now have is that our footlockers did arrive the other night and I now have a full set of pictures of you. I opened the picture album now, because I just couldn't wait till Christmas to do it. Sweetie, that picture of you in a bathing suit on our honeymoon does give sort of a seductive, chorus-girl effect, but then you are a chorus girl aren't you? . . .

Good night, darling. I wish I could kiss both you and all your dimples, but I still love you very, very much.

Jim

Last month my taxable income was 166.67. For November it was $175.49. I personally received 109.52 for Oct. and $105.06 for Nov. The latter included some overseas pay and had my meals subtracted from it.

Letter number thirteen
3 December 1944
Somewhere in Great Britain [Velindre, Wales]

Dearest Liz: Today was a quiet Sunday. I went to bed at eleven last night and didn't get up till ten this morning. Also got in a one hour nap this afternoon. I made a trip over to the Station Hospital after lunch and that was the extent of my work for the day. A majority of the officers and men are in London on pass, so things are very quiet here.

. . . Incidentally, the holly leaf in yesterday's letter is a little corsage from me to you. I hope the censor doesn't remove it. Since I can't send you flowers, I'll try to send you a little something green in a letter every now and then. . . .

Tonight I played poker for the first time this month. We played for a three-pence limit. . . . Three-pence is worth about a nickel. . . .

Good-night sweetie. I love you something terrific.

Jim

If you want to knit me a pair of wool socks (heavy) I sure can use them.

On December 1, Himmler ordered the crematoriums and gas chambers of Auschwitz Concentration Camp dismantled and blown up. On the third, the British Home Guard stood down, signaling an end to the threat of German invasion of the British Isles.

Letter number fourteen 3 December, 1944
Somewhere in Great Britain [Velindre, Wales]

Dearest Liz:

Since it is only twenty two days until Christmas, I'm going to make this your Christmas letter.

Merry Christmas! Darling, I sure wish I were there with you to give you a great big Christmas hug and kiss. It won't be Christmas for me today, because I'll not only be away from home but away from you. From now on Christmas is where our family is, and that can only be where we are together.

. . . The best present would be to be with her today, but, failing that, just having you for a wife is the best thing that ever happened to me.

I don't know where I'll be this morning, but I'll be thinking of you and loving you with all my heart. . . . Away from you I just feel as if all I ever want out of life is just to live in peace with you. . . .

Don't feel lonely today, darling, because I'm going to be right there thinking of you and with you every minute of the day. . . .

Somewhere in Great Britain [Velindre, Wales]
4 December, 1944

Dearest Liz:

. . . When your husband heard he had a letter, he went running around like a little bird dog on the scent of a covey of running quail. Finally he tracked it down and you never saw a feller as happy over getting a letter from his "steady." Boy! . . .

Letter Number Sixteen [Velindre, Wales]
6 December, 1944

Dearest Liz:

. . . I took another ride in the pouring rain. Fletcher was having some pleuritic pain so I drove part of the way. I sure hope that he doesn't get sick. He's the best driver in the battalion. We missed supper, so here your husband sits without supper, having ridden in the rain all afternoon, with a bad cold, etc, etc. Oh Gawd! Life with you was never like this. . . .

On board LST [Landing Ship, Tank) off LeHavre
13 Dec., 1944

Dearest Liz, . . . At the moment I am still on the boat waiting to get off into France. It is foggy so we have been unable to dock for fear of hitting a mine or other submerged obstacle. . . . Our trip across the channel was smooth during the first half and pretty rocky during the second half. . . . Have also been playing quite a bit of poker in odd moments and am now twenty four dollars ahead so far this month! . . .

One thing I never wrote about was the apparent relaxation of morals in Britain. Any soldier who wanted to find a girl to sleep with has little or no trouble in doing so from what I observed and heard. There is, as a result, a big venereal disease campaign directed at the civilian public and especially the women. . . .

On December 10, the whole 75th Division shipped out from Dover to Le Havre. After waiting offshore for three days for favorable weather to land, they travelled to Rouen, bivouacking in a muddy field near Yvetot on December 14. A concurrent account from another battalion describes their first view of war-torn Europe: "The entrance into the harbor at Le Havre had a profound effect on us, for it brought us in close contact, for the first time, with the ravages of war. The dock facilities and the city were in shambles—piles of rubble and twisted steel. The damage we had seen in England did not begin to compare with Le Havre."[1]

From Yvetot they went by train and convoy to Tontres, Belgium. The 75th was called the "Diaper Division" because of the predominance of young 18- and 19-year-old soldiers. At the ripe old age of 27, Jim was well up the age ladder. These raw young men were soon to participate in the Ardennes, Central Europe, and Rhineland campaigns, spending a total of 94 days in combat.

The 75th Division consisted of the 289th, 290th, and 291st Infantry Regiments, the 75th Reconnaissance Troop (Mechanized), the 275th Engineer Combat Battalion, the 375th Medical Battalion, the 897th, 898th, 899th, and 730th Field Artillery Battalions, the 775th Ordnance Light Maintenance Company, the 75th Quartermaster Company, the 575th Signal Company, the Military Police Platoon, and the Headquarters Company, a total of about 10,000 men. The various battalions were assigned to different places as needed, and often the 75th was not together. More than 60 units from other divisions were assigned to the 75th at one point or another, and every combat unit of the 75th was assigned to other divisions at some point, for as little as one day, or as much as ten days. It could be whole regiments (1,500 men) at once, or a single platoon (50 men).

Chapter Three

Into Combat: December 1944, Belgium

Jim's unit, the 275th Engineer Combat Battalion, moved from Yvetot to Charleroi, Belgium, just south of Brussels, spending a night in a large barracks. The next night Jim was at Gulpen, just west of Aachen on the road to Maastricht, where they first came under fire by a strafing German plane. The battalion was commanded by Colonel Hannston, with a major who was Executive Officer. The battalion had three companies plus the headquarters company. Each company was normally commanded by a captain, and Jim commanded the medical detachment of the Headquarters (HQ) company. He was in charge of the six men at the aid station, plus the aid men (medics) in the companies. Companies A, B, and C were each assigned to support the 289th, 290th, and 291st infantry regiments, respectively, with engineering work where needed, and the HQ company set up in a fairly central spot to stay in contact with the other three companies, which were scattered over as much as 20 miles. Each company had three platoons, each with a medic, and each infantry battalion had its own doctor and aid station. The battalion surgeon sent casualties on to a clearing station for minor stuff or emergencies. The more serious cases went to the "Evac Hospital."

Each battalion filed a Monthly Action Report to division headquarters for every month it was in combat. The first covered December 1944.

15 Dec 1944

Dearest Liz: Just finished censoring all the boys' letters to their wives, so now I guess I'll have a little time to write mine. We are now somewhere in France [Yvetot] in bivouac. The battalion is in a field and we are about a hundred yards off in a little granary in the corner of a farmyard. The weather and the ground are both cold and damp, only this time there is no opportunity to get warm except by crawling in my bed roll at night. My feet are almost continually cold, though the galoshes help a lot. They have also issued them to all the men which I am glad to see. Our granary is ten by fifteen feet with a hard dirt floor—about half wet and half dry. We have covered the floor with straw bought from a neighboring farmer

SECRET

HEADQUARTERS 275TH ENGINEER COMBAT BATTALION
A.P.O. 451, U. S. ARMY

L-104

13 January 1945

APPENDIX NO. 2: CONDENSATION OF DECEMBER JOURNAL

December 1 to 20, 1944: Preparation and movement into combat.

December 21, 1944: Battalion CP located at Rickhoven, Belgium.
Platoon of Co. A ordered to join CT 289th Inf. Regt.
Platoon of Co. B ordered to join CT 290th Inf. Regt.
Platoon of Co. C alerted for attachment CT 291st Inf. Regt.
Four Engr. Reconnaissance parties departed with assigned missions in sector of Tongres, St. Trunde, Liege and Huy for Division.
Battalion moved by motor convoy to new concentration area at Chardeneux, Belgium.

December 22, 1944: Battalion closed in at Chardeneux.
Reconnaissance element sent out along L'ourthe River.

December 23, 1944: Three parties departed to reconnoiter area along L'ourthe River from Grand-Hon to Hamoir for possible vehicle crossing sites.
Received Field Order No. 1 from Division.
Liaison Officer brought message: Four German paratroopers dropped in area. Ordered to send out patrols.

December 24, 1944: Platoon of Co. C ordered to join CT 291st Inf Regt.
Co. B ordered to protect bridge at Petit Hon.
Rec'd orders to reconstruct bridge at Durbuy. Co. B assigned task.
298th Engineers attached to this battalion.
Co's. A and B attached CT 289 and 291 respectively.
Co. A ordered to construct bridge at Barvaux to carry Div. load.
Bridge at Petit-Hon strafed — no damage.
CO, Co. B reported bridge at Durbuy completed at 2030.
G-2 message rec'd: Prisoners of War in area may attempt escape with aid of paratroopers — be alert.

December 25, 1944: Co's. A and B attached CT 289 and 290.
Co. B relieved of guard of bridge at Petit-Hon.
Co. C finished Bailey bridge at Barvaux.
One platoon Co. C attached Co. B.
298th Engineers relieved of attachment (except B Co. reinforced) to remain as bridge security.
Message rec'd: Air attack expected in vicinity between 2100 & 0100.

December 26, 1944: 1ST platoon Co B reported Lt. Klacik evacuated because of shock.

December 27, 1944: Closed in town of Heyd.
49th Engr C Bn in support.

December 28, 1944: Closed in 3/4 miles NE of LaForge, Belgium
Co. C reported 3 EM killed & one man wounded by German machine gun fire in laying mine fields on 290th Infantry Regimental sector.

- 1 -

SECRET

Monthly Action Report of the 275th Engineer Combat Battalion for December 1944.

for ten francs (twenty cents) a big bundle. The men who are sleeping in pup tents in the field have also been able to make themselves straw beds. I only wish I thought we would continue to be so fortunate. Our farmer is a husky, handsome guy with flashing black eyes and a deep black moustache. He is very genial and friendly, offering us homemade brandy and cider all the time. The boys say the "brandy" is like corn liquor at home. I have had neither as they are made under conditions which scarcely could be described as sanitary. If no one gets sick from the cider, I think I'll tackle some of it as I am again suffering from your "change of residence" disease!

The French we have seen all appear poverty-stricken and confused in the sense that they seem to be just living a tough life without any aim or idea as to for what or why they are going on. In the larger towns the poorer children have obvious dietary deficiencies—though I imagine there was a good deal of that even before the war. The country kids appear considerably better off. Most of the adults look poverty-stricken and miserable, but physically pretty well off. The securing of brandy and other local delicacies is less a matter of money than of making presents of precious cigarettes, chocolate, and soap. All the women seem to be well-rouged and lipsticked, so I guess that angle has already been worked to the bone.

Our gasoline lantern just ran out of gas, so I will adjourn for a few minutes till we get it going again. While I think of it will you see if you can get some "mantles" for Coleman Lanterns — Those are the little net bags which Pop uses for his gasoline lanterns on the boat. They catch the vapor & get very bright and give off all the light. We have trouble getting them. Also, I really acutely need some heavy wool socks, size twelve. Have been absolutely unable to get any. . . .

The 75th Division had been assigned as reinforcements to a planned Allied attack to reach the Rhine in Holland, but the Germans counter-attacked first, unexpectedly, on December 16, in what became known to Americans as the Battle of the Bulge. By late 1944, Germany was unmistakably losing the war, with the Soviet Red Army closing in on the Eastern front, Allied armies advancing rapidly across France, and strategic Allied bombing wreaking havoc on German cities.

The Battle of the Bulge, so called in the US because of the westward bulging shape of the battleground on a map, lasted from December 16, 1944, to late January 1945. It was the biggest single battle ever fought by the United States Army. More than a million men fought in the battle—600,000 Germans, 500,000 Americans, and 55,000 British. Another 400,000 GIs had supporting roles. About 19,000 GIs were killed, another

20,000 captured, and 40,000 wounded. The battle was fought on an 80-mile front running from southern Belgium through the Ardennes, and down to Ettelbruck in the middle of Luxembourg. The Ardennes is part of a high region that includes the Eifel on the German side of the border, and is a picturesque mix of farmland and forest, streams and steep-sided valleys, with small villages and winding roads. The Ardennes region includes eastern Belgium, all of Luxembourg, and a small region of France. Americans refer to the tough battles fought in the various forested parts of the Ardennes region as the "Ardennes Forest"; to Europeans, this battle is known as the Battle of the Ardennes.

Hitler's real target was the British-American alliance, which he did not believe would withstand a major defeat. The surprise attack would supposedly divide British and American forces, leaving the way wide open for the Wehrmacht (German army) to swing north and seize the port of Antwerp. Thus they could cut off the main supply base for the Allied armies on the Western Front.

Hitler correctly predicted that such factors as bad weather, bad terrain, and the Christmas holiday would help him catch the Allies by surprise. The Ardennes was lightly defended by a thin line of American troops, while the bulk of Allied forces prepared for offensives in the north through Holland and in the south through Alsace. At the battle's beginning, the US Army had 80,000 men, 400 tanks, and 400 guns in the Ardennes, while the Germans attacked with 200,000 men, 600 tanks, and 1,900 guns.

On the morning of December 16, under cover of heavy fog, 38 German divisions struck along a 50-mile front. The key to German success was to be rapid advance to the Meuse River, where they could swing north into favorable terrain toward Antwerp. American resistance proved more stubborn than predicted, and shortages of war matériel, men, and especially gasoline slowed the Germans to a crawl. In the first week, they managed to push a narrow bulge into the American line back nearly to the Meuse River at Dinant and surround the town of Bastogne in Belgium. The American defense of Bastogne has become legendary.

The fighting was affected by heavy snow and record-cold temperatures, often well below zero. Hitler thought the weather would be an advantage to the Germans, who had fought through severe winters on the eastern front. The newly arrived soldiers of the 75th Division (and many others) did not have winter boots or gloves. Many casualties on both sides were from severe frostbite and hypothermia.

The 75th Division fought as part of the First Army along the Ourthe,

Aisnes, and Salm Rivers, along the northern flank of the Bulge. The 275th Engineers supported a fierce battle at Soy, Belgium, on December 16, just four days after arriving in France. The soldiers were then pinned down in very cold, snowy weather for several days.

[Rijkhoven]
Finally found it out—
20 December 1944

Dearest Liz: At this point I don't know the date or how long since I've written you. We have been very busy moving around since I last wrote and have averaged about three to four hours sleep a night only. . . . Tonight we are billeted in a country village [Rijkhoven, a few miles from Tongres, on the Maastricht-Brussels Road]. The men are in the lofts of barns and we are in rooms around town. Hagie [Jim's sergeant] and I are together in a bed just a little wider than the one we had in New York. . . . This incidentally, will be the first time I've slept in a real bed between sheets since I last saw you. . . .

Right now Hagie and I are sitting in the dining room of the people with whom Vest and McCormick are staying writing our wives as is Vest. The wife is a young woman of twenty-four who lost her arm (right) when she was hit by a German bomb. She wants to give us everything they have and is certainly succeeding in making us feel comfortable and at home. She hauls out the best of everything for us and will accept no payment. They went out and bought us cognac which is hard to get, put a clean linen table cloth on the table and give us cocoa, apples, hot water for shaving, etc. We have all shown them our pictures and they are very struck with how pretty you are, sweetie! I told them I agreed, but think you need to put on a little weight. — Incidentally, how much do you weigh now? I want to see you up to one hundred and twenty when I get back. A hundred and eight or ten is not enough for you. [Jim had been a specialist in dispensing long-distance medical advice, particularly to his mother, ever since entering medical school.] . . .

Sweetie, I bought you a birthday present in England as I mentioned before. As yet I have been unable to get it wrapped and mailed. It is a piece of tweed for a spring suit for you. There are five yards and it is thirty inch width. [Jim somehow carried this bundle of cloth through two months of combat before he got it mailed!] . . .

I spend all my sitting time while traveling thinking about you, remembering happy days spent with you, and thinking about those to come. I console myself on cold, wet, supperless nights by thinking about what we would be doing and eating if we were together, and how cozy it would be.

Good night sweetheart, I love you.
Jim

On December 21, Jim got notice of his promotion to captain from first lieutenant, as of December 16.

21 December, 1944

Dearest Liz:

Today was really a red letter day. . . . there were THREE letters from you. . . .

The other reason that today was such a red letter day was because my promotion came through! . . . All the boys in the detachment seemed greatly pleased about it as did the men and officers in the rest of the battalion. . . . One of the first sergeants, in congratulating me, said I could be a major in his army any time. That was a real compliment as he is a darn good man.

. . . we are now somewhere in Belgium and on the eve of going up into the front lines. Don't worry, though, Liz, because I will be in the very back of the front lines most of the time. I was talking to a bunch of officers from a Corps Combat Engineer Battalion the other day. They have been here since D-Day and have seen action all the way. They have had only four men wounded and one killed. The one killed was an eight-ball who was originally in the two-seventy-fifth. He was killed when he thought he'd be funny one night and scare an already shaky guard on a lonely post. He succeeded, but also got a bullet through the heart. . . .

The first night we got up into this area [Chardeneux], part of the battalion, including the medics, got lost and went up to within ten miles of the front. We had quite a thrill when a German plane strafed the road and bombed a nearby hill. His ammunition was entirely wasted, thank God. [This was the first time Jim came under fire.] . . .

The Belgians make the British, French, and Dutch look sick as far as hospitality is concerned. Here is a people which really looks upon us as its liberator and is not afraid to show it in deed as well as in work. They don't have much, but believe me, they not only want to give it to you, but insist on it. An American soldier could walk through Belgium living off the fat of the land and not pay a thing. Not only that, but he probably couldn't pay anything. Very rarely, these people will accept a gift in return, never any money. . . . There are always at least two people in each town who come out with wine, bread, or fruit (apples or pears) which they insist on your taking. . . . Believe me, the Belgians are people we don't mind helping out in a war. We KNOW they appreciate it, and it's not because they say so. If there are any square deals handed out at the end of the war, Belgium is certainly one country the fighting man is interested in getting it for. They deserve it.

We have seen a lot of beautiful country. Night before last we stayed in an enormous Victorian country chateau [near Vise] which held most of the battalion without doing much bulging. It was at the head of a beautiful grassy valley, had a big barn attached to it, and two large ponds teeming with fish, which alas, I had no time to catch.

My German is standing me in pretty good stead, and I find that my French is more than enough just to get around with. I expect that the German will come in handier and handier as we get nearer there. . . .

Belgians in the Ardennes experienced the battlefront passing through their villages four times. First the Germans rolled through in 1940. Then, in September of 1944, the Allies recaptured the area. The German counter-attack in mid-December 1944 was followed by the final liberation of the Ardennes by the Allies in January 1945. An account of the capture by the Germans of the village of Grand Halleux, Belgium (two miles north of Vielsalm), by a young resident of the village lends perspective to the scene that Jim's division was thrown into, less than a week into the German offensive. The Battle of Grand-Halleux began on December 21 and ended on December 23, 1944. Grand Halleux was re-captured by the 75th Division in murderous fighting three weeks later, when Jim's aid station was nearby. This account comes from the "Centre de Recherches et d'informations sur la Bataille des Ardennes."

My name is Marcel Jeanpierre. I was thirteen when the following events took place in December 1944. . . . Since 18 December, we had been hearing the sound of artillery and heavy weapons. . . . The intensity of fire was increasing as the days went by and the detachment of US Engineers that was billeted . . . about 200 meters from our home, . . . had suddenly set off on Sunday 17 December 1944. We had heard from a soldier, Max Pervolsky, who used to spend his evenings with us, that the German Army was counter-attacking and already was in Saint-Vith. . . . On 21 December before noon, my dad and I had gone to the center of the village where we saw US Paratroopers arriving in trucks. . . . It was very cold and the soldiers had lit wood fires in front of the town hall to keep warm. There I met a Hispano-American soldier who gave me some chocolate.

In the afternoon of 21 December, we saw coming to our house (about 300 meters from the village center to the East) a Sergeant and a party of about ten men who went to set up an outpost facing the direction of Wanne. During the evening they settled in the heated kitchen where we used to sleep on mattresses laid on the bare floor. All through the night, mamma made coffee given by the soldiers and dad discussed in German (learnt at school) with the officer of the outpost, Sergeant Willie Beaty; he was 24 and told us he had fought in Sicily, Italy, Normandy and Holland. Each time a patrol of three or four men was going out for rounds, we dimmed the oil lamp (there was no more electric current). We, that is to say, my father, my mother, my grandmother, my sister and I, did not sleep, kept awake by the curiosity and the movement. At dawn, the US soldiers rejoined their unit in the village. On that day, 22 December 1944, around midday, they came but they decided to set up in the neighboring house that was empty of its occupants.

In the afternoon, while the US Sergeant and dad were talking . . . a man was seen in a wood situated about 300 meters to the north, who was observing us; the Sergeant immediately sent a jeep to the top of the hill (cross of Ennal) on the road but in vain then he called in artillery fire. . . . It was getting dark about 1700 hours and, while the soldiers were in the house next door all the family was around the stove with an oil lamp lit on the table. About 1915 hours, bursts of submachine guns pierced the silence. My father pushed us all into a corner of the kitchen under the staircase of the first floor and that was more or less protected by a closet. A few seconds later, we are deafened by the explosion of hand grenades, the door is broken open to the road then a second explodes in the middle of the room wounding my mother and my grandmother. The table is broken, the oil lamp is hurled onto the floor, a chair lands on the stove and starts burning. Grenades explode simultaneously in the corridor at the first floor (over the kitchen-cellar) and demolish the staircase that leads down into the kitchen. The attacking Germans are howling their first names: "Johann, Manfred, Hans, etc." to the point of making our hair stand on end. Once the assault against the outpost is finished and the noises of the fighting are getting further from the village, dad starts picking up the mattresses covered with rubble and carries them to the cellar adjoining the kitchen. We grope our way into the cellar in pitch dark and we carry my grandmother who has lost much blood. About midnight, noises of boots and guttural voices echo into the kitchen, the door to the cellar is pushed then a kick throws it open. There appear three German soldiers, the first one who is a non-commissioned officer pointing a pistol forward. . . .

My father tells him then that my mother and mainly my grandmother have been wounded. The noncom says: "let me see that!" He examines briefly and concluded that it is not severe. Next he says "there are many partisans (underground men) in the area." My father: "I do not know." The noncom: "Yes, there were some in the next village (Wanne), we killed them." As a matter of fact we learned later that the SS had shot six men in Wanne on 20 December 1944. . . . After a short time, he gives a military salute and leaves the cellar. We had a narrow escape.

The next day, 23 December 1944, a radiant sun is shining but nevertheless it is cold. . . . My father and I step over the rubble in the kitchen and go and take look at the road and the neighboring houses. A lonely SS officer sees and calls us. He waves to follow him along to the house next door where the US parachutists were billetted and shows us the body of the unfortunate Sergeant curled up and holding a clod of earth in the right hand. The helmet had rolled beside him. The German tells us: "Here is the Schweinhund!" that fired at us yesterday evening when we attacked. He turns up the body by an arm and gives him a kick then he empties his pocket, takes his billfold and, after searching it, takes his comb knowing that this object is not to be found in Germany. He also steals the photo-wallet that he throws along the wall.

Another US soldier is laying [*sic*] dead in a door entrance collapsed by grenades. It is in fact the Hispano-American soldier who had given me a chocolate on the town square on 21 December. . . . we had to leave the area by order of the German Authority to go about twenty kilometers from there to Ottré, on snowcovered roads and then await the American counteroffensive.[2]

23 Dec 1944

Dearest Liz:

. . . We are in a country village [Chardeneux] so small that there is not even a store. It makes the last one practically seem like a city. I can't say I mind though, because it just makes it that much less a probable target. The Medical Detachment is set up in a small barn. We have a central part with a clear floor about thirty by fourteen feet. On one side is straw stacked from the floor up with several levels on which the men can sleep. On the other side we are separated by an eighteen inch stone and brick wall which separates us from the stable where the cows are. Over the cows is a hay loft which is reached by a ladder from our central part of the barn. We have rather a dim electric light (twenty five watt bulb), but our Coleman lantern gives off a pretty good light. We have our trailer with us, containing most of our supplies. Fletcher and Mirando sleep on the truck some distance away.

The weather has turned clear and cold. It makes it cold in our dispensary, but I don't mind it too much because it may help our troops advance, and the sooner we do, the sooner the war is over, the sooner I see you again, and therefore the sooner I can relax and be happy again.

About a week ago we were issued sleeping bags by the Army. They consist of a soft blanket bag with an inside zipper and a lightweight outer canvas. It is damn good because there is a hood on it & it can be fastened right up so as just to leave a small hole for your nose. I have put it inside my other sleeping bag.

The old Belgian whose barn we are using is friendly and hospitable as anything. Unfortunately he only possesses a three room house (all small) or we could have a real inside dispensary. However, the boys can go in and warm up from time to time.

A lot of the boys are buying wooden shoes to send home as souvenirs. If you don't mind, sweetie, I'm not going to. They are heavy, bulky, and of no earthly use. . . .

This business of being a captain is not so bad in a lot of ways. The boys really step around a lot more for you than for a lieutenant, whatever the color of the bar on his shoulders. It's amusing to watch the first lieutenants I've never seen before hop around when a CAPTAIN starts to let off steam—how are they to know he was only another lieutenant two or three days ago! . . .

Darling, I feel like rambling on all night to you, but I'm getting cold as an Alaskan rock and still have to censor the boys' letter so they'll go out tomorrow. There is also an almost perfect half moon outside which I want to look at again to remind me of you, you moonstruck female girl that I love.

Jim

Chardeneux remains a small village to this day. When I visited in 2014, it was clear that the whole village knows well the story of Christmas 1944, when every building in town housed soldiers of the 275th.

Through the cold, cloudy weather during the first week of the German advance there was no bomber support. Jim remembered the boys in the battalion deriding the Air Force crews, comfy in their English bases, calling them "fly-boys." Christmas Eve found the 275th at Barvaux Sur Ourthe (about seven miles east of Chardeneux, where Jim maintained the aid station), where they constructed a Bailey Bridge across the Ourthe. It was the second clear day on the Bulge and there was a huge air raid. The soldiers watched as bomber after bomber flew into flack from a big German anti-aircraft battery just ahead. Plane after plane went down but the bombers kept right on coming to deliver crucial air support to the hard-pressed infantry below.

That stopped any criticism of the "fly boys." The raid noticeably lessened the pressure from the Germans.

[Chardeneux]
Letter Number twenty-four (I think) 24 Dec. 1944

Dearest Liz:

Christmas Eve! . . .

It is a beautiful, clear, cold day. We have certainly not been thinking Christian thoughts this noon, but they have still been cheering to us—they are that there shouldn't be a very happy Christmas in Germany. We have been watching the U.S. Army Air Force's Christmas present to the German People go over and believe me, no one is unhappy about it. When you get over here and undergo the discomfort and unpleasantness of what this war has forced upon us and think of how different it is at home, you really boil. You feel that truly nothing is too bad to wish on the people who have wished this on us. I'm sure that the cold and discomfort of a winter campaign are going to make the fighting just that much more vicious. From our standpoint it is a good thing, because we have been, if anything, too easy on them.

Bill Mauldin cartoon, *Stars and Stripes*, US Army, 1944, from author's personal collection.

One good thing about fighting in Europe is the thickness of the population. That means that we should almost always be in reach of some sort of building for shelter. Though it is cold in the barns, it is a lot better than being outside. The family whose barn we are using have invited us in to share their warm front room with them. It is certainly appreciated, because it does give us a chance to get really warm now and then.

The family are farmers. There are the father, mother,

and eighteen year old daughter. They are very nice, simple, straightforward, hard-working people, who are scared stiff of the war and the Germans. I can't say that I blame them. . . .

The people here speak no English at all, so our French has been getting a real workout. I find that I can get along very well with mine and carry on a conversation. I get along better than anyone else in the battalion other than those who really speak French. I have trouble because I keep injecting German words into the conversation. Needless to say, they are neither understood nor appreciated. It presents quite a problem to explain to these people why I lived in Germany instead of some other country when I was in Europe before. . . .

I am enclosing the Mauldin cartoon that I think is so good. Will you please hang onto it? The guy talking in it is a personnel clerk who never comes closer than fifteen or twenty miles behind the lines and yet receives combat pay. The other is an aid man who lives in and in front of the front lines. . . .

Many people have described their wartime experiences in letters home. But very few have chronicled war for the people doing the fighting. Bill Mauldin, World War II's most famous cartoonist, is one of them. In 1943, when he was 21, Mauldin's division shipped overseas to North Africa. Mauldin had been drawing cartoons since he was a boy, and he was quickly assigned to cover the war for the *45th Division News*, and then for *Stars and Stripes*. His cartoons, featuring a scruffy pair of foot soldiers named Willie and Joe, scored an instant hit with the soldiers who saw them. Within two years, Mauldin won fame—and a Pulitzer Prize—for capturing foot soldiers' everyday experiences.[3]

Somewhere in Belgium [Chardeneux]
24 December, 1944

Dear Ma and Pa . . . Tonight is one heck of a way to spend Christmas Eve, but it could be a lot worse. We are sitting in a little Belgian village waiting for battle orders, which we expect at any time.

Christmas Day: Had to quit last night to censor the boys' letters for them so they would get off yesterday afternoon. We did not move after all, so we spent a quiet and quite pleasant Christmas Eve. It is now noon on Christmas Day. We are "in the front lines" now, but for us it is not bad as we are in the rearmost part of the forward echelon. We are close enough to know there is a war going on and to be ready to duck at any moment, but apparently we will actually be under fire very little of the time. I think this is probably the safest spot there is in any combat unit. We were bombed and strafed once at night, but we had plenty of warning. It wasn't so bad, though it does make the heart beat a little faster. Our battalion and detachment morale is very high, and I think we're going to do all right.

Our aid station is in a Belgian Village so small that there is not even a store. There is an eleventh century church, however. We have the station in a barn with straw on one side of us and cows and horses beyond a wall on the other side. The people are very friendly and we now spend all our time in their kitchen, which is nice and warm. It is a great relief as we have been thoroughly cold and wet for some time. I hope that we will be able to get a building with heat and light for our dispensary from now on. The Belgians really appreciate the Americans and seem glad to let us share anything they have, and when we get to Germany we will just commandeer what we need.

My French is getting a good workout here, as the people speak no English. We really like the Belgians. They don't have much but they're willing to share the shirts off their backs with us. Every time we go thru a town, there are always at least two or three people who come out to give something to the American soldiers.

Yesterday and today have been beautiful clear days, which have enabled our Air Force to give the Germans a nifty appropriate Christmas present each day. As one of the officers said, when those boys start coming over up here you're so glad to see them you don't care if they make them all generals.

Last night, not having a Christmas tree to trim, we spent the evening giving each other haircuts and shaves. We had quite a hilarious time doing it.

Our food is very good and they keep it coming right to us. My health is excellent.

In a later letter Jim describes how the Belgians obtained tinsel for their Christmas decorations. "When the bombers fly over little strips of the thin metal covering them are torn off and are perfect tinsel. So the kids just gathered it up in the fields and decorated their trees with it!"

In contrast to the cheerful tone adopted in his Christmas Eve/Day letter to his parents, Jim's Christmas letter to Liz was a downer. He was in combat, grumpy, missing home, and frustrated with the waste of war. He saw his first battle wound on Christmas Eve, a shrapnel wound of the shoulder that had laid bare the scapula and muscles of the back. That same night an officer was brought in raving mad, having broken under the stress of having been ordered to send some of his men into almost certain death, for the third time that day. The medical detachment had not moved after all and was still on the small Belgian farm, though now sleeping in the house instead of the barn. This was at the height of the battle for Grandmenil, and they probably didn't move because the Germans had pushed the Allies back from Grandmenil on Christmas Eve.

Christmas Day, 1944
Somewhere in Belgium [Chardeneux]

Dearest Liz:

Well, Christmas Day turned out to be another beautiful clear day. Your husband, contrarily, has been in a terrible humor all day. I suspect that it's because he is upset and fed up that he is not with you. Also there is a certain amount of nervous strain connected with this war business. . . .

The war is funny. The destruction of war is as remarkable in its absence as in its presence. The impression we have at home of a countryside completely laid waste is not true at all. There is always a great deal more time and space where it is safe than there is where it is not. . . .

Our Belgian farmer continues to be very cooperative and hospitable. Most of us are sleeping on the floor of his two small front rooms. . . . All the boys are impressed with how hard the daughter, Angéle, works.

The farmer and his wife and other old people in the town have never seen a typewriter and are now busy watching Hanna type out a requisition on it. . . .

I had hoped to meet Angéle Breda on my visit to Chardeneux on April 16, 2014. Unfortunately, she died in 2012, but her son Marc Breda was there, living in the house where my father and his comrades once stayed. The barn my father described has been converted into a community café, but retains the original structure. Marc called Suzanne Vierset, a longtime friend of his mother, who joined us at the barn/café. Suzanne was only eight at Christmas in 1944. She remembers the chocolate the soldiers gave the children, which was momentous because they had not seen chocolate since the Germans invaded in May of 1940. And she remembers the room in her house where no civilians were allowed, which must have served as battalion headquarters that week. Small children at the time, Suzanne and a friend were able to sneak a peek and saw the walls lined with maps.

Marc disappeared into the house and emerged with a framed photo of his mother as a young woman, and another of her in later years tending sheep. As I read them the description my father had written of Angéle, Marc and Suzanne confirmed her sunny disposition, which she retained all her life. I was thrilled to make this connection to my father, sitting in the barn/café and easily able to picture it as it was, with stacks of hay filling one end and cows just on the other side of the wall.

[Chardeneux]
26 Dec 1944

Dear Sweetie:

. . . It is now nine o'clock and I have been going continuously since about seven thirty this morning. I organized an SOP (standard operating procedure). . . . Afterward I had sick call. Then went up to the front lines to see how the aid men were doing in the companies. . . . Getting back here was like getting completely out of the war. We really have it made where we are. . . .

The whole aid station gang has been watching Angéle all evening. She is spinning wool yarn with which she knits herself socks and sweaters. She has also knitted herself a dress! . . .

Jim was in charge of the 15-man medical detachment, nine of whom were out on the front lines as aid men during combat, one with each platoon. The three companies of the 275th Engineers were each supporting one of the infantry regiments of the 75th Division, namely the 289th, 290th, and 291st (references to Combat Teams, or CTs in the battalion reports refer to the infantry regiment plus any supporting units such as a tank battalion or engineering battalion). These green regiments were facing their first combat as they were parceled out to other divisions and arrayed along the defensive line of the road between Manhay, Grandmenil, Érezée and Hotton. Facing them were the divisions of the Sixth Panzer Army, whose mission was to fight their way northwest.[4]

On December 27, the Headquarters company relocated to a crossroads just north of La Forge, a collection of houses a little north of Fanzel, where they ate their Christmas dinner a few days late. Jim got slight frostbite on his toes, which he attributed to his own carelessness while in the motor convoy.

Somewhere in Belgium [La Forge]
28 Dec. 1944

Dearest Liz:

Sorry I couldn't write last night . . .

We hated to leave our "home" and they hated to see us go. The women bawled all over the place. We were really one big family there. Last night we stayed [in Heyd] with an interesting woman . . . one of those strong-charactered looking people. . . . She was living alone with her three little boys ranging from three to six. She took us (eight) in with the greatest good cheer and what she had was ours. She was one of the cheeriest souls I ever saw. She'd have to be, because I guess she's had a lot to bear up under.

Tonight we are in the kitchen of a cross-roads pension [in La Forge or Les Aunais], whose owners have taken off for God knows where. It is very comfortable but the home like atmosphere is missing. . . . We are in beautiful wooded country where it looks like the trout ought to abound.

We are getting now so that we move with relatively little effort and great efficiency. . . . The discomforts of war may be terrific but there are also a surprising number of comforts. For one thing, the H & S mess sergeant doesn't like to serve cocoa, because most of the men bitch about the absence of coffee when he does. So we carry a good supply of cocoa, milk powder, and sugar and are able to have cocoa several times a day when we have a place where we can make hot water. When we don't, your husband has been forced recently (oh the shame of it!) to drink coffee! . . .

What's the news from the home front? What are the ration shortages now? Are you getting cigarettes? We are still getting very few—were supposed to get five packs per man a week, but aren't getting them. Hershey bars are non-existent. We got four "candy bars" ten days ago, none since. Of course, I imagine when we are a little less active, extra-curricular supplies will come thru a little better.

Just took time out to make up a little cocoa. — My fifth cup today! Thats two and a half quarts! . . . .

In the early morning hours of December 28, units of the 2nd and 12th German Panzer Divisions attacked from the woods into Sâdzot, which is a hamlet of about a dozen houses, about four miles south of La Forge. The area was defended by several units of Jim's 75th Division. The account of this attack is typical of the confusion and poor communications that plagued both sides. Attacks and counter-attacks were constant as units along the ragged Allied front tried to maintain contact while German units probed for gaps in the Allied lines. On the night of December 27–28, German troops apparently exploited such a gap and came quietly down the hill into Sâdzot. Company B of the 87th Chemical Mortar Battalion, which was supporting the 289th Infantry in the forest above Sâdzot, was billeted in the houses, thinking they were a mile behind the front line. The Germans entered the first two houses, slitting the Americans' throats. The lone guard, Corporal Bill Cummings, spotted them and ran down the road raising the alarm while the Germans attacked behind him, machine-gunning Cummings and entering each house on the run, tossing in hand grenades as they went. There were many green replacement troops in the 87th, who were unprepared for sudden combat, and were killed quickly. The veterans knew to sleep with their boots on and their hands on their rifles. Some of these were able to respond quickly enough to escape down the hill toward the 509th Parachute Infantry, which was bivouacked in the fields. In the dark and confusion, the 509th started firing at the Americans running toward them before realizing they were friend, not foe. The 509th then advanced back up the hill with superior force and armor and nearly annihilated the German attackers. When it was all over, 53 of the 70 men of Company B had been killed, along with 120 soldiers of the 509th. The retreating Germans left 250 dead around Sâdzot.

During the fighting, two residents of Sâdzot fled with their nine-month-old daughter to shelter in a basement. A stray bullet struck the baby. After American forces secured the village, they rushed her to an aid station for medical treatment. Fifty years later, she was the English teacher in the village of *Érezée*.

As I climbed the hill above Sâdzot 69 years later, it was easy to imagine units of the two armies feeling their way in the darkness, not sure of each other's location in the dense forest. Before long I came upon a sign marking a tree plantation dedicated to the 75th Division, a suitably lasting memorial from the Belgian people. A little farther along I spied a brick hunting camp with a plaque on the side memorializing Sergeant James D. Deane Jr. of Connecticut, and Staff Sergeant Robert V. Myers of Company G of the 289th, who had left their foxholes on Christmas night to try to make contact with the next company on the line. Their bodies were found the next morning, together with those of five German soldiers. Nearby, I could detect a row of foxholes along the upper edge of a slope, where I could picture this bunch of scared young men, half frozen on a frigid moonlit night, watching through the trees for Germans to advance up the hill toward them.

Whether to spare Liz the gore he was facing, or to clear his own mind by writing of other things, Jim almost never wrote about the men he treated in his aid station during combat. He almost certainly helped deal with the very heavy casualties of the fighting around Sâdzot and other nearby battles. The fighting in this area between Grandmenil and Hotton was the turning point in that part of the Bulge. From there on, the 75th Division and the other units were pushing the Germans back toward their own border to the east, where they had begun this desperate offensive.

Somewhere in Belgium [La Forge]
29 Dec. 1944

Dearest Liz:

"Well" said I, pulling out this sheaf of paper "you guess you'll write your durned old wife!" chorused the boys. They get a great deal of amusement out of my sitting down whenever there's a chance to write "my durned old wife." . . .

Wow! Time out for ducking! We just got strafed with no casualties except our electric light system. Some damn fool was flashing a light near our building about half an hour ago, and I imagine that drew the fire. We are so safe compared to the boys in the line, tho, that it's not even funny. We get enough to make us keep our eyes and ears open, however. Yesterday it was artillery fire in our area for a couple of hours. It was very sporadic and never came within a hundred yards of anything or anyone. We did get showers of shrapnel, tho. . . .

The Center of Military History of the US Army published a comprehensive history of WWII in several volumes, known as the "Green Books."[5] Much of the background offered here is taken from that history.

By the third of January, 3,724,927 Allied soldiers had come ashore in Western Europe. They were disposed tactically in three army groups, nine armies (including one not yet assigned any divisions), 20 corps, and 73 divisions. Of the divisions, 49 were infantry, 20 armored, and four airborne. Six tactical air commands and thousands of medium and heavy bombers backed up the armies.

The organization of US Army units was as follows: army group made up of three armies; armies made up of two or three corps each; corps made up of three or four divisions each. In early January 1945, the 75th Division was assigned to the 1st Army.

[La Forges]
31 December 1944

Dearest Liz:

. . . Just had another little interruption. Some damn fool just came in here and left the safety off on his rifle with a bullet in the chamber—a tracer, too. So of course the thing went off and everyone scrambled for the floor, thinking that someone had thrown a grenade thru the window or something. The only harm done was that it ripped a lot of plaster off the wall and covered everyone with dust and debris. Boy, everyone really hits the dirt around here when anything goes off. We all figure we'll have a hell of a time on the fourth of July when we get home. . . .

Tonight is New Year's Eve. I sure hope the coming year will see the end of this war. I still think my original prediction of May or June will be right. We got some non-denatured alcohol yesterday and are going to make lemon punch with it and the lemon from our C rations. We tried and failed to get fruit juice. We can't get wine, beer, or cognac.

The boys all want to use the table for supper so will have to quit.

Good-night, darling. I love you.

Jim

Working at home in New York, Liz was bombarded with war news as the Battle of the Bulge raged, which must have been nerve-wracking. Jim admonished her in his letters not to brood on the situation, suggesting that his company was relatively safe. But in his New Year's Eve letter from the front, Jim's tone darkened.

Somewhere in Belgium [La Forge]
January 1, 1945

Dearest Liz,

. . . Last night we played poker most of the evening and drank a gallon and a half of punch made with a pint of Hagie's whiskey plus a half pint of straight ethyl alcohol. We used our dried lemon powder for flavoring. It made a damn good, though somewhat weak punch (equivalent of one bottle of whiskey to five of water as compared to two bottles of rum to one and a half of water in our old Med School punch).

Late (about 11:30) the Col. called us over to Battalion Headquarters for a drink of whiskey and cheese and fruit cake. We had that and then listened to Hitler speak at five minutes past midnight. The accent did not sound like Hitler to me, but then I haven't heard him speak for five years. Whether it was he or not, it was a defiant speech and a good one to keep the Germans fighting. . . .

You really made me jealous to hear about a steak cooked by my best cook. We have darned good food, but it just isn't what she puts out. Incidentally, we had turkey again for New Year's dinner today. They spoiled it by boiling it, but I guess didn't have facilities for roasting them. The turkeys at least seem to be one thing the folks at home are giving up that the boys overseas are getting. We also got five real chocolate bars today on our PX issues—3 Hersheys, a Nestle, and a Suchard. We also got a stick of gum, a box of matches, and a pack of cigarettes apiece. There was also a little pipe tobacco, tooth powder, and one cake of soap to be divided up among the detachment. The PX up here at the front is free when we get it. It is given out as a regular issue with the rations.

If [my brother] Dan goes to a Navy Yard on the Pacific Coast, it should be nice for him and Alice. The chances of their being in California would be good, and I'm sure they'd both like that a lot. As yet I have only scattered bits of information about your apartment and its furnishings. . . .

You said in your letter written Dec 21st that you hoped we wouldn't be feeling bitter and thought that I wouldn't. But I do. Liz, until you're right up there you have no conception of how terrible war is. It is not only the suffering of the killed and wounded and their families, but what the men go through in the way of mental and physical agony. I tell you, there is nothing too bad for a nation that has started two terrible wars in twenty-five years. It is the people who let it and wanted it to happen. If it were practical, the whole damn nation, men, women, and children ought to be wiped out. You can't afford to spare baby rattlesnakes just because they're babies. They're just as dangerous as the big ones—probably more so, because they have a longer life ahead of them. I don't want our children in a war, but, if Germany isn't ground into the dirt with a spiked heel till she can never rise again, they'll be in one. The Germans are fighting this war as a case of win or be wiped out and I think they should get their wish. The boys talk about making up for this lost time when the war is over, but that is impossible. Everything in war is a total loss, that can never be made up for. When you see or think of individual Germans you may be inclined to be sorry for them, but when you think of what they as a whole have done to the world, all they get in the neck is not nearly enough. The phrase "the disillusionment of war" contains words than which never truer ones were spoken. — Excuse the outburst, but we're pretty close to things over here and feel them strongly. I don't think now that anything is too bad for anyone who won't do all in his power to stop a war as well as not to start it. That applies to people at home as well as here. And starry-eyed idealism means nothing to the ruthlessness of people who are directly and indirectly responsible for it.

. . . Darling, excuse me for being so bitter. Don't let it upset you. I'll get over it and am probably not really as bad as I sound. I think getting back to you will sweeten me up considerably. It's too bad all the boys are not so fortunate in their wives. I sure am and I love her very, very much.

Jim

This very harsh condemnation of Germany was written following Jim's first week running an aid station close to the front lines. He was one of the few Americans with firsthand knowledge of the military, cultural, and professional sophistication of the Germans, having spent four months with a family in Frankfurt in 1935 and nine months in Munich in 1937–38. He had German friends and a great deal of respect for the accomplishments of the German people. Yet his exposure to the horrors of war was rapid and lasting. He knew all about the Malmedy Massacre of 80 American POWs that had occurred on December 17, just north of the 75th Division sector. He told in later years of the profound effect of his experience of walking through a snowy field in

Belgium, confirming the identities of three dead soldiers and tagging them for the Graves Registration Unit that would pick them up. I think this was on December 27, when three members of his battalion were killed while laying mines in a valley near Hotton and Soy in support of the 290th Infantry. He undoubtedly saw horrific wounds. He saw Belgian villages utterly destroyed, and Belgians who had just been liberated from four years of severe privation at the hands of the German occupiers. It was also extremely cold that week, with temperatures well below zero, and frostbite was affecting most of the troops.

Jim had witnessed Germany's preparations for war in the 1930s and seen how the German people acquiesced in those preparations. Now, after one week of combat, he was ready to vilify everything German.

Chapter Four

Cleaning up the Bulge: January 1945, Belgium

My father's battalion, along with all the other engineering units, was very busy as the new year began. The tide had turned in the Battle of the Bulge, but the fighting was still intense. Germans were being pushed back in very small increments, house by house, village by village, river by river. The engineers cleared roads and trails of mines, booby traps, and debris to allow the tanks and trucks to move up. The roads were always icy and the tanks were ill-suited to the conditions. The 275th spent many hours pulling stuck vehicles back onto the road, then sanding and salting to keep them there. At least one platoon of engineers was always at the front with their respective infantry units, responding as patrols found mines and booby traps along the desired route of advance. Jim went to the front most days to check on his medics and give them whatever they needed. At his aid station, the most common complaints were frostbite and trench foot. The engineers reported few battle casualties in their own battalion, but there were heavy casualties in the infantry units through early January, and many of those undoubtedly came to Jim's aid station at La Forge. The official 75th Division history, written just after the war, describes the events.

> At 2400 [New Year's] the 75th Division Artillery with other battalions with the [XVIII Airborne] corps presented A New Year's Greeting to Adolf. Every gun in twenty corps battalions, calibers ranging from 105mm to 240mm, fired three rounds into enemy territory.
>
> New Year's Day was generally inactive. The enemy withdrew south across the AISNE River, and was observed digging in. Our patrols mopped up pockets down to the river. The 291st Infantry relieved elements of the 7th Armored Division in the GRANDMENIL-MANHAY sector on 29 December, and the 517th Parachute Infantry Battalion at MANHAY on 2 January. The 1st Battalion was shelled by about 75 rounds of artillery and mortar fire at 1445 on 1 January. The 289th Infantry reverted to division control on 29 December. Combat Team 290 remained on the defense, attached to 3d Armored Division. The Division reverted to VII Corps at 0900 on 2 Janu-

ary. At 1500 Company F of the 289th Infantry attacked from CROIX ST. JEANNE south against a German company occupying the heights west of VEIUXFORNEAUX. After a stubborn fire fight, Company F withdrew to enable Division Artillery fire to fall on the entrenched enemy position. The artillery fire started at 1800 and continued during the night.[6]

Digging in meant clearing away about a foot of snow, then hacking through frozen ground with whatever implement could be found. In early January, the ground was frozen more than a foot deep in most of the Ardennes. Whenever possible, aid stations were set up in buildings to protect the sick and wounded from the weather. Consequently, Jim was usually in relative comfort while the front line infantry were shivering in their foxholes.

Soldiers from the 290th Infantry Regiment, 75th Division, near Amonines, Belgium, January 4, 1945. US Army Signal Corps photo.

Somewhere in Belgium [La Forges]
3 Jan 45

Dearest Liz: . . . . The day you wrote the Washington letter, you said you spent the last hour of the trip on your favorite day-dream—the day I get back. Darling I was traveling and doing just the same thing that day. Your vision and mine were just the same, too, Liz. . . .

My old Belgian with the carbuncle was much improved today after yesterday's operative procedure. He was very pleased and so was I. Also managed to wash out my ODs and a set of wool underwear today. That will bring my washing pretty well up to date, provided nothing happens to prevent it drying. I had worn the same ODs since leaving England.

Somewhere in Belgium [La Forge]
Friday 5 Jan, 1945

Dearest Liz: . . . .

Sweetie, I sure miss you. Reading your letter written on Christmas Day made me so full of longing for you that the tears threatened to well up beyond control. I love you so overpoweringly much that there are times that it gets me to be away from you.

I did not write yesterday. I had a long, trying, busy day. At the end of it the proprietor and proprietress of this pension-bar in which we are living returned. Since I am the only officer who speaks any sort of French at all, it became my job to oil the troubled waters and get everything straightened out and arranged. Madame turned out to be a case-hardened old female who was exceedingly difficult to deal with. They didn't go to bed until midnight and I was just too damn dead tired to write since I had to get up at seven today to do some physicals for battlefield promotions at eight.

To complicate matters, today Madame insisted that we move the aid station out of the kitchen-office which we were occupying. Hanna and I walked about five miles trying to find another house to put the aid station in without success. The alternative was to move into the big room occupied by H&S [Headquarters & Supply] orderly room over Steinbring's dead body. The Col. had already refused to let us in the kitchen in the mansion where he has his headquarters (command post) [Les Aunais] on the grounds that he doesn't want the aid station in the same place as the command post. Actually he wants a private place to cook and eat his meals. We ended up in the H&S orderly room after a harrowing morning. In addition, the Col. wanted these officer physicals (we don't have the equipment to do them in the aid station) done and typed up in five copies by ten this morning. Gawd. In addition we don't carry the forms for it in our equipment—for which I got bawled out, too. The hell with it! So after all the aid station mix-up I had to drive back to Division Surgeon's office and get the forms plus other information, supposed to be a matter of personnel and command. Ho-hum. I kept having to remind myself how lucky I was to be in the Engineers and not the Infantry. I really am, though. Those boys really have it rough.

We are now allowed to say that we have participated in stopping the German push into Belgium about which you have been hearing so much in the papers at home. We've been right in there, too, and our outfit acquitted itself very well. I think a lack of overconfidence led to the greater use of grey matter with consequent good results. Everyone feels like an old combat soldier now and morale is very high.

This letter was just interrupted while I went over and doctored Simmons, who has a little staphylococcus food poisoning and Chivington who has a touch of the grippe. It was interrupted earlier by three other patients. I have four civilian patients at the moment, too, including one pediatric case. One is the proprietor who had a hernia repair done in October in his bedroom by a "specialist." Naturally he ended up with an infection and the wound is one hell of a mess. I'd be a sharp doc here, anyway.

Hanna took me over today and introduced me to the medical officer of his old outfit from which he came to us on cadre. Their outfit is right near us now. The guy was a very good egg from Montana. He gave the enlightening information that Missoula was medically "sewn up" by the "Western Montana Clinic" there. He said it was an ideal place to live, though.

Sweetie I sure hope it won't be long before we are living someplace together. That is the thought and hope that makes life worth living for me, darling. Goodnight and I love you very, very much, Liz.

Jim

P.S. Enclosed is a photo of the proprietor & wife. He is a very decent, genial guy who wants us to have a souvenir.

On my 2014 visit to La Forge, I had been unable to locate the buildings described by my father. While walking the hills around the village, I found an elderly gentleman at work in his garden behind a barn. I screwed up my courage and, in my hesitant French, told him of my quest. Hard of hearing, he told me to wait while he came out to the farmyard. We chatted for a few minutes and suddenly he remembered. There had been an auberge (café-guesthouse) on one corner of the crossroads known as Les Aunais, just a few hundred yards up the road. And across the road from the auberge had been a mansion. He remembered salvaging materials when they both were torn down in the 1950s. The site of the mansion is now the local football field.

January 6 found the Battalion moving back from the front for a few days' rest at Fraineux, after two weeks of combat. Soon they moved south and east again in more snow, with temperatures not quite as cold as at New Year's, into the thick of the fighting. Jim's aid station moved back a few miles to the vicinity of Remouchamps on January 6. His letters during these days portray the trying process of moving all the men and equipment.

The aid stations in all the combat battalions were busy. From December 24 to January 24, the 75th suffered 407 killed, 1,707 wounded, and 334 missing in combat. In addition, non-battle casualties, largely trench foot and frostbite, numbered 2,623 men. This total amounts to one third of the entire 75th Division in their first 30 days of combat. By the end of hostilities five months later, more than half of the Division were casualties.[7]

Somewhere in Belgium [near Remouchamps]
6 Jan 1945

Dearest Liz: We are just starting another move which I expect will take at least four or five hours, so I will start a letter at the same time and figure on getting it finished by the time we reach our destination. It seems as if two thirds of the time on convoy is spent in meaningless halts. Of course, we are at the rear of the column, so we never know the reason for them. This place we are leaving is the first one at which we have arrived during the day, but it looks as if we'll hit the next one when it's dark again.

Just stopped along a beautiful dirt road thru a snow covered forest of pine trees. We are moving along the side of a hill with a brook winding through a narrow meadow on our right. It all seems so beautiful and peaceful and far from war. . . .

We have now reached the top of the hill we were climbing and have stopped again. I've been sitting here thinking about you and about getting home to you if and when this damn war ever ends. It sure seems like a hell of a long time already, even though it is not yet quite two months.

There are a few good things about being in combat. One is that we never wear neckties. Another is that no one says much if you don't shave for several days—the chief reason being that that's about the most often you get a chance to. There is a lot less emphasis on the "soldiering" you had to do in garrison. It has its good and its bad points.

Last night I again failed to get much sleep. I had a man with severe lumbago to whom I gave morphine a little after twelve. I'd no sooner given it than he informed me that he had had a morphine reaction last winter. So that meant staying up an extra hour to make sure he was OK, which he was. Then they woke us up at 6:30 this morning to say we were moving. I was running around like a chicken with his head chopped off trying to locate things the men had taken and the owners of the place were complaining about. Being the linguist among the officers has both its advantages and disadvantages. It got me a couple of shots of cognac last night but also a lot of anguish night before last and this morning.

It seems as if every time I pull out my pen and paper to write, the convoy starts to move again. Apparently it's just one more of those G-I frustrations. It is getting colder now, and I am now trying to write with my gloves on. I hope you can read it. We have been climbing. Up where we are now there is about as much snow as there was that day we went skiing out at the Belmont Country Club two years ago. It has been a beautiful drive right along. . . .

Well sweetie, this letter is getting so difficult to write that I think I'll close and try and write another tonight—I hope. From the looks of the map I doubt if we have any indoor quarters at this next place. Some fun with five or six inches of snow on the ground.

So long, darling. I'll stop and just think about being with the girl I love so much.

Jim

Chow is served to soldiers of the 347th Infantry Regiment on their way to La Roche, Belgium. Nine months before, most of these boys were in high school eating in a warm cafeteria. Photo by Newhouse, January 13, 1945. National Archives Record Group 111-Series SC-photo 198849.

At this point the front line was moving back and forth. Tracing the movements of the battalion is difficult during this time. The three regiments of the 75th Division, the 289th, 290th, and the 291st, and battalions within those regiments, were being assigned to different places under different divisions. Casualties had been so high during the first two weeks of the battle that Allied commanders tried to shore up the front lines with any resources they had. Even companies of the same battalion were assigned to different units on some days. Jim's aid station moved less than the infantry companies, which were frequently bivouacked wherever the fighting took them. As the division regrouped in the Remouchamps area, they prepared to fight under their own command structure for the first time.

Somewhere in Belgium [near Remouchamps]
8 Jan 1945

Dearest Liz: Last night we had six to eight inches of snow, so this morning we figured when we got up that we would probably be here in this nice place for a week longer. But no such luck. Turner came back from Battalion Headquarters a little while ago with the word that we would probably move this afternoon. . . .

Somewhere in Belgium [near Remouchamps]
9 Jan, 1945

Dearest Liz: Today was a good one because it brought another letter from you. We didn't move either and spent a day reminiscent of one on the farm in the winter with deep snow around. We got the buzz saw hitched up in the barn and sawed up a stack of wood, having used up all of these people's cut available supply. It reminded me of cutting wood on the farm with you. . . .

We had quite a field day on rations today—boned chicken for lunch and roast pork for supper—pancakes for breakfast.

You really made my mouth water with your talk of blue cheese and pabst beer. The only beer I've had since leaving England was the night I was promoted—two glasses of lousy. I sure hope that when we hit Germany, the Germans will fail to evacuate or destroy their beer. I could really do with some.

Liz, don't worry yourself reading casualty lists. They are never released in this war until after notice has gone out from the War Department in Washington. . . .

The boys have gotten such a kick out of my sitting down to write my "durned old wife" that they've all written home about it and it has become a standard phrase in the detachment. . . .

V-Mail
FROM CAPT Robert J. McKay, Jr. D-435325
Med Det 275th Eng Bat
APO #451 0/1 PM
New York, N.Y.
Somewhere in Belgium
9 Jan, 1944

Dear Pop:

. . . Would you please get Liz a dozen nice pure yellow roses for her birthday on February fifth from me? If you can't get real yellow ones, get small dark red ones.

Things are going fine with me. Have had a lot of snow the last few days. This morning we spent cutting wood on the farm we are living on at the moment! It seemed quite like home. Had a dandy letter from Alice yesterday.

Lots of love to all,

Jim

The 275th worked with the 291st Infantry Regiment south of Trois Ponts, clearing roads as the weather allowed. January 10th they were in Basse Bodeux as the 291st pushed the Germans southeast, toward the Salm River.

Somewhere in Belgium [Froidville]
11 Jan 1945

Dearest Liz:

Yesterday I again failed to write. We were on the move, and it was impossible. It was too cold to write in the truck as I did on the last one. It is cold as hell now with deep snow on the ground. Last night was the first night we've had to sleep out since we were in France [near Froidville]. It was rough. We had a little shed for the aid station, but it wasn't very good. I have an idea that we'll be sleeping out quite a bit from now on. Read about the cold weather at home, but you don't know what cold is until you actually have to live out in it.

We have been reading the last few days of Admiral Ingram saying the Atlantic Coast might be V-bombed. The G-I soldier over here hopes it will happen to perhaps bring it home to people at home that this war is still going on. Believe me, no gains over here are fast. Every one of them is sweated out and paid for in blood, no matter how rapid they may seem to people at home. If some of these people at home who wonder why we can't do any better over here could see the men who are doing their best and winning a tough war, maybe they'd be able to change their minds about who the war is tough on. I see just enough of the front line soldier to know what he is up against. It's a miracle how he does what he does and my hat is sure off to him. The next time you hear someone bitching about how tough things are at home, just ask them how they'd like to spend just a week at the front in this weather without shelter and fighting a tough enemy at the same time, dodging either small arms fire or shrapnel at all hours of the day and night. Most of the bitchers at home would just fold up and give up if they had to live for a week in what we consider A01 billets. Nuts. Thank God it isn't absolutely continuous. No human could stand that—which is the reason why it isn't, I imagine. The nice warm apartment we were living in last year would sure look good about now.

Sweetie, excuse me for carrying on so. I guess I'm not feeling so hot today. On the other side, the latest G-I joke is what the boys at Bastogne said when they were surrounded: "Well, they've got us surrounded now, the unlucky bastards!" That is no lie either. The American Soldier with his back to the wall is a tough customer to deal with.

It's getting too cold to write any more, so I'll quit. However uncomfortable things are sweetie, I still miss you and love you with all my heart all the time.

Jim

The fighting was intense and was making the news at home. Jim apparently received a telegram from his mother. He replied by Western Union cablegram: "ALL WELL AND SAFE. MY THOUGHTS ARE WITH YOU. TELEGRAM RECEIVED MANY THANKS." The cablegram was sent on January 11 and received on the fourteenth.

The Battalion moved again on the eleventh, this time to the tiny village of Goronne, a few miles west of Vielsalm. En route south, the two or three trucks of Jim's medical detachment got separated from the rest of the battalion. Jim finally saw a tent down in a field with lights on and went down to find out where they were. It was an infantry command post, and they informed Jim that the road he was on would get him where he needed to go, but that the Germans were very active and had been cutting the road periodically with patrols. While Jim was there, a soldier came in with several German prisoners. The soldier was obviously very cold and tired and asked what to do with the prisoners. He was ordered to march them another couple of miles to the POW gathering point. The soldier was not at all pleased with the order, but went back outside. He was back within fifteen minutes reporting that the POWs had been delivered. Jim suspected that he must have shot the Germans rather than walk another four miles.

In Goronne, for the first time, Jim's aid station was located near the infantry aid stations in the same village, reflecting the intensity of nearby fighting and the intermingling of the engineer companies with the infantry companies as the engineers worked to bridge the Salm and clear the mines left by the retreating Germans.

Three days earlier, 196 Americans had been killed in a bloody battle one mile to the east, in the gentle gap on the west end of the ridge known as Thier-du-Mont. I visited the monument that marks the site in April 2014, and looked down across the peaceful green fields at Goronne where my father had his aid station in a house on the south side of the village. The fighting along Thier-du-Mont was continuing as he arrived there on January 11, 1945. It was cold and the ground was blanketed with snow, although that snow must have been trampled and stained with the blood of so many dead and wounded soldiers. The old man who now lives in that house remembers the jeeps coming into the village bringing the wounded to the aid stations, with guns booming from up on the ridge. My father makes no mention in his letters of the gore that must have been all around him. I stood in the field near the monument, tears welling up, imagining the medics performing triage and sending the quickly bandaged men back to Goronne, where my father waited to do what he could. I guess they were tears of sorrow, and of pride. There was no need to explain my tears to my new Belgian friends who had brought me to this spot. They instinctively put their hands on my arm or shoulder and silently shared my emotions.

Somewhere in Belgium [Goronne]
12 Jan 1945

Dearest Liz: . . .

I had no sooner started to fold yesterday's letter than one of the men came in with the order to move, which we did. We are now located in the same town as the Infantry Aid Stations in this neck of the woods—never thought to see that day, but such is life in the Army. We have a big kitchen with wood floor and a good stove, so it is really quite a good set-up. It is cold as the dickens—I would estimate between ten and twenty above, so it is good to be indoors.

Your mention of the newspaper article on American Women Forces to "fraternize & mingle" with the soldiers here amused me, too. You'd better watch out. . . .

You spoke of making cocoa and sitting around and playing records after the movies on Dec 30. We play a little poker every night that we aren't too busy and have cocoa afterward. Our cooks are not very ambitious and are glad to give away cocoa so they won't have any to make. I still haven't seen a movie or had any beer except once since England. . . .

An incident occurred in this village that was a precursor of things to come. A paragraph in a V-mail described it.

Somewhere in Belgium [Goronne]
13 Jan 1945

Dearest Liz:

. . . Last night I had a little minor adventure. I went out about ten to go over to shoot the bull with the boys at headquarters and see if there were any news. Outside the door, the guards were having trouble with some civilian, because they couldn't decide whether or not he was bona fide or not. I tried to help them out by talking to him in French. We ended up in a house occupied by an infantry major and owned by a man who is suspected of collaboration and whom the civilian had given as his reference. My french is pretty voluble by now, but still not up to the german, which the suspected collaborationist speaks very well, so in the middle of the conversation, I switched over to german. The people there spoke only enough of each to know what we were speaking and to think I was all too conversant with both. So I ended up by having to show all my identification and clear myself of suspicion, too! . . .

Goronne sits in the midst of farmland, about two miles up a gentle rise west of Vielsalm. Vielsalm is the main town in the area, located on the east bank of the Salm, which is a small river flowing north to meet the Amblève. Upstream a mile or so is the village of Salmchateau, and downstream a couple of miles is the village of Grand-Halleux. The American strategy was to cross the Salm at these two smaller villages and then close in on Vielsalm from the north and south.

Jim's battalion was clearing mines while the 51st Engineering Battalion built a Bailey Bridge at Grand Halleux. Bailey Bridges consisted of prefabricated steel components designed to be easily trucked in standard army trucks and assembled on site with hand tools and minimal machinery. The bridge could be assembled on one bank of a river and then moved into place by a squad of men over an ingenious mechanism of rollers and cable. Next to the placement and removal of mines, assembling Bailey and other types of bridges was the most common task assigned the 275th and other combat engineer battalions.[8]

On January 15 the battles to control the area around Vielsalm were intense. C Company of the 275th moved with the 291st Infantry toward Grand Halleux, where the Germans held the high ground east of the river. A difficult three-day battle ensued with high casualties. In the cold, snowy conditions with fighting all over the fields and woods of the area, medics frequently used improvised sleds to pull wounded men back to a passable road for transport to the aid station. South of Vielsalm, elements of the 289th Infantry crossed the Salm River in the early morning hours, took Salmchateau, and continued up a brook to Beche, turning north up a steep ridge toward Vielsalm. Another company of the 275th worked to install a bridge in Salmchateau late in the day.

A medic pulls a sled with a wounded man toward an aid station. US Army Signal Corps photo, 1945

Somewhere in Belgium [Goronne]
16 Jan 45

Dearest Liz: Today has been unpleasantly exciting. For the last twenty-four hours we have been hitting the floor regularly in response to the whistles of German shells. So far we've been lucky and hope it continues. We'd be even more satisfied if the shelling discontinued. It has its humorous side as well. Vestal was just in here and we all heard one go over and sort of ducked. He didn't hear it and was scoffing at us. A split second later one came over closer and he hit the floor so hard he scattered a chair and a table and its contents all over the place. We couldn't help but be amused audibly at his headlong discomfiture. Things are still a little nerve-wracking, tho.

I have pretty well recovered from the drizzles but still feel pretty weak and lousy. It sure takes it out of you. I must have been getting fat because I was able to take my belt in about an inch and a half this morning. . . .

This letter is having a lot of interruptions as we hug the floor intermittently. We are in pretty good position except for a big window in the room which we are going to cover up pretty carefully tonight to keep away from glass splinters. Our fatigues really do double duty today soaking up the dirt we get off the floor.

John Green had a copy of the Paris Herald today. It was quite different from the Stars and Stripes, the service paper also published in Paris. The emphasis in the Stars and Stripes is on the war we are fighting over here, whereas the Herald took a much broader view of world news in general. Actually the Stars and Stripes is a pretty good paper and almost everything in it is interesting to a man in the service over here. . . .

The war and people are funny. All the men are convinced that they not only don't want another one, but won't fight another one. Yet I don't believe any of them are willing to be one iota less selfish in order to prevent another. They just want George to carry the load. I'm beginning to come to the point where I doubt that the human race is worth saving.

Good-night darling. Excuse me for getting gloomy again. Don't let it upset you. A good deal of it is just nervous strain. Incidentally, I found my fountain pen about half an hour after mailing yesterday's letter.

I love you, Liz. Jim

Somewhere in Belgium [Goronne]
16 January 1945

Dearest Liz: This is in the way of being a birthday letter from me to you. I'm afraid that your present is going to be several months late, as it hasn't been mailed yet. . . .

Sweetie, I was walking up the street early this afternoon and suddenly it reminded me of you—because it was such a beautiful snowclad winter day with a clear blue sky. It reminded me of your white skin, and clear blue eyes. . . .

The Germans withdrew to the east from Vielsalm during the night of January 16–17, leaving the town heavily mined. The 275th spent the day clearing landmines, a task made easier by a sketch map of the mines' locations that had fallen into their hands. A cooperative German POW helped interpret the map.

Letter Number 16 Somewhere in Belgium [Goronne]
17 Jan 45

Dearest Liz: Here your husband sits at the window on the dental chair using, of all things, the January copy of Esquire for a writing board. Things are much better today than they were yesterday. Jerry has stopped throwing his shells into this town so far today. I think and hope that our artillery got the guns that were doing it last night. I'm not anxious to get any closer to danger than we were yesterday.

. . . I usually do write you in the afternoon now as that is the best time. It's our slackest time of the day and there is still light to write by. The light in the evening from the Coleman lanterns is not too good and the flickering hurts my eyes for any finer work than playing poker or taking a bath. . . . Last night . . . I took a bath—oh joyous day!—put my accumulated socks and underwear in to soak and went to bed. . . .

I've been trying to do some reading without success—both medical and otherwise. There are almost always ten to fifteen people in this room the size of the kitchen at the farm and there are just too many interruptions. . . . I have read about thirty pages of John P. Marquand's "So Little Time" which the Colonel found in a paper bound copy at our last stop and turned over to me when he finished. The November 30th copy of the New England Journal of Medicine also arrived. . . .

On the back of this Esquire I'm writing on is an advertisement which is really tough for me to take. It is for Pabst beer. . . . We are able to get a little hard liquor every now and then and occasionally wine, but they don't appeal to me like a good beer, or rather several, would. . . .

At one time or another all the boys have said to give their love to my "durned old wife" so consider that it has been sent by all of them. The Colonel also asks frequently to be remembered to you. . . .

The land rises quickly north of the Salm to the Grand Bois, a large forested area along a high ridge between Vielsalm and St. Vith. The shelling Jim experienced in Goronne likely came from this ridge. On my visit in 2014, I stood on the spot where the German guns had been on those days, at the top of a steep rock slope rising from the Salm between Salmchateau and Vielsalm. Gazing west to Goronne, I imagined the action and the noise as the guns boomed, spotters watching with their field glasses where the shells were landing, telling the crews how to adjust their aim for the next round. On January 18, the front was about two or three miles east of Vielsalm, four or five miles from Goronne.

"Allies Press the Germans Back along Western Front," *The New York Times*, January 18, 1945.

Somewhere in Belgium [Goronne]
18 Jan 1945—Thursday

Dearest Liz:

This is being written . . . before a prospective move. . . . The Colonel apparently has it in his head to make an absolutely front line battalion out of the Engineers. . . .

You probably will know where we are fighting by the time you get this letter. We were mentioned yesterday for the first time in the Stars and Stripes, so I guess it's now public property and you'll be able to follow a good deal of our progress from now on in the papers. . . .

The aid station moved again, into Vielsalm, on January 18. From the nineteenth to the twenty-first, the infantry regiments fought their way east through the Grand Bois against well-entrenched German positions and knee-deep snow. By the twenty-second, the Germans had been pushed back to Commanster, then Aldringen and Maldingen.

On January 20, Jim was able to set up a decent aid station in Vielsalm, where the battalion took a breather, having bridged the small Salm River. The town was in relatively good shape and the aid station had the luxury of one electric light bulb, the first electric light Jim had seen in a few weeks. The Engineers were still close to the front and could hear small arms fire, but were not being shelled.

Members of the 275th Combat Engineers sweeping a snow-covered road for mines before tanks advance to attack Commanster, Belgium. Liz cut this photo out of the *Herald Tribune* and kept the clipping. US Army Signal Corps photo, 30 January 1945; National Archives, College Park, MD.

Somewhere in Belgium [Vielsalm]
21 January, 1945

Dear Ma & Pa

. . . Ma, if you should make your Christmas cookies that keep so well, would you send me a box? Our food continues good and I am in good shape. We have been getting pretty good places for our aid station due to my ability to speak enough French to get in ahead of the others. We have now been under all sorts of fire except small arms, but what we've had has been enough. The Colonel is keeping us right up front. My last aid station [Goronne] was right along with two infantry battalion stations! . . .

Anti-tank gunners from the 7th Armored Division at Rencheux, near Vielsalm, December 23, 1944. US Army Signal Corps photo.

V-Mail
TO: Mr. Robert J. McKay
c/o INTERNATIONAL NICKEL CO.
67 WALL ST, NEW YORK CITY

FROM: CAPT Robert J. McKay, Jr., D-435325
Med Det 275th Eng Bat, APO #451 0/1 PM
New York, N.Y.
Somewhere in Belgium [Vielsalm]
23 Jan, 1945

Dear Pop:

. . . I am in beautiful, snowclad, wooded country now which would be grand on a skiing trip, but this is not a skiing trip. My health and general welfare continue excellent, but I sure miss Liz and home. Our food is very good and as yet we haven't really had things too tough. However, home would sure look good about now. It doesn't take long to get good and sick of this combat stuff.

Yesterday I entered civilian practice, arriving just too late to deliver a baby! Also was called in to see an old woman of 84 who probably has cancer. There wasn't a thing to do for her. The one doctor here, who used to run the out-patient maternity clinic at a nearby city, seems to be pretty competent. He and a priest have just opened up a hospital in a nunnery here. They are really laboring under adverse conditions. The Germans took all his instruments, and they have no light or bandages. We are trying to help out all we can, but we can't give him too much for fear we will get caught short ourselves. These Belgians are made out of good stuff, though. They haven't thrown up their hands at all. They're still in there pitching. If anyone asks you to contribute to a legitimate Belgian relief, do it. They really need it and at the same time they are really trying to help out the American soldiers who are over here.

We are all much cheered by the present Russian successes and hope that they keep up. The only hitch is that the nearer victory comes, the more tantalizing is the thought of going home. As short a time as we have been in, we are awfully eager to get the darn thing over with. . . .

The local doctor Jim mentioned was the only doctor for about 15,000 people in the area. The Germans had taken not only all his medical supplies and instruments, but also had taken three cars from him during the war, so he was unable to get around.

I visited Salmchateau and Vielsalm in April 2014. I had sought out contacts ahead of time, and soon after my arrival two local men visited me at my B&B. One was Francois Dutroux, a 25-year-old WWII enthusiast, who spent many hours helping me before, during, and after my visit. The other was Odon Jeunejean, a 69-year-old who was born in September 1944, just three months before his father was killed while trying to help a wounded American captain. Odon led us to the mine shaft (now closed) where the residents of Vielsalm sheltered from the German attack. There is an abandoned trolley bridge just below the entrance. Odon stood on the spot where his father was killed as he tried to reach the captain on the bridge. Tears welled up as he described his own search for that American captain. He has never found any trace of him.

The next day I was picked up again. After a visit to Goronne we arrived at city hall in Vielsalm, walked up the stairs, and were greeted by about 20 local folks, including the mayor, who were there to welcome me and thank me for my father's service in liberating their town. The most distinctive local was a man with a large handlebar mustache and a cowboy hat. His name is François Frank, 69 years old, and he is the baby that my father almost delivered. A beer was pressed into my hand, the local reporter snapped pictures, and before I knew it the mayor called for everyone's attention, made a short speech about the debt forever owed to the American soldiers, and presented me with a framed certificate naming my father an honorary Freeman of Vielsalm. Then he called François Frank forward and presented each of us with a framed certificate validating François's birth on January 22, 1945, in a cellar in Rencheux, a hamlet just across the Salm. I was able to make a short speech of appreciation in French, saying how impressed my father was by the Belgian people's courage, hospitality, and generosity. Then it was back to the beer, more photos, and conversation with these wonderful people.

Also in the room was Joseph Lambert, who, in my mind, should have been the guest of honor. An "ancient combatant," or veteran of the Belgian Army, Lambert was captured in the first days of the German attack in 1940, and spent the rest of the war in Germany. I sat down with Mr. Lambert and we had a good talk with the help of an interpreter. Wounded when captured, he was taken along with the rapidly advancing German army to France. Then he and 200 other POWs were taken back through Belgium to Germany. Most of the POWs walked, but Joseph and the other wounded rode in trucks. The convoy passed right by his home in Vielsalm as it wound its way to St. Vith and then into Germany. They were loaded on box cars headed for Frankfurt. He broke down as he described 48 hours in that boxcar without food or water, 74 years earlier. I put my hand on his shoulder in silent comfort. He gathered himself, obviously wanting to tell me the whole story. He spent a year in an unpleasant POW camp, but was then sent to work on a farm where he received bed and board in exchange for his labor. He spent three-and-a half years on the farm, living a fairly normal life, and thankful for the food he received. As the Americans closed in on that part of Germany during the first week of April 1945, he was locked in his room at night. When the village was shelled, he remembers being terrified that the house would be burned and he would be unable to escape. On April 7, he was set free by the Americans. He worked his way home to Vielsalm, where he discovered that his parents had been killed. He bears no malice toward the German farm family with whom he spent those war years, and in fact keeps in touch with them.

Eventually Odon reminded us that we were due at the restaurant, so we stopped talking and moved down the street to the local fancy eatery, where I was treated to an enormous Sunday dinner. I sat across from Bertrand Goosse and his father, Jean Pierre, both of whom speak English. Bertrand is at military school and is another WWII enthusiast.

After lunch five of us went across the river to Rencheux to see the cellar where François Frank was born. François had heard stories of the circumstances of his birth from his mother, and a man whose father had been in the cellar and remembered the event well also joined us. There were 20 local people in the cellar at the time of the birth. This was where they spent the nights during the fighting. The birthing bed was a bin of potatoes. The cellar is about 16 feet by 24 feet and looks unchanged; my hosts confirmed that the stairs and walls are the same, and pointed out the grates above the cellar windows to prevent Germans from tossing in grenades, which they were in the habit of doing. Once again, I imagined my father coming down the stairs into the crowded cellar, just as François was delivered, helping the young mother as 19 of her neighbors gave her moral support. Apparently the story has come down over the years of how 20 people went into that cellar, and 21 came back out.

By late January the Germans had been pushed back to the Siegfried Line where they had started their counter-offensive in that area of Belgium. Jim's letters home continued to understate the combat situation, although now there were a few days without many casualties.

During the war, Liz lived in Greenwich Village on 13th Street, near the subway station, within walking distance of the senior McKays' apartment on 5th Avenue. Liz was splitting the apartment on the third floor of a doctor's house with another woman. It was very crowded. The kitchen was a hotplate in a cupboard. She had one large room, looking out the back over a yard.

Somewhere in Belgium [Vielsalm]
Jan 23, 1945

Dearest Liz:

. . . We got the welcome rumor today that we may be pulled back for a rest period. I hope so, because I, for one, wouldn't mind a bit to get a real shower, see a movie, and drink some beer. . . .

Your letter of Jan. 8th was written "curled up in my big chair." I was interested to get the plan of the room as you have it set up and to picture you in it . . .

You said the apartment was cold but would probably seem warm to us. We usually manage to maintain a heat of about fifty five to sixty degrees. That is not too bad for us since we wear long wool underwear, OD pants with fatigues over them, a flannel shirt and one or two sweaters. . . .

Somewhere in Belgium [Vielsalm]
25 January 1945

Dearest Liz:

. . . Sgt. Hanna got back from Paris last night with a glowing description of life there. It apparently is a regular G.I. paradise. He got three full days there and had a wonderful time. They are also giving out a few trips to England and the French Riviera. I'd really like to get one of those Riviera jobs. . . .

Somewhere in Belgium [Vielsalm]
26 January 1945

Dearest Liz: . . .

Yesterday, I almost got a shower. Major Furst has one rigged up for his patients and asked me if I didn't want to use it. I did but had a meeting in Col. Davis's office with the regimental surgeons and me that lasted three hours and took all my potential shower time. Today the showers are closed.

It's snowing like the dickens now. It would be wonderful weather for skiing but isn't for war—if any weather can be said to be good for war. . . .

The last few days I have been awfully low and depressed and missing you especially. Every once in a while I get that way and feel as if this damn war and separation from you will never end, though actually it has only been about eleven weeks. It seems like eleven years already. . . .

The hoped-for rest period was not to be. The Germans had been pushed back from one bulge in the American lines, but there was another at the southern end of the line in the Alsace area of France, known as the Colmar Pocket. The whole 75th Division was moved from Belgium to Alsace (about 300 miles) to help finish pushing the Germans back across the Rhine, a task that would involve 10 days of combat for the 75th. The convoy pulled out of Vielsalm on January 27. As usual, the medical detachment trucks were in the rear of the convoy. The official history of the 75th Division, written in 1945, describes the move:

> The division's month of cold and combat in the ARDENNES had earned it a rest, but on 25 January the proposed rest period near LIEGE was cancelled. The entire division was ordered to move to the Seventh United States Army area south of STRASBOURG, France. Rail movement of the infantry and

a portion of the rear echelon commenced the afternoon of 26 January from PEPINSTER, BELGIUM, southeast of LIEGE. . . .

The motor movement of all the motorized elements of the division, including Division Headquarters, commenced at 0800 on 27 January. Approximately 8,000 men and over 1,400 vehicles moved from BELGIUM to FRANCE. The move started in VIELSALM and vicinity and proceeded north of TROIS PONTS, BELGIUM, thence south through HOTTON, MARCHE, and ROCHEFORT, BELGIUM, to SEDAN, FRANCE. The trip through France, except for the severe cold, was extremely interesting. Elements of the Maginot Line as well as such famous World War I battle grounds as VERDUN and ST. MIHIEL were passed en route. Most of the journey was completed with strict blackout driving. Continuous and heavy snowfalls made the roads dangerous and slippery, but all the convoys negotiated the journey over the mountains without serious mishap. The same day the division was attached to XXI Corps; to French First Army for operations; and to Seventh United States Army for Administration and supplies.

The XXI Corps consisted of the 3rd Infantry Division, 28th Infantry Division, 75th Infantry Division, and 5th French Armored Division. As part of the French First Army's drive to wipe out organized German resistance west of the RHINE in the COLMAR pocket, the Corps objective was to seize NEUF-BRISACH, block the RHINE, and maintain contact in the Vosges Mountains.[9]

Jim's detachment reached Sedan, France, where they probably spent the first night. On January 28 they had a beer in Verdun, then traveled on to Nancy where they stayed in a fancy opera house, which was comfortably warm. From Nancy they drove through the night in severe cold and snow south and then east into the forested Vosges Mountains above Colmar. They spent a freezing day in the snow at Saint-Marie-aux-Mines. The next night they drove over the mountain pass to Ribeauville, one of the lovely villages that sit at the edge of the Alsatian plain. The division set up their command post in Ribeauville. Jim's battalion waited on the road for a very cold four hours before moving southeast a few miles to bivouac in a wood near Ostheim. They dug foxholes at 3 a.m. in the frozen ground under 16 inches of snow while "the artillery thundered around us." They were camped in the woods a hundred yards off a road, from which they could hear the sounds of both US and German patrols as they probed back and forth. In April 2014, I visited Ostheim with my family, our friend Dennis Thalmann who lives not far away, and Lise Pommois, a local expert on the battles in Alsace-Lorraine.

We met at the old church wall, a landmark in the village. The church was destroyed in the fighting, but one peaked wall stood, with a stork nest on top. From my father's collection, I had the 1945 topographic map showing where houses, fields, and woods were, and from the Battalion Monthly Report I had the coordinates where they bivouacked that night. The spot lies just east of Ostheim. The E25 highway now separates the village from the woods, but once we got on the other side we found the layout unchanged in 69 years. The outlines of the fields are the same, as are the small roads that provide access to the forest. We drove to the designated coordinates, parked, and got out. On the Alsatian plain, all the good land is farmed intensively. What is left is wet forest. Many of these woods have been drained with ditches over the centuries, including this one. This is the Forêt Communale de Colmar, and we found it carpeted with wild leeks on a lovely spring day. We walked into the woods, fanning out in search of signs of the two cold days and nights that the 275th spent here.

Jim's granddaughters Sarah and Jess exploring remains of foxholes in the woods near Ostheim, France.

It was hard to imagine the 500 men arriving on that dark, cold night, spilling out of their trucks, no doubt parked on the same little road we had just parked on. They must have been exhausted, stiff, and cold from sitting in the backs of trucks for several hours. My father described artillery thundering around them as they dug in. In their first days of combat in Belgium, my father's detachment complained when ordered to dig themselves foxholes for the night. They had learned fast, however, that their only protection was down in the ground. Artillery crashing into woods shatters trees, sending shards of wood at high velocity in all directions. My guess is that they didn't complain now as they cleared away 16 inches of snow and hacked their way through eight inches of the frozen ground until they could finally lie down in the relative warmth and safety of un-frozen soil in the pre-dawn hours of January 30, 1945.

As we walked through the leeks, small craters became evident. Some were probably shell craters, and others were foxholes (or both, as shell craters made handy, pre-excavated foxholes). My daughters were moved that this was where their grandfather had spent that night and the next. We picked a hole and declared that it was his foxhole. The trees in these woods today are mostly less than 69 years old, with just a few big old ash trees that would have witnessed the men digging and the explosions all around them. We got back in our vehicles and drove on through the woods to the east.

Somewhere in France [Ostheim]
Tuesday, 30th January, 1945

Dearest Liz: As you can see from the heading, I have again changed place of operations. I can't tell you just where I am in France, but I am still at the front. We did get away from it on the way here and it sure seemed funny to see real civilian towns. On Sunday, instead of going to church, I was able to get a couple of glasses of beer and did [in Verdun]. Unfortunately it was lousy beer. Last night I had a glass of fair wine. Saw a lot of beautiful country and snow and cold weather. It has been impossible to write until today.

At long last we have actually "gone into the field." We are in a woods (not evergreen). There is somewhere between fourteen and sixteen inches of snow and I have spent a good deal of the day digging myself a nice deep trench to sleep in tonight. It is cold and uncomfortable as hell, but I manage to make out all right, except that I've had no mail from you for five days. . . .

This afternoon, among other things, I sawed wood with Fletcher and Turner. It reminded me of you and I boasted to them that you were the only living female who could begin to saw wood decently.

The life here is more camping out right now than it is anything else. We are really fighting the elements and, I think, winning. Camping out will sure be old stuff after the war, but the five man staff which makes it easy will be missing.

Liz, I've thought about you a lot in the past few days, even though it has been impossible to write you. I passed through a place that had two perfect big slopes for skiing with beautiful scenery etc., but no you there to make it really enjoyable. The full moon through the pine trees reminded me of you. . . .

The men were suffering from dysentery, which became severe. They were terrified that the Germans would attack and they would be unable to defend. No attack came, and before long they learned from captured German correspondence that the enemy lines had suffered too, the same disease paralyzing both sides.

The weather suddenly changed on the night of the 30th, and a thaw set in. Jim moved the aid station to a drier spot nearby. It started to rain, and the streams and rivers rose. Once again, the weather would play a role in the fighting, as the 75th was attacking across the seven-mile-wide Alsace plain and had the Ill River to cross to reach the Rhine east of Colmar. The 275th would help accomplish the required bridging.

Jim writes frequently about food, and one can imagine the quality of the cuisine near the front during a battle in frigid conditions.

Somewhere in France [Ostheim]
31 Jan 1945

Dearest Liz: . . .

We've been trying to do a little housecleaning today—throwing out accumulated junk and repacking the rest. We found we had eight cases of C rations, enough for us for eight or ten days. At first we ate them about as fast as we got them, but, like all soldiers, have gotten pretty tired of them. I drink a cup of good lemonade (contains sixty milligrams of Vitamin C) almost every day. I make it from cast off C ration lemon powder. It is really very good, but no one seems to want to drink it. We had oranges a couple of times last week and had apples three times this week. The apples were good, but frozen when we got them.

Fletcher says to tell you hello, that there's plenty of good beer, steak, bananas, french fries, fried oysters, hot buttered rum, and blond-headed girls—waiting for us when we hit New York! I've invited the boys to a party at the Farm when we get home. I'll send you a more consolidated menu later. Every time we get hungry, I start telling Fletch about the dinner you're going to fix when I get back. . . .

Last night we all went to bed at eight o'clock and slept till eight this morning. I had had a total of about fourteen hours sleep in the four previous nights. . . .

Chapter Five

Disputed Ground: February 1945, France

On our visit in 2014, Lise Pommois showed us the site of the temporary bridge built to cross the Ill. The site is only a couple of miles from the 275th's bivouac in the Ostheim woods. Flanking the modern bridge are concrete abutments just to the north, possibly of the original bridge that had been blown up. Stone revetments just to the south are probably the abutments of the temporary bridge built by the army engineers. This was the only crossing for several miles at the time, and I stood on the bridge imagining February 1, 1945, my father with his medical detachment crossing the river in their two trucks, one carrying the planks they had picked up to serve as the floor of their next spot. They would have turned right after crossing the bridge, driving a mile or so south until they entered the woods north of Holtzwihr, where they bivouacked for the night of February 1. A typical passage from the 275th Battalion Monthly Action Report for February describes the situation:

> 1 February 1945: Battalion bivouacked ¼ mile NE of Ostheim, France. Materials remaining at bridge site (771449) across Colmar Canal sent to XXI Corps for use in construction of another bridge. Battalion convoy left Ostheim and bivouacked ¼ mile NE Holtzwihr, France. 11th Engr Combat Bn given mission to maintain MSR rear of Colmar Canal. 275th Engr Bn Commanding Officer and S-2 with one platoon of Company C (reinforced) attempted to feint construction of a bridge across Colmar Canal between Horburg and Colmar. Purpose was to draw enemy attention in order that 28th Division troops could advance and enter city from the northern flank.[10]

This is the Forêt Communale de Holtzwihr, and is the spot where, a week before, Audie Murphy had climbed up on a burning tank to use the machine gun to single-handedly repel 100 German infantry and six tanks while sending his men to take cover in the woods. The next day Holtzwihr was liberated. The following description is from the History of the 75th Division:

The Colmar Pocket
1–7 February, 1945

To the people of France, the continued German hold on a pocket of Alsace in the Colmar district was an intolerable threat to national pride and security. A month of tough fighting had pushed the Germans east through the Vosges Mountains and out onto the Rhine Plain. The French First Army was accordingly directed to liquidate the remaining pocket. The 75th Infantry Division, battle-hardened by its month in the Ardennes, was assigned to assist in this mission. The battle of Colmar was characterized by the peculiarity of the terrain. The Rhine Plain at this point is about seven miles wide, the greater portion lying on the west side of the Rhine. High mountains overlook the plain from both sides of the river and are inter-visible. Excellent enemy artillery observation into the valley is provided by these mountains. Cover in the plain is provided by deciduous forests and villages. Short range cover is provided by a slight rolling of the ground. The action began with about a foot of snow covering the plain, and one to ten feet lying in the mountains. It was completed in a mid-winter thaw that resulted in severe flooding. After the thaw, tank action was not bogged down because tanks sunk through 8 to 12 inches of topsoil mud to a gravel bed underneath. The infantry, however, had to deal with mud at every step. The mission of the 75th Division was to cover the right flank of the 3d Infantry Division in its drive south along the Rhine.[11]

1 February, 1945
Holtzwihr, France

Dearest Liz:

This letter is again being written on the truck while we are stopped along—Now I'm no longer in the truck but sitting in our tent in a new woods which makes the old woods look like a palace. This place is about like the swamp on the farm with all the big trees cut out. It is thawing like the dickens. Tonight we have one of those warm breezes like the ones in Munich I have told you about. It's just like a spring breeze and really thaws things out. It seems as if every time we are in France we have mud. Some fun. We are getting on to it now, though. We picked up a small stack of lumber at our last area and now have a nice floor for the aid tent made out of sixteen inch planks plus some smaller stuff which we lay on the ground and then pitch the pup tents over them. The boys have two pup tents end to end and four of them sleep in it while one of them and I sleep in the aid tent. I feel like a stinker sleeping in it every single night, but it is the practical way to do it since any patient who comes in at night is a patient whom I'll have to see. . . .

I've been getting a lot of good use out of the muffler, sweater, and helmet you knitted. They are all dandy. The sweater is going to be worn out by the end of the year at the rate I'm wearing it. In cold weather I have eight layers of clothes on my back! . . .

All this outdoor living has been good for us, despite the hardship. We've been living too close inside up to now and had no appetite at all. We're eating fine now. Your husband, for one, is toughening up on all the wood-cutting we do. . . .

The battle of Colmar was fought by French, British, and American forces. The French 5th Armored Division took the small city of Colmar and five nearby villages on February 2. British forces then occupied Colmar. The 75th Division was attacking in a southerly direction just east of Colmar on February 1 and 2. Jim's aid station moved into Wihr-en-Plaine on February 2, just hours after the village had been cleared of Germans.

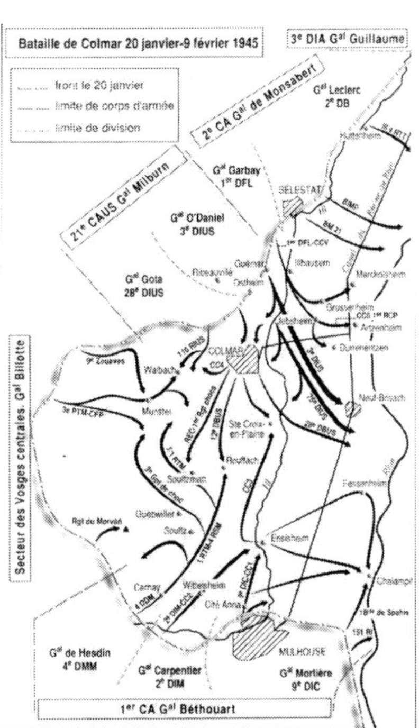

French map of Colmar Pocket action. Musée Mémorial de la Poche de Colmar, Turckheim, Alsace, France.

Jim drove into the city of Colmar once to see it, but otherwise was in Wihr-en-Plaine, a village of about 2,000 people on the plain just east of Colmar (merged with Horbourg in 1993, now called Horbourg-Wihr). He describes the British forces in Colmar stopping for tea in the afternoons and always sleeping comfortably at night, while the Americans, French, and Germans continued working or fighting into the night.

In 2014, I crossed the bridge my father must have used to cross the Ill to reach Colmar. It is a single-lane Bailey Bridge, still in use, just south of Horbourg and about two miles from his aid station in Wihr-en-Plaine.

Somewhere in France [Wihr-en-Plaine (now the eastern part of Horbourg-Wihr)]
2 February 1945

Dearest Liz:

Tonight the battalion received fifteen bags of mail which as yet has not been sorted. . . . We are again in a house. We have a fair sized room with an adjacent room with two beds in it. There is a room upstairs with two dandy beds, but no one is very eager to sleep in it. Our downstairs rooms are good. They are at the front of the house which is set down about six inches in the earth with a stone wall two feet high in front of a garden four feet wide. If we stay on the floor during any shelling, it would therefore take pretty close to a direct hit to do us any damage. Gawd only knows where the proprietors went.

This morning the Colonel found some raw liquor in a cellar in another town and made off with about five gallons of it. It is just plain liquid fire and I won't touch it, but he is having quite a time on it. In prowling around the house we are in, we found a barrel about half full of very good Burgundy type red wine, of which I had three glasses with our spaghetti supper. It really tasted good.

The thaw is a real one. Today was just like a beautiful, clear, warm, early spring day. Most of the snow is gone and the mud is terrific. The worst, tho, is that we are entirely too close to Jerry for comfort, as usual. . . .

The Colonel asked me if I'd try to get him some trout flies if he fixed it for me to go to Paris. Of course I said yes. . . . [He never did.]

Somewhere in France [Wihr-en-Plaine]
3 February, 1945

Dearest Liz: . . .

We now have our home pretty well fixed up. We have the big room—about the size of our bedroom in the apartment—all cleaned up. The little room next to it with two beds sleeps four of the boys. We cleaned out the kitchen today, boarded up the windows, fixed the pump and the drain of the sink it pumps into, installed our own stove and now have an A-1 bathhouse. We also found a little stove and a great big pot to stand on it and boiled up our fatigues this morning and our socks this afternoon. . . . I put name tapes in gloves, marked nine pairs of socks and attended a meeting, thus thoroughly consuming the afternoon. . . .

Things have been pleasingly quiet around here. We just hope that they stay that way and that we stay here a while. . . . One thing I've been doing is to darn the holes in the cashmere lining of my civilian gloves.

The Germans surrendered Colmar on February 3. The contrast between life at battalion headquarters and the front lines just a couple of miles away is striking at times. February 3 was a busy day for 75th Division infantry as they fought for Wolfgantzen as part of the drive toward the Rhine across the broad, flat plain. The division advanced a mile some days, but on February 3 the line only moved about one quarter mile.

Somewhere in France [Wihr-en-Plaine]
3 February, 1945

Dear Dad & Mom . . . The snow has all melted where we are now and we've had regular spring weather yesterday and today. It has finally given my toes, which were frostbitten the end of December, [a chance] to completely recover.

We are now set up in a little village with a small house to ourselves. It is the best set up we've had, so I hope we are able to stay a week or so. Some guy came in this morning and asked how things were going on the front lines, so I told him to walk over to the edge of the village and see for himself. You can see we aren't exactly staying in the rear.

Somewhere in France [Wihr-en-Plaine]
5 February, 1945

Dearest Liz: . . .

At the moment I am the only member of the aid station group still drinking wine regularly. Smitty never drank it at all. I've been drinking it only with meals and still enjoy it. The other boys have been drinking too much and so don't enjoy it anymore!

The village we are in contains, I imagine, about two thousand people. It is very muddy and dirty. In peace time it might be picturesque. We have a barn out in back of our house which is full of tame rabbits. We have been pirating turnips from the fields to feed them. . . .

Somewhere in France [Wihr-en-Plaine]
Liz's Birthday [Feb. 5], 1945

Dearest Liz: . . .

Liz, I wish so much I could be with you today and every day. It's really just about the only thing I look forward to and wait for. The first printed hint of the foreboding I have had for some time appeared today in the Stars and Stripes. That was that the bulk of the soldiers now in Europe would be transferred to the Pacific just as soon as the war here is over. It's a long, weary task to be followed by another. . . .

The fighting was fierce around Neuf-Brisach, an octagonal fortified city built in the early 18th century, across the Rhine from the ancient town of Breisach. Neuf-Brisach is about eight miles southeast of Wihr-en-Plaine and was captured on February 6. On the seventh, the 275th constructed a treadway bridge across the moat into the city. On the eighth, the Germans had been driven back across the Rhine and were off French soil for the first time since the war began.

Somewhere in France [Wihr-en-Plaine]
9 Feb 1945

Dearest Liz: Today was another nice spring day with occasional spring showers. It is beginning to dry out a little which is nice. We are still in the same place. The war is getting further and further away. The people are coming out and back, so that the place almost seems like a normal village again.

Last night I slept upstairs in one of the two beds there. When we first arrived I didn't want to sleep up there because of the danger of shells. Then we had a couple of patients sleeping there. It really gave a good night's sleep. . . .

The whole battalion is in this town tonight, so all the boys came over tonight and we have had a full poker game all evening. I played till ten o'clock, then dropped out, having lost a dollar, five cents. After all I still had to write my sweetie and we have to get moving early tomorrow morning as I'm going to try to run through a physical inspection of the entire battalion. At the same time Hagie is going to do a dental survey. As usual, a rest period will probably mean more work for us all the way around. . . .

Somewhere in France [Wihr-enPlain]
10 Feb, 1945

Dearest Liz: . . .

Tonight the Engineers are getting a real treat. They are actually showing us a real genuine moving pitcher show! It's a Humphrey Bogart in "To Have and to Have Not." Apparently we are going to get our rest period right here. Really, it is not a bad place for it. There are two shows. . . . I had a long, hard day running the battalion thru a physical inspection under anything but optimum conditions. I should have been able to do it in two or three hours, but it took seven or eight. What a chore! However, it is done now, and it is the first unit in the division to be done. . . .

By February 12, the worst of the fighting was over in Alsace and the whole division had been relieved and had moved about 75 miles west to the French town of Luneville for a rest period. The 275th was in the village of Essegney, about 15 miles south of Luneville and Nancy. Within a few days, the 75th was ordered back across Belgium to Holland, where they would join the 9th Army in the effort to push the Germans back across the Rhine near the northern end of the front. The logistics of moving an entire division were imposing. The bulk of the troops moved by train, while all the motorized units, including the medical detachment, drove in convoy. The motor convoy left Essegney on February 15, stopped for a night somewhere near Sedan, France, and a night in Ligny, Belgium, before stopping for two days at Zichem, Belgium on February 17.

Somewhere in France [Essegney]
12 February, 1945

Dearest Liz:

At last it has come! We are on that long-awaited rest period. We are actually in a rear area and it is wonderful. We are in a nice clean village which has hardly been touched by the war and where there is no question about where the inhabitants['] sympathies lie. . . .

We have the aid station in a house owned by a woman who has a small cafe. Her husband was the blacksmith before he died. She has five children. One son is married and lives nearby, one is an enforced laborer in Germany from whom she has not heard in six months, a son who is here, a daughter who is here, and another daughter whom I don't know about. They are very nice. We have their living room for our aid station and sleep out back in a very comfortable barn which we reach by going thru a succession of indoor rooms. We really seem way removed from the war, and it is good. . . .

Night before last, at our other place, they did have a movie. . . . It was Bogart and Bacall in "To Have and Have Not." It was good and just the thing for the boys on the front line. They showed it in the ex village dance hall with the stars shining thru the holes in the roof. . . . We sloshed through about a hundred yards of five to six inch mud to get to it and had no heat in the place and no seats except what we could improvise by removing the shutters from the building and boxes and gas cans. It was a real luxury just the same. . . .

I mentioned Anelli's getting the Bronze Star day before yesterday. If you remember, he is the older (thirty six) good-hearted, simple one that we had such a question in our minds whether to bring along or not. In combat he continues to be the sloppiest man in the battalion. We were notified about eight-thirty that the General was coming to pin the ribbon on, so I had the boys go up to get Anelli and bring him down to the aid station and get him cleaned and polished a little for the General. They had quite a time. It was like trying to get your pet dog ready for the show at the last minute. They bathed & shaved him, cut his hair, and got out clean clothes for him. . . .

Somewhere in France [Essegney]
14 February, 1945

Dearest Liz:

Happy St. Valentines Day! . . .

For several weeks we have had a new General, General Porter. He is really on the ball. He has done more since he's been here than was ever done for the division before. He doesn't take or make excuses, he just believes in getting things done. He expects more of us, and I think he's the man to get it out of us. . . .

Don't worry too much about my being shelled and strafed. It doesn't happen too often. The worst night I've spent was one in the woods when a German patrol got within about two hundred yards of us and the bullets were ricocheting through the trees around us. I don't think that will happen very often. Incidentally, when I speak of "we" or "us" I mean the Medical Detachment Aid Station Group. Sometimes it means the battalion or the part of it we're with (H&S and Headquarters). "The boys" refers to the Detachment and to the aid station group in particular. I live with them and not with the officers. We have had Sgt Hanna, T/3 Smith (Smitty), T/5 Duff, Cpl. Turner, and Fletcher in the aid station. . . . Duff has been getting quite unbearable. He is thirty-seven, used to his own way, always blowing off, and much more bustling than efficient. . . . The result is that I've started alternating him with Garcia, the other one who went to Army Surgical School last summer. Chief (Garcia) . . . is very good in every way. . . .

Somewhere in Belgium [Sichen (now part of Scherpenheuvel-Zichem)]
Sunday, 18 Feb, 1945

Dearest Liz: Again we are in a new place, still in a rear area. This time I am really living in luxury. Our aid station is in a big room which used to be a small store. It is a good set-up. I am living at the local doctor's house two doors up the street. I have a literally enormous room with a beautiful soft double bed with clean sheets and eight foot blankets! How I wish you were here to jump into it with me. It is some luxury. The family consists of the doctor, his wife, his mother, and two daughters aged twenty-one and sixteen respectively. The older one is rather solidly built, the younger has about a five inch nose, but both are very nice and have a good sense of humor. They practically kidnapped me into the house at first, but their ardor was somewhat killed when I announced I was married and showed them your pictures. That properly impressed them that the competition was out of their class. (I don't guess I should flatter you like that, should I, sweetie?) They have an enormous house but they only have heat in the kitchen. Coal is a hundred and twenty dollars a ton and butter six dollars a pound here!—if you can get either.

It is much more like living at home here, because the people live more like we do. There is the common knowledge of Medicine, the girls play the piano, etc. Always before we have been in the homes of relatively poor and uneducated people, who have nevertheless been very kind and goodhearted. This afternoon we had coffee and cake(!) and then the girls played me a little piano concert and the doctor discussed the treatment of pneumonia and meningitis with me. I sure wish we would stay here, because they want to do all my laundry tomorrow, but I fear we'll be moving out. You would be amused at the conversations which are conducted in Flemish, English, German, and French. Between everybody, it is always possible to find the right word in one of the four languages. Two EM were here for coffee this afternoon who just left after staying here seven weeks with an ordnance company. Boy, do those guys have it easy. They work pretty hard, but they live well and have most of their evenings to themselves. . . .

The 275th Battalion moved to Beringe, just west of Panningen, Holland, about three miles from the west bank of the Maas, about six miles west of Venlo. The Germans still occupied the east bank of the Maas, and continued their strategy of using rivers as lines of defense as they retreated. They still controlled dams on the Roer and the Rhine, and released water to create flooded conditions on both rivers, thus slowing the Allied advance.

Somewhere in Holland [Beringe]
19 February, 1945

Dearest Liz:

. . . We are now in the land of canals and windmills and dikes. . . . It is really low, flat, and sandy. H & S is set up in a small town which is well back of the lines for a change. We can hear the artillery in the distance, but that is all. The aid station is set up in two front rooms of different owners next to each other in sort of a long brick tenement house along the main street.

. . . This morning I had an interesting experience. One of the inhabitants took Sgt. Hanna and me down below the town in which we were into a maze of rooms and tunnels hewn out of sandstone. We entered through a small, inconspicuous hole in what looked from the outside like the entrance to a small cold storage cellar. We went down three flights of ladder (about 40 feet) in a narrow shaft and ended up in a room hollowed from the sandstone. We went through a number of such rooms in many of which were carefully tended mushroom beds just lousy with mushrooms. They mix sand and horse manure together, heap them into rounded mounds about twelve inches wide, ten inches high and ten to twenty feet long, water them and let 'em grow. All the buildings in the town are built of sandstone taken from these rooms. They saw it out with a crosscut saw and then let the blocks harden in the air. Each house has its own such cave-cellar from thirty to eighty feet underground and all communicate with each other. There are also tunnels running out into the fields and even to the next town. They can bring cattle, trucks, and everything else in thru some of the field entrances. The air shafts are variously concealed. The one we saw was a dummy well. Incidentally, they have wells in the caverns with very fine, clear, fresh water. The guy told us that as far as they know the caves were dug in 1037 AD! They are still being enlarged as they take out blocks for building. He said there are a lot of dates cut in the walls and that is the oldest one. That is approximately the first mention of it in the town records, too. I really wish you could have seen it. Unfortunately, I didn't get to eat any of the mushrooms—which is the town[']s chief industry. The whole village sleeps in the caves every night as protection from the vicissitudes of night life during a war. . . .

Somewhere in Holland [Beringe]
21 Feb 1945

Dear Pop and Mom, . . . We are having warm spring weather and not much activity at the moment. If we stay here a while, I should be able to get some reading and some laundry done. We have the aid station a quarter mile outside a village now in a small room with another room in the house across the road for the boys to sleep in. The place across the road belongs to a well-to-do farmer who has four daughters who are tickled pink to have us there, so we have the run of the house. They all have a dandy sense of humor and we have a lot of fun. . . .

Somewhere in Holland [Beringe]
22 February, 1945

Dearest Liz:

. . . It's about five-thirty now and the boys are just coming in from throwing & kicking a football around on the road between our two houses. . . . It's very peaceful sitting here at the table looking out over the flat Dutch landscape with the sun setting on the grey horizon over a farmhouse across a black plowed field which is immediately across the road. . . . To add to how good things are, I had a thorough shower this afternoon in our own shower unit which we have set up now. Afterwards I changed all my clothes and gave them to one of the Farmer's daughters to wash, together with my last piece of laundry soap bought on the boat coming over. . . .

The Allies were preparing to pursue the war across the Rhine into Germany itself. The gathering force was massive and the coordination of its various parts was difficult. A combination of the need for secrecy and the inefficiency of army communications meant that units like Jim's battalion were usually ignorant of the movements of the overall force. And those at home, who desperately wanted to know where their loved ones actually were positioned, were only able to grasp at clues they might get in the newspaper.

Somewhere in Holland [Beringe]
24 February, 1945

Dearest Liz:

. . . We heard on the radio this morning that the Ninth Army had started a drive. I hope it is true and that it does the trick, tho I'm afraid the fighting from here in will be inch by inch, foot by foot stuff. . . .

As you know by now, from now on I will be where I'm supposed to be. The Col was just like a little boy wanting to use us as infantry, but I think he's pretty well under control now.

We sure hated to leave France just as it looked like we might be in trout country during trout season. Alas, there is no fishing at all here! You amused your husband when you disgustedly said that due to our frequent movements you were just going to read about the whole damn front from now on.

You asked what I thought about the big three conference. The answer is, I don't. I don't see that it or the war have solved a solitary problem and I'm sure the war has created a lot of new ones. . . .

Anna, the farmer's daughter who did my laundry, really did a dandy job. It sure looks beautiful. She even ironed my fatigues! I gave her the laundry soap, two bars of Lux, two chocolate bars and two packs of cigarettes for doing a set of ODs, one of fatigues, underwear & a pair of socks. . . .

Jim's letters to Liz often reflect his concern over Liz's relationship with his parents, known as Ma and Pop. Liz's apartment in New York was right around the corner from the senior McKays', and they spent a lot of time together. After a rocky start to their relationship on Liz's first visit to Basking Ridge, they obviously were doing better all the time. No doubt their mutual concern for Jim helped the process. Liz's letters reflected her concern for not being a burden on her in-laws, and Jim's letters and those from the senior McKays reassure her that she is a pleasure, not a burden.

Somewhere in Holland [Beringe]
25 Feb 1945

Dear Ma,

. . . Our present stop in our comprehensive tour of western Europe is a small town in Holland. It's not storybook Holland at all, except that the people sure do do a lot of scrubbing of floors. There are lots of canals and a few windmills, but in general it is a poor and relatively un-picturesque countryside with no signs of the fields of tulips you hear about. . . . The boys (five med. det. EM) sleep across the street in the house of a well-to-do farmer with four unmarried daughters. We call them our "woman-power" and utilize it for laundry etc. One of them did a beautiful job on mine—the first I haven't done myself since we've been over here. She even ironed it, which is luxury deluxe. . . .

I've been glad to hear from all reports that your blood pressure is down, that you're looking and feeling better than you have in years, and that you're actually taking it easier. . . . That's the sort of thing which is very important. . . .

Mom, you've really been wonderful in taking care of and doing things for Liz and I can't tell you how very much I appreciate it. She really appreciates things like your getting her a little bouquet because "you're sure I would have if I'd seen it." . . . She really seems to like both yours and Dad's company and it's a great comfort to me that you hit it off so well. . . .

My health remains excellent and my spirits hold up pretty well most of the time. Our food continues good and we're practically at peace with Germany up here compared to what we've had before. The end of the war still looks a long way off over here. . . .

Chapter Six

Across the Rhine: March 1945, Holland and Germany

Duty in Holland was routine as the 275th Engineers waited for the Allied push to the Rhine. They were assigned to the VIII Corps of the British Second Army, defending the west bank of the Maas near Venlo. Patrols were sent across the Maas every night. An excerpt from the 275th Battalion's monthly report illustrates the preparations that were underway for crossing the Rhine:

> 1 March 1945: Beringen, Holland (479059). Ferry training with 440th AA [Antiaircraft Artillery] Battalion and 772 TD [Tank Destroyer] Battalion for crossing on Maas River. . . .
>
> 3 March 1945: Left Piej, Holland and arrived 4 miles NE Venlo, Holland (948148). Companies attached to respective CTs [Combat Teams].
>
> 4 March 1945: Companies given mission of clearing all roads of mines in the division sector. . . .
>
> 6 March 1945: Technician sent to Company B, 275th Engineers with twelve flame throwers and fifty filling to train 290th Infantry. Billeting party dispatched to vicinity of Lintfort, Germany (RA1823).
>
> 7 March 1945: Battalion departed in division motor convoy en route to Lintfort, Germany. 75th Division to relieve 35th Division and defend sector along Rhine River. Companies given mission of clearing all roads of mines within division sector.
>
> 8 March 1945: Reconnaissance made of all roads along Rhine River.
>
> 10 March 1945: Complete reconnaissance made of Moers-Beckerworth bridge (railroad). Bridge guards placed on all bridges in division sector.
>
> 11 March 1945: Camouflage net constructed across arch in Orsoy to conceal and obstruct the enemy's view in line with important road. . . .
>
> 13 March 1945: Infantry and engineer patrols to be sent across Rhine River nightly. . . .
>
> 14 March 1945: Class 40 timber bridge constructed at RA212289. . . .

Camouflaged dummies of boats and bridge materials to be constructed under supervision of camouflage officer from 84th Camouflage Bn. Class on mines and booby traps given to 17th Cavalry Group.[12]

This period saw the first heavy use of the first jet fighter, the Messerschmitt 262. Hitler was counting on the superiority of these jets and the V-1 and V-2 rockets to turn the tide of the war. The 75th was one of the first to shoot down a jet fighter.

In Holland, there was even time for a steak that Jim cooked up in a manner he would become famous for in later life. His disgust for war surfaced again, along with his daydreams about getting home to Liz.

Somewhere in Holland [Beringe]
1 March, 1945

Dearest Liz:

. . . We had a real treat for lunch today. One of the cooks gave me a two and a half pound chunk of beef today which we ate at lunch. I cut and cooked my own—a five by six inch two inch thick piece fried with onions and red in the middle. . . .

The war news is looking awfully good around here right now. I just hope it keeps up and that this turns out to be the final drive. That Iwo Jima fight really sounds tough. I was also glad to read that the US occupation area would be Southern Germany. Fraternization will be a big problem there, but there will be a lot fewer soldiers shot in the back and other difficulty than elsewhere. I wonder if that includes Austria?

. . . I have continued to do some medical reading and reading "So Little Time." It is very good. One very appropriate passage I'll quote. He is speaking of books & writing about World War One: "They tried to give dramatic significance to something in which significance was utterly lacking. They tried to give an interpretation to something which actually offered nothing for an artist to interpret." That is so true. War is nothing. It has no sense, no meaning, no purpose, and no use.

. . . From what you say, I'm sure our dreams are very similar about when we get together again. I certainly long for the day. You don't have to worry about things being tough for me right now. They are extremely easy. I keep busy with one thing or another, but very little of it is real work in any way.

One interesting thing is that in the past year, if I haven't learned anything about medicine, I've learned a good deal about its practice. I'm sure that lots of things which used to bother me are just routine now. . . .

Somewhere in Holland [Piej]
2 March, 1945

Dearest Liz:

. . . It was a typical March day with wind, rain, sleet, snow and sunshine. It was the coldest day in about a month and we all nearly froze, having become so accustomed to the soft garrison type life we have been leading. . . .

The aid station is now located in an ex. bar in a small town. It is a large room for which the stove is grossly inadequate, especially, as now, the glass is out of the many big windows which are boarded up leaving big cracks through which the wind whistles merrily or nastily. . . .

Last night we had a gay evening sitting around with the four farmer's daughters and his wife drinking cocoa and wine and singing. We sang English, Dutch, German and American songs until I was hoarse. I went back to the aid station about ten-thirty but got very little sleep what with one thing after another all night. Tonight I'm going to try to hit the hay early. . . .

The 275th crossed the Maas at Venlo and on into Germany on March 3, as part of Operation Grenade, which was designed to push the Germans east across the Rhine. For the first time the Americans had to confront the local people as occupiers rather than as liberators. Jim was set up about a mile from the border, just east of Venlo, probably in a tiny village called Louisenburg.

When I visited in April of 2014, I found a productive agricultural area with no distinction between the Dutch and German sides of the undefended border. In the midst of flat fields drained by a system of ditches, I found the farm that had served as battalion headquarters on March 3. The border here is a drainage ditch 650 meters west of the farm, a ditch that serves fields on both sides of this artificial frontier.

Somewhere in Germany [3 miles east of Venlo, probably Louisenburg]
3 March, 1945

Dearest Liz:

Well, sweetie, here we are at last in Adolf's home country. We are in some houses at a little country crossroads which haven't been touched. It is sure easy to tell you're in a country where the war has not been actually fought. The houses are better and the people have so much more of everything. Almost all of them have moved out, taking their valuables with them. There are just three civilians in the group of five houses where we are. The medics have one six room house all to themselves! Some luxury. Supper was supposed to be K rations, but we had ham, eggs, & wine, courtesy of the guy who owns the place. There is a big coal pile out back, so everything is OK except for no electricity. I hope we continue to be so lucky, but doubt that we will.

The war news continues to be extremely good. I just hope the drive continues right on thru. When it's over, it will probably just mean being packed off to the South Pacific, but we're all hoping they'll send us via the USA with a month's furlough. I doubt that they will, tho.

Actually, being in Germany certainly gives one's morale an uplift. You feel as if you're actually getting on with the war. The civilians here talk about the hardship of the war, but they don't know what war really is. It's hard to be hard on them, especially when they're so eager to oblige, but I think we should give every one of them a taste of what the people in Belgium, Holland, and France have had to go thru under them. These people are still living in comparative luxury. I don't know if it is as true of those in the cities as it is here in the country.

The countryside is still flat here, but not so completely so as in Holland. Then there are the woods which are scattered so thickly all over Germany. . . .

Somewhere in Germany [probably Louisenburg]
4 March, 1945

Dearest Sweetie: For a change, I really earned my keep today, but not as a medical officer. Since I'm the only one who speaks German well, they just appointed me the local military government until the regular one can take over. Boy, it is a real job and very interesting. I would like to do it, I think. It presents a real challenge, both in the matter of wits and good will. I think I could do it well in Germany because I really believe I understand the people well, aside from knowing the language. I must have interviewed well over a hundred people today. What a job! At least it got us a telephone. This morning I went around to all the houses within a kilometer of here to register the inhabitants and notify the people of the regulations we're setting down. The big problem, however, are the people coming through, mostly [censored] either returning to [censored] after being freed from forced labor in the part of Germany we've taken, or else coming to buy milk from the farmers here. The [censored] all have the idea they can move as they will and do what they will, which creates a problem. The Germans are scared stiff and doing just what we tell them to. We're trying to get everyone to stay put for a few days, but it is difficult. It seems like an impossible task to separate out any Nazi sympathizers. I don't believe that any of the people left here really are, but I'm suspicious of some of the people coming thru with [censored] papers.

Our rules are: that they must stay in or around their own house and barn, no visiting at all, one person allowed out one hour a day (eleven till noon) to do any necessary outside errands. I'm telling all the [censored] to stay on their side of the border or we'll pick them up as Germans.

Last night I checked a number of houses but didn't get any names. While I was doing it the wife at one of them started to talk about how hard the war was. I told her rather sternly that they didn't know what it was here; that if she wanted to find out about it we'd be glad to imitate the German soldiers. That shut her up. When I went up with a group of armed men this morning to get their names, I called that family and another out in the yard to do it without saying why they were being called out. All were scared stiff, wringing their hands and crying, obviously thinking we were going to pick out a couple and shoot them. If we'd been Germans we probably would have and they were thinking about what I'd said the night before.

When the Germans left [censored] they took every single cow and horse they could find with them, leaving some of them with the farmers here. Today a group of [censored] Home Guards came over to get them back but I think got a little carried away with themselves. I had to calm them down and make them realize they were not a law unto themselves and at the same time convince them we were on their side, not the Germans. They were very reasonable, once convinced that I meant business, and we were able to find a number of cows and horses for them with [censored] brands on them. The farmers admitted all of them and even showed us a few we didn't spot. They went back to [censored]. I'm afraid that we'll have to arrest a few [censored] for crossing the border tomorrow to convince them they can't do it without proper authority.

One thing that will interest you, sweetie, is the amazingly large number of pretty girls here. There are four really pretty ones within a half mile radius. The prettiest one Reen explained by saying "You know, her features are a lot like Liz's!" So I'm afraid you're still my acme of perfection, darling. That is going to make the "fraternizing" a problem, because these people are so anxious to make friends and we are not supposed to talk to them except on business. . . .

P.S. All the cut out places are by yours truly. They all refer to the name of a neighboring country or its inhabitants. Jim

The next day's discoveries brought on some ranting and philosophy.

Somewhere in Germany [Louisenburg]
5 March, 1945

Dearest Liz:

. . . Today I found out that three households here have foreign "forced labor" servants. It makes a problem about what to do with the servants and also throws a new and unfavorable light on their employers, since I imagine that anyone who has pressed labor probably requested it. Something new I discovered is that the Germans have made forced laborers out of Polish women as well as men. Those people are real genuine minus fourteen karat swine. They ought to put up the whole damn nation on an auction block and sell them all over the world as slaves.

You will be surprised to hear that your husband attended a church service tonight. I went because I think very highly of the chaplain (MacArthur). I believe I mentioned him as being very good back at Breckinridge, and he has continued to be just as good since. He hasn't had very good attendance lately and I wanted to help boost that and also hear him preach. . . . It was a good talk, but he's still missing what I believe is the fundamental, the one basic fundamental, which would automatically stop wars, avoid a lot of hit-run accidents, and solve innumerable little unpleasantnesses and unhappinesses. That fundamental, I believe, is just plain everyday thoughtfulness and consideration of the other fellow. That is still not a basic teaching by parents and church. If everyone practiced it, minor disagreements could never build up to war, nor would the head of any state permit his people to enter a war. And the world would be rich in material goods because everyone would not destroy something just because he couldn't use it, but would preserve it for someone who could. I've seen so much wanton waste and destruction where a little thoughtfulness would have prevented them, and not only that, but would actually have made less work. That, it seems to me, is the trouble with our whole individual, group, national, and international life. Everyone is grabbing at everything he can get, whether he can use it or not, thus depriving someone of the use of it, to whom it would do some good. That's the trouble with our present-day civilization. It is trying to do good, allegedly, by groups, but that's the wrong place to start. If you don't have thoughtful, considerate individuals you cannot have thoughtful considerate groups. That's why I still think Roosevelt has done more harm than good. His policy has been that as long as the group aim was good, individual integrity is unimportant; that the end more than justifies the means. But I don't see how that is compatible, because in the long run the group is just as much a self-centered, lying, cheating, killing, harmful organization as its leaders and individuals are as people. A lasting peace, a good union, a good government, a happy people—all are automatic if every individual is saturated and believes in the tenets of ordinary practical thoughtfulness & consideration of the other fellow which he practices. The wrongness, futility and danger of unions and other forms of group pressure become obvious when you think and realize that they would all lose their reason for being if men, as individuals were thoughtful and considerate of the other fellow in practice.

They are dangerous because they attack the problem at too high a level—group instead of individual, and obscure and delay the discovery of the true issue which is individual. Their improvements are all surface and artificially maintained as they now stand. They mean less than nothing because not only have they used lying, cheating, killing, and force, but they have endowed these methods with not only an aura of respectability, but of laudability. This, naturally, put the day of true improvement even further off. The place to stop labor troubles, war, hunger, poverty, etc is by proper education <u>and</u> <u>example</u> in homes, schools, churches, and daily life. That's the point they're all completely missing these days. That's the weakness in the extreme conscientious objector's stand, too, I think. It contains too many elements of selfishness. He's not out there <u>sharing</u> the hardship when you get right down to it. He is refusing to do his part to ease the <u>other</u> fellow's load in order to better follow his <u>own</u> ideas. Refusal to fight or take life doesn't answer the question, because it's still self-centered and not basic enough. With the right attitude and education you'd never have to refuse to fight or take life. "Brotherly love" doesn't meet the real issue. It becomes too much of a surface affair. A man can live in <u>physical</u> peace and harmony, yet be an absolute dirty bastard when you come right down to it. It's the difference between being within the law or really fair, between being really ethical or as ethical as you have to be or as the next fellow is. Everyone had lost sight of the fact that because someone else does something a little off color does not make it all right for us to do it; nor does the fact they get away with it or do it "in a good cause" or "because they had to" make it a right or desirable way.

Excuse the sermon and I hope you've lived thru it. You might hang onto it, because I think it expresses fairly intelligibly what I believe in. It ought to make Democracy work, if done.

Jim's beliefs were sometimes difficult for Liz, with a Quaker mother and a brother who was Quaker and a conscientious objector serving time in a prison in the State of Washington for his refusal to serve in the military.

Somewhere in Germany [Louisenburg]
6 March, 1945

Dearest Liz:

. . . I started to get the knotty problems of military government today—lack of uniformity of the authorities' regulations in different places, people wanting to go here and there for good but questionable sufficient reasons, etc. It's a job which offers a real challenge. One of the military government teams came down this afternoon and watched me at work, complimented me and said they would honor any passes I wanted to give and to use my own discretion about the exceptions to the rules. That was a real compliment.

Tonight I got back some laundry I gave the family down the road to do night before last. They really did a beautiful job. As far as these people are concerned I'm the local dictator, so they're really anxious to please. . . .

They are now attempting to reclassify and reassign to the right spots all the medical officers in the European Theatre. Today I made out a questionnaire and then Col. Hansston has to make out a form with his opinion on it. On the bottom of my questionnaire is a box where the senior medical officer of my organization (Col. Davis) is to give his opinion as to the Army job I'm best suited for. He gives a first and second choice. The second choice was the type of duty I'm doing now, the first was "Medical unit commander." That means commanding officer of a medical battalion or similar unit or in other words a Lt. Colonel's job! Wow! I've said before that everyone keeps mentioning further promotion to me, but I've thought it was partly in fun, partly just trying to be nice because they like me. . . . I hope I'm not in the Army long enough for it to come, but it's nice to think about. . . . The job I don't particularly want and which I'm afraid I'll get is that of Regimental Surgeon, a major's job. I know that Col. Davis thinks a couple of the men in those jobs now do too much bitching and make too little give and take effort to make things run smoothly. I get along fine with everyone. . . . I don't particularly want to leave the engineers.

On March 1, the 75th Division was assigned to the XVI Corps of the US Ninth Army and on March 7 moved up to relieve the 35th Division, which had fought to cross the Roer River and advance to the Rhine. The 75th was assigned a sector along the Rhine, from opposite Duisburg on the south to opposite Wesel on the north. The Germans still held a bridgehead west of the Rhine at Wesel, where they had been using a railroad bridge and a road bridge to evacuate men and matériel across the river. On March 10, they completed that withdrawal and blew up the last bridges just as the Americans rushed in.

Rivers are numerous and confusing in this part of Europe. The Rur rises in Germany in the highlands of the Eifel region and flows northwest into the Maas at Roermond, Netherlands, where the name is spelled Roer. The Maas is the Dutch name for the Meuse. The Meuse rises in France, flowing through Belgium and the Netherlands. From Nijmegen to the sea south of Rotterdam, the Maas parallels the Rhine. At one point the two are less than half a mile apart and are connected by a canal. The Ruhr River is a completely different system from the Rur (Roer) and is on the east side of the Rhine, flowing west to enter the Rhine at Duisburg. The Moselle rises on the western slopes of the Vosges Mountains in France and flows north through Metz, France, and then northeast through Trier to enter the Rhine at Kologne. All these rivers formed defensive lines for the German armies, and formidable obstacles to the Allies. The Germans destroyed all bridges as they withdrew to the east.

Although Berlin, the political heart of Germany, might constitute the final objective of the Allied armies, the region known as the Ruhr with its coal mines, blast furnaces, and factories—the muscle with which Germany waged war—was the more vital objective. Without the Ruhr, Germany's case would fast become hopeless; taking Berlin and all other objectives then would be but a matter of time. No political or geographical entity, the Ruhr takes its name from the river flowing through the heart of the region. The Ruhr region can be fairly accurately described as a triangle with its base along the east bank of the Rhine River from Cologne northward to Duisburg, a distance of some thirty-five miles. One side of the triangle extends eastward from Duisburg along the Lippe River to Dortmund, for thirty-five to forty miles; the other side about the same distance southwestward from Dortmund to the vicinity of Cologne. The region encompasses major cities such as Essen, Dusseldorf, and Wuppertal.[13]

Somewhere in Germany [Lintfort]
7 March, 1945

Dearest Liz:

. . . We are now set up with all of H&S [Headquarters & Supply] Co in two big buildings across the street from each other in a small German city whose exact size I don't know, but it does have a trolley line. . . . There is no light and water. . . . This battalion still doesn't know how to run a billeting party. We would much rather live in the country than in the town, too. It is so much cleaner. The latrine facilities are almost non-existent, the men careless, and there's no place to dig one outside here. We have one toilet which doesn't flush for forty men. . . .

For the first time in God knows how long, I have seen a hill, a small one, to be sure, but nevertheless a hill. It looked wonderful. Germany in general is a lot prettier than the other countries. There are lots of pretty girls—relatively speaking—but the boys are sticking to the no-fraternizing policy very well so far. The Germans see you on the street and want to speak and smile but we give them the stony-stare treatment. They're tired of war and beefing pretty hard about it and being chased out so we can billet troops. The situation here, though, is nothing compared to Belgium, France and Holland. There is plenty of coal and there seems to be enough food and cattle feed for everyone. There is no doubt but that

> they've been living off the fat of the land at the expense of the occupied countries. They're tired of the war right now and a lot of them are glad to see us come for that reason, but I don't think hardly any of them regret the war for a minute. This country really needs to get the works in occupation. . . .

Lintfort (now Kamp-Lintfort) sits on higher ground between the Maas River and the Rhine, about 10 miles northwest of Duisburg. On my 2014 visit, I found a small, undistinguished city, with no sign of WWII having passed this way. Down the road lies the Rheinberg War Cemetery, holding the remains of more than 3,000 British airmen, killed on bombing raids to the Ruhr region. It is a sobering reminder of the cost of those glorified bombing runs. Row after row of graves with crews buried side by side, distinguishable by their identical dates of death. I saw one crew shot down on December 24, 1944. That day had been the first clear day in two weeks, and the Allies sent thousands of bombers out on the famous Christmas raids. My father described seeing hundreds of them fly over where he was that day and watching them go down as they flew over the German anti-aircraft batteries. Seeing these 3,000 graves brought home the horror of those raids, on both sides.

It is a short drive down to the Rhine at Rheinberg and Orsoy. In the National Archives, I had discovered maps of this section of river drawn by the 275th with potential crossing sites inked in, so I concentrated my exploration there. The river is lined with a dike about 30 feet high. The cross-sections drawn by the engineers in 1945 show a dike only 11 feet high. I found a spot to park outside the dike near an apparent coal depot, about half a mile downstream of Orsoy. I climbed the dike and suddenly the sweep of the great Rhine River unfolded in front of me. Huge power plants upstream and downstream as well as the coal depot reminded me that this is still the industrial heartland of Germany. The map showed the coal depot, and from my father's description of patrolling the riverbank in a spot with big pipes lying around, I decided this could have been the site where he had his closest call with a mortar shell (described later). The banks of the river are now lined with rock or concrete, with about 50 yards of grass leading to the inside foot of the dike. I dropped down from the dike and walked along the bank, imagining his experience. Where I looked downstream a few miles in hazy sunshine at the cooling tower of a power plant, he would have been looking at the smoke screen from the constant effort to screen Allied preparations for the crossing. Whenever the wind blew the smoke clear, anyone on this side of the dike, including my father, would have been under fire from the German side of the river with small arms, mortars, and strafing planes.

It was clear from the maps that the 275th had zeroed in on a crossing at the site of a ferry at the upstream end of the village of Orsoy. The ferry is still there and is the only way to cross the Rhine in the 15 miles between the bridges at Wesel and Duisburg. I walked through the peaceful village, finding it hard to imagine that the place was essentially rubble by the end of March 1945. My father had his aid station in a bomb shelter here for three days while the 275th cleared the streets and tried to construct a boom across the river. I walked along the dike that isolates the village from the river. The dike here is landscaped with trees and a pleasant walk, affording an excellent view of the ferry going back and forth, dodging river traffic, overseen by the enormous cooling tower of the Walsum power plant.

Somewhere in Germany [Lintfort]
8 March, 1945

Dearest Liz:

. . . The town we're in now is full of people and military government continues to be the biggest problem. There is still a lack of organization and coordination between the official military government and the occupying troops. The people and the occupying troops are both ignorant of what the exact regulations are and the result is that some troops operate according to one set of rules, others according to others and what a mess. However, it is getting straightened out and should be OK as soon as everyone gets to know what problems will arise and a good idea of routine procedure. We have to be strict as hell with them and yet not antagonize them. They take a mile if you give them an inch, yet they're scared stiff at first. It's very difficult to be strict and at the same time just. If we fail in either I think we will lose their respect and have that much more difficult a job. . . .

Jim was learning administration, and discovering that not only was he good at it, but that he enjoyed it. Dealing with US Army bureaucracy was good training for his future in dealing with university bureaucracy.

On March 10, the 75th Division relieved other units of the XVI Corps along the west bank of the Rhine between Wesel and Duisburg. Jim's aid station stayed in Lintfort while preparations for crossing the Rhine progressed. All the army engineering units were kept very busy, including night patrols across the Rhine behind enemy lines to reconnoiter the engineering needs when the troops got across the river.

Somewhere in Germany [Lintfort]
15 March, 1945

Dearest Liz:

Your Christmas card (!) and a letter written Dec. 10th arrived today along with the November copy of the Babies Hospital News Bulletin. . . .

It was a beautiful warm, clear spring day today, the warmest yet. This afternoon I chaperoned twenty men to a town about twenty miles from here where we heard Andre Kostelanetz conduct a very good orchestra made up of G-I Army band members, Lily Pons sing, and very good piano and flute playing by two other USO artists. . . . While there I ran into a boy named Harry Fraker whom I knew at Lawrenceville and Princeton. He is the first old acquaintance I've run into over here. . . .

Somewhere in Germany [Lintfort]

Dearest Liz:

. . . There is a rumor out around the battalion that the Colonel may be promoted out and Major Fore take his place. If that happens, I'll probably ask for a transfer. About a week ago several people came to me and told me to be on my guard because there was a lot of talk going around about me being pro-German and even pro Nazi! Apparently the good Major had quite a bit to do with it, though he hasn't dared to say anything to my face. With that knowledge I've found him checking up on me behind my back several times after I had been talking to Germans for him or others. . . . He mistrusts me chiefly thru narrow mindedness and ignorance, I think. . . . I don't want anything to do with a unit he is in command of. The present situation is extremely unpleasant, to say the least. I'd like to smack his smug mouth, but I'm afraid it would cause more trouble than it would be worth. . . .

The push to cross the Rhine was underway with the 75th Division now part of the Ninth Army, assigned to the northern crossing, which would occur between Rees and Duisburg, centered on Wesel. Duisburg is at the confluence of the Ruhr with the Rhine and was a vital port and the entrance to the Ruhr Valley, the heart of industrial Germany. The crossing concentrated north of the Ruhr and the effort was code-named Operation Flashpoint. The railroad bridge at Wesel was the last to be destroyed by the Germans as they retreated, on March 10. The army engineering battalions had a crucial role to play, building crossings of various types to get the armies across the Rhine. The 275th Engineer Combat Battalion was sent upstream to construct a boom across the Rhine to catch floating mines sent to blow up the floating bridges that would soon be put across by the Allies. The Rhine is over 1,000 feet wide at this point, and the flow was high and cold in the spring of the year. The ground was a little higher on the east side where the Germans covered the river, leaving the men working on the boom highly vulnerable. Arrangements were made with 75th Division headquarters for both artillery and infantry support during the boom construction. On March 23–24, the 75th Division artillery poured a massive barrage across the Rhine to soften up the German lines for the crossing and provide cover for the 275th's efforts to build the boom. Smokescreens were constant along the west bank in an attempt to hide Allied preparations. Jim set up the aid station close to the river (probably in Orsoy) to better serve the squads working on the boom. They were under all types of fire most of the time, so they worked at night as much as possible. Men had to cross in small boats under cover of darkness to attempt to secure the far end of the boom on the German side of the river. The first boom was launched upstream of Orsoy on March 24, at the same time the main assault was launched a few miles downstream. The boom was nearly complete when it was hit by enemy artillery and lost. A second try to put a boom across at the same location the next day failed due to the strong current. A third attempt was made downstream near Orsoy on the twenty-sixth. This one failed when the cable snapped after having been hit by enemy strafing. The recoiling cable (about an inch in diameter) snapped back and cut off the leg of an unlucky enlisted man. Jim remembers he had surprisingly little bleeding due to the shock, and he applied two tourniquets and sent him back to a hospital. A fourth attempt, on March 27, using powerboats also failed due to current.[14] Nonetheless, all the activity diverted German attention and strength away from actual crossing points downstream, near Wesel.

Members of the 275th Engineers building a temporary bridge for the Rhine crossing 24 March 1945; US Army Signal Corps photo by JD Karr; National Archives, College Park, Maryland.

During this action along the river, the Colonel commanding the 275th thought that the medical detachment could wear their medic armbands and move along the river to scout things out, without being fired on. Jim recounts his closest escape of the war, which occurred here, when the Germans apparently had not heard about not firing on medics. He and a few others were scouting when they came under mortar fire. Jim was near a foxhole, which he dove into, while the others took cover in some large concrete pipes lying nearby. The foxhole was about six feet long by two feet wide by four feet deep, with some boards covering the top except for a small space to climb in and out. When the shelling had apparently stopped, Jim tried to hoist himself up through the entrance, but the canteen on his belt caught on the cover, so he dropped back into the hole. Just then a mortar landed immediately outside the hole, right where he would have been if the canteen had not caught.

His letter to Liz near the end of this action shows the strange juxtaposition of a soldier dealing with combat, while trying to write his sweetheart and sound as normal as possible.

Somewhere in Germany [west bank of the Rhine, vicinity of Orsoy]
26 March, 1945

Dearest Liz:

This will have to be short because I am dog-tired. It is now one o'clock. Last night I got four hours sleep, the two nights before one hour of fitful. It seems literally like six days since we started. During the day I've been working and again at night, too. We've been on a river problem and I've had the aid station in a bomb shelter about three hundred yards from where the front is. I've been shelled, bombed, strafed, pinned down by mortar fire, and under direct small arms fire. I've had two narrow escapes and have no desire for more. I'm still not eligible for the purple heart, thank god.

. . . Don't bother about the razor brush. . . . We've had beautiful weather until today when it rained about half the day. A lot of the trees are coming out and I've seen loads of daffodils, other small flowers and overgrown pussy willows. I picked a sample of each for you during the past few nights but no longer have them due to various types of damage. . . .

By March 29 the entire 75th Division was across the Rhine and participating in the intense fighting north of the Ruhr. The mission of the XVI Corps was to eliminate the Ruhr industrial centers. The 75th was assigned to sweep from the Rhine at Dinslaken, east toward Recklinghausen, and then south to the Ruhr to isolate Dortmund.

My own Rhine crossing was on March 29, 2014, exactly 69 years after the 275th built their bridge at the same spot. I awoke early and got to the Orsoy ferry shortly after it started its day. I drove down the paved ramp on the bank and onto the ferry, and was the first of three cars and one bicycle to ride this run. The five-minute crossing was so easy and peaceful on this lovely, cool morning. I tried to imagine the scene 69 years ago. The 275th had just built a bridge after two weeks at work on the west bank as a frontline unit, while the infantry waited behind them. At least one of the three companies of engineers crossed first to sweep for mines, followed by the 75th Infantry regiments, now able to cross a bridge. My father's medical detachment would then have loaded up their gear and driven across to find a new spot to set up the aid station east of the Rhine.

31 March, 1945 [Brassert section of Marl]
Somewhere in Germany

Dearest Liz: Tonight we . . . have a nice six room house in a medium sized town. . . . They finally sent me on a quartering party so I got houses in the good part of town instead of the poor. The owners seem to be solid Nazi Party members, too, from the looks of things. . . .

I'm also sending you a money order for four hundred dollars sometime in the near future. It is pay which has piled up on me. We also had to change all our money into marks. That meant quite a bit right there as I had retained a good deal of each country's money in case of sudden moves. I also turned in twenty seven dollars of American money which I had kept so as not to have to stand in line to get money if and when I get home.

. . . Yesterday was busy as hell and then we spent the night in a field. I slept in the aid tent which we had dug in against German artillery fire. We didn't get any, though. Today was payday and I've been busy dashing around trying to get all my men in the various companies paid off. Tonight I've been swamped again with civil affairs and civilian requests for medical aid. . . .

I can't say when we move, Liz. You'll just have to gather it from my letters if you can. The present place is our fourth billet in Germany, tho, if that is any help. . . .

Chapter Seven

The Last Fighting: April 1945, Ruhr Region, Germany

The 275th Battalion was busy in April supporting the rapid movement of the infantry regiments in their maneuvers to surround the Ruhr industrial area. Many roads had to be swept for mines and cleared of debris, and bridges had to be constructed over the canals. Over the next two weeks the medical detachment moved the aid station every few days as the infantry battalions pushed the Germans into the shrinking Ruhr pocket.

I drove the same route, more or less, 69 years later. I stopped in Recklinghausen for a stroll into the town, sitting at a street-side café with a croissant and coffee, imagining the town as my father saw it. Large areas of the Ruhr had been flattened by the saturation bombing, so he likely saw mostly rubble as the engineers worked to clear roads for the troops and supply convoys. I hopped on one of the several autobahns in this heavily populated area, and drove down to the Ruhr River at Witten. This was where my father saw his last day of combat. As opposed to the northern Rhine with its broad floodplain, the Ruhr runs down a valley with steep bluffs on either side, making it easy for the Germans to inflict heavy casualties on the American troops along the river below.

An excerpt from the battalion's monthly journal describes the activity:

> The 75th Infantry Division was continuing its attack to the East; objective, the Zweig Canal. The 275th Engineer Combat Battalion supported the advance. Company A was in close support of the 289th Infantry Regiment, Company B in close support of the 290th Infantry Regiment and Company C the 291st. Engineer support consisted chiefly in clearing road blocks, bridging and constructing culverts or bypasses over small streams and canals; removing mines from roads and marking and clearing intermittent minefields. . . .
>
> Fortunately, the 291st Infantry Regiment was able to gain a small bridge-

head across the Zweig Canal in Datteln, during the night of 2 April. This bridgehead enabled Company C to construct a much needed causeway in that vicinity on the afternoon of 3 April. Construction was started at 1500 and by 2000, vehicles were crossing. . . .[15]

Jim's name appeared in the 275th's Monthly Action Against Enemy Report for April, when he was awarded a Bronze Star for meritorious support of his battalion under combat conditions. In the midst of intense fighting, Jim's correspondence continued to downplay the details of his combat experience. Letters home to his parents tended to be weekly, rather than the daily routine Jim maintained with Liz. He was a bit more graphic with his mother than his wife.

Somewhere in Germany [Brassert section of Marl]
3 April 1945

Dear Mom, . . .

You spoke in your letter about how much Liz seemed to like the Farm, so much so that you said it wouldn't surprise you at all if we ended up settling there. . . . That would be funny, wouldn't it, after all our talk about the far west. . . .

Our last operation was on a big river. I got closer to the war during it than I have so far. I moved the aid station up to give direct support. We were about a mile forward of the infantry aid station and had quite an exciting time. I was up all night three nights in a row, working as an engineer officer one of them. The morning of that night I got caught out on the exposed river bank with some other men when our smoke screen blew away and the enemy opened up with direct small arms fire. Everyone got away without a scratch, though. Two days later I was pinned down by mortar fire twice in twelve hours. The first time five shells lit within fifteen feet of my foxhole, one of them being only two feet from it. The second time I had no foxhole, the closest one hitting about twenty feet away. Some fun, but not even a scratch. A bomb also hit seventy feet from my aid station, which was in a bomb shelter. I have no desire to get any closer to the war, thank you. . . .

The fighting along the Ruhr liberated tens of thousands of slave laborers in the many factories there. Allied doctors and all the hospitals were inundated with terrible health issues, with local medical needs in addition to their own soldiers' injuries and illnesses, and were forced to restrict whom they could treat.

Somewhere in Germany [Brassert section of Marl]
1 April, 1945

Dearest Liz:

. . . Happy Easter, sweetheart. I sure hope I'll be with you for the rest of them. I started to go to church, then didn't. I was also a thorough stinker. A German woman with a very sick 9 months old baby came in and asked me to see him. It sounded like diphtheria so I went to see him, tho we aren't supposed to treat them. The kid was very sick but I couldn't tell what he had and had nothing for further diagnosis or treatment. There are no doctors in this town and all civilian hospitals are full and we have orders to only take care of immediate life and death cases and not to transport anyone more to civilian hospitals. The damn Nazis have been taking the doctors with them here. Under the circumstances there was nothing I could do, tho the mother begged me to take her to one of the civilian hospitals and she'd make them take the baby. The trouble is that they have no diagnostic facilities now either and nothing would be gained. I still feel like a heel for not even trying, tho. I did call up every possible source of diphtheria antitoxin or culture as I think it's probably nasal diphtheria but may be pancreatic fibrosis, in which case hospital admission would be a waste of time. I've also had to inadequately treat a couple of other civilian emergencies. Needless to say tonight I feel I've done my bad deed for the day rather than my good. On the other hand, the Germans let seventy-eight babies starve to death in one of the Dutch cities the last week of their occupation, and a Russian mother came in last night for milk for her month old baby who hadn't had any for four days, but that's no excuse for us behaving the same way. There is an enormous amount of slave labor which is more frequent the further into Germany we get. They've really had a tough time of it, too. I found papers today proving that the owner of our house is a party member, so I don't feel at all bad about booting him out of it. . . .

The medical detachment with their aid station was able to stay much more comfortable than the infantry soldiers. They had the luxury of speculating on their future whenever the war should end. They had been told that most would be sent to the Pacific to fight Japan, but rumors were rampant about leave in the US on the way. They also knew that many medical officers would be needed in occupied Germany.

Somewhere in Germany [Brassert section of Marl]
2 April, 1945

Dearest Liz:

. . . You were talking about me being more useful as part of the Army of

Occupation than in the Pacific. I don't know if that's right. The Colonel certainly wouldn't agree. He was telling me tonight how hard it was to get a surgeon who had the complete confidence of the men, how much it meant for morale, and how I had it. If that is true, this is probably where I belong—in a combat outfit where I can do something immediate for the men who are really doing the fighting. . . .

Your saying that you wouldn't need or want any other heaven than for us to be together the rest of our lives put me in mind of a little wood motto I saw in a German home the other day. It read:

Die Liebe ist,
Wenn zwei Personen
uf Erden schon
im Himmel wohnen
Literally translated: Love is when two persons on earth already live in heaven

There is only one surviving letter from Liz to Jim during this period, her 144th letter since his departure.

58 W 9th St. Wed. April 4th, '45—no. 144

Jim darling—This morning there was no mail again, but when I got home I was much surprized to find a letter, as they almost never come except in the morning mail. It was written March 27th—5 days after the last of March 22nd. When I first read it a wave of fear went over me. You said I could stop worrying, that things were better—but that you were still woozy: I couldn't tell whether you'd been sick or wounded, as you spoke of the field Hospital, or were just exhausted.—Am re-reading, I think it was just the latter. You said you'd had four bad days on the front lines, which means I guess you crossed the Rhine on the 23rd (the day after your last letter) when the main crossings were made. I had read that the 9th Army front had met stiff resistance, but I had hoped that as you were not mentioned you were not in the thick of it. I guess I was wrong. I know it's foolish to worry after a thing is all over but I can't help it, till it is <u>all</u> over and you're home again. . . . [T]oday the paper said you were

A 1945 portrait Liz sent to Jim.

on the northern edge of the Ruhr—southeast of Haltern. That makes my psychic or intelligence service correct again, as I had guessed you were in that general region. I guess this means that you are one of the inf. divisions left behind the spearheads to hold the Ruhr pocket. I hope you won't be involved in too strenuous activity in clearing it up. Also I hope the couple of intervening letters I think are missing between the 22nd–27th show up soon, so I can know what happened. Oh God, what will it be like to live without fear again?

Something happened today which is a good example of how much I think about you, even when I'm not conscious of it. This afternoon I was sitting at my desk reading through a chart, concentrating on it, quite oblivious of the clinic noise. All of a sudden I was conscious of a slight noise behind me & I glanced round and saw a pair of white shoes and white pants. Darling, crazy & unrealistic & impossible as I knew it was, my heart dropped & started pounding, as I instinctively thought it was you. It was just the way you used to drop into my office. Actually it was Henry Doyle being cute, & I think he must have been surprised at the look I'm sure I must have given him—startled & hopeful & disappointed. It was all such a completely unconscious reflex action, but it took quite an effort to pull myself together & carry on a normal conversation. I don't suppose that ever happens to you, but it does with me, because I'm in surroundings that are full of associations with you & I think so much in terms of when you come home again. Like last night, the apartment door was open, & I heard a man's footsteps coming up to the floor below, & I had a sudden feeling like I used to have when I heard you clumping up the stairs in Henderson.

Jim, I wonder if anything more has happened on the status between you and Fore. The more I think about it the madder I get. I hope someone has told him off. . . .

Sweetie, I thought I had a lot to write about tonight, but getting your letter describing your tense condition puts everything out of my mind, just as being in it makes it hard for you to write. Everything but what is happening with you just doesn't seem to matter—& I feel, emotionally, as though I'd been through what you have. Having re-read the letter about 10 times I feel a little better though. — There is a poem in the last New Yorker, which says what I feel:

"At first I was quite brave in war
Fear of defeat kills fear
But death is difficult to face
When victory is near."

In my terms, your continued danger is difficult to face, & becomes more so the nearer to the end it gets. . . .

Goodnight, darling. Please God keep you all right. How I wish I could do something about it myself, cause I love you, I love you, I love you, and even more I love you.

Liz

This is the last of the series of Coleman mantles.

Liz writing of her hope that someone had "told off" the battalion executive officer, Major Fore, highlights the tension between Jim and Fore. Jim recounted an incident that would have lasting consequences for him. As the 75th Division marched through the German towns, the pattern was to take over the houses and apartments of working-class Germans for use of the GIs. Jim thought they ought to be using the houses of obvious Nazi sympathizers instead. He deplored the tendency of American soldiers to be destructive of commandeered German homes where they billeted. Jim felt the best way to get to the Germans was to exhibit discipline and control, and he instructed his men to be respectful of the German houses, most of which were those of middle-class working families. Upon the soldiers' departure from one house, the owner returned to see how badly the GIs had damaged it, only to discover that Jim's detachment had left it in good shape. He volubly thanked Jim for not wrecking his home. Major Fore, who had continued to resent and distrust Jim, overheard this, and reported Jim to CID as a German sympathizer. He was suspended from duty for several days while the accusation was investigated. The enlisted men under Jim staunchly defended him, and he was cleared. The incident apparently went on Jim's record, and dogged him into civilian life. During the McCarthy era, his phone calls were tapped, particularly calls to his brother, Dan. He could hear someone breathing as they listened in. His complaint to FBI authorities in Albany apparently stopped the taps.

From the crossing, the 75th went east. Moves were frequent as the armies advanced rapidly to surround the Ruhr region. Caught in the Ruhr pocket was all of German Army Group B with its Fifth Panzer and Fifteenth armies and part of Army Group H's First Parachute Army. For two weeks they fought fiercely to break through the American armies. The 75th Division Command Post shifted across the Rhine from Lintfort to Hiesfeld after their crossing on March 29, then Imloh on the thirtieth, Marl on April 2, Erkenschwick on the fourth, Mecklinghoven on the sixth, Ickern on the ninth, Castrop-Rauxel on the twelfth, and Braumbauer on the fifteenth. By April 18, all German garrisons had surrendered, and Field Marshall Model, commander of German Army Group B, committed suicide. Still, the hard-core Nazis were not admitting defeat.

Somewhere in Germany [Ickern]
11 April, 1945

Dearest Liz:

. . . I've been awfully jumpy and irritable lately. Guess I need a vacation. Or perhaps it's the disappointment engendered by Gen. Marshall's recent statement about direct transportation to the Pacific. Vestal being back in headquarters is no help. It's all I can do to sit at the table with him. I just literally can't stand him. Then the men have a radio which they keep going full blast all day on the second story of our house and you know how happy that makes me. . . .

I sure like Major Sutton [new Battalion Commander]. His idea seems to be to be as reasonable and cooperative as possible with everyone. He'll have a hell of a time being that way in this battalion, but I hope he swings it. As you know, there are some people he'll have to get rid of and I sure hope he does it. The Colonel [Hanstton] never would. . . .

The 75th was sweeping south around Dortmund in mid-April, as the combined Allied armies tightened the noose on the German armies trapped in the Ruhr pocket. The troops found an absolutely desolated landscape, the result of months of saturation bombing. The US Army *Pictorial History of the 75th Infantry Division, 1944–1945 Campaigns* describes the scene:

> The most famous cities of Germany no longer exist as anything but rubble and waste. Back as far as October, 1943, German officials stated that 1,200,000 civilians had been killed or were missing in the spectacular air raids over Germany. The total destruction you will view . . . is Dortmund. A city of some 50,000 houses, only 2,500 are now habitable. Our cost was great, but here is Dortmund.[16]

Somewhere in Germany [Castrop-Rauxel]
12 April, 1945

Dear Ma & Pa:

. . . Everything continues to be well with me. I'm having things easy again after our little river problem and in general we have the life of Riley in the homes we take over from the Germans. The campaign seems to be going great guns and the resistance we get now lacks the organization and spirit it had before. . . .

It's full spring here now. It is like it usually is at home the first week in May. I just hope the good weather holds so we can get Jerry polished off. If we only didn't have the little yellow rats to settle with after we're through here! . . .

Somewhere in Germany [Castrop-Rauxel]
12 April, 1945

Dearest Liz: . . .

I'm more and more pleased with Major Sutton. He is young, reasonable, and cooperative without letting anyone run him. His ideas about a lot of things such as looting and handling of civilians coincide with mine. I think this battalion may turn out to be a much better set up than before now. The best thing is that he is really a reasonable man. I just hope he's able to keep it up. . . .

We are seeing hundreds of slave labor now. They've just been released and are walking back. Most are mere scarecrows. Tonight we had an old Dutchman who had been in Germany for three years with his eldest son. His wife and four other children stayed in Holland. He had blisters which covered half the soles of his feet which we patched up. We gave him food and talked to him for awhile. I really boil when I see what people like that have been through. We have it easy compared to them.

Congratulations on your raise, darling. Are you trying to make more than your husband so you can maintain your independence as a career woman? . . .

It's drizzling out now, just right for us to go to bed early and sleep a long, sound night's sleep. I sure miss you and just can't seem to get really relaxed without you to hold tight before going to sleep and to feel right there when I wake up during the night. . . .

Jim was seldom located close to Division Headquarters while they were in Belgium and France, but once in Germany they were usually co-located. From his description on April 13, he was probably in Castrop-Rauxel, a coal mining center. The "little combat problem" Jim described was actually the assignment of the 275th to combat infantry duty, relieving the 3rd Battalion of the 289th Infantry Regiment. The action was an operation to split the larger Ruhr pocket into two smaller areas as the US Army tightened the noose on 325,000 surrounded soldiers of German Army Group B and four million civilians. The 275th's combat role was brief, less than one day. The area east of Witten surrendered two days later.

Somewhere in Germany [Castrop-Rauxel]
13 April, 1945

Dearest Liz:

. . . After writing you last night that my days at the front were over, I spent the day there [at Witten] during a little combat problem the Engineers had to carry out. Things were pretty active with three shells bursting within a hundred feet and inability to use the front door of the house the aid station was in because of sniper fire. The son of a gun never hit anything but damn fool civilians who went up the street anyway. I'm back safe now, sweetie, and don't expect to go up again, so don't worry.

It was a beautiful day with warm sun, the fruit trees all out and other trees almost so. We are in pleasanter country now with a few low rolling hills. Still no trout streams, tho. I passed thru two beautiful quaint old towns set on the side of small hills crowded with blossoming fruit trees.

Last night we were in terrible quarters. McIntyre was the billeting officer. As usual when he is, we had lousy billets. He seems to hate to take the good houses where the party members live. He put us right in the worst type of old dirty smelly tenements. I kicked like a steer, bawled Mac out and told Major Sutton that aside from the unpleasantness I considered the places a health hazard. Obligingly, two officers turned up with bug bites this morning, so we moved to a very good place early this morning. . . . The medics have a nice, clean, neat, small modern house with a fair sized kitchen. . . . News of President Roosevelt's death came very suddenly tho I was not too surprised. I can't say I wept any bitter tears, but it certainly comes at an inopportune time. Truman, whom even the vocal New Dealers consider a political twerp, is certainly not the man for the job at a time like this. I hope he can rise to it. In a way this may have been an opportune time for Roosevelt to fade from the picture because I think he favored relatively short occupation of Germany. I believe we should occupy it for fifty years with complete control of education and the press as far as emphasis on or incitement to things military. . . .

Major Fore I think was reprimanded by the Colonel several weeks ago for his suspicions. Since Major Sutton has come, he has just quietly completely changed the official attitude on a lot of things which were the basis for Fore's suspicions. . . .

We got hold of a keg of German beer tonight, but, alas, it is not very good. We did get a few bottles of good Rhein wine down at the front today. . . .

From the sounds of it, Roosevelt's death on April 12 was not the momentous event for soldiers busy fighting a war that it was for the folks at home.

The Ruhr campaign had been victorious, with the surrender of 325,000 German troops of Army Group B and the ruin of this large industrial area.

Somewhere in Germany [Brambauer]
20 April, 1945

Dearest Liz:

. . . I re-read and burned some more of your old letters today. I hated to do it, but the pile had grown too big to carry around, especially as space is shorter now that a lot of the winter clothes are being put away.

The Colonel never was impressed by my "pro-German sympathies" and I think Fore has pretty much gotten over his suspicions. With the beautiful weather, beautiful countryside, and attractive girls, the Army better get those WACs here soon or there's going to be an awful lot of "fraternizing" of a certain type. It is such beautiful weather and so peaceful right here after the terrible times which have gone before that it is only natural for the young men and women to be attracted to each other. It seems such a waste that they aren't allowed to carry it through in a normal way, but then, as I've said before, all war is a waste. And on the whole the non-fraternization policy is a good one. I'm sure a lot of these pretty girls may be willing to forget it for a little while but still are ardent Nazis at heart and in the end would make a lot of trouble. . . .

As I wrote you at the time, I wept no bitter tears at Roosevelt's death. In contrast to you, I think that just before his death he was backtracking on what he was supposed to be so strong for. Specifically, he was avoiding the issue of whole hearted US participation in world affairs when he advocated that we only occupy Germany for ten years when any fool can see it will take a lot longer time than that to do any permanent good. . . . I'm convinced that England is just as selfish and imperialistic as ever and I'm afraid Roosevelt was countenancing it and willing to countenance it further. . . . I think the fact that our country will continue to carry on just fine in spite of Roosevelt's death and the more or less acknowledged lack of size of Truman will prove to those with the brains to see it that Roosevelt was not at all indispensable. . . .

The boys did an enormous washing last night and this morning. This afternoon we had a Polish woman in from the foreign workers camp here and she ironed them all. We gave her chocolate, cigarettes, etc. of which we are the only source over here. Those people haven't had them for three years! We are now feeding the starving slave labor our left-over food which salves my conscience somewhat. Don't think the Germans weren't literally starving them, either, especially the Russians and Poles. We have a few Russian boys working as KPs in the kitchen now. They really keep things spick and span. We work them rather than Germans because we're supposed to feed the people we work and feeding ANYBODY over here is doing them a hell of a favor.

Well, sweetie, I better quit rambling on. I do it because I love you and miss and want you so much, especially right now while we're sitting still in this beautiful weather. We're having beautiful clear nights, too. The moon was just a half moon last night. I hoped you were looking at it, too. The lilacs are just out today.

That reminds me of home and the time you came to the Farm while I had the mumps. I loved you then, but I love you LOTS more now that I really know what a wonderful (and AWFUL) girl and wife you are. Living with you sure looks like heaven from here.

. . . [Last paragraph of the letter was cut off.]

Somewhere in Germany [Brambauer]
21 April, 1945

Dearest Liz: The news just came over the radio that the Russians are only four miles from Berlin! I hope they smear the place—and quick. You'll have to excuse my writing and a short letter tonight. I hurt my arm playing volleyball tonight and can hardly write. . . .

Today both the preacher and his wife who own the apartment in which we are living were here. I had only met her before. They are certainly nice people, the kind you'd like to know better if things weren't as they are. It's too bad.

I finished my Nero Wolfe today and plan to start on "Leave Her to Heaven" tonight. . . .

Major Sutton continues to wear well. He doesn't say too much, but I think he is smelling out the four flushers much better than the colonel ever did. He continues to be a real nice guy, too.

I've had quite a busy week medically with our being quiet. Many come in under such circumstances with their accumulated ills. Also they are starting to think about trying to get out of the Army before being possibly ordered to the Pacific. I'm going to have a hell of a job with that situation when the time does come.

Good night darling. The length of this letter is a poor measure of how much your husband loves you. If it were, it would be as long as "Gone With the Wind," because he does love you so VERY VERY much. Jim

It was full-blown spring, and the 275th moved east of the Ruhr into the hills, where they were ensconced in the lovely town of Plettenberg. The war steadily moved away from them as other armies quickly pursued the last German army units. Set amid wooded hills, Plettenberg was centrally located among the 34 German military hospitals in the region for which the 75th Division was responsible.

The tasks of occupation were beginning. Jim related yet another frustration with the army:

Each doctor in the division was assigned one or two of the hospitals to over-

> see except for the division surgeon and his assistant, and me. . . . Only two of us spoke German: the division surgeon, and I! True military efficiency. God! It burned me so. Some of them were doing interesting things medically. For instance, the idea of repairing a fracture with a steel shaft in the marrow was originated in Germany in one of those hospitals. . . . I had the opportunity of going to a couple of these hospitals . . . that were doing interesting things, but most of the time I was sitting in Plettenberg, playing bridge with the division surgeon and my CO.[17]

This was perhaps another illustration of army thinking, or perhaps it was a strategy to keep together the bridge group of Jim, the surgeon, another officer, and their commanding officer!

Somewhere in Germany [Plettenberg]
22 April, 1945

Dearest Liz: . . . We have new and better living quarters tonight—except that we still have a God-damned radio. I'm really getting to HATE radios and cigarettes. They don't listen to the radio, but just like to have it on full blast. They don't smoke the cigarettes half the time but hold them so the smoke blows in someone else's face or else put them down on a table or ashtray and let them just smoke the place up until they burn the table or burn themselves out or both. GAWD!

We have a big six room apartment now which belongs to a doctor who has his office on the ground floor, the apartment being on the third floor. . . . We have no hot water or central heating yet, but will as soon as we get the coal for them. The dining room and living room are connected by sliding glass doors. I have all my books out on the nice desk in the living room plus Thomas Mann's "Magic Mountain" in German, which I found in the bookcase. The aid station is in the kitchen. Our living room windows face east toward a couple of beautiful green hills. There are lots of lamps, nice furniture and indirect lighting in the living and dining rooms with thick oriental rugs on the floor! I have my own big bedroom with bed. What a set-up! Let's just hope it lasts for awhile.

Today was a typical April day in Germany with rain, sun, snow, sleet, and hail. Incidentally, I have high hopes of getting to do some trout fishing soon, provided all the streams are not contaminated too much by industrial waste or sewage. . . .

Jim's hatred of radios lasted the rest of his life. It was a source of silent friction with Liz, who liked to listen to Vermont Public Radio. Jim's hatred of cigarettes went against the grain in that era, when a very high percentage of adults smoked. WWII soldiers received free cigarettes in their rations (a practice that continued until 1975). Jim claimed that he had quit smoking at the age of 12, but his feelings had to be suppressed when he got home. Liz, having smoked since her mid-teens, continued smoking until she went into the hospital for the birth of their fourth son, Tim, in December of 1954. At that time Jim showed his attentiveness by welcoming her home with a new carton of cigarettes, not having noticed that she had quit! Liz burned them in the fireplace, and never smoked again.

Plettenberg lies halfway between the cities of the Ruhr to the west and Kassel to the east. There was nothing of military importance in the town, but bombers returning from a run that had not dropped all their bombs on Kassel looked for any target to use up their bombs. Frequently those secondary targets were rail lines and bridges. A rail line ran up the Lenne River from the Dortmund area through the village of Eiringhausen, in the northern part of Plettenberg. Consequently, the area was bombed regularly in the final weeks of the war.

In early April 2014, I spent three days in Plettenberg. I had been exchanging emails with Markus Schmellenkamp, a local man interested in the war. Markus had arranged for me to spend the day with the two men most knowledgeable about Plettenberg and the war, Horst Hassel and Rolf Wilmink. They picked me up at the Hotel Klinger at noon, and we drove up the valley to Herscheid, where they had reserved a big table at a very nice, very German restaurant. Markus and Rolf carried in a large bin laden with documentation that they have collected on the 75th Division. While it was the 86th Division that took the city on April 15, 1945, it was the 75th that arrived to occupy it for the next two months until a British unit took over. I think Horst

Jim in front of his Plettenberg aid station / apartment in April 1945.

The author in April 2014.

and Rolf know more about the 75th's time in Plettenberg than anyone in the United States. Some of the research that they have done was spurred by the desire to recover certain historical artifacts that are important to the city, which they believe were taken home as souvenirs by members of the 75th. In fact, the town fathers hired Rolf in 1994 to go to the US to try to recover some 19th-century flags and the Mayor's Chain, which is a ceremonial necklace, traditional in all the old towns and unique to each one.

We headed down into the valley to visit all the sites relevant to my father's stay here. The first stop was the building where my father lived and had his aid station during his seven weeks in Plettenberg. He described it in detail to my mother, and I have a photo of him in front of the building. I had sent the photo to Markus a month before. The building has been altered, but thanks to their social media network, Markus and Rolf found someone who knew all about the renovations done thirty years ago.

I stood on the sidewalk and looked up at the "cone-shaped hill" that my father described in a letter, quietly imagining him doing the same thing in the same spot. Across the street is the old hotel that housed more of the Headquarters Company, as did a big house across the street. We moved on to see the Shooters' Hall (Schutzengesellschaft), which served as the German military hospital during the war, then becoming the American hospital. Down the street are the site of the POW camp that housed 3,000 Russians, and the old Rathaus (city hall), which can be seen in a photo of a ceremony on V-E Day. All my guides were natives of Plettenberg, so as I got to know them I started to ask them about their own family stories of the war. Rolf's father was in the army in 1945 at the age of fifteen, serving as a helper with an artillery unit defending the city. After telling them about the military cemeteries I had visited in the last week, I asked if there are comparable German military cemeteries. They didn't know of any. That was a time that the Germans do not want memorialized. After a little more prodding, however, they took me to the oldest church in town (12th century), where there is a small plot holding the graves of about fifty soldiers, all under 18 at the time of their deaths in 1945. Rolf showed me the graves of four of his father's friends who were killed in Dortmund in an explosion right next to his father. I stood in silence contemplating this quiet, shaded corner of an ancient cemetery, which holds a bunch of kids who had the misfortune to grow up in the wrong place at the wrong time. About a thousand Plettenbergers (out of 16,000 residents) died in the war, but this little hidden group of graves is the only memorial. I guess we know who won the war.

Rolf and Horst told me that on April 12, American artillery shelled the town as troops came over the hill from the west. The only defenders were two artillery crews, both made up mostly of 15-year-old boys. American artillery shot back and scored a direct hit on one of the German guns, killing seven young boys who were "manning" it. Rolf's father was in the other crew. On April 13, the 86th Infantry Division took possession of the town. Historians in the town say that the citizens were terrified. When the troops moved out of the town on the afternoon of the 13th, rumor spread that the town was about to be "carpet-bombed." Most of the inhabitants fled into the hills for the night. Returning the next day, they began to realize that the war was really over in Plettenberg. On April 22, the 75th Division settled in the area to begin the job of occupation.

The reports of the 275th show how their function had suddenly shifted to rebuilding the infrastructure that Allied bombs had destroyed. They focused on rail lines, which would be vital to keep supplies rolling in occupied Germany. Much has been written about the over-kill of Allied bombing in the last few months of the war, and the unnecessary destruction of non-military infrastructure.

Somewhere in Germany [Plettenberg]
23 April, 1945

Dearest Liz: . . . . The town we are in now is really a pretty place. It lies in a basin surrounded by high wooded hills which are really small mountains. The one our windows look toward is cone-shaped with fields and houses running about halfway up. The rest of the way is a symphony in multi-shaded green. In back of us a dirt road runs up a little cut into another higher basin surrounded by hills. The town itself is pretty and quiet with a number of nice tree-shaded residential streets. Battalion Headquarters is in a big mansion and the rest of H & S distributed between this apartment house, a small hotel across the street, and a good-sized house next door.

The weather was cold and cloudy today. We got the steam heat and hot water going this afternoon. Tonight I had a deep tub bath which reminded me of those we used to have in our apartment in New York. I missed you telling me what I did wrong, tho, sweetie.

We have a regular mess hall now downstairs in the hotel with a separate room for officers mess. It makes a very nice set-up. We even eat off plates and have civilian tableware! . . .

Plettenberg turned into a very pleasant interlude for the 275th. The next letter gives a good indication of Jim's daily activities.

Somewhere in Germany [Plettenberg]
25 April, 1945

Dearest Liz:

. . . At breakfast I amazed myself by putting away two fried eggs! Afterward I held sick call, followed by a visit to a sick soldier at one of the companies, after which I did a bunch of physical examinations. This afternoon I went to "Experiment Perilous" with Hedy Lamarr, Paul Lukas, and George Brent. . . . I studied a little and gave some booster shots, then had supper. We were supposed to have an officers' volley ball game after supper. I had to see a couple of patients and, by the time I got down, there were eight men on each side with a gang of EM [Enlisted Men] playing. . . .

Steinbring has gotten together some beer barrels and is going after beer soon. I hope it is fit to drink, but I doubt it. Some of the guys have been getting US beer in cans in their packages. If you can get any canned beer, would you send all you can? You could get Ma & Pa & D & A to send it, too. Steinbring said tonight they thought I missed my beer more than sleeping with a girl. They're right as long as the girl isn't you, sweetie.

Last night one of the boys brought us in half a dozen bottles of white wine, the first we've had in about two weeks. All we need now is that canned lobster to go with it. I don't like to drink wine alone.

Hanna, Garcia, and Cohen walked up to the top of the cone-shaped hill this afternoon. I'm planning to start doing a little fishing in a few days, but I'll sure miss you, because it will make me think of both our honeymoons—at Cambridge and on the Jersey lakes. I guess that's what's getting on my nerves—being someplace like this without you where we could have so much fun together.

The war was only two weeks from the end in Europe. The machinery of the US Army ground on, and Jim describes the arrival of a new Evac Hospital unit. Spare time was beginning to be plentiful, and the men's morals were sorely tested.

Somewhere in Germany [Plettenberg]
27 April, 1945

Dearest Liz:

. . . Today I spent the whole day going back to an Evac Hospital and back. It was a long hard trip. The hospital is one which has just come over and they really don't know the ropes yet. Being more or less veterans now, it was the first time I'd had the chance to see how obviously green new outfits are.

. . . The officers at the hospital were very hospitable and asked me to come to a party they're having tomorrow night. I'd like to go but am afraid it would probably get wilder than I want to mess with. I enjoy the fun of a good uninhibited party up to a certain point. That point is where you either have to leave or join in the wild part and that always embarrasses me. . . .

The war news is sure good these days. The rapid advance to the south is very encouraging. I was afraid they would meet a lot more opposition. Of course they haven't hit the toughest parts yet.

Somewhere in Germany [Plettenberg]
28 April, 1945

Dearest Liz: . . .

Tonight I went over to the CP [Command Post] after supper to play bridge. In the middle of the game Lt. Johnson came in and they gave him his captain's bars and the Bronze Star Medal. Major Sutton then told me to stand up and much to my surprise presented me with the Bronze Star Medal, too. Was I floored! I'm enclosing the citation, and will send the medal when I get it. I just got the ribbon tonight. The Sergeant Major told me the Colonel wrote it up himself the last night he was with us. He certainly wrote me a good one, too; at least I think so. Everyone seemed very pleased that I got it, and that was nice, too. To top everything off, Leo Walker ran into a brewery today and got a whole stack of beer which is pretty good. We're drinking it now.

Jim receives a Bronze Star from Major Sutton. Photo: author's personal collection.

. . . This business of a Congressional Medal for Roosevelt really burns me up, especially one clause of the citation "his everlasting contribution to world peace." In my opinion that should read: "his failure to make the everlasting contributions to world peace he could have made." You wrote about the German people in relation to the concentration camps: "That acceptance of what has been happening—I am sure must be partly due to lack of knowledge. If you feed the average person only one story, as the Germans have been fed, they believe it and don't question it. A great many of them probably don't know what's happened, and what they do know, they've been deadened into accepting. The psychology of the whole thing terrifies me—that what we've come to feel is an innate sense of right and justice isn't innate, but can systematically be trained out of ordinary people." I think the above is just what the New Deal has done to the American People. It has put the aims and desires of the "Leader," Roosevelt, and the party above honest right and justice. Right and justice became what accomplished those aims without regard to whether there was anything right or just about those methods. Call a man like Lindbergh a traitor for patriotically telling a few unpleasant truths about our relative unpreparedness and for asking that something be done about it—then two years later claiming credit for far-sightedness in those very matters and saying that they had told us of this situation but had been hog-tied so nothing could be done about it. The public disgracing of Lindbergh came direct from the White House and was one of the worst examples of dirty, low, contemptible political chicanery I've ever heard about. To give such a man the Congressional Medal is a slur on our national honor, honesty, and sense of justice and fair play. I fail to see that the type of prosperity and improvement we've enjoyed under Roosevelt has been worth the abandoning of our sense of decency, justice, and fair play any more than the undoubted prosperity and improvement Germany has enjoyed under Hitler has been worth it. Roosevelt was President with almost unlimited influence and power for almost eight years before the war started. Did any man ever fail so miserably to do something toward stopping what was obviously coming if he didn't act? He might have failed, but it would have been a glorious failure in the right direction instead of an inglorious political capitalization on the world's misfortunes. And they cite such a man for "his everlasting contribution to world peace." Phooey!

Excuse my tirade, darling, but injustice has always made my blood boil, and I still don't think a permanently good end is accomplished by unprincipled means.

What General Marshall said was that they'd need all the troops they could get to the Pacific just as soon as they could get them there after V-E day and without an hour's delay. He said it would mean a quicker and less costly victory. I think he's right. It's the fair and just thing. The war here now is relatively easy and the boys over there have been there as long or longer than any here. . . .

Jim

Jim talks about studying in many of his letters. He had left his internship at Babies Hospital in New York when he entered the army, just one year out of medical school. His pride in his growing abilities as a doctor shines through. He was proud of his ability to treat the men in his battalion and get them back to their unit within days, rather than evacuate them to the rear and lose them for a month or two.

Somewhere in Germany [Plettenberg]
30 April, 1945

Dearest Liz: . . . .

Fletch and I made another trip back to the Evac Hospital to pick up a couple of men I had left to get G-U x-rays and to get a couple more looked at. It's a new unit, as I said before, and some nincompoop amateur psychiatrist tried to evacuate one of my men to the rear as a psychoneurosis who couldn't take duty with our outfit. It was a lot of bologney and not what I had the guy there for in the first place. The psychiatrist . . . has taken the N-P school course and has had no army experience outside of hospitals, let alone in combat. . . . I was able to get the man back. I also made a diagnosis of calcified hematoma irritating the quadriceps muscle sheath on a man and took him there to be x-rayed. Everyone was very impressed with your husband's diagnostic acumen, but it was the most logical answer to his symptoms. The x-ray proved it. . . .

After four weeks, I've found out what started my psychic vomiter vomiting originally! I already wrote you he was OK now and also a new member of the detachment. He told me yesterday how his younger brother had always come along right after him and shown him up at everything and how much it had bothered him. His previous attacks coincided very well with periods when he said his brother's successes particularly bothered him. I had thought right along that it was a subconscious effort to draw attention focused on his brother to himself but had been unable to find out why. I'm pretty sure that's it now. If I can get him to relate the vomiting and the envy of his brother up now, while at the same time getting him reconciled to having a smarter younger brother, I think he'll be permanently cured. I'm encouraged.

Tonight I took my third deep, hot bath in a week. What a luxury! Also sent out a big laundry. It sure is wonderful to be able to bathe and change clothes with relative frequency again. Perhaps the greatest thrill was in sending SHEETS to be laundered.

Chapter Eight

Occupation: May 1945, Plettenberg, Germany

Jim's relations with the other men in his detachment were variable. They were a small, tight unit living in close proximity. None of the men were highly educated, and none were of his world back in the States. He was several years older than all of them, and he was an officer and their superior. He referred regularly to visits to Headquarters where he could play cards and socialize with other officers. Luckily, his right-hand man, Sergeant Hanna, was competent, and his driver, Fletcher (Fletch), was faithful and easy to get along with.

The 275th Medical Detachment in Plettenberg. Jim is second from the right; author's personal collection.

Somewhere in Germany [Plettenberg]
2 May, 1945

Dearest Liz: . . .

Fletch and Belanger, the psychic vomiter, now in the detachment, finished fixing up our German jeep today and we got it registered and legal, so we're all set now. We're lucky as they haven't been letting anyone take over anything but trucks. It's painted US green with regular US star insignia on the hood and each of the two rear doors, and Geneva crosses on both front fenders, both front doors, and each side of the back. . . . Now that Fletch is a T/5 [Technician Fifth Grade, equivalent to a corporal] and we have two vehicles we are calling him the detachment motor officer.

We are all wondering today over the announced death of Hitler, whether it is true or just a dodge so he can escape capture and punishment. None of us take stock in the possibility of a Himmler peace offer, because he of all people has nothing to gain by it, and we can't see him sacrificing himself for the sake of his people. The surrender of the Germans in Italy was encouraging and we can't help but hope that other sector commanders may do the same in the near future.

Yesterday I sent you a copy of the Mule [the 75th Division newspaper] which may give you a little better idea of where I am and what I'm doing.

Tonight Fletch and Belanger made some good noodle soup and fried bacon and onions. Together with beer it made a very pleasant ten o'clock supper.

I'm getting a little studying done steadily every day now, which is all to the good. If I could only get some clinical work, too, it would be fine. . . .

Concentration camps were being discovered as Germany was conquered. The sector around Plettenberg had no camps, sparing Jim the treatment of those extreme cases. He makes no mention of the "displaced person camps" in Siegen referred to in the Battalion records. Nor does he mention the discovery nearby of a cache of art treasures by a 75th Division medical officer. The cache at Schloss Alme in Brilon was one of several in the area where art had been taken to protect it from air raids. Most of it was art from the Ruhr area; some had been stolen by the Nazis in other countries.

In the immediate aftermath of the war, engineering units played a vital role. From transportation infrastructure to the construction of POW camps, the 275th and other units became the heart of army operations. The monthly summary of the activities of Jim's battalion describes the range of work they performed in May 1945.

> Early in the period it was realized that the greater part of the engineer's time would have to be spent in the rehabilitation of the local rail net and the public utilities so thoroughly devastated. . . . [A] detailed reconnaissance was initiated to determine the extent of the damage to these facilities and to plan for whatever work would be necessary to supply the troops and civilians with food, water and power. Coincident with the proposed plans, "B" Company moved to Altena in the north, to assume control of the rail net, with approval from Corps to use all the civilian labor necessary to the task ahead.
>
> As the reconnaissance continued and work on the railroads commenced, "A" Company was constantly engaged in the destruction of captured enemy explosives for which dumps were established within the area. Signs were posted in every town of any consequence as well as along all usable routes, and several hundred civilians under engineer supervision were repairing roads.
>
> At this time, the appalling conditions existing at displaced persons

camps were called to the attention of the engineers who began work at once to see that the water supply and sanitary conditions were adequate. The two camps at Siegen, housing approximately 21,000 Russians and 7,000 Polish and Italian civilians received the most attention. The camps were greatly overcrowded. Water and sewerage facilities had been damaged considerably by bombings. "C" Company was charged with the responsibility of restoring mains, plumbing and sewerage systems. As a temporary measure, sufficient latrines to provide four holes for each 100 persons were to be constructed. Using German labor, the water mains, plumbing and sewerage system were speedily repaired. In constructing the outdoor latrines, long and deep pits were dug by camp labor and the engineers constructed the boxes and latrine houses. . . .

The declaration of the cessation of hostilities made necessary the construction of additional prison of war enclosures. This work was done by "C" Company, who as yet hadn't been ordered to open the railroads' southern branch. "B" Company by this time had enough rail opened and operating to supply coal to the power plants and waterworks in the north, "A" Company worked the railroad from Werdohl to Plettenberg and "C" Company commenced to work on the line from Siegen in the south to Finnentrop in the middle east.

In keeping with the Division's policy, recreational facilities were established by the engineers at a lake near Stottnort. . . .

Now toward the end of the period [May], with some 30,000 civilians working under the Battalion's supervision, three to eight hour shifts a day, approximately 225 miles of rail in the Division area are in operation, supplying troops and moving them and keeping the utilities going twenty-four hours a day with the necessary fuel, otherwise unobtainable.[18]

Somewhere in Germany [Plettenberg]
3 May, 1945

Dearest Liz:

. . . My old appetite has come back lately and I sleep like a log. My mind is starting to function again so that studying doesn't come too hard. Most of the medical officers have been pretty busy supervising the cleaning up of concentration camps and the care of the unfortunate people in them. Apparently they were unbelievably bad. The reports of them couldn't possibly exaggerate how bad they are. . . .

This afternoon Fletch drove me over to Clearing in our new "jeep." I dropped in to see Major Furst and discuss the further handling of Belanger, the psychic vomiter. He spoke of the great new field offered by preventive "mental hygiene" in pediatrics and agreed that the age group I'm interested in was a wide open field with great possibilities. He suggested that I apply for a Commonwealth Fellowship after the war in psychiatry. I don't believe I want to be a psychiatrist, tho. I want to be a damn good doctor who is able to give his patients psychiatric as well as medical treatment when they need it. I think it's a mistake to divorce the two. . . . I want to practice the combination of medicine and psychiatry rather than neurology and psychiatry. It is so much larger a field.

Weekend passes were now coming through. After six months without a day off duty, Jim was offered a three-day pass to Brussels. While disappointed that it wasn't Paris, England, or the Riviera, he decided to take it. He worried over whether there would be plays, concerts, good movies, golf, tennis, or good beer. He wasn't interested in going just to raise hell for three days. In the meantime, life in Plettenberg was getting quite enjoyable.

Somewhere in Germany [Plettenberg]
5 May, 1945

Dearest Liz:

. . . I've never been to Brussels, I like the Belgians very much, the beer is said to be the best in Europe at the moment, wine is good and a third the price of it in Paris, and it is a shorter and less tiring trip. One hitch is that everyone wears an overseas combat jacket instead of a blouse and you need one or the other. The combat jacket costs about twenty-five bucks and I've just hated to spend the dough on it.. . . I'm about the only officer in the battalion who doesn't have one now, except Reed. The trip should be a change, anyway, and I need that. . . .

Tonight we went to the movies, seeing "A Tree Grows in Brooklyn." . . . Fletch, Hanna, Smitty, Belanger and I drove over in our jeep. We felt very sporty. The jeep isn't really as good as the American ones, but it looks sportier. We felt like a bunch of high school kids going out in their Model T on Saturday night. When we got back we ate some fudge Smitty had made and drank a bottle of champagne . . . from some captured German stuff. It was a very pleasant little party. . . .

Germany surrendered on May 7, 1945. For folks at home who had been reading nothing but war news, mostly about battle after battle, the surrender was greeted with great jubilation. It wasn't quite the same feeling among the troops on the ground.

Somewhere in Germany [Plettenberg]
7 May, 1945

Dearest Liz: . . .

On getting back, I went immediately to a Company Commanders' meeting where Germany's surrender was announced, together with plans to return to strict garrison life. How we all dread it. . . .

I imagine New York went wild over the news. It was received quietly here at first, but there has been a good deal of noisy celebrating during the evening. They turned on some street lights and ordered everyone to break black out. I didn't see any lighted windows in the civilian houses, tho. Personally, I didn't feel much like celebrating, because there is so much still ahead. Apparently they really are going to go right at discharging a lot of men with disabilities or long service. It looks to me as if perhaps most men will be discharged as they attain five years of service or if they are over thirty-eight or forty. It still means a long time for me however you cut it.

I have been very busy all evening getting all the aid station business straightened out to run while I'm away at Brussels . . .

Tomorrow is going to be a holiday here with none but the necessary work being done. We're having breakfast from seven-thirty to eight-thirty instead of the usual six-thirty to seven-thirty. I'll be driving most of the day. . . .

V-E Day was momentous for the countries freed from Nazi occupation so recently. Jim's pass to Brussels turned out to coincide with the huge celebration.

Somewhere in Belgium
8 May, 1945

Dearest Liz: . . .

I'm spending the night at a rest camp on the way to Brussels. We left our area as soon as the mail came and arrived here this evening. It is some sort of permanent barracks with straw-mattressed cots in a town of about fifty thousand people. . . .

It's quite a night—practically like Mardi Gras. Flags of all the allied nations are flying from every house and building. The main square is jammed with a band going full swing at one end. A civilian band is marching around town, passing under balconies which line the ways, and whose occupants cheer and throw confetti down on the crowd. It is a great fête to celebrate the victory. . . .

Nothing if not persistent, Jim searched Brussels for a tennis club. He found it in the southern suburbs, the Albert Jer Tennis Club in what was then Luxor Park (now Parc de Woluwe), on boulevard du Souverain. The club is still there, though not as luxurious.

Brussels, Belgium
10 May, 1945

Dear Sweetie: Today is another beautiful day and I think I have things lined up now to get the most out of it. After asking heaven knows how many people yesterday, I finally found a Belgian girl in an American Red Cross Office who knew where there was a tennis club. This morning I hopped a trolley out there. There was no one there but the grounds-keeper's wife, but she talked as if it would be possible to play there if I came back this afternoon. So just as soon as I eat lunch I'm going to hot foot it out there. It is in a nice suburb of town just across the street from a big park. It looks like a nice club and the courts looked very good. If I can borrow shoes, racket, and balls out there now, all should be well. If not, it's still a pleasant place to spend a sunny afternoon. There are several large ponds in the park. One of them has rowboats on it and I can go rowing if nothing else and then sit in an outdoor restaurant near the pond and drink a couple of beers.

The Hotel Central, where I'm staying, is right across the square from the stock exchange. The square seems to be the central gathering place in town for the people celebrating victory, just as Times Square is in New York. From my balcony I can look out on the square and watch all that goes on. My room is on the fourth floor.

Brussels is a nice place, but two of the things I'd like to get here—good food and good wine with it—are out of the question unless you pay terrific black market prices—about twenty dollars for a meal. I don't want to pay the price or patronize the black market. We can get good champagne in the night club downstairs for about four-fifty a bottle, which isn't bad at all. But no food. The Skyline Club, as it is called, has a good orchestra and a lousy floor show. It is open <u>only</u> to American Officers and nurses and WAC Officers here on pass. The only civilian girls allowed in are those with a Red Cross Hostess card. The ones there last night looked like a pretty nice bunch. Apparently what they do is see how many officers are there and then ask about half as many hostesses and introduce them to some officers. Most of the nurses here are awful battle axes. Personally I prefer 'em awful nice—like yourself, for instance.

. . . It's eleven o'clock now and I just got back about half an hour ago and have been sitting in the cafe across the street having a few beers.

I really had fun at the club this afternoon. I was introduced to the secretary, who in turn introduced me to a very nice boy of twenty or so named Jean de something or other who is a darn good tennis player. He and I hit the ball around for a while, then he beat me a love set. Afterwards he and I played four sets of doubles with two other very nice boys a little younger than he. We interspersed our sets with sitting in the club garden and drinking a beer and talking to other people there. We stopped playing about eight o'clock and changed clothes. Then we had a very good supper of soup, steak, french fries and beer. They were just as hospitable as they could be and made me be their guest on everything except supper for which we went dutch. It cost three dollars and fifty cents, including the tip, which will give you some idea about the black market here. Apparently the wealthy can get EVERYTHING they want on the black market. No one seems to think there is anything wrong with it, either. Europe sure is decadent. Tomorrow I'm going to one of the boys' houses for lunch, after which we plan to play tennis all afternoon. I guess all of them are very wealthy. I saw Jean's house, which is a small palace on the order of the Merrills' house at Pride's Crossing.

Tennis balls here cost about nine dollars apiece when you can get them. They have tennis rackets but good gut costs thirty dollars. They can't get shoes. Will you send me my black-soled sneakers I got in New Orleans and three or four cans of tennis balls if you can get them? Send one can at first and I'll let you know about the demand. Also send any real gut I have left in those two big tin cans. Dad can tell you which is and which isn't.

They are celebrating out on the square tonight again. The damn fools shoot off rockets, roman candles and fireworks right in the middle of a big crowd.

You have no idea what a pleasure it was to talk and be with gentlemen again, Liz. I guess I must be a snob at heart. This business of playing tennis and sitting around outside a nice club in good company was just what I needed—aside from you.

Well, darling, it's getting late, so I'll hit the hay in preparation for all that prospective exercise tomorrow. I hope you'll forgive me for some of the extravagance it may involve to keep up with these guys, but it <u>is</u> doing your husband a lot of good. . . .

Brussels
11 May, 1945

Dearest Liz: Today was another beautiful day and I had a good time to go with it. After being wakened several times during the night by celebrants, I got up about eight-thirty and had breakfast. I then went over to the officers clothing store and bought a new shirt so I'd have a clean one to go to lunch in. I bathed, got my shoes shined, and went to a photographer and got my picture taken. I should get them in about three weeks and will send them to you then.

After getting the picture taken I went out to the de Smets' for lunch. They are a family of three: Madame deSmet and her sons Pierre and Jean. Pierre is about twenty-two or three and Jean eighteen or nineteen. Their father was a major in the regular army and died in a German PW camp. They live in a medium sized house about like a small edition of a New York brownstone only modern and in a good neighbourhood. Madame de Smet turned out to be very nice (her sons were the two boys I played doubles against yesterday) and boy did we have a good dinner. We started off with Benedictine before dinner. We had a very good potato and greens soup, then asparagus garnished with eggs and a sauce, followed by <u>three</u> <u>inch</u> broiled steak, french fries and green beans cooked deliciously with onion and some other herb. For desert there was custard pie. With the meal we had plenty of good beer and good burgundy. It was really wonderful, because I've been starving for a real meal.

After lunch Pierre and I played ping pong for a while, then went out to the tennis club and rallied the rest of the afternoon. Madame de Smet had invited me back for supper which consisted of an enormous cauliflower, asparagus, lettuce, egg, onion, and other unknown herb salad with a delicious dressing of completely unknown vintage; boiled ham, some delicious wurst, french fries, pudding for desert, white burgundy and beer to drink. It and the lunch were the two best meals I've eaten since eating one of yours.

We ate and talked until ten minutes of ten. Pierre, Jean, and I raced to the trolley stop, but I missed the last one. They stop at ten. So I walked over to the club where the men are staying to get a lift back downtown on their shuttle truck. . . .

On getting back to the hotel I ran into . . . a Harvard classmate, Dick Betts, here on pass. He is an artillery battalion surgeon. . . .

So far I've spent just about sixty dollars, but thirty of it was for clothes, seven for the pictures, five for a present for my sweetie which she may get sometime, so the expenses haven't been too bad, considering that I've been throwing it around quite a bit buying drinks, shoe shines, tipping heavily, etc. . . .

After V-E Day, the folks at home were anticipating Jim's return, not realizing how long it would take. A letter from Liz to her in-laws right after V-E Day describes the celebration in Southwest Harbor, Maine with church bells ringing and boat whistles going off.

Jim could finally reveal the details of where he had been. One letter gave a detailed itinerary of his movements around the Bulge, the Colmar Pocket, and Rhineland campaigns. Another filled in the details of his first weeks after leaving New York.

Somewhere in Germany
16 May, 1945

Dearest Liz: The news just came in tonight that we may now give our exact location. I am in Plettenberg, Germany. . . . I don't know just how long I've been here, but it has been several weeks. It is the place where I'm living in the doctor's apartment. . . . I can't remember just every place I've been, but will try to give you an idea.

When I first got to France we stayed for five days in a field near Yvetot. . . . From there I went to Charleroi, Belgium. . . .

Plettenberg, Germany
18 May, 1945

Dearest Liz: . . .

The biggest news of today is the lifting of censorship on our mail! I imagine they will continue occasional spot checking at the base post offices, but unit censorship is a thing of the past for the ETO.

Don't worry too much about our being among the combat troops sent straight to the Pacific. I'm pretty sure they will be units which have never been in combat. . . .

Now I can also give you the details on the first part of my overseas experience. I was at Camp Shanks. I boarded the boat, the "Aquitania" on the 13th [November 1944] I believe, and sailed the 15th. We had a very easy, pleasant trip with no excitement. We came up the Irish Sea in a fog and into the Firth of Clyde, landing at Greenock, Scotland, near Loch Lomond and Glasgow. It was a beautiful harbor. I went by train to Velindre, Wales, which was the village I wrote we were staying in. It is about thirteen miles west of Cardigan Wales and about halfway between there and Carmarthen, where the Station Hospital was. . . . It was beautiful country. You would have loved it. The city I went to once was Cardiff, Wales. We took a train from Velindre to Portland and sailed on an LST about Dec. 11th or 12th—I don't remember just when. . . .

Jim's social life began to get in the swing after his return from Brussels. The 275th opened up an existing building as a "club" on a lake called Veresetalsperre, about 10 miles by road, via Herscheid, west of Plettenberg. On my tour of the Plettenberg area in April 2014, I visited the lake now called Versetalsperre. However, it did not match the postcard that my father had brought home. I quizzed my local guides, and the mystery was quickly unraveled. The lake bearing that name today was not there in 1945. The original Versetalsperre is upstream, and is now called Furwiggetalsperre. We drove up

Versetalsperre in Sauerland in 1944. This lake is now called Furwiggetalsperre. Postcard from the author's personal collection.

The author at Furwiggetalsperre, April 2014. Author's personal collection.

there and the scene is exactly as it was when it was photographed for the postcard. We walked across the dam and re-created the picture. Then I stood outside the picture windows where my father described sitting while eating the trout that he had caught in the lake, or sometimes in the stream below. The old lodge building looks exactly the same, but is now abandoned. I could understand how my father reveled in this quiet spot, well away from the everyday hubbub of army life.

A non-fraternization policy had been in place since the army had entered Germany. The next letter reflects the conflict Jim felt over the policy—his desire to see army discipline maintained, and his recognition of human nature. In his words as the letter goes on, you can hear him working through the conflict as he "talked" to Liz, ending the letter with a notably different position than that expressed at the beginning.

Plettenberg, Germany
20 May, 1945

Dearest Liz: Tonight's letter will have to be short, too, as your husband is pooped, in a hell of a humor and it's late. Also I can't find your two letters received yesterday which I intended to answer.

Last night's party at the Evac Hosp was fun. It was held on the ground floor of a castle which was very nice inside. There was lots to drink and it was sort of like a med school party—lots of drinking but mostly good clean fun with it. I danced a couple of times and sang with a big group for two hours. I got to bed at two-thirty, having left the party at two. They had a busy night in the hospital and I watched an operation a while before going to bed. They are set up in tents and I slept on a litter in the shock ward! This morning I was busy all morning plus the hour and a half ride back here.

Right after lunch I took off for another Evac. about 28 miles from here to pick up the CO, a buddy of Col. Davis and some nurses for our party. The CO was a nice guy but we got only four nurses, three of whom were terrible. Gawd! None of the girls from the other Evac could come. The place is beautiful, tho and well fixed up. We had drinks, rode around the lake in a motor boat, had more drinks and then a trout supper cooked by German cooks. It was VERY good. The whole works was spoiled by a lot of open fraternization by the men, led on by the extremely bad example of several officers whom you don't know. This lake is apparently a very popular place and there were stacks of people, especially girls there. They sure made those nurses look sick. You have no idea how nice it is to look at a decently and femininely dressed woman. Those damn uniforms are awful to see girls in, too! Unless something is done, and quickly, the whole non-fraternization policy is going to be a miserable failure. The trouble is that it is bucking human nature on both sides. The officers sympathize with the men and if they don't fraternize themselves, they do not discipline the men for doing it. It has gotten now so that they do it openly which is very bad. If they had to do it all in secrecy it does cut down a lot on the amount they can do. The policy is good in principle but it just doesn't work out in practice, especially as it is now being run. There are a lot of angles to it which I can't discuss, but they all add up pretty much to one thing—an untenable and contradictory situation. The big shots get enough extra-curricular mixed social life that the policy doesn't bother them, but the average junior officer upon whom the real enforcement of the policy rests more than sympathizes with his men and condones fraternization. I'm beginning to think the whole idea was a bad mistake. It did work in combat, but it doesn't now. Most of the people, the pretty girls and the soldiers all want to be friendly—a normal and laudable reaction under normal circumstances. These facts are too basic that any army policy can successfully defeat them, I'm afraid. I think it would be better to let the men associate with the people but at the same time drum incessantly into their ears the tricks of propaganda which the Germans will try to pull on them.

Well, sweetie, this has turned out to be a long letter. Excuse my blowing off, but you're my best safety-valve. I thought about you and missed you so much today. I sure hope we'll be together soon for a while, at least. When I think of surprizing you by appearing suddenly, it seems so wonderfully possible now.

Good night, darling. I love you very very very much.

Jim

Soldiers were starting to eagerly anticipate actually going home. Rumors and speculation centered on whether troops would be sent directly to the Pacific theatre, known as the CBI (China, Burma, India) in army parlance, or go via the US with two weeks or a month's leave at home. There was no expectation that Japan would surrender.

Plettenberg, Germany
25 May, 1945

Dearest Liz: . . .

With the specific announcement in the papers today that four infantry divisions are on their way home via the US, our spirits have improved a lot. I think now they'll probably send all the infantry divisions home on the way to the CBI. When you stop to think it over, it is logical as it will definitely save shipping space. They'll have to have more training and training over here just means that much more shipping diverted from the Pacific to supply them.

We were all conjecturing when we might get home today and almost everyone guessed a date during your vacation time in August! Here's hoping we're right! If I get home this summer, let's really plan to go up to Cambridge [New York, where they honeymooned]. I think I'd like that. How about you? I'm going to write Mrs. Blackfan and maybe sort of pave the way. . . .

The routine of administering the needs of the troops in an occupation force was becoming established. The three companies of the 275th were scattered around the area, with H&S (Headquarters and Service, of which the medical detachment was a part) and Company A in Plettenberg. Company B was in Laasphe at the beginning of May and Company C in Kreustal, then Altena. The companies were working in different parts of the region on railroad repair, dealing with captured explosives, and constructing a POW enclosure.

Plettenberg, Germany
26 May, 1945

Dearest Liz: . . . I was busy with a showdown inspection of the men's personal equipment and with sick call till eleven. Then I drove to B Co for lunch, inspected their mess, barracks & the aid men's equipment. Then we drove to C Co and did the same there, eating supper and getting back about 8:15. I made my weekly medical report to Major Sutton, shot the bull a while, returned to the apartment, read the letters and today's administrative distribution and am just getting down to writing my sweetie at 10:10. I'm really pooped, too. We drove about a hundred and fifteen miles. . . .

I'm planning to spend several nights at the lake next week if it warms up and do some early morning fishing. . . .

I would suggest that you send no more boxes after receiving this letter unless you receive information to the contrary. I don't know, but I'm getting very suspicious and hopeful that you'll be keeping me from catching those early morning fish before the summer is out! . . .

Jim included with his letter to Liz a letter he had received from his mother-in-law, Eleanor Tyson Cope Foote. She and her Unitarian minister husband (Padre in the letter) were in Charlottesville, Virginia, where Harry was acting minister to a new church for two years.

Mrs. Henry Wilder Foote
1009 Wertland Street
Charlottesville, Virginia

May 14 – 45

Dear Jim—I have a feeling you may never receive this, but I did want to send you a line for May 30th. Tho I realize I am much too late in getting this off—especially if you are sent to the Pacific without coming home first. I am hoping they will keep you in Europe because you speak German—but Liz writes me that is not at all probable.

We happened to spend V.E. Day at Hampden Institute, a quite ideal place to be—at least outwardly peaceful, tho we divined a spirit of great unrest among the student body. Mr. Bridgeman, the President, told us that a strike had been very narrowly averted just before our arrival. He is very forward looking, and wholly conscious of the necessity for change in our whole outlook & handling of our minority problems in this country—& in the world. After listening to Pres. Truman on the radio, we went across to the Chapel for a short service which had been prepared in advance for this day. It was fairly adequate—and Bridgeman address splendid—really Lincolnesque in its tone & spirit. But—how far we are from the end—and what difficult & really terrifying problems are facing that San Francisco Conference! We have heard nothing directly from Wilder & are eagerly awaiting his first reports. The news we get on the radio is pretty thin. . . . I fear our friend [ ] is sadly missing his leader & advisor, F.D.R.

Enough on problems. I have no very late reports on Liz, except that her boss, Miss Thornton, was down in C-ville about 2 weeks ago, and told me she thought Liz looking & seeming much better. Her father thought so too when he saw her in N.Y. in April. (I find he is writing too—so has doubtless given you his views on this all important subject). I know that young Wilder had the thrill of his life on that weekend in N.Y. . . . Just now we are hourly expecting a wire from Caleb—announcing the arrival of "Heshe." It seems to be nip & tuck which happens first, his trial or the babe's arrival. [Caleb and Hope's first child, Robert, was in fact born May 26, 1945.]

Padre and I are planning to leave here June 11th, and are hoping we may be privileged to see Basking Ridge & your Pop & Ma—not to mention Liz. We [ ] to Camb. where we expect to stay about a week at the Merrimans, before going on to Maine. We don't expect to come back here next fall, unless the A.U.A. fails to find a successor, which begins to look dubious as time goes on. So—like everyone else—we are waiting to see what happens.

I know I don't need to send you my congratulations for the anniversary of the great day, which brought so much happiness to our little girl. Again I thank you for that alone, and send you both my blessing & the ardent hope that before another May 30th comes round—you will be together again and starting the home you have planned & hoped for in a sane and peaceful, and let us hope, more enlightened world. Liz writes that you have received the Bronze Star—for which hearty congratulations. But—I echo her wish—that she "wants her man more than the medals"! Just the same we are very proud of you.

Always affectionately,
Mother F.

Now that Jim's unit was settling into a pleasant routine in Plettenberg, uncertainty began to creep in as to the fate of the division as the army tried to consolidate and deploy units for the occupation, as well as assemble full divisions to send to the Pacific.

Plettenberg, Germany
Monday, 28 May, 1945

Dearest Liz: . . .

We're all getting the feeling that it's about time the British started to take over and the air is full of rumors as to our fate, tho no one, including the General knows. The thing we're all afraid of is that they'll split the division up and use us as replacements. Personally I don't think that will happen, but you never know. My present guess is that I'll be home the first of August, tho that is undoubtedly being optimistic, so don't get too dependent on that—but also don't be unprepared, should it happen. I'm hoping that we'll get sent home soon and do our Pacific training in the U.S. I sure don't want to do it here. . . .

Versetalsperre
29 May, 1945

Dearest Liz: What fishing! I came out to the lake just before supper and then fished from seven to 9:45 with half an hour out for a rainstorm. I caught four trout. Two were about eight inches and two twelve or thirteen—really nice fish. My luck wasn't very good until I adopted the little boy tactics you find so amusing—i.e.: worming up to the pools on my belly. I fished the brook below the dam of the lake. It is VERY similar to the brook where we caught the trout on our honeymoon and I kept looking around for my mosquito (not flea) bitten wife whom I love. . . .

Jim was constantly trying to keep up with holidays, birthdays, and anniversaries at home. This required considerable advance thinking, given the time it took for mail to go back and forth. His anniversary letter to Liz was written May 8, marked "DO NOT OPEN TILL MAY 30th." Jim and Liz were married May 30, 1943, in King's Chapel, Boston, by Liz's father, Henry Wilder Foote II. They honeymooned at a camp on a lake near Cambridge, New York. Jim's father, Robert James McKay, was born in nearby Shushan in 1887, while his grandfather Daniel Graham McKay was minister there. The McKays were good friends of the Blackfans, who lived in Cambridge.

Somewhere in Germany
8 May, 1945

Dearest Liz: I've been waiting for ten days for a beautiful day, so I could properly write you commemorating the second anniversary of another beautiful day just two years ago from the time you are reading this. I'm glad I waited, because this morning is JUST like the one on which I got up in Chestnut Hill and got all dressed up to go down to King's Chapel and hold hands with the girl I loved while her father married us. That was a beautiful and happy day, darling, and has been and will be followed by many more.

To me you are just like a beautiful May day—lovely and sunny and warm (!) and giving life beauty and meaning. . . .

I wish we could be together today, Liz, but since we can't, I'll be thinking about my pretty little bride in her green dress with the white frills and how I couldn't keep from looking at her with love-filled eyes on the train, so everyone knew she was a bride; about how funny it felt—and yet how right—when Mrs. Blackfan drove off, leaving us alone at the camp; and just about how sweet and "bridey" you were in every nice way.

In spite of your being a relatively worn old married woman after these two years, I still long with all my heart to see you and know there will never be enough time to be with you enough.

I love you very very much, Liz, and always will. I'm really glad that you're my sweet wife with whom I'm <u>in</u> love.

Jim

While Jim longed for his absent wife, the inevitable result of the fraternization he was so concerned about was now in evidence among the soldiers under his care.

Plettenberg, Germany
31 May, 1945

Dearest Liz: . . .

This morning after sick call I wrote my monthly medical report and left afterward for lunch at Attendorn on my way to Siegen where I went to get the name & address of a girl who gave gonorrhea to one of our men. V-D is getting to be a real first class nuisance. The line of duty now is yes under any circumstances as long as they report it when they get it, so they just don't seem to give a damn. . . .

Troops were now starting to return to the US as fast as ships could carry them. Jim was still clinging to the hope that he would get home that summer.

Plettenberg, Germany
1 June 1945

Dearest Liz: . . . About five o'clock Fletch and I left for the lake where I fished in another brook for a couple of hours, catching four ten inch trout and two smaller ones. It was a lot of fun. Got back about eight-thirty to the lodge where Trudi, the girl who does the cooking, had a nice supper of trout, German fried potatoes, spiced & onioned stewed tomatoes and lemonade ready. I ate looking out over the lake. It was really very pleasant. After dinner we came back here for the night.

Your letters of May 23rd & 25th arrived today to keep your husband cheered up and more or less in contact with the girl he loves.

I now have an idea of what we are going to do in the near future, tho I can't tell you yet what it is. It looks like it may keep us here at least 5–6 months longer. We will not be staying in Germany. So don't get excited or worried if there is a letter gap soon. It will just be the usual one attendant on a major move and setting up in a new place. . . .

Another package arrived from you today. It contained olives, sardine paste, lobster, and anchovies. Thank you, sweetie. We are hoping to maybe get American beer over here before too long on the ships coming back after taking troops to the U.S.

I think you might as well plan to go ahead and take your vacation as you had already figured to do. [Liz planned to go to the Foote summer home in Maine in August.] What I'll do is too uncertain for you to change that. . . . I thought if you were in Maine when I got back, we might meet halfway in Boston to speed up getting together. Of course, as you said, I'll probably be tied up a day or so at one of the P.O.E. (Port of Embarkation) camps before being released. If I could call you, you could then start right down.

We have not gone back to as strict garrison life yet as I had anticipated, but we probably will soon. Garrison life means keeping your shoes shined, reveille, retreat, always wearing the proper uniform, trip tickets for vehicles, and keeping all sorts of little records & paper work which we were allowed to skip in combat. In combat a good many of the annoying little petty check-up activities are suspended. You are able to live a "freer" life.

Plettenberg, Germany
Sunday, 3 June 1945

Dearest Liz: . . .

This letter won't be mailed until after our move is an accomplished fact, so I can tell you about it now. We are leaving for France early Tuesday morning, turning the area here over to the British. We expect to end up somewhere in the vicinity of Rheims. Rumor has been consistent for some time that we are going to operate the 17 redeployment and processing camps there. That, if true, will probably mean we will be over here for 5–10 months longer.

Today I had sick call, read the paper, had lunch, played volley ball, and then went out to the lake to fish. It was a beautiful day, the nicest we've had. I fished another section of brook I hadn't fished before and got five—1 ten incher, the rest about 8 inches. It was a very pleasant way to spend Sunday afternoon. I ate the trout for supper at the Lodge, and got back to Plettenberg about 8:15.

Liege, Belgium
5 June 1945

Dearest Liz: Last night I missed writing because your procrastinating and disorderly husband did not get through packing until 2 AM and had to get up at five. We left Plettenberg at 7:15 and arrived in Liege late this afternoon. We have been assigned a bivouac area here. I've just spent an hour or more putting up and ditching my pup tent, as it looks like rain. It's 9:30 now and I'm sitting in the truck writing this as I look out over the city of Liege. We are on a hill southeast of the town. . . .

Yesterday I splurged on a $20 combined birthday & Christmas present for Pop. It is a set of very powerful German artillery observation glasses with a sunglass attachment. I thought he could rig a frame or tripod for them and use them on the boat. I'm going to send them to you. Will you paint them blue and then put "Rebel Lass" in white on them and give them to him as soon as possible so he can get the use of them this summer? . . .

Today we came through Cologne, Duren, and Aachen. They are all really "kaput." I don't see how they can be rebuilt on the same spot.

Chapter Nine

Re-deployment Camps: Summer 1945, Chalons and Reims, France

The 75th Division was sent to Chalons sur Marne (now Chalons-en-Champagne) for three or four months to work on embarkation (re-deployment) camps. Mourmelon-le-Grand, about 20 kilometers from Rheims (now Reims), was headquarters of Oise intermediate section (army command area), and the center of gravity for camps to be constructed. Immediate work was commenced, with each engineering battalion being assigned to four camps, where they worked until they were themselves re-deployed. The engineers set up and operated numerous supply dumps, gravel pits, etc. Several thousand German prisoners of war were employed on unskilled and semi-skilled labor under the supervision of enlisted personnel. The camps were completed on the scheduled deadline of October 1. Each camp had a capacity of from 15 to 17 thousand officers and men and was capable of housing an infantry division while it was being processed for embarkation. Five of the camps were winterized with pyramidal tents on concrete floors for troop housing, plus necessary temporary housing for messes, ablutions, supply, administration, etc. The camps were known as the "city camps" because each was named after an American city.

Records of the city camps are sketchy. There were about 20 of them, spread over the French province of Champagne. In April 2014, I visited one of the sites, at Mourmelon-le-Grand, which—along with three others—lives on as a French military base. The camps were enormous, covering about 20 to 30 square miles each. You can still see the network of roads that lace what is now abandoned land used for military training.

Camp Norfolk, where the 275th worked, was in Mailly-le-Camp, just south of Sommesous. The site was a French air base before the war. It was used by the Wehrmacht during the war to train artillery units, and was bombed to smithereens late in the war.

There were some 1.9 million soldiers waiting to return to the US, and relatively few ships. Soldiers were being sent home according to a point system known as the Adjusted Service Rating Score (ASRS), one point being given for each month in service home or abroad, twelve points for each dependent child, and five points for each combat engagement and medal. Jim had entered the army near the end of the war, so had few points, although he had 15 points for his service at the Bulge, the Colmar Pocket, and the Rhine Crossing, and five for his bronze star. He wrote Liz and his parents of his hopes for going home, but knew he was well down the list. For a while he was afraid of being re-deployed to the Pacific.

Camp Norfolk
Sommesous, France
7 June 1945

Dearest Liz: . . .

We got to Camp Norfolk, about 18 miles south of Chalons, France (southeast of Rheims) about 6 o'clock last night. It is a tent affair. The men sleep in pyramidal and squad tents and the officers each have a wall tent which is about an 8 x 7 foot affair. The weather is hot and glaring. The countryside is dry and rolling—almost just like around Breckinridge. In other words, it is unpleasant country for anyone with your or my tastes. The heat, the glare, and the dust are terrible. As yet we don't know just what we are going to do. We will either be split up into platoons and divided among a number of camps, or else we will take over a camp and run it, keeping the battalion together. We expect to know tomorrow. If the battalion is broken up I don't know what I'll do. Probably I'll run a dispensary in one of the camps. The current rumor is that a lot more people are going direct to the Pacific than we thought. It does look like we'll be here at least until Oct. 1st, tho. Some of the men are going on pass to Troyes, 35 miles south, tonight. I don't know what there is to do in these towns. This is all World War I battle area. — FLASH! Major Sutton just came in and said that no combat divisions will go direct to the CBI. Keep your fingers crossed, Liz!

In a letter to his sister-in-law, Alice, Jim describes his feelings about the new trend for women to enter the workforce, having been forced to do so during the war, and discovering this new aspect to their lives. Alice had written Jim a couple of months earlier to ask advice about raising their son, Mike, known as Reb.

Camp Norfolk
Sommesous, France
10 June 1945

Dear Alice: . . .

If all parents educated their children by precept and example in the ways of kindness, thoughtfulness, consideration, and industry, there would be no wars and no oppression. I also think that is the only way to stop war, greed, and oppression. Too many people, especially women, have lost sight these days of the fact that they are already entrusted with the biggest part of the world's most important job, the bringing up and education of children. And it is the home environment, the family life, and the example parents THEMSELVES personally give their children which is the most important and deciding factor in that education. If a woman turns out just one child who by his qualities contributes positively to the goodness and welfare of the world in a small or large way, she has done more than the woman who selfishly carves out a successful career for herself, even though it be nominally one which helps others. Her ultimate contribution to humanity, I am sure, is greater, and I am also sure that her personal satisfaction is greater. In a "career" where she does a man's work and competes with men, a woman leaves undone a job which only a woman can do, and therefore leaves humanity that much poorer. Though it is something I have always known, the war at first hand has given me the knowledge of how irreplaceably important women are to the world, but they are only important as WOMEN. I have seen how the company of fifty nurses and WACs does less for morale than the presence of one woman talking to or just being watched by the same group of soldiers as she does their laundry or their cooking. The latter, dressed and behaving like a real woman, changes their whole outlook. For several days afterward they will not only be happier, but they will kill less, steal less, lie less, drink less and in general be less vicious and better men. . . . The same thing is true in civilian life, though it is not there so obvious and striking, but it is on a larger and more important scale there.

Jim settled into their new situation in Chalons-sur-Marne, France. Duties were routine, the men bored, and mischief common. Two companies of the 275th were a half hour south. Reims was less than an hour away to the north, and Paris less than three hours to the west. Jim was often annoyed by the stupid decisions the engineers made, resulting in more work for him. He was beginning to look for his favorite diversion, tennis.

Chalons sur Marne
19 June 1945

Dearest Liz: . . .

This morning I saw a few patients and then went down to Mailly-le-Camp to inspect a new mess run jointly by B & C Co mess personnel. While there we were able to buy 2 bottles of Piel's beer apiece and did it ever taste good! This afternoon I took a long nap, played a set of lousy tennis with Col. Hall, took a bath, ate supper, played volley ball, & am now seated in my under-shorts writing my sweetie.

It sure looks to me like they'll dissolve some of these headquarters groups, including ours, which are sitting around doing nothing. That might mean one of three things to me—1) Joining a unit on its way straight to the Pacific 2) Joining a unit going via the States 3) Going straight to the Pacific as a replacement (most probable). Here's hoping it doesn't happen, especially after we had gotten our hopes up so high.

Chalons sur Marne
26 June 1945

Dearest Liz: . . .

The aid men all came in this morning. This afternoon we all went over to Reims & went thru the Pommery Champagne Factory and visited the Cathedral [Notre-Dame Saint-Jacques de Reims]. The architect who designed it really had something. It impresses & awes even the most ignorant & lecherous G-I with no artistic or other sensibilities at all. There is really an awesome quality to Gothic architecture which is peculiarly suited to the building of churches. I think the most beautiful part of the church is looking back toward the entrances down the side naves from the back end of the cathedral.

After supper Hagie & I took our bottle of gin & our bottle of scotch apiece up to H&S with some of our groceries from home & had a nice little party which broke up about ten when the men went on to a dance & we came home. There is no moon tonight as it seems to be blowing up a thunderstorm.

Our footlockers arrived a few days ago. It really surprised me as I honestly never expected to see mine again. [The battalion's footlockers had been diverted in England when they first arrived 8 months earlier.]

Darling, I wish so often for you and all that being with you means—it is all of life for me. . . .

Chalons sur Marne, France
27 June 1945 (Wednesday)

Dearest Liz: . . .

Day after tomorrow I'm going to Paris again for the day. . . . God knows when I'll go again. I hope to hell I do well in the AAC tennis tournament on July 9, 10 & 11 as it will probably mean an opportunity to go to Paris and/or London for several days to play winners of other local tournaments. There is nothing much to do, yet the complete uncertainty of my situation keeps me in enough of a nervous uproar that I can't get down to doing any work. Damn the Army! This business of being unable to make <u>any</u> plans really gets me down.

The only cheerful thought today, sweetie, has been of you and of methods of surprizing you without scaring you when I get home, assuming that it will be before going to the Pacific. . . .

Chalons sur Marne, France
28 June 1945

Dearest Liz: . . .

. . . Col. Davis . . . and all other Regular Army medical officers are leaving within a few weeks to go direct to the South Pacific. They are also sending a bunch of high point officers directly home to staff the increased hospital facilities there. . . . Col. Davis said, tho, that most of the direct to Pacific units would probably be gone within 6–8 weeks & that if I hadn't been snapped up by then there would at least be a chance of going back thru the U.S. . . . Of course, being in one of the direct to Pacific outfits would have its advantages as far as safety is concerned as they are almost without exception strictly rear area units. It will seem unfair, tho, if the medical officers in this division are sent direct, because it will mean arrival in the Pacific ahead of the 86th even which has seen about a tenth the action we have. I'm especially vulnerable as my job here is in <u>no</u> sense essential. Of course the thing we all hope for is just to be forgotten. That would probably mean staying here till the AAC job is completed, then going home with the division for demobilization which looks to be what will happen to it. I've been terribly in the dumps all day and felt even worse when I read your letters which looked forward so cheerfully & confidently to my coming home. I've been so optimistic about getting home soon for a little while & it has meant so much to me that the outlook gets me down worse than anything else ever has. Perhaps it will work out all right in the end. . . .

I went to Reims on business & also to pick up my new tennis racket, which I did. I then decided to drop in at the Reims Tennis Club. They have very nice courts and I ran into a little group of good players—mostly EM—who are being organized for a sectional team. They want me to join it and the officer in charge is going to call Major Sutton with the idea of getting me over there every day for practice for a week or so, after which the team would tour a number of tournaments and have matches with other sectional teams. It sounds ideal but I doubt if I make the team in the long run & also am sure that such a rear echelon arrangement will go over very poorly with the CO of a combat outfit like ours. I hope it works out though, & I did get an hour of good tennis this afternoon.

. . . That's another thing that gripes hell out of me which is not taken into account by the Army—that is how DAMN much it means to us to see each other again while so many can't REALLY care too much on either side when they do. It gripes me so to see men to whom going home means nothing doing so, when people like us to whom being together is EVERYTHING get gypped out of it. Well maybe we won't get gypped out of it, so let's not gripe too much before we come to that bridge.

I have to get up at five to go to Paris tomorrow, so will close this & get to bed now. Darling, I love you and miss you so much & wish & hope with all my heart that it won't be direct to the Pacific, because I want to hold you in my arms & kiss you & tell you in person how terribly much I love you. — and soon.

Jim

Paris, France
29 June 1945

Liz Darling: This is being written at the ENSA Theater. ENSA is the British USO. The show I'm waiting to see is Laurence Olivier & Sybil Thorndike in George Bernard Shaw's "Arms & The Man." I'm now back at the Red Cross Independence Club for officers. It was hard writing in the theatre. . . . I was interrupted by the playing of the Star Spangled Banner, the Marseillaise, and God Save the King for which we all stood at attention. . . .

This has been repeatedly aggravating with about half of it spent waiting in line [trying to get tickets to an opera, then other shows]. . . . I ended up at the Place Pigalle, the Scollay Square of Paris. There I ran into one of the men we brought in on the truck this morning. We had a few beers & talked & watched the thriving business enjoyed there by the "oldest profession." It was really amazing.

Chalons sur Marne, France
4 July 1945

Dearest Liz: . . .

Tonight the Battalion paraded thru Chalons & really looked very well, I think. There was a big crowd out to watch. There was to be a band concert afterward followed by a public dance in the market place with music by our division dance band. . . . I do wish I'd get to know some French people well here. So far the only opportunities of doing so have been via getting to know unmarried daughters, but I can't see that because they're short of men & want to get married so can't waste their time on "platonic" friendships. So far the only people I might have made friends with turned out to be collaborationists & I don't want to mess with them. Hell!

Playing tennis is doing me good. I'm looking & feeling much better both physically & mentally. I'm sleeping much better, too.

I find I can hardly put "Earth & High Heaven" down. . . . It made me feel that maybe I was holding you down in a way with a lot of my ideas & prejudices. I think when I come home you'll find me a lot less prejudiced than before on racial problems—I've seen so much blind, unreasoning, contradictory prejudice in this war. On the other hand you are also prejudicial if you refuse to admit & criticize the faults of a race or group just because they are that group. . . . It's just as illogical to me to privilege a minority as a majority & leads to no good. I, personally, have no trouble with racial groups, but I've seen cases where negros were allowed to get away with things no white soldier would, because of the fear of starting a race riot. That's just as bad as starting a race riot, tho, because it causes just as much ill feeling as if it were the other way around.

Sweetie, I'm glad we don't have any particular problems of that sort to cope with, because I love you & it will save a lot of heartache. Fundamentally we agree pretty well, tho the architecture of our finished thoughts may be a little different. . . .

Chalons sur Marne, France
5 July 1945

Dearest Liz: Darling, I don't know quite how to console you in the hour of your great bereavement—namely the death of Ronnie [the Footes' pet collie]. I know how terribly unhappy it would have made a little girl 13 or fourteen years ago and I know there is enough of that little girl left in you for it to be real crying news. . . . The Germans have a word for that longing you sometimes get for that which is past and was beautiful & you hate to see gone forever, whether you really wish it back again or not. I remember crying my heart out at the age of 20 on reading the original of the "Student Prince" because it hit me at a time when I was particularly growing up in relation to responsibility. . . . I felt like the Prince—that the beautiful days of my carefree youth were left irretrievably & beautifully behind. . . . I'm sure that Ronnie's death marks for you the passing of the last of that era of happy, carefree girlhood. . . .

Tonight I've been busy as hell. Major Sutton suddenly decided to move into a hotel down by Div. Hq. Hotel tomorrow. We will add 6 QM officers to our mess there. It is . . . a mess for me to get straightened out. I'll now have to manage the hotel manager, his wife, and 9 other employees. . . .

Chalons sur Marne, France
6 July 1945 Friday

Dearest Liz: . . .

I spent all morning working on moving to our new quarters & setting up the mess there. This afternoon I worked some more on it, then went to Reims & got in two hours of sun & tennis, & then picked up an AWOL in Ay near Epernay, getting back about 7 o'clock. . . . There is a dance at Div Hq tonight. I plan to go, not having been since the first one. . . .

We're moving to the hotel tomorrow. I have a nice big room to myself with bed, table, chairs, wash basin & douche bowl (ALL French toilet facilities seem to give A priority to douche bowls!). It looks out on the court in back.

With the help of archivist Pascaline Watier of the Biblioteque Georges Pompidou in Chalons-en-Champagne, I located the Hotel Moritz, which is now a somewhat dilapidated building. It is on rue Lochet, just steps from the northern entrance of Le Petit Jard, the major park in the city. The site is about four blocks from the main bridge into Chalons, which carries rue Jean Jaures over the Marne River. This bridge was destroyed by retreating Germans in the summer of 1944. There was substantial damage in the city, but as usual, Jim made no mention of it. It was a lovely sunny day when we visited, and as we

Jim's granddaughter Sarah and the author's wife, Betsy, at Hotel Moritz, April 2014.

sat in Le Petit Jard, I could imagine my father striding by from his quarters 100 yards away. I could not, however, imagine him sitting in the sunshine as we were doing. He was a man who strode, not sat.

Hotel Moritz
Chalons sur Marne, France
Saturday 7 July 1945

Dearest Liz: . . . .

. . . Today saw the advent of another very cheering custom—namely the arrival of two cans of American beer apiece. I managed to phenagle 5 instead of two, so did pretty well. I have a perennial deal with Smitty to give him my coke & I get his beer. . . .

The dance last night was rather fun and I spoke a lot of French. I met three girls who, believe it or not, seemed to have somewhat the same grade of background our friends have at home. . . . Their dancing is impossible for me, tho. They ALL jitterbug or semi-jitterbug—to them that is the way Americans dance. Do people do that in the good places at home now? Maybe I'm just old-fashioned.

Having been a tennis teaching pro for two summers in college, Jim was quite comfortable taking charge of all matters having to do with tennis. His involvement would offer welcome opportunities for travel, exercise, and social contacts over the coming months of his deployment.

Hotel Moritz
Chalons sur Marne, France
8 July 1945 Sunday

Dearest Liz: . . .

This afternoon I went over to the Terrain des Sports here and became captain & manager of the Mailly Sub-Area tennis team (4 men) which I will take to Reims tomorrow for the AAC tournament. . . .

I'm going to a French movie in about 1 minute. . . .

When I got back Hagie said that the Special Service officer had called to say that we don't go to Reims tomorrow, the tournament being postponed till the 24th. . . .

Occasionally, when Jim's life and work were quiet, he would write a real love letter to Liz, rather than the usual daily letters that read much like journal entries. On July 10, he wrote a three-page love letter, remembering their early dating days when they began to realize they were very much in love. Liz had a boy (Petrie) she needed to break off with, and Jim was, for the first time in his life, interested in only one woman.

Chalons sur Marne, France
Tuesday 10 July 1945

Dearest Liz: . . .

In fact, I was sure your reaction to Petrie after our Gloucester trip would tell the story and I was pretty sure things would go the way you told me they did on Sunday night. If they'd gone any other way it would have been awful, because the one absolutely clear wish & desire & purpose in my whole mind & being then was to marry you. From the time we started that fall it was just like being caught in a current which carried me relentlessly (in a nice sense) toward the port I knew I wanted most in all the world—marrying you. At first I was just adrift on the current, being carried pleasantly along without realizing its strength. By the time I did, I also knew it was carrying me to just exactly the right place. After living in the port, to which the current carried me, for two years and more, I'm surer than ever that it's the RIGHTEST one to which ever a man was carried and that it will prove to be even more so as the years go by.

. . . Darling, I guess this letter turned out to be sort of a love letter, but I mean every world of it and more which can't possibly be expressed by words or anything else but a lifetime of being together. That must be one of the satisfactions of old couples—to have, by a long happy married life, expressed their love for each other. Right now I feel as if I'll bust with the love for you which fills me and which I can only express in person. I want so much to hold you close & tell you by word & deed of all the love in my heart for you. Goodnight, Liz. I love you.

Jim

Chalons sur Marne, France
11 July 1945 Wednesday

Dearest Sweetie: Your debauched husband is sitting here in his room now eating olives and drinking Haig's Gold Label Scotch Whiskey from the bottle & writing the woman whose lovaire he is. Isn't that AHFUL? . . .

I played tennis, beating the No. 3 man on our team 8-6, 6-2. The entire afternoon was spent in inspecting Engineer units at 5 different camps. . . .

You can stop sending potato substitutes now. We now have lots of macaroni. Anchovies, olives & lobster & shrimp are still high on the list. Hagie has plenty of saltines for all now. Lots of fly streamers would be very welcome. . . .

I, too, have so far been favorably impressed by Truman. I'm afraid it only proves, tho, that machine politics are less vicious than the class & racial politics of the last 13 years. Whatever one's opinion of Roosevelt, it is more of a return to government by the people as compared to government by one man. I think Truman is a relief to everybody because of the relief from fear of a dictatorship which I think even his supporters often wondered about with Roosevelt. I think Truman is a better representative of the people because he is less egoistical, humbler and, like any common man, holds opinions which will be common and sympathetic to both sides. . . .

Jim really missed meaningful relationships with civilians, particularly in family settings. During combat they stayed in common houses, and a few times he had greatly enjoyed the family atmosphere, so different from the army social life. Since moving to France, Jim had been starved for such contact.

Chalons sur Marne, France
Tuesday 13 July 1945 Friday

Dearest Liz: . . .

Tomorrow is Bastille Day. All the public buildings were lighted up tonight & the people were working themselves into the holiday spirit. At last it looks as if I may get a little congenial social contact. Louis Le Conte, who runs the Chalons tennis team asked me to come over & play bridge & meet his friends tomorrow afternoon. I believe his family should be nice. I sure hope it works out well.

Chalons sur Marne, France
14 July 1945 Saturday

Dearest Liz: . . .

This morning I went down to Camp Norfolk with Chivington and Major Sutton on an inspection trip. This afternoon I took a nap & loafed around until 4:30 when I dressed up & went over to Louis Le Conte's house. The front looks like any other hovel up a narrow, dirty little street. In code, tho, it is a small palace with a big formal garden for a back yard. He had in 3 French boys & 2 girls all in the age group 20–25. We talked, ate tarts, and played bridge till 8:30 when we went downstairs & I met his mother & father & 2 sisters (Louis has 3 brothers & 3 sisters in all). I really felt this afternoon that my French was progressing. I talked as much as anyone there & didn't get stuck enough to keep me from saying or understanding almost anything I tried to. . . . One of the girls was very pretty and made me long for you terribly. Not only did she look something like you, but was there with her fiancé and kept looking at him the way you look at me.

Tomorrow at two we're playing tennis with the French team. Louis has already written Epernay asking for a match with them.

Once again, Jim was finding that his social and athletic skills were his ticket to building relationships. The next day he wrote Liz about the day's tennis followed by champagne and cake with the French team. "Tennis & bridge sure are a great help socially if you can play them well."

Most letters contain responses to something in Liz's latest letter, as well as Jim's own news. On July 16, he filled her in on his new tennis duties and then responded to her news that her brother Caleb, who was a conscientious objector (CO), had been sentenced to another two years in prison. Caleb had finished serving a two-year sentence for refusing to serve, had then refused to serve once again, and been sentenced again.

Jim related how a general of the 75th Division saw him playing with Louis one day in Chalons and called Jim over. Jim thought he would be balled out for being out of uniform, but the officer instead asked him to form a tennis team for the division. Jim formed the team and spent many enjoyable hours that summer in competitions with other units.

Chalons sur Marne, France
Monday 16 July 1945

Dearest Liz: . . .

Last night I received a call to report to G-1 at 9 o'clock this morning. I was afraid that meant transfer either to one of the camps or out so I didn't mention it last night in my letter. When I went down there this morning, it was to find they just wanted me to run the tennis part of the AAC [Assembly Area Command] athletic program. I'll be put on detached service to Div. Hq. & given a jeep to use. Actually I'll continue living right here and will continue to perform my regular duties as battalion surgeon except during tournaments. I will run an AAC tournament in Reims next [week, and will] pick the four best players to compete in the Corps tournament Aug. 3, 4, & 5th. The team which wins the tournament will send its manager (coach) to England with the winner & runner up in the singles and the winning doubles team who will go to play in the Theater finals in England the 15th, 16th, 17th, & 18th of August. . . . One thing is that I don't think I'll be transferred out as long as the job is active. . . .

Was sorry to hear Caleb had gotten so much this time. However, I think he has gone about putting over his ideas the wrong way. Whatever the principles behind it, he is refusing to carry his share of the burden. No matter how often he gets thrown into prison, he is given a term and he knows he'll be out in one piece and with his wife & child then. We don't know that and never will. I think the COs should go into the medical or chaplain's corps of the Army. . . . after the war, the word of a CO who stayed home in or out of jail isn't going to count for a tinker's damn. If he has been out with the men who fought, they'll listen to him. As I said before, it's too negative an argument the way he's doing it.

Poor sweetie, I hope you don't have too tough a trip to Maine with Agnes & the baby. I do think restricting civilian train travel is right, tho. I don't believe people at home know what "40 and 8s" are. They are box cars—40 men or 8 horses. If the men are lucky there's straw on the floor. There's no water, no heat, & no toilet. That's what the soldiers not lucky enough to be motorized have ridden in over here. Quite frankly I don't think a soldier would mind the old day coaches—they're better than a lot he's ridden in—if he didn't see PWs & civilians riding in comfort & luxury at the same time. Have people griped much about it? . . .

Chalons sur Marne, France
19 July, 1945 Thursday

Dearest Liz: . . .

I went to Reims, planning to play off the Suippes Sub-Area tennis entrants. On arriving, I found that all but two of the Oise AND AAC rackets had broken strings. I did manage to get it played off by 1 o'clock. Canda & I left at 2:30 for Paris to try to trade off tennis balls for good rackets. We have 3 ordered at 5 balls apiece. The Army issues lousy rackets (strung with grade C silk) and then gives you absolutely no strings to maintain them with under the heavy use they receive. . . .

Last night Louis Le Conte's 7 months old niece died. After thinking about it all day today I wonder if it wasn't an intussusception. It was probably too late to save her when I saw her, especially with the facilities available, but I wish I could have been more sure of it at the time. Actually it wouldn't have made any difference because even if there were a competent enough surgeon here, her condition was too bad for operation. . . .

The baby was the daughter of Louis's sister, who came to visit during the summer with her husband, a French armored corps officer named Armand d'Evry. The d'Evrys became very good friends of Jim's. Medicine was not taking up much of Jim's time, between managing the battalion's headquarters facilities and the AAC tennis team, and attending various social events.

Chalons sur Marne, France
Saturday, 21 July 1945

Dearest Liz: . . . .

The dance last night wasn't much. I knew very few people & found myself interested in none, so I only stayed an hour. Tonight the Engineers are having a party in the hotel garage which has been fixed up as an officers' nightclub for us. It gives me a pain. Major Sutton is bound & determined now to move the owner & his family out so the Engineers can have the whole place to themselves to raise all the hell they want. If he succeeds, I'll be swamped with the work of managing a 25 room hotel with dining room for 40 people. Another of his reasons for moving the French out is that they keep two pigs in the back of the Garage & it smells up the nightclub a little. Why the hell we need one is beyond me. Division already has a nice place set up which is almost never crowded, & is only across the street from us. Major Sutton just wants to be his own little king, I guess. This business of being in the Army as an officer is sure producing an excess crop of self centered egotists. I'm getting bad enough, & I'm meek as a lamb & considerate as hell compared to the rest. They keep the jeep drivers up half the night driving them around on dates, then if I want to make a trip early, the driver is asleep & I hate to wake the poor guy. Tonight Louis Le Conte asked me over to play bridge. I accepted since there'll be no sleeping with this party right outside my window. Then I find I have a blind date with a nurse for this party! The hell with it. I'm going on & play bridge & if there's any kick, I'll really raise one about getting a married man a blind date he not only doesn't want but wasn't even asked if he wanted for a party he doesn't want to go to, & then giving him hell for not wanting anything to do with it. I'm tired as hell and coming down with a cold. . . .

Darling, forgive my blowoff. It looks like you're going to have a hell of a time going thru life listening to me do it. Maybe we better just emigrate to a desert island or the wilderness. . . .

Chalons sur Marne, France
Sunday, 22 July 1945

Dearest Liz: . . .

Last night at the Le Contes' was very pleasant and the Engineer party was pretty good, too. The nice married nurse I told you about meeting at the picnic last week was there with Van Vreede & I danced with her (she's a good dancer !!!!—amazing in a nurse) a couple of times. Then Van, she, & I came up to my room & consumed a K ration I had hidden away. She & Van returned to the dance & I hit the hay about 12:15.

This morning & evening I've spent making the draw for the AAC tennis tournament tomorrow. This afternoon we went to Epernay & our combined American-French Chalons team won 8-1. They were lousy. Epernay is really a nice place with more pretty girls—not painted ones—than I've seen anyplace in France. They have a nice club on the bank of the Marne with 3 tennis courts, sculling facilities, & swimming. All these pretty girls were out in their bathing suits of the 2 piece variety. They looked to me as if they must have really been out to conserve cloth when they made them. I wonder if yours looks the same way? Send that picture! . . .

Jim got to know Louis well during his tennis "assignment." It turned out that the Le Contes had been an important family in Chalons for centuries. The palace was rich, with original Aubuchon tapestries and the like hanging on the walls.

Chalons sur Marne, France
Tuesday, 24 July 1945

Dearest Liz: . . .

We had beautiful tennis weather again today & we played off the 75th Div–AAC tennis tournament as far as the finals which are tomorrow. I play Canda (he beat Bennett who is supposed to be our best player) in the finals of the singles & he and I play Bennett & Buchstaber in the doubles final. We will then practice (the four of us will make up the Division team) for the XVIth Corps tournament at Auxerre the 3rd, 4th, & 5th of August. . . .

Chalons sur Marne, France
28 July 1945 Saturday

Dearest Liz: Well here it is one AM again already . . .

I played 3 sets here with the No 3 man on our team M/Sgt Moritz of the OM Co. I won 1-6, 6-4, 6-1. After lunch I took a two hour nap, went down & got my PX supplies for the week, read Time & Newsweek & your letters, and looked Louis up at the office where he works. I ate supper at 5:30 sharp, then went out & played tennis with Louis, beating him 4-6, 6-1, 6-0. After playing we went back to his house for dinner of soup, omelet, green beans, wurst & salad, cheese, dessert red wine, & champagne. After dinner we fooled around with his sister's 6 & 7 year old sons for a while, then Louis, Madame Le Conte, Robert, & Nicki, & I played bridge, taking turns dropping out for a rubber. I've just returned from their house which is about 3 blocks from here. . . .

Jim's roughhousing with Louis Le Conte's nephews may have pushed his own family plans to the forefront of his mind. Given the long separations of couples during the war, the baby boom immediately following the war was no surprise. Not only were there millions of couples in their twenties who had postponed children, there was the incredible longing of the soldiers for a simple family life after the surreal existence of soldiers at war. Jim and Liz were no exception.

Chalons sur Marne, France
Wednesday, 1 August 1945

Dearest Liz: . . .

Sweetie, I beg to contradict you, you will be pretty when you're pregnant, as you always are and will be to me. I, too, have done some serious thinking about your getting pregnant if I go to the Pacific via the U.S. and have come to the conclusion that it would not be a good idea. Our present finances aren't so much against it, but I do agree about the absence of the father (me) being an almost all important psychological component both for you and our baby. Also I think our children will be much better off to come into the world after you & I have been together again long enough after the war to get stabilized. I'm afraid that inevitably the presence of a baby the first few months after I get back would make us wish at times we weren't tied down just then, whereas later it wouldn't bother us. And I think the only time to have children is when you can & do want them wholeheartedly ALL the time with no regrets as to what you may be missing by being tied down with them, as we unquestionably will be. . . .

I'm enclosing a clipping from the Stars & Stripes "B-Bag." It expresses pretty well what goes on here, the impression people here get of us, & why. It is probably actually true of at least 30% of the soldiers—really a staggering percentage & it is the attitude which has been getting me so terribly disillusioned & disgusted & hopeless with & for the human race & its future. I'm sure a lot of U.S. soldiers will read that, take it literally, & agree with each other that the author is "damn right."

* * *

Dale Carnegie II

Hurrah for us! All except a few damn fools will agree that my program for the spread of good will in Europe by our troops is bound to succeed. It consists of five well defined "musts."

1—We must hate all foreigners. . . Jews. . .Negroes.

2—Treat all women as prostitutes (including our own females in uniform), and on the make. A few may not be, but why should we discriminate.

3—We must do all possible to keep black markets flourishing, even to selling the clothes off our backs. After all, why not? If people are suckers enough to pay. And a little "reverse lend-lease" is a good thing.

4—We must treat children with kindness (God knows why) but at the same time we must agree that they are all illegitimate and the offsprings of either German or American soldiers, according to the age of the child.

5—We must connive to cheat, steal and drink our way into the hearts of our Allies. Since we saved them they ought to be on the ground kissing our feet, and if they refuse force may be necessary.

I ask my fellow soldiers to continue this ambitious program. A better world is sure to be the outcome of such action.—**Angelic, 325 Reinf. Co.**

Sarcastic look at racism in the occupying forces, published in *Stars and Stripes*, US Army, 1945.

The eagerly anticipated tennis tournament to determine champions of the XVI Corps, which included the 75th Infantry Division, began in Auxerre, 90 miles southeast of Paris, on August 3, 1945. Later in August the winning teams would travel to England for an army tournament being called GI Wimbledon, to be held at the famous All-England Lawn Tennis Club courts.

Auxerre, France
2 August 1945

Dearest Liz: Well here we are in Auxerre! We left Chalons at 10 this morning & arrived here about half past two. We spent till about 4:15 getting settled. The men are in a house about a mile from the Hotel de l'Epee where Canda & I have a very nice room with 2 three-quarter beds and SHEETS! It is really very nice. Our window looks out on the back of a small church. . . . I hear they only have three lousy courts to play the tournament on. The 101st Airborne Division is running it & they are just arriving here now! It's a true Army snafu.

On the way down today we came through Troyes which was interesting as it is a small city of narrow streets & houses dating back to the middle ages. You can imagine easily the knights & men at arms riding down the narrow, muddy streets smiling up at the ahful girls in the second story windows. The country from Troyes on down here is much like that around Basking Ridge & Boston—many small wooded hills with low, almost swampy, land between. . . .

Auxerre is quite a large place with much old architecture still there too. . . . Auxerre must have a 100,000 or over population. . . . There should be a tennis club, but apparently we are playing on the public parks courts. There is a cafe right across the street from the hotel where Canda & I drank beer & played gin rummy for an hour before 6 o'clock dinner. The latter was good—bologna, salami, potatoe [sic] salad, macaroni, tomatoes (canned) & chocolate cake. I stuffed myself. . . .

Auxerre, France
Friday, 3 August 1945

Dearest Liz: . . .

At the drawing of the tournament last night Canda was seeded first, I was second, Lt. Beeman (Captain & No 1 for Univ. of Michigan) 3rd, & a guy named S/Sgt Moore 4th. . . . My man looked awfully good in his match this morning, but I was playing well and polished him off 6-1, 6-2. . . . the sun got too hot for me at 2-0 in the second set & I lost two games & almost fainted on the court. Fortunately a breeze came up & I walked into the shade at every opportunity & came back OK. . . . Canda and I are seeded in the doubles & so got a first round bye into the semifinals (there are only 6 teams entered—there were 12 singles players). . . . The courts were very good. . . .

Chalons sur Marne, France
Sunday, 5 August 1945

Dearest Liz: . . . your husband got wiped all over the court 6-1, 6-1 in the singles final at Auxerre. . . . Being runner-up puts me up for the Wimbledon Trip, tho. I leave Tuesday morning for Chantilly near Paris, practice there till the 10th, then leave for England. The only hitch is that I think a Pfc named Nusblatt in the other half of the draw is better than I. If so & if they won't take him to England anyway, I think I'll withdraw so he can go. We'll see.

The latest dope is that starting about August 23rd they're going to transfer out all the men & officers with below 85 points out of the division. Where we'll go nobody knows. . . . Major Sutton, who has 131 points is going home the 9th of August.

Chantilly, France
Tuesday, 7 August 1945

Dearest Liz: Here sits your husband at Chantilly [about 20 miles north of Paris]—a rough life. He & Capt. Fitzgerald of the 17th Airborne have a room on the 5th floor of the Hotel du Grand Conde overlooking the Chantilly racecourse. . . . The room is rather bare. . . . We have one luxury—a private bathroom with plenty of hot water. There is a tub & wash basin but no toilet or douche bowl. The latter, I have found, is what the French use for contraception. That was what I had guessed & several of the guys who get around have lately confirmed it. . . .

The story about the new atomic bombs broke in the papers today. I assume that is the secret project Pop has been working on. Is it? [It was.] I sure hope it helps end the war sooner. That explains the apparent lack of American interest in developing "V" bombs.

"Pop" refers to Jim's father, who worked as a chemical engineer for the International Nickel Company, which was a leader in the development of metal alloys. Pop did indeed work on developing the alloys for the atomic bombs.

Paris, France
Wednesday, 8 August 1945

American Red Cross [stationery]

Dearest Liz: The team has been practicing in Paris today at the Jean Bouain Tennis Club out near Porte St. Cloud. . . . Tonight we're staying in Paris & catching the 10:29 train out to Chantilly. I have a ticket to see Edgar Wallace's play "The Case of the Frightened Lady" at the British Theatre. . . .

Liz, I had a long dream about us last night. I dreamt we had three children about 7, 5, & 3, the oldest & youngest girls. . . .

I wonder if the Vatican would oppose the atomic bomb if it were a solid Catholic country using it. Personally I don't see how the Pope has a leg to stand on in such a protest considering the weak-kneed if any opposition the Church has made to wars present & past. The church has certainly failed. It isn't even a power for peace in peacetime. . . .

Chantilly, France
Thursday, 9 August 1945

Dearest Liz: . . .

The big news of the new bomb, followed today by the entry of Russia into the Japanese war makes us all very hopeful that it will all be over almost any time or within 2–3 months. Of course, if they try, they can probably hold out for 12–18 months. Here's hoping!

V-Mail
Friday, 10 August 1945
Chantilly, France

Dearest Liz:

. . . We're all really getting our hopes up that the atomic bomb and the Russian declaration of war may mean it won't be too long now. If the war does end, I'll probably be among the last to get out of Europe—i.e. sometime next spring but at least it would be something definite to look forward to. Darling, I hope you're having a really good vacation in Maine with a good family reunion, plenty of sailing, swimming, lobsters, & sun. . . .

London, England
Saturday Night, 11 August 1945

Dearest Liz: Tonight is just 9 months to the day, including the day of the week, since my sweetie & I were last together. . . .

Yesterday we went out to the flying field about 10 miles south of Paris, only to find the plane wasn't going. We managed to get rooms in a hotel in Paris & spent the night there. This afternoon we got the plane all right & flew over in an hour and a half. . . .

The news of Japan's offer to surrender came yesterday afternoon, so everyone celebrated last night. Fitzgerald, Van der Bosch & I wandered around, had drinks in 3 nightclubs & saw the floorshow in one of them—not very good. Since the Metro closes at 11 I had a long walk home & got there at 2 o'clock to find someone else in my room! After some difficulty & unpleasantness (It was a drunken tech sergeant) I got him out & got to bed about 3. . . .

We are quartered in the Lincoln House here in London. It is an Army Officers Quarters—for leave personnel—near the Knightsbridge Underground Station just south of Hyde Park. Van der Bosch & I have a fairly nice room together. . . . We ate with a man & woman who work for OWI in London & had a long discussion about the contradiction of the G-I liking for the Germans & disliking for the French with its various implications. . . . We then bathed & spruced up & went up to Piccadilly to watch the crowds celebrate the questionable V-J day. The English were sure letting both their hair & their reserve way down. I was spotted by a group of medical students who made me join in their song, snake dance, & cheer of "Hooray for London Hospital!"

Very few of Liz's letters to Jim survive, although she wrote him faithfully every day. Three of the surviving letters tell of her hearing of the end of the war. In the first, she went on to describe an idyllic summer day with the Footes. She was in Southwest Harbor, Maine, on vacation from her job as a social worker at Columbia Presbyterian Hospital in New York. The Footes had been summering at their house on Connor Point for over 30 years, and Liz grew up spending carefree summers surrounded by siblings and many cousins who summered nearby. A sail out to one of the nearby islands for a picnic was a family tradition throughout the 20th century. It is a reminder of how little Jim and Liz really knew each other that Jim had not yet been to Southwest Harbor.

Liz with members of her extended family in Southwest Harbor, Maine, August 1945.

Southwest Harbor Sat. Aug 11th '45 no 272

Jim Darling—There was no mail today but I can't expect any with your last of only Aug 3rd. But oh darling, how I've wanted to call you up today and talk to you. We went off on a picnic, to Cranberry Island, with some cousins who live in Northeast. As we were sailing out someone went past us & said the war was over. Actually, when we got back at 6 tonight we found that wasn't true, but it certainly sounds as though it were going to be. And I keep thinking—Thank God, Jim won't have to fight in the Pacific. Oh sweetheart, sweetheart. I can't believe it, & I won't until I know it's true. In fact I don't think I will till you come home. Do you suppose you will get home this year? Christmas is only four more months. Do you suppose?!!

Today was a beautiful day—quite hot for here. I slept as though someone had hit me over the head last night (with a blanket and a quilt), but woke up about 7 with the beginning of the household noise. I dozed till 8 when we all had breakfast—raspberries & fish. We got off on our picnic about 11—Wy, Marty, young Wy, Judy & I in the sailboat, the others in a launch. It was very light sailing out—it's about 2 1/2 miles, but we got out about 12:30 & had a swim. The tide is right, now—being high at noon. Then lunch, during which there was much discussion of world events with Wilder holding forth. Then we walked along the outer shore for a while. It was fun to jump from rock to rock, skip pebbles, & play with the kids going out on the rocks & getting wet from the waves. Then I sailed the boat in with the kids—Wy & Judy, & two of the young cousins. The breeze was nice & fresh—in fact one puff healed us over so far we took bucketfuls into the cockpit. — We had supper of chicken, rice, beans out of the garden, & blueberry pie (blueberries from the point). The garden is wonderful this year—the best raspberry crop I've ever seen, beans, head lettuce, onions, peas just coming & corn in the future. I guess I told you Mother & Dad brought a colored girl up from Charlottesville. She's only 19 but a very good cook. I must say it makes a vacation much more of a vacation, especially with this crowd.

Tonight we went over to the Browns. Joe has been here for two weeks, has to go back tomorrow. We listened to music, talked, & had delicious raspberry ice cream & cake. At this rate I ought to get fat, but I'd dropped back below 112 before I came.

Well sweetie, it's after 11 & I'm so sleepy being out in the sun all day. I'm sure your tan is better than mine, but mine has rapidly improved the last two days. Oh Jim, how I wish we were having this vacation together. It would make it so perfect. As it is half of me is enjoying it, & the other half of me is just wishing so much for you I can't stand it. You said in one of your letters you missed me more when things were pleasant, & that's the way I feel.

[The rest of the letter was censored by Liz]

London, England
Sunday Evening, 12 Aug 1945

Dearest Liz: You have a pooped husband tonight. He played five sets of tennis this afternoon—all of them pretty energetic.

I got up about 8 & had breakfast, walked over to the Athletic & Recreation Office & got a lot of information on the tournament, came back to Lincoln House, packed my tennis stuff, ate lunch, & went out to Wimbledon, which is a half hour bus ride from here. The courts are very good & a joy to play on. My game is showing slow improvement. They gave us new balls to practice with.

UNITED STATES FORCES
TENNIS CHAMPIONSHIPS
European Theater

ALL-ENGLAND LAWN TENNIS CLUB,
WIMBLEDON

15th—18th August, 1945.

Major Commands Competing :

THIRD ARMY	- Five Teams	U.S.S.T.A.F.	- Two Teams
COM. ZONE	- Five Teams	SIXTEENTH CORPS	One Team
SEVENTH ARMY	- Three Teams	G.F.R.C.	- - One Team
U.S. NAVAL FORCES	- - One Team		

TOURNAMENT CONDUCTED BY SPECIAL SERVICES WITH THE CO-OPERATION OF THE AMERICAN RED CROSS.

Program for the United States Forces Tennis Championships, European Theater, held at Wimbledon, August 15–18, 1945.

From the papers it looks as if V-J day is actually here. I sure hope so. . . . On the humorous side, sweetie, I was just thinking that the past 9 months is the longest time I haven't so much as kissed a girl since I first kissed one at the age of 16! . . .

We had a meeting of all players & coaches tonight. In the morning we got out to Wimbledon at 9:30 to get our pictures taken for the program & the home town papers. . . .

Southwest Harbor Tues. Aug 14th no 275

Darling, darling, darling—Oh Jim—it's true—the war is over. We got the news just after 7 tonight. Dad & both Wilders had gone to Southwest to take Abner to the bus, & as Marty & Mother & I were sitting at the table talking, we heard car horns blowing & turned on the radio & heard the National anthem—& then a rebroadcast of Atlee's speech. A few minutes later they came home from the village with the news that at least 150 people were out on the streets—& some beer with which to celebrate. I can't tell you the feeling I had as I stood out on the lawn, looking at the moon, and listening to the sound of the church bells & boat whistles coming across the water—the feeling I've had ever since. Chiefly I think it is deep thanks that it is over &

that you won't have to go to the Pacific, mixed with a[n] unbearable longing to be with you, to share with you the relief & joy of it. I feel the only way I want to celebrate is to be with you, to have you take me in your arms & hold me long & close, without any words being necessary: Oh Jim, darling—I can't bear not being with you tonight. I assume you are in London, & have been wondering what you have been doing, though of course it's late at night with you. But I know that whatever you are doing, you are thinking what I am, that your thoughts turned immediately to the fact that we will be together again. I have tried to think of what it is meaning to the whole world, & of the terrific jobs ahead, but I confess that the thought uppermost in my mind is of you—& of your coming home. I suppose it will still be some time before you come, & a long time before you are out of the army; but I feel that so long as we can be together, we can make the most out of that time. GOD how I want to see you & talk to you & feel you near me now. — I've been thinking of your parents tonight as they are the people who most of all share my feelings tonight, other than you. I think I'll write them tonight.

[censored by Liz]

Sweetheart, how is the tennis going. I take it from these letters that you definitely are going (have gone) to England. I wonder if you have been playing your tournament & how it is going.

I had a good sleep last night & woke up feeling fine. It was foggy so we had breakfast with a big fire in the fireplace. I went down to Sou'west to do the shopping & get the mail, & to get lobsters for a feed for Abner tonight. They were all sold out but said they'd have them in this afternoon. Then we went for a picnic lunch to Valley Cove—it cleared off in the morning—a cove where two mountains drop into the sea, one with straight cliffs—a very pretty spot. The Wilders rowed round, fishing on the way; & I walked there with Abner. We had a fish fry for lunch, frying the cunner they had just caught. We got back about four & I sailed over to the Southwest fish wharf with Dad to pick up the lobsters—8 one lb. ones. We had a[n] early supper as Abner's bus left at 7. Sweetie, I wished for you as we all dug into our lobsters, cause I know how you would have loved it.

This evening we have celebrated by sitting around the fire with beer listening to the celebration reports in various places. At Mother's suggestion Dad read us excerpts from the peace service Dad had prepared for the American Unitarian Ass[ociation]. They are all still in the living room talking, but I retreated to the kitchen to write you—as it's with you that I want to do my "celebrating." I still won't believe it till you're home, nor has there been time for me to realize the relief of the fact that you won't be fighting in the Pacific. I know it but I can't really know it till you're home. Jim, do you think you may be home by Christmas? That's the time I've sort of set my mind on because it would be so wonderful to have you here by then. I wonder what you'll be assigned to. Just so long as it's in this country; at this point I don't care what it is. I hope, though, for your sake, that it may be a hospital.

I can't write any more now except to say over & over again how thankful I am & how much, how terribly much I'm longing for you now—not so much the physical longing that sometimes comes over me, but a longing simply to be with you & share the happiness of this hour with you—because the happiness can't be complete without you. I can't stand not being with you. I guess I'd better go to bed—& when I'm alone in the dark I will be able to feel you with me, cause I know you are in everything but person. Goodnight, my darling. Please God may you get home soon cause I love you, I love you, I love you, I love you—oh God, I love you so terribly awfully ahfully much

Liz

London, England
Tuesday, 14 August 1945

Dearest Lizzie: We're all still waiting for the official announcement of Japan's surrender. . . . This evening Beeman, Fitzgerald & I went to a dandy play "The Cure for Love" . . . we walked home past Buckingham Palace where a crowd had gathered & was yelling "We want the King!" . . .

Jim on the courts at Wimbledon, August 1945.

Jim was knocked out of the tournament early, but had a great time and would always brag of having played at Wimbledon, with a twinkle in his eye. While in London he visited the Griffiths, friends of his father from the International Nickel Company, whom Jim had visited in 1938. He got them tickets to come out to Wimbledon. There were two Griffith daughters, and true to form, he took one of them out to the theater while he was in town.

London, England
Wednesday, 15 August 1945

Dearest Liz: It's 8:15 & we just got back from Wimbledon. It rained all morning & they didn't get started playing until almost 2 o'clock. I met one of the seeded players, Bill Anderson, & he beat me 6-3, 6-1, but it was a good match, most of the games being deuce. I played well so didn't mind losing. It's sure a joy to play on grass. We had British umpires & G-I linesmen.

We woke up this morning to find that the news of Japan's surrender finally came thru at midnight. What a relief. . . . Truman's promise to get 5,000,000 out in the next 12–18 months still leaves 3,000,000 in the Army I think. . . . I think they should go right into a program of compulsory military service to split up & divide the job of occupation which will probably require a million men at least for many years. . . .

We're all going out to eat in a Chinese Restaurant in a few minutes, having arrived too late for the G-I mess. Liz, I wish so much you were here to go with me in your grey sweater & skirt so I could hold your hand & smile into your eyes & come home with you after supper & hold you tight & close in my arms because I love you so very very very very much.

Jim

Liz's oldest brother, Wilder, was working for US Secretary of State Stettinius, who was due in London to participate in talks.

London, England
Thursday, 16 August 1945

Dearest Lizzie: . . . I just got back from the Griffiths'. I called them, asked them out to the tennis at Wimbledon this afternoon & they asked me to supper tonight. Patsy, the oldest girl (about 20–21) is in the WAAF & had to leave at five to get back from her 48 hour pass. Betsy, about 2 years younger, Mr. & Mrs. Griffiths & I stayed till about 6:30 & then drove back to their house at Kenley in their Daimler. We had a drink, I showed them my pictures of you & Dan & Alice & Reb and then we had supper. . . . We talked a lot about England & America & their similarities & dissimilarities & about the continental countries. After supper we talked till about 11, then they drove me back into London where we rode up Whitehall etc & looked at all the floodlighted public buildings. Trafalgar Square & Piccadilly were relatively deserted. I guess everyone had a hangover. It was also raining.

Last night I had quite an evening. We had supper at the snack bar here instead of going to a Chinese restaurant as we heard all the restaurants were jammed. We then proceeded to the Dorchester bar for a couple of drinks, then on to the Piccadilly area where we went to a "club" —London edition of a small, expensive bar—for a couple more drinks. The whole West End of London was jammed with celebrants. Streets were blocked off for half a mile around Piccadilly. Girls were out in full force & kissing everyone in sight—your glamorous

(& naughty) husband himself was kissed 3 or 4 times during the evening. Every time a girl saw a G-I soldier or officer whose looks she liked she'd yell "I've never kissed an American soldier!" or some such thing, dash up, throw her arms around your neck & kiss you before you knew what was going on. Wow! The same was true in the bar. I left the others in the bar the other side of Piccadilly about 11:30, wandered around for half an hour or so, then wandered home, arriving at one. One of the sights of Piccadilly was a girl without a stitch on (jitterbugging) dancing with a group of guys on top of a port-cochère! I've never seen anything like it. The only hitch was that the whole thing was sort of empty for me, because the whole meaning & happiness of V-Day for me is wrapped up in you and we weren't together. Every time one of those girls kissed me it made me wish that much more it were you. Believe me, it would have made some difference in the response they got. <u>You</u> would have gotten the ahful response from me that I'm sure a couple of them wanted.

This morning I thought for a little while that you & I might get into more direct contact through the medium of Wilder. The Stars & Stripes said Stettinius was here for a United Nations Conference. I went to the Embassy to find Stettinius & his aides won't be here till the end of the month. It's too bad. I was looking forward to seeing Wilder in person & you by proxy thru him. [censored]

Southwest Harbor Sat. Aug 18th '45 no 279

Dearest Jim— . . .

Last night when I went to bed, I was feeling awfully blue as I told you—in fact I cried. But before I got into bed I went out & looked at the moon from the upstairs balcony (this house has a porch across the front on both stories, & most of the bedrooms open out on it.) It was so peaceful & beautiful sitting there on the rail—with the moon off & on covered by light clouds, & its path reflected in the water—& the lighthouse on Baker's Island blinking off & on—& the only sound the distant put-put of a lobster fisherman's boat & the squawk of a night heron flying up into the cove. The peace & beauty seemed a connecting link to you—so when I at last went in & crawled into bed I quickly went to sleep, thinking about you.

. . . Jim, today while Marty & I were doing house work, we were talking about apartments & houses & furnishings, & I got thinking about the stuff we'd want to get, & about getting our various & sundry wedding presents together & in use. I've almost forgotten what we have. Gee, that will be fun. I think the thing to do is to start with the minimum until we see what we're really going to need & want. I also got to thinking about getting an apartment up-town. Unless the housing in N.Y. improves, it will be hard to do. I

almost feel as though I ought to start looking now. It wouldn't be bad if I got it before you came home, but on the other hand it would be silly to do it if we weren't going to live in N.Y.C., or weren't going to live there for a year or two after you got back to the U.S. What would your guess be, as to when you'll get back, & how long you'll be in the Army after you do get back? If the Army discharged 5 million men in the next year, they're bound to discharge a lot of doctors, but I suppose the older guys will go first. I'm still finding it too good to believe that you won't have to go to the Pacific—that there won't be months more of that [g]nawing fear to go through.

Darling, I wish so much you were here to enjoy these nice days with me, to see the beautiful sunsets, & to look at the moon over the water with your romantic old woman. I want to hear you make fun of me running around in old blue jeans or shorts or a bathing suit, . . .

[censored]

London, England
Saturday, 18 August 1945

Dearest Sweetie: . . . I just got back from the tennis banquet at the Grosvenor House. It broke up at midnight and, since the buses & Underground stop at 11, we walked back to Knightsbridge.

. . . This morning I went down to the old City of London (St. Paul's area) and saw St. Paul's and the damage done to the district by the blitz. There was a lot, but nothing like in Germany. I also went to Westminster Abbey. The most interesting part of the latter was closed—the part behind the choir where the Stone of Scone & the tombs of the early English Kings are. There was an enormous number of people at both St. Paul's & the Abbey—more English civilians than soldiers, too. . . .

I was surprised today to come out of Westminster Abbey & find myself facing a statue of Abraham Lincoln! Had you noticed it? I still find Nelson atop his pillar on Trafalgar Square the most moving statue I know & also England's greatest hero. . . .

With the war over, it is now time for us to think about what we're going to do in the immediate future. I wish to hell we could talk about it together. Right now, I'm inclined to think I should try to get a 1 year rotating internship at the Medical School Hospital (whatever it is) in Portland, Oregon. That would give me a general background for my specialization & doing it immediately after I get out of the Army seems the best time as otherwise it will probably mean extensive moving around while you are right in the midst of having kids—and I have no intention of going off away from you someplace for a year ever. . . .

As it turned out, the longest separation Jim and Liz endured for the rest of their marriage (53 more years) was three weeks, when my father and I drove to Alaska. Having already driven to Alaska twice with Jim, Liz stayed behind in Vermont and then flew to meet Jim in Anchorage.

Jim's departure from London was delayed by rain for a couple of days. He finally got back to the 75th in Chalons sur Marne on August 21.

Chalons sur Marne, France
Thursday, 23 August 1945

Dearest Liz: . . .

The battalion has a new CO, Col. Grauch, who seems very nice. He is about 40 or 42 & appears to be less addicted to alcohol & women than our previous two. Maj. Sutton & Col. Hansston both went home while I was in England. . . . Col. Davis is returning to the States tomorrow for an ulcer. I hate to see him go.

Today they told all men & officers with over 65 points to be ready to leave on short notice at any time, so it looks like they will be sending everyone home in the order of their points. That means I'll be among the very last IF I'm not actually caught in an occupation job. I could kill these God Damn Senators who are yelling to stop the draft and that we don't need & aren't going to have compulsory military service. If they succeed, it will mean that I and a lot of others like me are going to have to stay in the Army for occupation purposes. . . .

I agree with you on how good it is to look back on our life at 128 Fort Washington. . . .

I'm afraid you're probably over-optimistic when you think the change of governments & even greater social upheaval will change British imperialism. Germany had a pretty true & complete socialism & it certainly didn't do much but magnify the undesirable national tendencies heretofore called "imperialistic."

As you can see, we are still in Chalons & there is no more talk about moving, thank God. Enclosed are some pictures taken at Plettenberg & just now developed. Things are better now with the Engrs. I try to get out of doing & avoid doing as much of their dirty work as possible, so I don't have so many irritations. Of course, I've been completely away from them for almost 3 weeks. . . . I was very sorry to hear about Mrs. Mountain being replaced by Miss Geyer whom you don't like. If she stays & irritates you much, why don't you quit & try to get another job. . . . I've met some other members of the Auchincloss family & have always considered them Class 1 unpleasant snobbish drips. . . .

Chalons sur Marne, France
Sunday, 26 August 1945

Dearest Liz: . . .

Louis just called and I'm playing tennis with him tomorrow evening & going to his house for dinner Tuesday. Tonight at 9 I'm going over to the party at Tommy's girl's house. What a gay whirl!

Sweetie, you be careful about climbing sheer cliffs. I don't know what I'd do if anything happened to you. It would just take life away from me. If Wilder can do all the exercise he seemed to at Southwest he must have a very mild myasthenia or a complete remission.

Chalons sur Marne, France
Tuesday, 28 August 1945

Dearest Liz: . . .

They got a quota for another pass to Brussels & no one wanted to go but me & since Maj. Fore isn't here to say I can't go, I'm off at 7:30 AM tomorrow for Brussels! . . .

This morning I did some inspections at Mailly and arranged for a stack of immunizations. This afternoon I did some more administrative work & played 3 sets of doubles. This morning I had a man come in . . . his back had been hurting for 5 days & he'd been to two different camp dispensaries & "just hadn't gotten any satisfaction" so he thought he'd come in "where he knew he'd get it." . . .I found he had a pilomidal sinus which was giving his trouble, explained it to him, told him how not to aggravate it, gave him his prognosis, & was able to send away a very satisfied customer. It always makes me feel good to do that. The trust the men have in me also is a source of pleasure. Hanna says every man in the battalion really considers me "his" doctor, which is the way I like it to be. . . . Every time I go on pass to Paris, London, or Brussels I'm stopped by one or more of our men who'll spot me across the street & come over to talk & ask me to have a drink with them. . . .

Jim had word that Dr. Rusty McIntosh, his boss during his internship at Babies Hospital in New York before the war, was going to be in Brussels. Jim very much wanted to talk with Rusty about his future. At home, Liz was obviously thinking about it. They had talked a lot about settling in the Northwest after the war, and Portland, Oregon, was a good possibility.

Brussels, Belgium
Wednesday, 29 August 1945

Dearest Sweetie:

This morning we left Chalons about 8:15 and arrived at Brussels at 3:30. I went right out to the American Embassy to try to locate Dr. McIntosh. Neither they, the consulate or the Belgian Ministry of Health knew anything about his arrival. . . . Despite that disappointment, I still had & still have my "home" in Brussels "Chez de Smet."

After failing to locate Rusty I went out to de Smets to find no one at home, but the maid said Pierre was at the tennis club, so I went out there. We greeted each other like long lost buddies & played 2 sets of singles which I won 6-2, 6-4. . . .

The source of the de Smets' good food supply, I discover, is a group of farms they own in southern Belgium. I brought Madame de Smet 2 lbs of lump sugar (bought at Breckinridge), a bottle of olive oil, a box of Quick-Mix Chocolate, & half a bottle of stuffed olives, all of which she seemed glad to get, but didn't want to take. They are certainly nice to me. They are going to their house at the shore near Holland on Sunday for a week & want me to try to get leave & come with them! . . .

Brussels, Belgium
Thursday, 30 August 1945

Dearest Liz: . . .

At the tennis club, I met a very nice American officer, Capt. Ben Lane from Pleasantville, New York. He was class of '38 at Dartmouth and commands a company of engineers in a former amphibious, now corps, combat battalion. He came in the 3rd wave on D-Day in Normandy. He came back with us to de Smets' for dinner. He went to both Smith & Vassar quite a bit while at Darmouth & agrees with me! . . . I . . . ate a lot of cauliflower, ham, tomato, & egg salad, delicious fish & parsley potatoes with sauce, baked creamed mushrooms in big sea shells, melon, egg pudding, & 3 kinds of wine plus beer! We only ate for 2 1/2 hours! Wow! . . .

Tomorrow I'm going to Antwerp with Ben Lane . . .

Chalons sur Marne, France
Saturday, 1 September 1945

Dearest Liz: . . .

I got up just in time yesterday to get shaved & dressed before Ben Lane arrived at 8:15 to go to Antwerp in his jeep. It was a pleasant trip, tho a bit chilly, since it was foggy & cloudy. I got a good look at Antwerp, which was not beaten up nearly so badly by the V bombs as one might think. Of course, as Ben & I decided, whereas the inhabitants of London & Antwerp think in terms of what has been destroyed, we who have seen Germany & the towns in the Bulge & around Colmar think rather in terms of what is left standing. That may give you an idea of the destruction the war has wrought in the hard-hit spots. After seeing big towns & cities virtually flattened except for a few walls & fewer houses left standing, and small towns with not even a wall (or maybe just one or two) standing, the absence of a house, or a block, or of several blocks means relatively little.

In Antwerp we rode around in the jeep & saw the town, including the harbor, the fountain in front of the old city hall, & the cathedral. Where Brussels seems like a little Paris, Antwerp reminded me of Hamburg, Bremen, & Frankfurt am Main—ie: more German than French. We got back in time for lunch & the beginning of a drizzle which lasted all afternoon. . . . After lunch, which lasted an hour and a half, Pierre & I went out to the Albert Club where we met Ben Lane & decided we couldn't possibly play tennis. I collected the racket I had ordered. . . . We then went to the movies, seeing an old one, Ida Lupino & Jack Benny in "Artists & Models," produced in 1937. Afterwards Pierre, Mme. de Smet, & I went to "La Dame de Chez Maxim," an amusing play, starring Florelle, a Parisian actress of about 50 who still retains her "it" & verve. We got home at 11:30 & ate till 1:15 when we went up to bed. . . .

Going up [from Chalons], the road was very rough. . . . we turned off at Rocroi & went up to Dinant—Namur, Brussels. It was a beautiful, interesting drive along the Meuse river, which apparently is a resort for vacationing Belgians, of whom we saw many. Coming back today we went way out of our way to keep off the bad road, travelling the route Brussels, Namur—Marche—Bouillon—Voriziers—Chalons. We got on the wrong road to Namur & came through Waterloo, Napolean's Waterloo. I had never realized before it was just 6 miles south of Brussels. The Belgians have really taken the brunt of a lot of wars. We corrected our error & got to Marche OK, but then got all mixed up & went way east to St. Hubert toward Houffalize before coming back to Bouillon. It was really beautiful country & well worth getting lost to see. I wished you and I were bicycling thru. I've been so envious of the French couples I've seen all during the month of August taking their vacations with a bike trip together. Bouillon (I wonder if it's where bouillon was originated?) is a quaint town, set down in a narrow river valley topped by an old fortress atop a razorback ridge overlooking the town in true feudal fashion. . . . I'm really taking an evening to writing you—first because I want to and second because the Engrs are throwing a dance out back which makes me (a) long for you, and (b) unable to sleep! . . .

As you said, "God how I want to talk to you" about the Portland business. I think you analyzed the situation much better than I, & I'm convinced going back to Babies first is the best way if OK professionally speaking. That is what I want very much to talk to Rusty about. It's too bad I couldn't locate him in Belgium. He apparently didn't come after all. I'll write Wilder tomorrow & hope to get to see him. . . .

A week later another tennis tournament was scheduled in Brussels. Jim expressed reservations about going, tired of travel and feeling some resentment from his battalion for his long tennis binge. Nonetheless, he went.

Brussels, Belgium
Friday, 7 Sept. 1945

Dearest Liz: . . . We got off from Chalons about 6 o'clock yesterday morning while it was still dark & raining. It was cold & wet & very foggy thru the Ardennes, but when we came down out of the Ardennes, it was sunny & beautiful. . . . In the next round I play a British Lt. Col. Saunders tomorrow & Pvc Johnny Makepeace if I beat him. Makepeace is a nice guy, even tho he did go to Yale. . . . Today Buchstaber & I won our 1st round doubles 8-6, 6-3. . . .

Brussels, Belgium
Sunday, 9 Sept. 1945

Dearest Liz: Tonight your husband has joined the ranks of the defeated again. John Makepeace beat me 6-4, 7-5 in the quarter-finals of the singles this morning. Afterward Buchstaber & I beat a Belgian team 7-5, 6-2, then met Makepeace & Ben Lane, the engineer Capt. with whom we are staying. They beat us 3-6, 6-4, 6-4 in the quarter-finals of the doubles. Afterward we stayed at the club & had dinner of soup, ravioli, & steak before coming back. We stopped off downtown on the way back to enable Buchstaber to get some much-craved ice cream. We then were stopped by some MPs who asked us to take a G-I who'd gotten drunk, insulted a Belgian woman, & then been beaten up by some Belgian civilians, to the hospital. That took an hour, so it's now 11 o'clock. Some of this G-I behaviour is inexcusable. They just don't differentiate between decent women & prostitutes.

Operation Magic Carpet was the massive effort to bring troops home after the war. There were over 3,000,000 US personnel in Europe, and over 2,000,000 in the Pacific. During the war, an average of 148,000 troops were transported to Europe each month. During the 14 months of Operation Magic Carpet, an average of over 435,000 troops were brought home each month. The operation had been in planning since 1943, and it was an enormous challenge, both from a shipping and an administrative standpoint. Servicemen were transferred in and out of divisions to maintain staffing as those with the highest Adjusted Service Rating Scores neared their day of departure.

Chalons sur Marne, France
10 Sept. 1945

Dearest Liz: As usual my wife did NOT disappoint me & there were five letters and a package here on our return from Brussels. The V.J. newsletter of Ruth Plimpton's which you had already received was here, too. . . .

The big news of my return is that the division is going to start concentrating in one of the AAC (Assembly Area Command) camps on Oct. 1st when Div Hq & we will move there. That should mean coming home in November & possibly October even! The bad news was that a service outfit of engineers to which Reed & Steinbring have been transferred and which has been transferring a lot of men to us (officers) has a high point medical officer who is due to be transferred in someplace else. I'm really sweating it out as to whether he might replace me & I'll get his job. That 45 points they all talk about is as of VE day when I had 41. When the V-J count becomes effective, I'll have 47. You're quite right that I must have more than a lot of them, but kids count an awful lot. . . . It's almost unbearable to think that we <u>may</u> be together again in as little time as 6 weeks! It's equally unbearable to think that it might be a year or more. I sure wish you'd remembered to say Rabbit, rabbit, rabbit. On the other hand, we can't kick. We've been very lucky.

We left Brussels at 9 this morning & got to Chalons at 2:30 after a relatively easy trip. It's 197 miles the way we go. Under the circumstances, I would suggest that you stop sending packages Oct 1st unless I let you know otherwise. They're taking about 3 weeks now. . . .

So far, <u>nothing</u> I've done over here has counted as leave. 3 day passes don't count & the trips to England, Auxerre, & the Brussels tournament were on duty orders!

. . .Will you please send some olives, crackers, & shrimp or lobster?

I love you.

Jim

Chalons sur Marne, France
Thursday, 13 September 1945

Dear Mom & Dad:

. . . . My trip to England was very enjoyable, despite my being put out in the 1st round of the tournament. I saw the Griffiths several times and enjoyed their company. He had just been made Chairman of the British Company, so I guess I was floating around in pretty high company society. Griff looked very sleek & prosperous, Mrs. Griffiths seemed to be happier & less of a mouse, and the girls were both attractive. Patsy is in the WAAF. Betsy, the younger one, is starting to school to learn to be a dispenser (unskilled pharmacist) in a doctor's office. Griff seemed a little cool at first, but I got the impression it was just that he is a little unsure of himself socially & has a social inferiority complex. . . . I had the whole family out to Wimbledon for the 2nd day of the tennis & went back to their house afterward for supper. I had Betsy out to Wimbledon for the finals and took her to a play another evening. . . .

Our present status is that we will move out to one of the camps of AAC (Assemble Area Command) Oct 1st to start closing the ten non-winterized camps. When that is completed, we will be processed & head home, probably about Nov. 1. The big IF is whether I'll be in the division when it leaves. . . .

Chalons sur Marne, France

Dearest Liz: . . . We are starting a new VD campaign, which I think will be a good one in view of the fact that we'll not only have command "cooperation" but also participation due to a letter on the subject from higher headquarters. It is really quite restful to have to worry only about my job & not the tennis team, too, for a change.

We are going ahead now with the transfer to AAC of our low point men. All the low point officers except Hagie & me have already been transferred out. Boy, how I hope I'm able to stay & go home with the division!

The medical detachment has been awarded the Certificate of Merit, which entitles us to wear a laurel wreath on our sleeves. H&S got it, too. Only "service" troops of combat units get it. It's just one more thing to sew on. . . .

Chalons sur Marne, France
Saturday, 15 September 1945

Dearest Liz:

Well, it looks now as if the axe is finally going to fall. Today they got a directive ordering all units to transfer out officers with under 70 points (V-J) before returning to the U.S. That polishes me off very neatly. So far I'm still here, but it looks as if it will just be a matter of time . . . it will probably mean I'll get home sometime between next June & September, as I'll most likely go to an occupying unit. . . .

Last night Dick Lillie, Don Sweeney (ex-surgical resident at MGH), 2 other medical officers, and I had a very pleasant but decidedly beery evening, starting at 4:30 and winding up at 11. This morning I had the "runs" from the beer & did little else all morning. This afternoon I went out to see Dick about getting 10 nurses for a dance the Engrs are having tonight. . . .

Chalons sur Marne, France
Saturday, 16 September 1945

Dearest Liz: . . . Last night June Kay screwed me up by getting me a date even tho I'd said I didn't want one. . . . Don Sweeney & his brother in law were along all evening, so I didn't have to bother too much with her. I went up to their party at the 177th for a couple of hours, then we came down to the Engr dance here. . . . Dick . . . & Sweeney asked me to come out any time & scrub with them in surgery (they do most of it for the hospital), so I plan to do it. If we get the cases, they're going to teach me some of the simpler operations & possibly let me do one or two if there are enough. It will be good practice.

. . . The thing that is bothering all us low point medical officers is that we hear they have stopped taking in medics & did not take the last class of medical students for whose education the Army paid. That, plus the disinclination of Congress to have a draft, has us not only annoyed but worried. We're also afraid that those who are over here will be stuck. None of us know of any medical officers shipped out of the States by the Army since V-E Day. The Navy has done it.

I was sorry to hear about Uncle Roger's death. Be sure to write your Aunt Doro whether you "know how to" or not. I'm sure she'll appreciate it & I'm sure you'll write her the right letter.

It was good to hear you were feeling a little better. . . . Dick & I were talking tonight about why Harvard is the best med school—and we're convinced it is both by our own opinions & by the obvious awe & respect in which it is held by graduates of other schools. We decided the most important thing was the selection of students with emphasis on interest in medicine & ability to understand people. . . .

Chalons sur Marne, France
Friday, 21 Sept. 1945

Dearest Liz: Today was a GOOD day with 4 letters from my own very best girl. . . . I worked all morning at the aid station but spent the afternoon out with

Lillie, bulling, playing ping-pong, & reading a mystery. Tonight I saw Abbott & Costello. . . . The Div. is having a football rally, street dance, & jitterbug contest on the main square tonight & we are going to watch the jitterbug contest which one of our sergeants has a good chance of winning. The 75th football team plays Oise at Reims tomorrow. . . .

If Alice [Jim's sister-in-law] is pregnant again, that is news. . . .

The purpose of the figuring on the cost of my & Dan's education is that Ma & Pop intend to give Dan the difference toward starting his boat yard. It should be quite a help as it is somewhere between 10 & 15 thousand dollars. That's only fair, don't you think? . . .

Chalons sur Marne, France
Wednesday, 26 Sept. 1945

Dearest Liz: . . .

Dick Lillie left Sunday for his new assignment to the 50th Field Hospital. . . .

Tonight Hagie reported from buddies at Division that Division plans to carry us as far as possible in hopes of getting us thru. That means we'll probably go clear to the port of embarkation & then be transferred. My chances are slight, but there's still one left. . . . It's more probable that I'll get occupation & be stuck for longer. We're pretty sure here now that the guys who've just come in or who have been sitting around the States will get out ahead of us 40–50 pointers. We really need someone to start talking for us. We're the forgotten men in the discharge system. Don't let it get you down tho, darling, & keep your stomach & fingers in good shape in case I do get home. . . .

Today at lunch it was announced that we would have an officers' meeting at 4 o'clock. I almost forgot about it, but did remember. The purpose of it turned out to be the public reading of a letter of commendation to me from General Mickle for coaching the tennis team! I think it helped out some on the annoyance of the Engrs at my tennis playing all summer, because it does give the Engrs some reflected glory. . . .

While Jim seldom mentions other letters in his writing to Liz, he was also receiving regular letters from his parents and occasional ones from his brother Dan. A birthday letter from his mother reads:

Wednesday, 26 Sept – 1945

Dear Jim: Happy Birthday. We all love you more & more & are sure anxious to see you & your grin walking in. Poor Liz is just on needles & pins &

of course you are. We are just hoping and being thankful for things as they are. We are all really very fortunate & know it.

Since I am staying at the farm a good deal, I miss Liz a lot, having her for dinner & hearing about you etc. Alice & Reb stayed up this week to make grape jelly. Reb is sure a big help. They are going to have their hands full with two babies as is June. And of course we are looking forward to yours & Liz's. I have just finished two baby afghans for Liz, in case of twins. However I hope you & Liz will have a nice vacation together before you have anyone else to consider first. Children sure change ones life a great deal. But they are an everlasting joy, anyway ours are. We have had a nasty, hot, humid wet summer. I am about to go to Arizona if it keeps up. But I am hoping for some lively Indian summer yet. I was so delighted with yours & Liz's pictures & the nice leather frame for my birthday. Well old dear, we are waiting for your return for your birthday gift, but we do send a heartfull of love.

As ever
Mom

Paris, France
Thursday, 27 Sept. 1945

Dearest Liz: This morning the 3-day pass group from Chalons left about 8:30 with your husband in charge. There were men from all the division troops in Chalons. . . .

We arrived in Paris about 12:30, having had a flat on the way. The first thing I did on arrrival at the hotel was to take a bath. . . . After lunch I went to the Opera . . . to try to get tickets. . . . All I was able to get was an aisle folding seat for "Lakme" tomorrow night at the Comique. So I got a seat here at the hotel for the Casino de Paris tonight. After finishing with the tickets, I saw a French comic mystery movie, "Le Mystere de Saint-Val," returned to the hotel, read the Saturday Evening Post, got a haircut, had my picture taken to show you what the ribbons look like, ate supper, went to the Casino de Paris, returned & am now writing my best girl.

The Casino show is the same stuff as the Folies Bergere, but I don't think it is nearly as good. I think you could beat any of the girls in it on all three counts—looks, figure, & ahfulness! I did have a very good seat—third row orchestra in an armchair!

The number of G.I.s in Paris has gone way down. There are few enough again that the city is able to at least partly absorb them. It makes it pleasanter. There are more things in the shop windows now, too, tho prices remain sky-high.

While in Paris, Jim was right in character, seeking out culture—including museums and opera—and taking advantage of his free time there. He was quite familiar with Paris from his visits before the war, and had favorite spots he wanted to see. The Louvre had been closed in 1939 as the German invasion began. Its works were dispersed around France, mostly to individual chateaus. The Louvre re-opened under the Nazi occupation, but was virtually empty. Since liberation, the collection had been returning to the museum.

Paris, France
Friday, 28 Sept. 1945

Dearest Liz: . . . After napping this afternoon I walked down to the Louvre to see my favorite statue, the Victory of Samothrace. The museum was jammed, mostly with French civilians. Only part of it is opened as yet. The only really well-known pictures I saw were the Mona Lisa, Manet's "Olympia," & Ingre's "Le Source." The Venus de Milo is also there now. They seem mainly to have just put up what they have without much arrangement into schools.

. . . I tried to find out . . . about a 3-day trip to the castles of the Loire sponsored by the French government. I'm going to inquire further tomorrow as I'd like to take it. They advertise French cooking & wine with it & it's given by the French Anglo-American Good-will Committee, so it should be a dandy trip if I can get it some time. I've just finished supper now & am writing you before going to "Laknie" at the Opera Comique, which starts at 7:45.

. . . I'm resigned now to the fact that I won't get home this fall.

. . . If it's a nice day I think I'll hire a bike & go for a ride out to the Bois de Boulogne. Tomorrow night I guess I'll either have to find a Red Cross Dance to go to or else go to the movies someplace.

Paris, France
Saturday, 29 Sept. 1945

Sweetheart: I've been so lonely for you all day today that it's actually almost been a physical pain. I've really hit a new low in loneliness & longing for you—and that's saying plenty. . . .

Then I got a bike from the Red Cross here, rode out the Champs Elysees, around the Arc de Triomphe, & out the Avenue Foch to the Bois where I rode around for over an hour. It's pretty darn big. I sure missed riding around with you. . . . I got back at one for lunch, after which I napped for 2½ hours, waking myself up from time to time with loud snores. That's one thing—I really have gotten a good rest here. This afternoon I walked down to the Rue de Rivoli & into the Tuileries where the kids were sailing their toy boats, then up thru the

Tuileries & along the Champs to a theatre where I saw Jean Arthur, Joel McCrea, & Charles Coburn in "The More the Merrier" which I never saw before. After supper I went over to the Olympia Theatre, where there was a special service variety show. It was very good. . . .

The three days have cost approximately $25.

Jim's three days in Paris marked a transition. The euphoria following the surrenders of Germany and Japan, the exciting anticipation of going home soon, and the enjoyable hubbub of the GI tennis tournaments were over. He clung to the hope of going home with the 75th Division, but began to realize that he would likely be staying in Europe for an unknown period. Doctors were needed to serve the ever shifting population of bored, restless soldiers awaiting their tickets home, and the army found it easier to keep the veteran doctors in Europe than to bring replacements over from the States.

Chapter Ten

The 75th Division Awaits Transport Home: Fall 1945

In late September, the 75th Division was transferred to an embarkation camp near Rheims (Reims), France, to await shipment home. Camp Pittsburgh was one of the roughly 20 "city camps" built by the army's engineers. The camps were all within about 25 miles of Rheims. Jim described how his aid station was set up in an old school, and the waiting room was lined with school desks. On Saturday nights the desks would be full of GIs with small wounds from fights, and Jim would start at one end and sew wounds, etc., to the end of the line, and then go back to the first desk and start again. They sent the repaired GIs back to the camp in one of the two ambulances. One second lieutenant was in the habit of getting drunk and coming in to pull rank on the enlisted men to get an ambulance driver to drive him back to camp. Jim got wind of this and intercepted him, read him the riot act, and sent him the five miles back to camp on foot.

Chalons sur Marne, France
Monday 1 Oct. 1945

Dearest Liz: . . . The day has been cloudy & gray. It has been spent on administrative work—chiefly sorting out & destroying records. Tomorrow we plan to turn in our medical equipment.

This afternoon I went down to see Maj. Furst who is now Division Surgeon. He said I didn't have a chance of going with the Division but would be transferred out, probably at the last minute. Oh joyful prospect! It's better than Japan, tho.

I don't know anything more about how the occupation is going than you do except that they apparently aren't being tough enough. The men in the units say they arrest violators of laws, send them to Mil. Gov't. for punishment & they're back unpunished the next day. They need martial law with on the spot punishment still. Where they should be executing hundreds of Nazis with short shrift, they're executing an occasional one or two after long drawn-out superfluous trials. As you said, the war has only magnified the world's problems and at this point I'm sure another war will come soon because people individually are still unwilling to pay for peace by giving up a single one of their own selfish little desires & claims. Yet it's still OK with them to pay with their lives & their children's lives for a war. The utterances of the audible members of Congress are not only asinine, but disgraceful in their selfish tricks to get votes <u>now</u> at the expense of the future peace of the world—and I don't mean even <u>distant</u> future.

Chalons sur Marne, France
Tuesday, 2 Oct. 1945

Dearest Liz: . . . Whatever our fortunes, I think we'll always be able to be happy together, because we just <u>do</u> belong to each other. . . . Whatever the storms which pass over us, our marriage will always be a haven where nothing can touch us because everything about it is right. We're like two pieces in a jig saw puzzle who fit. . . .

Soldiers who wish to be a hero
Number practically zero
Those who wish to be civilians
Number way up in the millions.
[From a clipping included in the letter.]

Chalons sur Marne, France
Wednesday, 3 Oct. 1945

Dearest Mom: . . .

Alice & June are sure getting way ahead of Liz—especially, considering the ambitious program she & I have laid out for ourselves in the way of children. Liz & I do plan to take a little time off together before we start in. At the moment I think we both feel as if all we ever want to do is be alone together. It will take us a little time, anyway, to get readjusted & stabilized back to the point where we'd be fit for parenthood. . . .

Chalons sur Marne, France
Friday, 5 Oct. 1945

Dearest Liz: . . . This afternoon I studied for 3 hours, then packed up my maps to send home. I'll mail them to Basking Ridge tomorrow. We expect to move to Camp Pittsburgh on Monday or Tuesday. . . .

I'm enclosing a clipping from the AMA Journal on how the G-I bill of rights applies to us. It means for sure that we can get $75 a month for 1 year. . . . That will be quite a help.

Jim's duties at this point were very light, and his social schedule continued busy as he and the other officers essentially killed time waiting for the move to an embarkation camp. He describes playing bridge for five-hour stretches, drinking champagne (Chalons is the heart of French champagne country), and eating the canned lobster and other goodies sent regularly by Liz.

Meanwhile, the army was having difficulties transporting and processing for discharge the huge number of soldiers returning to the States each day. A shipping strike was causing bottlenecks in US ports. In France the army also had huge administrative hurdles, sorting out the men by the point system, transferring those with under 80 points to other outfits that would be staying in Europe, leaving only the higher-point men still attached to the division that was due to leave. At the same time, high-point men from other divisions arrived to depart with the 75th. This massive shifting of units caused great confusion. Families at home looking for their soldier's arrival would see the unit that he had been in through the war, but he would no longer be attached to it. The 75th Division's departure was delayed several times.

Chalons sur Marne, France
Friday, 6 Oct. 1945

Dearest Liz: . . .

It sounded to me in your letters, as it frequently has before, that you are doing more than your share of work on weekends at the Farm. It used to annoy me that your family let you do it at your house & I certainly don't want you to do it with my family. They know you work hard & nobody is going to get mad if you take things a little easy on weekends. Keeping your end up & doing all the work are two very different things & I don't want you to do the latter. . . .

[N]ow that it is night I'd like to call up my girl in Belmont & then go out & see her & drink a hot buttered rum & sit in front of the fire with her where she might be able to guess she loved me!

Even better would have been if I could have come home from the hospital for the weekend & we could have decided it was too bad weather for the Farm & would just have stayed cooped up happily & restfully together in our apartment. About this time we'd just be having beer & salami sandwiches after the movie, then would walk home with my wife holding tight to my arm & shivering from time to time. . . .

Chalons sur Marne, France
Monday, 8 Oct. 1945

Dearest Liz: . . .

Wilbur, Smitty, & Turner left today, leaving only Hanna & me of the original detachment which came overseas. . . . This afternoon Major Furst told me that as soon as we process the 8,000 men with 80+ points who are coming into the division, I will be transferred to Oise which will assign me to one of the units under its command. That means staying in France but might mean an AAC dispensary job, hospital job, field unit job or anything. We'll just have to wait & see. . . .

Camp Pittsburgh, France
Wednesday, 10 Oct. 1945

Dearest Liz: Yesterday your bad husband failed to write you, for which he apologizes. I was away all day, getting back just in time to get to Louis' for dinner. I wasn't able to break away from there till 11:30 & it was 12 before I got home & started packing to move this morning. I packed till 2 last night & from 7 till 8:30 this morning. In the process I found I still have far too much junk & will have to start cutting it down. Among the things were your old letters, which I burned today. I hated to burn them, but I'm rapidly getting converted to your belief in getting rid of everything you don't use. . . .

Camp Pittsburgh is a dusty unpleasant "winterized" tent camp. "Winterized" means stone floors in the tents, 3 foot tar paper side walls, & a small stove in each tent. All the tents are wired for electricity, but there's no juice & no bulbs, so that's not much help, especially since it gets dark about 6 o'clock now. It also turns out that I'm going to have to work my ears off on this processing deal. . . .

The officers have started a language clean-up. Anyone swearing or saying a "nasty" word pays 5 francs into a kitty. The last day on the boat they'll draw for it, & the guy who gets the lucky slip gets the kitty.

This business of getting so close but not quite making it is getting me down. . . .

Jim

Camp Pittsburgh, France
11 Oct. 1945

Dearest Liz: Today was a bad one with no mail from you. Last night was really grim. It was cold & I was cold because someone stole my sleeping bag & someone else switched G-I sleeping bags with me & I was afraid to use the one I have now because it's dirty as hell & I'm afraid I might catch scabies from it, the disease being rampant. There were no lights & I had no flashlight. . . .

Today I had a big sick call all morning & finished a physical inspection started yesterday. After lunch I went up & talked to the boys who are the static doctors here & they were unanimous in saying ANYTHING was better. They also said the camps weren't closing down till sometime between Jan 1 & June 1 & at the moment Oise is not assigning doctors to any field units. So this afternoon I went over to Reims & requested transfer to the 50th Field after & if I'm transferred out of the 75th. The guy over there at Oise Hq. said he thought I'd get home just as soon from there (50th Field). He couldn't guarantee me the job, tho. . . .

Camp Pittsburgh, France
Saturday, 13 Oct. 1945

Dearest Liz: . . .

This afternoon we gave shots to half the battalion. I also made out a report & examined 300 new arrivals for venereal disease, lice, & scabies. 1 out of 10 had lice or scabies! Tonight I itch all over just on general principles.

The Stars & Stripes today announced that the redeployment schedule was due to fall way behind due to the reclaiming of the Aquitania & Queen Elizabeth. All the G-Is today were running around cussing the British, tho I don't see anything to cuss them about. We cancelled lend-lease on them without warning & they want to get their own men home from the East. The thing which makes me most suspicious about the merits of the longshoremen's strike in New York & the Eastern Seaboard is the fact that any possible relation it might have to the shortage of ships was only mentioned briefly at the tail end of the article on the back page. That's the way the Nazis used to do it while still claiming they presented all the facts. . . . The radio estimated that 200 Victory ships were stalled along the East Coast due to the strike. That would be about 1,500,000 tons of shipping as compared to the 130,000 tons represented by the Queen Elizabeth & Aquitania. The longshoremen <u>may</u> have a legitimate bitch, but they're still trying to push something thru at the expense of a lot of soldiers who did a lot of fighting without which they wouldn't have jobs at all. The basic causes of war, trying to get something for nothing at the other guy's expense is worse than ever & it seems to me that the present leader of the school are the "New Dealers" & the unions. I was talking to five hot union men (G-Is) here today. They don't want socialism—which certainly is the best situation for the average industrial worker, because they still want to have unlimited ceiling on their demands for wages & privileges without regard for the effect it will have on other people: "the hell with them!" . . . I still think the Roosevelt machine wasn't worth it. It made a model of principles & methods which were and are reprehensible at best & in making social gains they have lost more than they made because they sacrificed honesty &

industry & consideration & justice on the alter of "the end justifies the means."

Pardon the tirade, sweetie, but I'm so god-damned disillusioned with my fellow Americans and, rightly or wrongly, an awful lot of the worst things I see look like they were born thru the acceptance of the rightness & justice of sacrificing everything that is right & just if they can get something out of it & get away with it. Morally . . . we have gone back 50 years to the days of the unprincipled "economic royalists." Now we will have to spend 30 years working back to where we were—which was in an age of increasing controls over unprincipled piracy & exploitation which by this time would have arrived at equal social improvements without the sacrifice of, but rather by use of our sense of what is right & just. . . .

Camp Pittsburgh, France
Monday, 15 Oct. 1945

Dearest Liz: Well, my orders finally came thru! I got back from Chalons about 3:30 and was in S-1 then when the Division AG (Adjutant General) walked in. I asked him if he knew when I'd be transferred. He said "Haven't you gotten your orders?" and showed me a copy. It seems the messenger failed to pick them up at the AG office this morning. The orders assigned me to the Halfway House (Oise transient billets in Reims) to await reassignment. I went right in to Oise Headquarters to see what Oise Unit I'd been assigned to, & also to put in another plug for the 50th Field. When I got there, they had already assigned me to the 178th General in Reims, so that is it. If it weren't for the fact that Lillie & Sweeney are in the 50th Field, the 178th would be the best assignment I could get. It is a big, new, fully equipped modern hospital. . . .

In Rheims, the capital of the province of Champagne, the dispensary was in the old Italian consulate and was relatively comfortable duty. The city had not suffered much damage. Jim worked there with Seymour Taffet, another doctor from New Jersey.[19]

178th General Hospital,
Reims, France.
Tuesday, 16 Oct. 1945

Dearest Liz: . . .

The hospital is a beautiful set-up. It is a completely modern 2,000 bed hospital on the outskirts of Reims. The physical set-up compares with Presbyterian [Columbia Presbyterian Hospital in New York], so you can see what I mean. Working here will be like working in a real hospital. I think that I will ask to be assigned to the surgical service as that is the branch in which I most need training that I won't get in the future without taking a special internship for the purpose. If I could learn to take out an appendix, do hernias and emergency surgery here while in the Army, it would be a good deal. That is another reason why I am disappointed at not going to the 50th Field with Dick Lillie and Don Sweeney. . . .

The dining room here is VERY nice with curtains, table cloths, napkins, waitresses and good food. I am just sleeping temporarily in a small ward tonight, but will be assigned a room tomorrow with running hot and cold water, central heating, and SHEETS! After supper I slept for an hour and a half, then went to the movies. . . . After that I went upstairs to the very nice officers' club, had a drink, watched a bridge game, played some ping-pong, and discussed books with Dick and another guy. It's sure been a heck of a time since I was able to discuss books with anyone I was stationed with!

Much of Jim's working time after the war ended was spent in non-medical army bureaucratic busywork, which was frustrating to a young doctor eager to learn all he could and get on with his career. However, the army did provide a great variety of medical complaints to address, and for someone willing to seek them out, there were opportunities for experiential learning. Jim showed great interest in the psychiatric aspect of the men's complaints, which was widely evident given the psychological and emotional trauma that the troops had endured. Jim repeatedly affirmed his conviction that the most important and interesting part of medicine was dealing with the patient directly.

Reims, France.
Wednesday, 17 Oct. 1945

Dearest Liz: . . .

The first day at the hospital was a busy one. I'm taking over a 60 bed ward. . . . I spent the morning walking around learning the setup. . . . One of the patients was at least a moral victory . . . he thought I was the first doctor who'd understood his troubles & even tried to help him! . . . His complaint is migraine headaches brought on by emotional upsets which he lets occur with even minor annoyance. . . . I dove right into his very confused personal life which is at the bottom of his troubles . . . & generally got him to think about his personal life indecisions which are driving him nuts because he has been refusing to face them.

It's sure nice to work in comfort again. This morning I had a nice hot bath & there is steam heat in the hospital. There is 3 day laundry service & 1 week dry cleaning. The officers' dining room is very pleasant & the food continues good with plenty of good salad every night. It is nice to be able to linger over ones meals & talk medicine, too.

There seem to be a lot of good cases as well as a lot of crud. About half of them are the Bn. surgeon's problem cases, only here I have the facilities to complete the cases one way or the other. The proportion of psychiatric problems remains enormous & even where pathology is present, the psychic component is great. . . . I still prefer medicine, tho I think I should get some surgical training. Surgery is just plain boring to me.

Soissons, France.
Saturday, 27 Oct. 1945

Dearest Liz: . . . Darling, I can still remember walking along 8th St. facing the prospect of not seeing you again for God knew how long & possibly not at all. At least now we know that we will be together again & probably sooner than we expected to be then. . . . The time between sitting on the couch holding your hand & looking at the misery in your eyes till I hit the corner of Fifth Ave & 8th St. is still in sort of an unpleasant fog. I sure hope we never do that again. This may sound silly & untrue, but the times I was really in danger I was mostly afraid of leaving you alone rather than of being killed. The latter wasn't so bad, but the thought of how you'd feel on getting a telegram from the War Department hurt worse than any wound or the prospect of dying. I could just see you becoming terribly quiet & shut up within yourself the way you do when you're hurt only worse and I wanted to live more so as not to cause you that than for any other reason. That's something I never told you before because I didn't want to upset you that I felt that close to death in combat, but it was one of the things that makes me absolutely sure that my love for you is the right kind. . . .

Good night Liz. I love you very, very, very much.

Jim

178th General Hospital
Reims, France.
Monday, 5 November 1945.

Dearest Mom and Dad:

Today I got transferred from the G-I and General Medicine ward and the female medical ward down to the hospital dispensary and admitting department. It's the same old stuff I did back as a battalion surgeon. It is easy but boring. . . . The hospital continues to be pleasant and comfortable, except that I expect to be transferred out and back to Germany within a few weeks, when they are scheduled to transfer all medical officers with under 55 points back there to service the Army of Occupation. It's a grim prospect. . . .

178th General Hospital
Reims, France.
Tuesday, 6 Nov. 1945

Dearest Wizabelf: At long last the mail started to function again today with the arrival of your letters of Sat. Oct 27th. . . .

The entire morning was spent in x-ray reading films with (Lt) Col. Levin, the x-ray man. This afternoon I took over admitting. . . .

I heard of a good job today which is open—CO of the PW hospital at Bar le Duc. The only trouble is that it would mean staying till the place closed which might be several years. They have all sorts of illness there, tho, & you are kingpin to do what you want with the enormous clinical material. The staff is all German. Needless to say, I'm steering clear of it. . . .

178th General Hospital
Reims, France.
Wednesday, 7 Nov. 1945

Hello Sweetheart!

That's what I wish I were saying to you as I walked in the door of Our apartment about now & kissed you hello after a whole day away from you. Won't it be wonderful when a day will be a long time for us to be apart? Today I've completely failed in thinking about you only once every half hour, because I've thought about you & missed you & wanted you about twice every five minutes, even in the midst of being busy. . . .

After working hard studying the past two nights, I'm going to take tonight off & go to the movies. The other guy on admitting is away tomorrow & until noon the next day & I am also OD tomorrow night. I sure hope it's less busy than it has been the last two times I was on.

The morning was again spent reading x-rays with Col. Levin. I'm learning a lot, too. Enough so that I'm starting to feel capable of reading the simple stuff myself. It's just like having a 2–3 hour private tutoring session in x-ray each time I do it. . . .

The last of the 75th embarked two days ago, so I imagine the first part is well on its way by now. Boy, I'd like to be with it! . . .

It looks like I still haven't completely lost my innocent look. The boys in the dispensary today were betting on my age. One guy knew how long it took to be a doctor & how many points I had, so he guessed right. The others guessed 22, 23, 24 (2 guys) & 26! . . .

178th General Hospital
Reims, France.
Friday, 9 Nov. 1945

Ma chère Sweetie: . . .

Last night really wasn't very busy, but I was kept up by a couple of behaviour problems, one a colored boy discharged only yesterday back to the guardhouse where he's serving a sentence for black marketing from a QM depot. He decided he didn't like it there as well as in the hospital, so faked an acute abdominal emergency & got back in. As soon as he was safe on the ward everything was OK. I tried to get him sent out again last night but was unable to get in touch with his guardhouse to come after him. The other one was a guy who likes to draw attention & disrupt the men around him by threatening suicide, which he did last night. When he finally saw we were going to stomach tube him or else, he admitted he had faked his suicide attempt, which we were sure was the case right along. So many of the real psychiatric problems are just "spoiled child" reactions gone wild, and could have been prevented by proper bringing up.

Today I was again pretty darn busy, so much so I only got to read x-rays for 15 minutes. Col. Levin said he thought he'd train me another week & then take a 3 day pass to Paris he wanted! I am catching on but have a lot to learn yet. Of course, I know nothing at all about technique. . . . Col. Steuer got his orders to Germany today & will probably leave the end of next week. He said he thought everyone under 55 points would probably get their orders to Germany next week, oh grim & horrible thought. Apparently the whole redeployment of doctors is terribly gummed up. There have been about 2,000 70 & 80 pointers sitting around doing nothing for 8 weeks waiting for transportation. Now they are being reassigned because a bunch of 90 pointers have just been released from their duties & have priority on going home. . . . Stars & Stripes today carried more bad news for us—that (MC) men with 30 months in the Army regardless of points would not be sent overseas. . . . In addition, we're beginning to wonder if part of this snafu isn't a political dodge to put thru State Medicine (not socialized medicine). If they keep us over here long enough we're going to lose our initiative, ambition, & ability to stand on our own feet, so we'll be willing to enter into State Medicine. In addition they will be keeping the chief opponents of State Medicine out of the way while they push it thru. I am thoroughly convinced now that <u>any State</u> controlled program of medical service is a mistake. The Army is the perfect example—there are more doctors per person by far than in civilian life plus almost unlimited technical facilities, yet I <u>know</u> and 9 G-Is out of ten will agree that medical service in the Army doesn't compare with what they themselves, rich or poor, have available in civil life <u>because</u> there is no incentive for the doctor. He doesn't work as hard or study as hard. There is no percentage in his taking an interest in his patients because advancement is not based on your skill as a doctor but on seniority, on pull, & on your paperwork—any of which take away from your patient's service to cultivate. As a matter of fact giving your patients good service under such a system is a drawback to the doctor. I am finding that out now, because my superiors are taking every opportunity to nag me about & obstruct really good medical service to the patients because they don't want to work that hard. I am now convinced that is why I've been relegated to the dispensary. There I have no opportunity to show anyone up or get too popular with patients, which means the others don't have to try to keep up a pace I set. That is just the sort of thing that State Medicine (meaning Wagner-Murray-Dingell bill medicine) will mean. It will lower, not raise, the standard of doctors & medical service. In addition, its administration will cost 5–10 times what it would cost to just give poor people the money to see a doctor under the present system. Will you find out the names of the New Jersey Senators & of the Congressman from our district for me?

Excuse the harangue, sweetie. This was really supposed to be a love letter, but we got to discussing things today & I got to thinking about the way things go here & suddenly realized that THIS is State Medicine, and it is NOT what we doctors OR the people want or is best for either of us. Cooperative medicine—yes. State Medicine—no. . . .

At the General Hospital in Rheims, Jim said he was assigned to the ulcer ward, where he diagnosed most of the problems as anxiety over waiting to go home. He discovered that the procedure was to ship home the patients who were discharged. He discharged 50 of the 70 patients, which did not please the "bean counters." As a sort of punishment, he was transferred to the dispensary in Rheims, where Jim and 10 men took the place of a much bigger staff. The building, at 50 Boulevard Lundy, was once the Italian consulate and only a block east of the Square de la Porte de Mars. When I visited in 2014, the building held the office of a local pediatrician. In 1945, army dispensaries were essentially walk-in clinics for the troops. At this point the dispensaries around France that had been serving troops waiting to go home were being consolidated.

Area Dispensary Headquarters, Oise Intermediate Section
APO 513 U.S. Army
Sunday, 11 Nov 1945

Dearest Liz:

Well, here I am installed in the dispensary—more or less. No one yet knows what the story is. 10 EM & I from the 178th are relieving a Medical Dispensary unit which relieved another Medical Dispensary unit yesterday. I assume that we will be relieved in the fairly near future by another one. They are the outfits set up to run a place like this. It is a big dispensary with pharmacy, lab & dental office. It was dirty & in a hell of a mess when we moved in. We have cleaned it up some—enough to use it, & will dig in again tomorrow. There have been 2 medical officers, a dental officer & 17 EM here & I don't know just how we'll get along with limited personnel, especially in view of the fact that none of them have experience with this type of work. . . . We may be here for 2 days or 6 months. We don't know. The building occupied by the dispensary is the former Italian Consulate at Reims & is quite a nice one. There are individual rooms for most of the men.

. . . will move down here tomorrow. It really would be a good set-up to be assigned here permanently instead of going to Germany. . . . The dispensary is in the middle of Reims, 5 minutes walk from the "Little Red Schoolhouse" & 10 minutes from the heart of the business district. . . .

Well, sweetie, there isn't much else to write except to repeat that the 178th is closing Thursday the 15th & I'm on detached service from it to run this dispensary in Reims.

As their predecessors left the dispensary, Jim realized his men had no food and very few supplies. He was told he needed passes for the mess halls. When he tried to get passes, he was told he needed a "buck slip." Always searching for ways around Army regulations, Jim realized that the whole supply system relied on "buck slips." A buck slip was a shortcut to requisition almost anything. Unfortunately, a buck slip had to be signed by a commanding officer. Jim had no idea who his commanding officer was at that point, so decided to sign the slip as his own commanding officer. It worked. The dispensary served 3,500 troops plus all USO, Red Cross, and British personnel in Rheims, and needed many things. The solution Jim devised was to use a buck slip to requisition more buck slips. He was then able to get all sorts of supplies. After a few weeks, the commanding surgeon showed up to inspect. Jim decided he should tell this guy what he had done to get supplies, as he had had no higher authorization to that point. The officer replied, "Everything looks fine to me Captain. Carry on."

Area Dispensary #3
Reims, France
Monday, 12 Nov 1945

Dearest Liz: . . .

This afternoon I went out to the 178th & packed up all my stuff & brought it back in. I also asked for another doctor for here & they are sending a guy named Taffet [Dr. Seymour Taffett] who was an artillery battalion surgeon (corps). I treated one of his men who had both legs blown off at Goronne last January! . . . The men I have are working out very well. Most of them are intelligent & interested & they've really done wonders at getting this place cleaned up & running, even tho none of them have ever worked in a dispensary before. It's a good setup for a small unit which cooperates & I think they realize it.

I wish I were going to stay here for a while. The living conditions are ideal. Our dispensary is nice, the quarters are good, there is a nice officers club with good free beer half way to the officers' mess, ten minutes walk from here, the mess is good, there are 2 GI & 2 French movies & an opera house within easy walking distance. It would really be a pleasant place to spend the winter & reminds me somewhat of Frankfurt & Munich. Unfortunately, however, I'll be going to Germany. . . .

Area Dispensary #3
50 Blvd Lundy
Reims, France
Friday, 16 Nov 1945

Dearest Liz: . . .

Taffett & I are doing a terrific business in Red Cross & USO girls. There won't be any we don't know at the rate we're going. We're the envy of the surrounding male population. Both the Red Cross & USO have their base for this area in Reims & our dispensary is the one they use! One of my patients (not the man-trap one) from the 178th got sick up in Luxembourg & came all the way back here to get me to doctor her! . . .

178th General Hospital
Reims, France.
Saturday, 17 November 1945.

Dearest Mom and Dad:

. . . 2 days after I got down here I asked for another medical officer and several more men, who are now here. It's a good thing, because we keep busy. The other medical officer is a guy named Seymour Taffet from Belleville, New Jersey (right on the edge of Newark). . . . He is a good doctor and in general we agree on methods of treatment. We both think we were railroaded down here for working too hard at the 178th, but it has turned out not to be too bad a deal. . . .

It suddenly occurred to me today that I haven't yet told you what to give Liz for Christmas, and that it is rapidly approaching. Ma, will you wrap into separate packages the piece of Pink tweed and the piece with the big herringbone pattern, the green compact I bought before leaving the US, and the plastic lace pattern brooch I sent from France? Also will you please get her a Bing Crosby recording of "White Christmas" and a recording of the song "Rum and Coca-Cola"—If possible the one which has been issued to the Special Services of the Armed Forces. . . . This coming Thursday is Thanksgiving. At one time I had hopes of maybe being home for it, but it begins to look now as if I'll be lucky to be home for it in 1946. However, according to our original calculations, that was about a minimum of time I expected to be away, so that is not too bad. It's awfully hard not to feel that there aren't a lot of people sitting in the States at our expense, tho. . . .

Today has been a beautiful sunny Sunday. I got up late and worked on a report all morning. After lunch I took a nap. Later Taffet and I went for an hour's walk along a specified route so the men could locate us easily if we had any patients, which we fortunately did not.

Mom, I hope that you didn't overdo it on your Jaunt to South Bend. Liz said your letters sounded as if you were leading an awfully gay life out there. What is your pressure now? How are you feeling, Pop?

Much love, Jim

Area Dispensary Headquarters, Oise Intermediate Section
Tuesday, 20 Nov 1945

Dearest Liz: . . .

Today was very foggy all day, as are about half our days now. . . .

As you probably read in the papers a new lowering of the point score for discharge has just been announced—to 55 points for EM. . . . The latest rumor is that they have stacks of ships at Marseilles, but just aren't getting the men on them. It is true, tho, that redeployment now is progressing fast enough to be noticeable for the first time. Men one knows are leaving right and left. It is going to make a lot of installations difficult to run. . . .

Area Dispensary Headquarters, Oise Intermediate Section
Thanksgiving Day, Thursday, 22 Nov 1945

Dearest Liz: . . . We had just about as good a Thanksgiving as the Army could possibly give us, but I still hope it's the last one I have to spend away from you, on account of you're my sweetie that I love & don't like to be away from at all.

I've been busy with patients all day coming in in dribbles. It was wet & foggy all day. We really had a wonderful Thanksgiving Dinner, the menu of which is enclosed. We put away a terrific amount of champagne by dint of flirting with the waitress, who kept pouring it into our glasses every time the head waiter & mess sergeant turned their heads! . . .

You spoke of how the clouds of war were gathering again and how "humanity's emotional want of peace evidently is not enough to make peace." I am convinced now that the human race has not progressed to the point of peace. The great mass of people are still such beasts that war is the only natural outcome. An inborn ability to follow the wrong lead doesn't help. The morals of the average man are still so bad that he will use any means he can to grab what the other fellow has if he thinks he can get away with it. . . .

The CQ has the G-D-X radio going so I can't concentrate. He would have it in the room with the only decent light. You know, I really don't like radios. They annoy me.

Things are getting busy again, so I'll have to sign off—this is my night on. . . .

Liz with her nephew Reb at the Farm, possibly taken the day this letter was written.

Liz spent a number of weekends at "the farm" in Basking Ridge. She wrote the following from there on Sunday afternoon of Thanksgiving weekend.

The Farm Sunday, Nov. 25

Dearest Sweetie: It's 5 PM & just getting dark. I'm writing now as it's a free moment & I know I'll be awful sleepy tonight as we're going in [to New York] on the nine o'clock tonight. This weekend has been quite winterish. Now looking out I see bare trees against a definitely wintry sky. There's been a skim of ice on the pool all day—the kind of day that's seemed very cozy indoors—good to come into after being outdoors. Pop has finished cutting an all winter supply of wood on the power saw he & Dan rigged up. In lots of ways I wish I could just stay here and hibernate all winter.

I've spent a fairly busy day for a Sunday out here. We all had breakfast about nine & after it was cleared up Alice & I went to get some apples & ci-

der & the Sunday paper. When we got back I did a big laundry—Reb's bed pads, sheets, diapers etc., napkins from Thanksgiving, one of your shirts I've been wearing & a few other things. Then I read the paper & wrote Mother before lunch. Lunch, like last night's supper, was simply setting out the left-over food and turkey. It sure makes cooking simple. After lunch Pop, Mom & Alice all went to sleep & Dan & I did the dishes, then he went back to his carpentry in the cellar & I took Reb out till about four. Since then Alice & I have been chatting in the kitchen while Reb played around banging pots & pans. Like all little boys, noise is the height of fun. Alice & Dan I guess will be starting back to Phila as soon as Reb has had his supper. . . .

Sweetie, taking Reb around today has made me miss you so. I find myself pretending he is our little boy cause of how I think it will be so nice when we have our little boy. I want him & I want to see you with him.

It's 7:30 now & DAR have gone & everything is cleaned & cleared. I'm so sleepy now I wish that train left at 8 not 9.

I've just read Truman's speech on health insurance & am sending it in case you did not see it. Much of it I think is valid—& I think there is a very definite distinction between insurance & socialized or state medicine. How else is the need to be met if not through insurance?

Gosh how I wish you were here—& that we weren't going back in town. We'd have some pop-corn & ginger ale by the fire & come up to bed very early with a good long night's sleep ahead. Can you close your eyes and see how it will be the way I can? I think I want to have at least a week here with you first—no matter what we do. How about you? Would you get bored & restless? I don't think I could ever get bored anywhere so long as you were there.

Goodnight, darling. Your wife is missing you something awful—& wanting you something ahful—& loving you more than she can ever possibly tell you, even in a long lifetime of living with you.

Area Dispensary Headquarters, Oise Intermediate Section
Monday, 26 Nov 1945

Dearest Liz: . . .

Everyone in the dispensary is being transferred for administrative purposes to the 193rd General Hospital. We will continue to operate the dispensary, however. The 193rd is to be the last General Hospital in this area to close. We are expecting a consolidation of the various headquarters & sections into one in about 6 weeks. They now have Oise (where we are), Seine, Delta, Chanor, & one other. . . .

Last night I got thru work about midnight. The men were having a party with some USO girls upstairs & invited us to come. I went till about 1:30. Today was my day off, so I didn't get up till 10:30! After lunch I drove out to Mourmelon [site of one of the re-deployment camps, about 20 miles southeast of Reims] to try to get some administrative work straightened out. On the way back to Reims we saw 3 wild boars along the road, the first I'd ever seen. One of them was a great big ferocious male, the others were smaller young ones. . . .

Reims, France
Tuesday, 27 Nov 1945

Dearest Liz: . . .

This afternoon I sent you a cable, giving my new address. They said it would reach you tomorrow morning! I'll be interested to see if it did. It cost $2.28. One is now allowed to cable the same way as before the war. . . .

Reims, France
Thursday, 29 Nov 1945

Darling: . . .

Last night my USO girl refused to go with Mason, but he & I both took her to the officers' club for about an hour's dancing. It worked out OK that way. The boys have been laughing at the way I ran away from her all day today. Thank heaven she's left for good.

. . . I had to get up at 3:30 to sew up a guy who had cut his face falling down while drunk.

Will you send some more anchovies, crackers, dill pickles, olives, & shrimp?

. . . All non-medical officers under 75 points have just been frozen till Jan. 15th. I imagine the cause is that they will be needed to instruct replacements & POWs in essential jobs over here. Many of the large QM installations in France which formerly employed 1500–1600 soldiers now have 20 US personnel and 1500 POW's to close them out.

It's not so much the trouble Russia is causing now as what seems to me to be a wrong attitude which points to future trouble.

The 193rd Gen. Hosp. seems to be much more on the ball in the matter of taking care of their personnel than the 178th. They now are giving leaves to the Riviera, Switzerland, Sweden, England, Paris & Brussels. I'm going to put in for the Riviera, Switzerland, & Sweden & should get one of them before the winter is over. I'd like to get Switzerland or Sweden at Christmastime. . . .

Reims, France
Sat 1 Dec 1945

Dearest Liz: . . .

I've had a hectic day all day. Sym left this morning. I've had the dispensary to myself since noon as Smith was off. I've been trying to get the weekly & monthly reports out, pay the men, readjust our personnel here, & see patients. What a job! This is going to have to be short as it is sandwiched in between the usual Saturday night parade of lacerations to be sewed up. I hear more work on the way in now, so I'll try to finish this before attending to it, as God knows when I'll be thru. . . .

2 days after the announcement that a Congressional Committee to investigate the holding of medical officers here was on its way, a telegram was distributed to all commands to get all medical officers out down to 69 points. Not only that, but they are not to go thru regular redeployment channels but are to go right to the port & if possible be out of the theatre within a week! If that's not an admission of guilt I never saw one. I only hope there's some action now on getting replacements over here, too. . . .

The congressional investigation mentioned by Jim apparently dealt with the fact that doctors were not being sent home with their units, despite the availability of replacement doctors trained under the Army Specialized Training Program (ASTP). The ASTP paid for soldiers to go to medical school to help fill the constant need for doctors during the war. The last class graduated in the summer of 1945, but these new physicians were never deployed overseas.

Reims, France
Monday, 3 Dec 1945

Dearest Sweetie: . . .

I weigh 147–148 now, the most I've ever weighed. Maybe I will be so fat you won't recognize me! I'm also the least active I've ever been.

. . . The setup now is as follows: Taffet & I are the MCs. . . . Costa is the dentist.

S/Sgt Harry Bowman—In charge
T/4 Martinez—2nd in charge
T/4 Moss—Lab & pharmacy
T/4 Stein—Pharmacy & lab
T/5 Heald—Dispensary technician
T/5 Whitaker—Dispensary technician
T/5 Molk—Dispensary technician

T/5 Steckhaln—Dispensary technician
T/5 Shapiro—Dental technician
Pfc Kooser—Clerk
Pfc Reickman—Driver
Pfc Senesac—Driver
Pfc Lenzo—Driver

. . . As you know by now, I'm staying at the dispensary with all my "beautiful" female patients. By the way, the package which arrived 2 days ago contained 2 bottles of olives, saltines, & lobster. . . .

It's getting pretty cold in the dispensary tonight. I'm on duty. We've had no fire since yesterday morning because the grate burned out of the furnace. It will be several days to several weeks till we get new ones in. We put in an emergency requisition & got two G-I pot-belly stoves with generators to burn diesel oil, but as yet have no oil. One of the drivers is out in Mourmelon now trying to get some.

Just went upstairs & put on a pair of those super hand-knit wool socks my wife knit. How wonderful they would have been last winter! As I got back down again the boys were just arriving with the oil & we are now heating the generator for 15 minutes prior to tuning it on, when the heat will really come. Fortunately we have a big fireplace with a chimney which draws very well.

. . . Please send popcorn, anchovies, dill pickles, blue cheeze. Send yellow popcorn if the white is hard to get. I'll have to pass a lot of it around & most people don't care which they eat.

Reims, France
Tuesday, 4 Dec 1945

Dearest Liz: . . .

Smith got his orders today & and a new medical officer arrived from the 195th Gen Hosp. His name is Stilman Davis. He is still a 1st Lt. tho he has been overseas 16 months. I hope he's just been gypped & isn't such a poor guy & MC he's never made Captain. Smith leaves Thursday. I've carried the dispensary alone for the last 2 days (he spent the day in Mourmelon today) so I got fed up tonight & told him he was on tonight—period. He didn't like it, but I'd had enough of his guff & didn't want to put Davis on the first night he was here.

The weather turned cold again, so we were sort of cool today without our furnace. I sure hope it gets going soon again. The Utilities Section was supposed to go to Paris & get the grate today.

Right now I'm at one of those times of being very tired & harassed where everything irritates you. Mason called up yesterday & said the Red Cross girl he had a date with tonight had a buddy in town she wanted to bring along. He asked me to help him out, so I figured I might as well. We're going to a USO Show and, if I have anything to say about it, right home to bed. I'm sitting in the Red Cross Club now waiting for them.

We had a nice new innovation at supper tonight—beer! That's a dandy idea. I only wish they'd sell wine at dinner, too. I also wish they would supply me 1 wife (Model LFM (Liz Foote McKay). . . .

Goodnight. sweetheart. I love you very very very much.

Jim

Reims, France
Saturday, 8 Dec 1945

Darling: Today was half good with the arrival of a package mailed about Nov. 10th containing ink, crackers, anchovies & dill pickles. The tragedy of tragedies occurred, tho, & the dill pickles had been busted. It's killing me not to eat them, but I tasted one & it tasted a little queer, so I decided to leave them alone, darn it! Please send some more, sweetie. That's the first time anything has busted. The package looked as if it had had very rough handling.

Last night I was a bad boy & ended up by going out & staying up late again. I dropped by Mason's on my way to supper to find him having cocktails with the two British Red Cross girls, Audrey & Sylvia. We all had supper together, then Mason & I took Sylvia to the movies, after which we went back to the 79 Club for a couple of beers. I got home about twenty minutes of twelve & was drawn into a bull session with Davis till almost one. Today I had a busy morning as Davis went to Chalons. He got back about two & I went over to the football game which Sylvia & Mason & I had a date for. The game was only fair. It was the semi-finals of the Service Forces Championship. The Seine Engineers beat the Oise Ordnance team 15-0. . . .

It turned very cold today. At the end of the football game it started snowing & reminded me so much of Christmas & Boston & you. . . .

You spoke of atom bomb control & universal training. I am of the opposite view from you—I don't think the secrets of the atom bomb should be shared with Russia, tho I do think that when it is controlled for peaceful uses, those should. I think we should have universal service, too. My basic reason is that I'm convinced that there will be another war in 20–25 years. Individual man is still too much of a selfish, cruel, lousy bastard for it to be otherwise. Hardly a one of them (men) wants peace if he thinks he can get more for himself by force, and they're too damn dumb to see that everyone loses in a war, especially now. From the looks of things now, that war is going to be basically Russia vs US, so I think we'd be foolish to increase their strength with the atom bomb or to weaken ourselves by not adopting universal military service. Whatever the sob sisters say, a man with previous military training can be trained a darn sight quicker & better than one with none!

In addition universal training at 18 will interfere relatively little with a man's life & it is fairer than selective service. The latter leaves too many opportunities for conscienceless individuals to bribe or cheat their way out of carrying their share of the load. With Universal Service EVERY one shares it & the opportunities for cheating it are relatively few. Liz, we have a lot to talk about & a lot of views to exchange. I'm at the point now where I think all we can do is to vote for keeping strong enough to survive and to do our little bit toward educating a few people into the sense of decency & right & unselfishness & consideration for the other fellow. You can't reform the world all at once. . . .

Reims, France
Sunday, 9 Dec 1945

Dearest Liz: . . .

Last night turned out to be a wild one. Half an hour after I finished writing you we had five emergency calls in quick succession. One was a drunk who banged up his leg in a fall, three were bad jeep accidents with 17 people hurt, 5 seriously, and the last was a USO trouper who fell from a ledge outside a third floor window to the terrace below. He was trying to get into his girl's room, with whom he'd been quarreling. I spent about ¾ of an hour calming her down—it was easy once I got the dramatizers out of the room. Then this morning I had to calm her down again after they told her as dramatically as possible that he had died during the night. The news didn't upset her half as much as the way it was told. People! I didn't get to bed till four as I had to write out a report of the case and figured I'd better do it on the spot. . . . I'm meeting Mason & Sylvia at supper & we're going on to the movies. These two British Red Cross Girls, Audrey & Sylvia, seem to be just what the doctor ordered in the way of feminine company. Both are nice girls & a lot of fun, both have steady fellers but still enjoy the company of the other sex on a purely social basis. It turned out that Sylvia's husband was killed several years ago in Burma. She is now engaged to an American captain in Seattle.

. . . Thank you for the copy of Truman's speech on health insurance. I noticed that the AMA finally came out in favor of the development of health insurance plans for regional areas & <u>not</u> under government control, making the statement that the administration & service would be better & cheaper under "private" auspices. I agree with that. Things are so bad in the Army that I've come to the conclusion that anything which possibly can be done out of government control, would be better so done. This bureaucracy is a vicious circle where paperwork becomes an end in itself & the original purpose of it becomes completely lost & forgotten. A lot of my reports now are a farce, because, in order to be able to cross check a lot of duplicating reports so they'll come out right, they now have rules which make the report worthless. For instance, a knowledge of the incidence of scabies is of great interest to the Army BUT they now say you can't report a communicable disease without putting the man in hospital or quarters, the only exception being gonorrhea. Therefore, since we treat scabies & trench mouth on a duty status, the whole Army could have them & no one in higher headquarters the wiser. In other words, the emphasis is now on the reports, not on the communicable disease. There are hundreds of similar instances.

Reims, France
Wednesday, 12 Dec 1945

Dearest Liz: . . .

The other day a French woman was in here asking me if she could buy some cognac from an American officer with which to make a grog which had been recommended for her ailing daughter. She also wished to talk to our pharmacist about pharmacy & new developments in it in America. I gave her a half bottle of cognac which we had around. Today she came in to see Stein, the pharmacist, who had been to Switzerland when she was here before. She also asked for me & asked me to come for the evening on Friday. I agreed. It should be interesting. She is a nurse. Her younger brother, age 28, is a doctor in the French Army. She has some relation to a pharmacy—whether she runs one, works in one or what, I don't know. Her husband is dead, I believe, & she lives alone with her daughter who must be 12 or 14. . . . Up till now I've made no civilian contacts in Reims. Tennis is my usual means of making them, but it is now out of season to do that. . . .

A guy was in here today from the A-G office. He said that they were closing the redeployment camps Jan 1st & completely reorganizing the service forces into a French Base & a German Base starting then. . . .

We had the typical criminal in here this afternoon. He was just out of jail for a similar offense, so he gets drunk, steals a truck & smashes it up. In here he raves about us letting the MP's haul a man off to Jail who is trying to go straight, etc. etc.! . . . He talked like a communist propaganda leaflet . . . he being a leaf caught in the whirlwind of oppression. I guess that is why "communism" is popular with the no-goods. It supports their own contention that their troubles are not their fault but someone else's. . . . At the same time it condones the use of force to take from those who have, regardless of whether they have earned what he has or whether the taker deserves any more than what he has. Ah me!

Communism had gained popularity during the Depression, and Jim had occasional encounters with communist adherents, later including one fanatic fellow medical officer. Jim wrote long condemnations of these people on several occasions. These encounters combined with his exposure to Russian militarism to engrain a strong mistrust of Russian motives and a real fear of a new war on the horizon.

Once again Jim and Liz spent Christmas apart, but this time their separation was eased by the knowledge that the war was over and sooner or later Jim would make it home. A year earlier Jim had spent the holiday near some of the worst combat of the war in very cold and snowy Belgium, while Liz spent the holiday tense with the fear that her husband would never return. Jim's 1945 Christmas letter included seven tiny envelopes with gift cards, each to accompany one of his gifts, which he had sent along in advance through his parents.

Reims, France
12 Dec 1945

My dearest Wife:

Merry Christmas! I love you, darling. Even tho again this year we are apart, I hope it will be the last Christmas we ever spend away from each other, because we belong together and only when we are together can we be "home for Christmas." This year for "our" Christmas present we have the certainty that we will be together again and probably before too many months pass.

Liz, in spite of the fact that we have spent almost half of our married life apart, I feel that in the best and truest sense we are husband and wife, that we have an inner bond which will never fail us and which will always be an inner fire of happiness, come what may. For that I'm grateful to you because—not underestimating the power of a woman—it is she who has the greatest opportunities to make a marriage a success or a failure, and you have made and will make ours outstanding as a success. Although we won't be together when you read this, we nevertheless will have a full and happy Christmas in a way, because we will know that we have each other and are thinking of and loving each other with all our hearts every minute.

I hope the time isn't too far distant when we'll be having Christmas with our children, because it belongs to children, and having them and making a good home for them and trying to bring them up in love and kindness and toleration and consideration will be the fruit of our love and marriage. I know they'll have a good mother.

Merry Christmas again, sweetheart!

I love you, Liz.

Jim

Reims, France
Friday, 14 Dec 1945

Dearest Sweetie: . . .

I was sorry to hear that your Ma wasn't doing so well. I thought perhaps the end of the war would ease her mental burden in that it would remove a lot of the tenseness of the situation of the members of her family. I suppose that now she is upset, & rightly so, over the complete failure or even willingness of the human race to cooperate for peace. If she could reconcile herself to the fact that the human race is still so lousy it doesn't even deserve the blessings of peace, it might help. But that is a pretty tough pill for a person of her beliefs & principles to swallow so late in life.

. . . a 1st Lt. wandered in half drunk at 1:15 & ordered the C.Q. to wake up the ambulance driver to take him home. Fortunately the C.Q. had sense enough to call me instead of the ambulance driver & the Lt. left walking & feeling lucky that he wasn't going to face a charge sheet today for conduct unbecoming an officer & a gentleman. He was lucky, too, because if he'd given me any back talk I would have thrown the book at him right into the general's lap. I don't usually pull my rank, but when some guy tries to use his to bully someone, especially an enlisted man, into something grossly unfair to the EM, I let them have both barrels of their own medicine.

I stopped after the last paragraph to keep my engagement to spend the evening at Madame Delarmare's. It was very pleasant. She lives with her daughter Micheline, who is 15 or 16 in a small apartment. Her husband has been dead 10 years. The three of us spent a pleasant couple of hours talking and they fed me some very good cherry pie. Two hours is about all I can take of continuous talking in French. Straining to catch every word becomes too tiring after that. She asked me to come again & eat some salad. I happened to mention missing it in the Army chow & that is one of the things they can get without much difficulty. . . .

Amidst the uncertainty of his immediate future, Jim was granted leave the week before Christmas. The army offered a variety of leave locations that soldiers applied to visit. Jim was granted a week in Switzerland but was obviously nervous about being away from his post if an order were to arrive to close the dispensary, transfer to Germany, or go home.

Reims, France
Sunday, 16 Dec 1945

Dear Sweetie: . . .

I'm still feeling lousy. . . . I sure hope it clears up entirely in Switzerland. . . . The entire day has been spent unpacking & repacking, just in case the dispensary should close while I'm gone. I'm all set now to take off for the U.S. tomorrow, should the opportunity arise. I'm on duty tonight & expect to take off about 8 AM tomorrow. We're going to Mulhouse by ambulance, then into Switzerland by train.

. . . It does look as if we're going to have to stay in your present apartment if we stay in New York. . . . If we can get a car to do it with, I think it would be fun to take an auto trip around the U.S. when I get back. We could have a nice trip & maybe get a better idea of where we want to settle. What do you think?

Swiss Leave Center
Mulhouse, France
Monday, 17 Dec 1945

Darling: Here is your husband getting all ready to take off for Switzerland. We (Sgt Moss, Lenzo (the driver), Johnnie (a Swiss guide who came back with Sym & spent the week in Paris) and I) left Reims at 8:30. We arrived here at 5:30 tonight after a pleasant & easy trip down. There was snow & ice on the road for the twenty miles across the Vosges, but the roads were otherwise good. We came thru Chalons, Vitry, Nancy & Thann to Mulhouse. Mulhouse is a large modern town, apparently little damaged by the war. It lies on the flat, swampy Rhine Valley plain about 20–30 miles due south of Colmar. . . . There is a large theatre with a vaudeville show at 7 and movie at 8:30. There is an amazing Px with free pressing, alterations and sewing, shoes shines, & haircuts all performed by POW labor. There are also manicures by French girl manicurists. . . .

I will probably take Johnnie's tour which goes to Geneva, Montreux (3 days), Bern, & Lucerne. At Montreux, there are opportunities for 2 days of skiing on the hills near town, tho it is not a regular winter resort. . . .

On the way here this morning I stopped in to see Louis LeConte in Chalons to say hello & to leave a Christmas present of candy, cigarettes, cigars, peanuts, etc. They seemed glad to see me and asked me to come spend New Years with them. If I'm not on duty, I certainly will.

As early as 1942, medical schools recognized the need to produce as many doctors as possible for the war effort. In response, many accelerated their programs to allow medical students to graduate in three years instead of four. Medical schools began offering courses geared toward the military needs that these doctors would face. For instance, at Harvard Medical School, where Jim graduated in 1943, a tropical medicine course was introduced in 1942 and all students received intensified surgical training. In 1943, the army began supplying students through the Army Specialized Training Program (ASTP). The ASTP mission was to provide a supply of replacement troops in disciplines requiring specialization such as engineering and medicine. Participants in the ASTP were inducted into the army and the army paid for their education. When the war ended, a large number of students remained in the pipeline. Those already serving overseas expected that these new doctors would be obliged to serve and would be sent to relieve the veterans. Naturally, the new doctors were not anxious to do that, now that the war was over.

The clipping Jim sent home to Liz was from the December 16 issue of *Stars and Stripes* and carried the headline "ASTP Doctors Must Serve 3 Yrs. after Getting Commission." The article described the "long burning question among military physicians as to whether the ASTP officers, most of whom remained in the U.S. after completing their professional training at government expense, would be released for civilian practices, while doctors who entered the Army from private practices would continue in active service." It was announced that ASTP Medical Corps replacements would arrive in Europe shortly "to permit the early return to private practice of additional medical Corps officers now overseas."

Swiss Leave Center
Mulhouse, France
Tuesday, 18 Dec 1945

Dearest Liz: . . . .

This trip <u>does</u> count as leave—7 days of it. That still leaves me 39 days leave coming as of Feb 25th, possible more, tho I doubt it.

The enclosed clipping is self explanatory. Boy, was I glad to see it. I figure they'll start sending them over in January. . . . There must be a hell of a backlog of them in the U.S. . . . I sure hope they'll get them over here thick & fast now.

Among other things this morning, I also got me a good genuine German haircut. While getting it I thought about letting my hair grow long just one time for you to see, but rejected the idea. It would be too messy & then you might turn out to actually like it. . . .

After lunch I went over to "Sad Sack's Swiss Shack" where they serve chocolate sundaes. Tres bons, aussi. . . .

Geneva, Switzerland
Wednesday, 19 Dec 1945

Dearest Liz: So ends my first day in Switzerland! They got us up at 5:30 AM on a cold, rainy morning. We ate breakfast & packed, then gathered under a shed at 6:45. From there we walked to the theatre where our visas were handed out, together with our food coupons—we had been separated into the various tour groups while under the shed. From the theatre we marched about half a mile in the dark to the train which took us to Basel, arriving there at 8:45. We went thru customs. . . .

Last night . . . I ran into a fellow named Bissini. . . . He was in my class at Carlisle. . . . He was with the 84th Div. Clearing Company. They fought just north of us in the final attack on the Bulge & have a very similar combat story. . . .

Sgt. Moss, Bissini, & I walked around Basel for a couple of hours this morning. . . . It was certainly amazing to be someplace not hit by the war. Basel is pretty much just another small German city, except that they have things like oranges which Germany didn't have under Hitler because of the use of all German foreign credit for war materials. . . .

The train took off at 11:30 for Neuchatel on the lake of the same name. . . .

The train followed the Jura for as far as Delemont where it reversed & came down thru Biel to Neuchatel. . . . We travelled 3rd class in clean, modern cars. All Swiss trains are electric, in case you didn't know. . . . After lunch Bissini & I went down to the lakeshore where we looked across at the Berner Alps with the Jungfrau directly across from us about 50 miles or more away. Bissini offered to take a picture of me, so I got up on the sea wall to oblige. A Swiss Miss comes along, Bissini grabs her, puts her up beside me, told me to talk to her in German for him & snaps a picture of us. . . . Now he says he's going to blackmail me with the picture. . . . The train left at 4:00, bringing us down to Lausanne where we changed engines to Geneva. . . .

The bright lights of Geneva were amazing after the coal-sparing dimont of the rest of Europe. Switzerland's water power makes electricity plentiful. We are staying in the Hotel Beau Rivage, a really first class hotel on the edge of the lake. Bissini and I have a nice room with private bath & twin beds. . . . [W]e went down to supper of soup, fish, potatoes, cauliflower, lettuce salad & pudding. . . . Monday, Wednesday, and Friday are meatless days in Switzerland.

What follows is a series of letters Jim wrote from his tour stops across Switzerland. A major hope on the trip was that he could connect with Liz by phone. They had not spoken in over a year. A Radiogram survives that Jim sent to Liz from Basel: TELEPHONE ME OPERATOR 19 MONTREUX SWITZERLAND IMMEDIATELY ALL MY LOVE, JIM. It was expected that it would take two or three days to get a call through once it was placed.

20 December 1945
Montreux-Palace
Montreux, Suisse

Darling: . . . We went by . . . the League of Nations. . . . Just above it is the Hotel Carlton which is now used by the International Red Cross as a 3 day quarantine spot for French children being brought into Switzerland to spend 3–6 months with Swiss families. A group of about a hundred & fifty arrived just as we were leaving the League Building. . . . Our next stop was the Headquarters of the International Red Cross, thru which all inquiries & information of prisoners of war & DPs passes. It seemed to be very efficiently run. The guy who showed us around said that Russia & Japan were the only nations who didn't belong, that Japan had occasionally made some effort to report PWs & missing persons, but Russia never. The more I hear of the instances of Russia's holding aloof from anything which

PLACES OF INTEREST

LOCAL TRIPS BY RAIL:

Montreux - Glion - Caux - Rochers de Naye is a memorable trip. The train ascends sharply through lovely mountain region to over 6,000 feet. The summit affords a breath-taking panorama, which will remain in your memory as one of the grandest views imaginable, snow-clad peaks, valleys and lakes stretching out as far as the eye can see. The adjacent mountain slopes are a popular resort for skiers, both beginners and experts. There is, furthermore, ample opportunity for buying refreshments and souvenirs.

Another suggestion is **Les Avants - Sonloup.** Les Avants is reached by the Montreux-Oberland railway, pride of Swiss railroads and known as the „Golden Pass". Thence, a funicular takes you to beautiful Sonloup, set amongst fir-tree forests famous for the superb view over gorgeous Lake Leman, its water-side charms and surrounding mountains.

Fares and suggested times-tables

8.43 a.m.	2.38 p.m.	Lv.	Montreux	Ar.	11.37 a.m.	5.35 p.m.
8.47 a.m.	2.43 p.m.	Lv.	Territet	Ar.	11.33 a.m.	5.34 p.m.
8.58 a.m.	2.53 p.m.	Lv.	Glion	Ar.	11.23 a.m.	5.22 p.m.
9.42 a.m.	3.36 p.m.	Ar.	Rochers de Naye	Lv.	10.42 a.m.	4.38 p.m.

Passengers from Territet change trains at Glion for the Rochers de Naye.

Non-stop entertainment:

A whole variety of smart restaurants and homely tearooms not only provide pleasant accomodation, but also give you a chance of sampling our domestic wines and culinary specialities. Entertainment up till the small hours of the morning is to be found in several snug bars; if it's dancing you want, there are plenty of dance halls where the bands are well up to western standards.

stic centre known as the Swiss Riviera for its benevolent climate, its romantic charm and ho

Palace Hotel

Railroads and funiculars are marked in red

A brochure Jim apparently picked up at the Palace Hotel in Montreux, Switzerland, in December 1945.

might let anyone know what they're doing inside of Russia, the more I think the rest of the world is a terrible sucker to trust them for 30 seconds. Like Hitler Germany they expect the rest of the world to cooperate with them, but they do not & seem to have no intention of cooperating with the rest of the world. From the Red Cross we went to the University of Geneva, the town hall . . . the old Arsenal, & the churches where Calvin & John Knox preached. . . . After lunch I took a 2 hour nap, then the 2 hour train trip here to Montreux where we are ensconced in a small double room in the biggest & finest hotel. Tomorrow morning I leave early to go up to St. Rocher de Naye to ski. They don't expect your phone call to get thru till day after tomorrow at the earliest, due to bad weather.

Friday, 21 December 1945
Montreux-Palace
Montreux, Suisse

Dearest Sweetie: About an hour ago just three years ago today I was so bursting full of love for a certain Liz Foote whom I was in the process of kissing that I just couldn't wait till my Michigan trip was over to make sure as I had intended and as I think she intended, too, but asked her to marry me. As I remember, she replied "I couldn't help it, Jim!" & made me the happiest & luckiest feller in the world not only then, but ever since. . . .

Last night after writing you, Bissini & I went down to the Montreux Casino, a nice bar & nightclub with one roulette table which gives it the name "casino." We stayed till midnight, seeing the floor show, drinking wine & playing casino, thus arousing the curiosity of the girls we should have been going after. A nice kid named Wayne Freedman, a 2nd Lt., joined us & profited by our casino playing to the extent of getting a date with the Parisian dancer in the floor show. She didn't speak English, so I interpreted for them about 20 minutes just before leaving.

This morning I got up at 7:45 & went out to Rochers de Naye skiing. It is 6000 feet up (Montreux is 1000) & is reached by a one hour ride in a cogwheel railroad. I rented skis & shoes here in Montreux for 5 francs. Johnnie, the guide, & I were there all day while others came out for varying periods. We had a lot of fun & I got very windburned. The hotel fixed a lunch to take out. The slope is wide & the middle of it was icy but it was quite easy to ski around it. I sure wished you were there to enjoy it. Liz, be sure & take a long weekend or whole week off & go skiing. You could probably get Peggy Greene or Alice (Ma could keep Reb) to go with you. I'm sure it would do you a lot of mental & physical good—but take care . . .

Most of the skiing here is open slope stuff. There were two guys from the Jap Embassy up there learning to ski. Nobody quite knew how to act, so they & the many G-Is just ignored each other. . . .

Ben (Bissini) wants to go out again tonight, but I don't if I can possibly get out of it. . . . There is no word on a phone call yet from you. They say there is a bad storm along the Atlantic coast with a lot of snow. That is supposed to be slowing up reception. . . .

Sunday, 23 December 1945
Bellevue Palace
Berne

Dearest Liz: Last night the phone rang at about 10:30 to alert me for an overseas telephone call, which, however, has yet to materialize. It doesn't look too good right now for its getting thru. By the alert I know that you are trying to get it thru. . . .

After lunch we went on a tour of Bern. We saw the Swiss Parliament, the Cathedral, the Junkergasse (the street where the patricians lived in olden times—they got the sunny side of the street), the bear pit where live the descendants of the bears of Bern, numerous fountains & landmarks. . . . I enjoyed the bears about as much as anything. . . .

On getting back from the tour I took a nap & am now waiting for our host for the evening to pick Ben & me up. The Bernese really go all out to make the G-Is welcome. There were 50 invitations of various kinds for our group of 88. Ben and I are going to the home of a dentist & his wife for supper & the evening. . . .

Hotel de la Paix
Lucerne, Switzerland
Christmas Eve, 1945

Sweetheart: This morning I got back about 11:30 from wandering around Bern & sat down in the hotel lobby to read. At 11:45 I was called to the telephone & the operator said a call from Cambridge, Mass. would come thru sometime in the afternoon. I told her that I was leaving at one for Lucerne, so she said she would try to get it thru by then. Everyone left the hotel for the station at ten minutes of one, but I figured I'd stick around till one. At one minute of one the bellboy called me to the phone and the operator said the call was coming thru. Darling, I was literally shaking all over with excitement and when your voice came thru it sounded like you were, too. It was wonderful to hear your voice, sweetie, but I'll sure be glad when I can see you, too, and when we won't have any 3 minute time restriction.

I was interrupted at the end of the last paragraph by the arrival of my host for the evening, & it is now 2:30 AM. When we arrived in Lucerne, they immediately gave out a bunch of Christmas Eve invitations. I took one which required someone who spoke German as I am the only one in the group who speaks it well. My host, Mr. Mathis, turned out to be a house painter. They were quite embarrassed at having an officer for a guest, but I still had a very pleasant time. . . . I got back to the hotel a little after midnight to run smack into the party the landlord was giving for those who didn't get private invitations. I joined Johnnie (our guide) and his parents, who had come down on their way to their home in Ascona. They are both of noble Russian families who fled the Revolution. It amused me no end to see an ex-Russian duchess dancing with a G-I sergeant! . . .

The landlord & his wife are real hosts rather than the owners of a hotel. We had a wonderful chicken dinner (chicken is the scarcest meat in Switzerland) and the wine & beer were on the house. Johnnie says our host is always like this. He enjoys being the host & giving parties for the G-Is without regard for his own profit. You can tell the sort of a guy he is by the look on his wife's face. She is a happy woman and is proud of him & in love with him. . . .

The Swiss had been expecting a German invasion early in 1945 and were very grateful to the Americans for defeating Germany and thereby saving their country.

Chapter Eleven
Changing Units; Medical Care of Occupation Troops: Winter 1946

Reims, France
27 Dec 1945

Dear Sweetie: . . .

The party Christmas night in Lucerne was enjoyable. There were about a hundred civilians and 600 G-Is there. Each G-I got a wallet & some travel folders of Lucerne. Then they had a lottery in which a hundred & seventy-four presents were given away by Santa Claus. The duplicate tickets were put in a butter churn which was turned up on the stage in front of the audience by—your husband! After each time I mixed them, a nurse drew 3 tickets & a local Swiss girl in native costume drew three, the numbers were called out & the lucky ones went up & collected. The Swiss girl looked, talked, & laughed enough like Alice to be her twin sister. . . . At the end of the drawing my number hadn't come up, so the audience started yelling "How about the captain?"—which amazed me coming from a bunch of enlisted G-Is. Anyway, they had saved me a gift which I will send you. It is a carved wooden ashtray with one of the bears of Bern on the top. . . .

After the gifts were all given out, we had beer & frankfurters. I went in the other big room of the Casino (Kursaal) to find a bunch of civilians. A girl & her brother asked me to sit down with them, so I went & got Ben & we joined them. They were very nice. Their names are Anselm & Hedwig Lauber & their father is a judge in Lucerne. We talked till one when the Kursaal closed, decided we still had more to talk about, so adjourned to their house where we bulled till 3 over a bottle of wine, cheese & cake. Anselm is 25 & just finished his final exams as an electrical engineer. Hedwig is 29 (blond with a Veronica Lake hairdo) and is one of the 5 chief editors of "Du" which seems to be one of Switzerland's better magazines. . . . She was cussing about men getting more than women for the same job and about the lot of Swiss women in general (they are not allowed to vote).

. . . On arriving [back in Reims] I found Sym all packed and ready to go to Vienna this morning. Half our detachment (all over 50 points) had been transferred out, and the dispensary was to be taken over today by the 254th Medical Dispensary to which the remaining officers & men from the Area Dispensary were to be attached. The full story is that all the dispensaries in Reims except this one have closed. . . . Things are further complicated by the fact that the medical officer of the 254th, Lt. DiLorenzo (23 points) is a first rate heel of minimal efficiency who thinks he's going to run things & from whom I couldn't take orders if he were a Col. Fortunately, the surgeon's office told me today that I automatically assume command because of my rank, tho only on DS (detached service). . . .

The dispensary will probably close about Jan. 15th. . . . Right now they are looking for a doctor to run the dispensary at the new Headquarters of German Base Section . . . at Bad Nauheim. I don't want the job as I want to get in a hospital, so I'm keeping my fingers crossed. . . .

To add to the confusion they are in the midst of devaluating the franc (the French promptly raised their prices 2–3 times) & all PXs are closed during the process & all money has been turned in for re-issue to G-Is. . . .

I love you,
Jim

Reims, France
28 Dec 1945

Dearest Liz: The worst has happened! This morning I was called over to the surgeon's office & told that I was to be the doctor for the Continental Base Headquarters Dispensary . . . in Bad Nauheim about 15 miles north of Frankfurt. . . . The trouble with the job is the politics of it. General Thrasher's mistress, Captain Kill (a nurse) thinks she runs the dispensary & with General Thrasher's backing she just about does. . . . . I suspect it will be Capt. Kill or me when we come to grips, as we undoubtedly will. I'll never put up with a nurse telling me what to do. I've already had one run-in with her when I refused to let her have a habit-forming drug (50 tablets of it) when she sent someone else over to get it. I could kill Taffet. He suggested my name to them yesterday. I literally figure there is a 50-50 chance I'll end up getting court marshaled. It makes me sick to even be among such people & such a situation, let alone to take orders from them. HELL! . . . The move to Frankfurt will probably take place the end of next week. . . .

Yesterday Madame Delamere asked me to dinner tonight. I went & really had a wonderful meal of roast duck, good soup, turnips, potatoes, salad, coke & red wine. . . .

Reims, France
Tuesday, 1 January 1946

Dearest Liz: Happy New Year, sweetie! . . .

Yesterday morning I was sick as a dog with a terrible cold & sinusitis but no fever. I was literally so weak I could hardly stand up. There was a lot to do, tho, so I did it. . . . Yesterday afternoon I went out to the 193rd to get my clearance papers from there. . . .

Twice during the afternoon I tried to call Louis to tell him I couldn't come last night, but was unable to get thru. When I got back here from the 193rd I felt like going in spite of my cold & did. The only available vehicle was an open 1½ ton truck. . . . It was very foggy & also freezing, so we hadn't gone half a mile before we had to just put down the windshield to see and go on. It was pretty good that way, but there was a $^{1}/_{8}$ inch coat of ice all over the front of me on arrival. I drove. Davis was with me.

The party at Louis' was very nice. We had dinner at his house, then sat around & talked till 11. Then Louis, Robert, Nicki, Jeanne, Armand (Jeanne's husband) & I all went over to their cousins' house for the regular party. There were about 20 people there in the 20–30 age group. All were very nice & we had a wonderful time. We danced to a phonograph till 12, then everyone (male & female) kissed everyone else on both cheeks & we sat down to supper of raw oysters (I didn't eat any because I was afraid of them) 2 kinds of fancy meat loaf, salad, cheese, dessert & Champagne, vintage 1934— the best year now available. After supper we danced, sang & talked till 3:30 when we went home. It was a really nice friendly, home party where everyone danced with everyone & a good time was had by all. I was the only American there, but felt more at home than I have for a long time. I knew about half the people there. Tommy's friend Nine was there with her sister Francoise, and I danced most with them. Francoise is the only French girl I've been able to dance decently with. Most of them bounce. Nine . . . and Francoise asked me to come to their house this afternoon for a party and to stay for supper & bridge. I accepted, but was unable to go when the time came because of lack of transportation. I slept at Louis' house (in pajamas!) till 8, then walked out to the 195th Gen. Hosp where I had left the truck & Davis & I drove back. It was nice being out so early. Sunrise is at 8:15. It was cold & clear without a cloud in the sky. A perfect New Year's Day. I wanted so much to enjoy it with you. . . .

Today I had a nice case of laryngitis, but in general felt better. I napped before & after lunch, did some re-packing, gave myself a couple of heat treatments for my sinuses & just loafed. We had a big turkey dinner both at lunch & at supper. We have mess cards at the mess downtown & also at a mess 2 doors from here. Actually only the duty officer is supposed to eat next door, but when there is an especially good meal the others do too. The town mess (Lion d'Or) has the big meal at noon & the one next door has it at night—thus 2 turkey dinners today. . . .

The mail clerk at the 193rd told me yesterday that they had NO mail in for 5 days. . . .

Liz, I wonder what you did on New Year's eve & New Year's. I pictured you at the Farm, at Cambridge, at Cedarhurst, at Port Washington, & even in New York. . . .

Jim returned to Germany from Rheims to be the doctor for the Continental Base Section Headquarters Dispensary in Bad Nauheim, north of Frankfurt. He took over and re-organized the dispensary, where once again he was understaffed with no supplies. As he had been taught by a savvy officer, Jim just needed to find the right regulation for the Army automatons to obey. That regulation read that for fixed dispensaries, the determination of staffing and supplies for requisition was up to "local needs." After that Jim could cite that regulation and was able to get whatever he needed, including three more medical officers to help him. He set up a large dispensary in a hotel, with 20 beds, two operating rooms, ambulances, etc., to serve the idle troops. It was the first "community dispensary" set up in Europe to serve as a clinic for both soldiers and their families. There were three doctors on rotating 24-hour shifts.

Bad Nauheim, Germany
Saturday, 5 January 1946

Dearest Liz: Your husband is just about all in tonight. I didn't get my business finished & into bed till 11:45, then was kept awake at least half the time until 5:30 when I got up. After a breakfast of grapefruit, rice crispies (2 boxes), 3 fried eggs (!) & bacon we loaded the 3/4 ton & ambulance & got away about 7:15. It was almost exactly 300 miles up here and we arrived about 5:45, an hour after dark. We had a terrible time getting settled in the right places, but finally did succeed. We were not supposed to arrive till tomorrow and, to add to the confusion, they didn't have a room for me as my name was not included on the list of officers they had up here. It appears to be a super deluxe plush set up—complete requisitioning of a big resort town, undamaged by the war. 15th Army Hq is here now but will deactivate soon & its men will probably join Continental Base Section. The billeting sergeant said: "Here every EM lives like an officer & every officer like a king." I have a small dimly lighted fairly nice room in a pension but have been told I'll be moved later to better quarters. There are sheets on the bed, which continues to be nice.

The wool socks & knit helmet you sent last year—as well as the sweater & scarf—saw stellar service coming up here today. It was cloudy & cold, freezing cold while driving the ¾ ton. As usual on long drives, I occupied myself with thoughts of you—all pleasant ones.

Jim was landing back in Germany, but not in the setting he had hoped for. Always a doctor to the core, he wanted to be in a hospital where he could see a wide range of patients and be challenged, rather than in a dispensary where the medicine was routine. And then there were the dreaded General Thrasher and his mistress Captain Kill. Jim quickly cheered up as he settled into Bad Nauheim. The city was untouched by the war, reportedly at the direct order of President Roosevelt, who loved the place. The Roosevelt family had stayed at the resort town for a month or two each summer from 1891 until 1900 so that Franklin's brother James could take the baths. In 1891, at the age of nine, FDR attended the German primary school there for a month. He later described this experience as his introduction to German militarism and discipline.

Sunday, 6 January 1946
Bad Nauheim, Germany

Sweetheart: What a spot this turned out to be! As far as living is concerned, it is wonderful—by that you can tell your husband is getting good food & drink. . . .

I am eating at the Grand Hotel—a first rate hotel with cooking literally comparable to Locke-Ober's—tho the stuff they have to work with limits them. All of the flavor is left in the food which is well served with clean linen table cloths & napkins every meal! . . . I noticed wine on the menu at 15 marks ($1.50) a bottle & ordered a bottle tonight. It turned out to be a really good Mosel, the best I've had since I've been over here. In fact it was so good I ate a second full dinner in order to finish the rest of the wine! . . . I've checked the other 4 officers' messes in town & none of them compare. Strangely enough, the Grand is the least popular, I think the "high-toned" atmosphere gets on the nerves of the Vestal type officer. That suits me. They also have very good dinner music. I was amused this noon when they played as Chamber Music, of all things: "Milkman, Keep Those Bottles Quiet!"! . . . Bad Nauheim is a beautiful resort town untouched by the war. Being here is just like living at a big resort. There are mineral baths & massages available, skating, golf course, tennis courts, & even one squash court! I see where I have the time of my life, except for your absence. The weather continues cold.

It was 12 above all day & is down to 5 above tonight.

This afternoon I went to a symphony, the program of which is enclosed. . . . I went chiefly because you would have wanted to go and enjoyed it chiefly because I mentally held hands with you all the time the lights were out. Tonight after supper I went to see Betty Hutton in "Incendiary Blonde." After that I went up to the station & waited around till the train came in with the bulk of the men & officers, took care of one sick man & came back to write you before going to bed. . . .

Jim had a former Luftwaffe pilot from Berlin as a driver for the truck he had available. He was amused by the man's disdain for Allied forces.

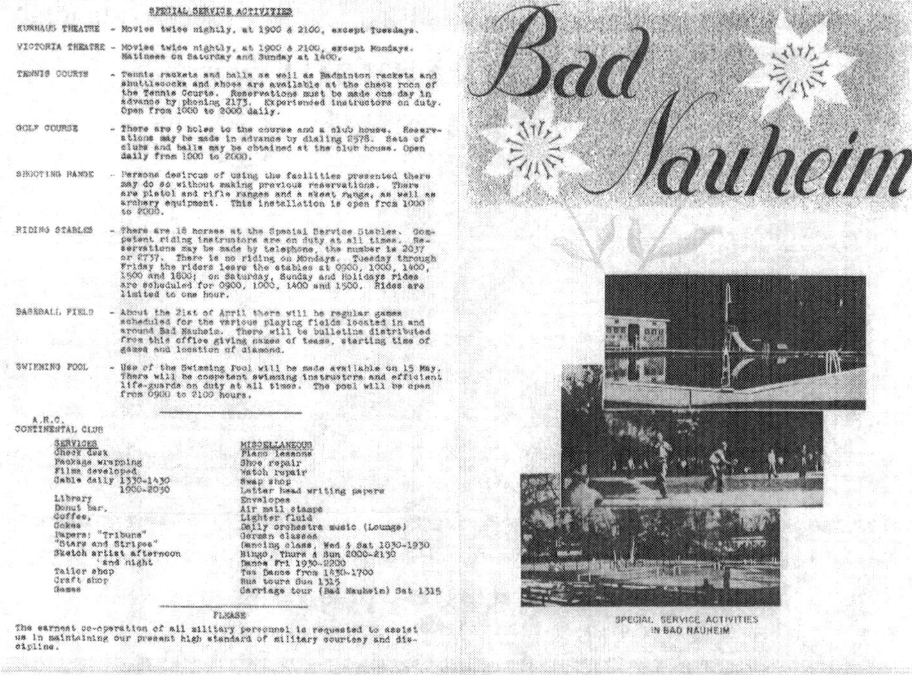

SPECIAL SERVICE ACTIVITIES

KURHAUS THEATRE - Movies twice nightly, at 1900 & 2100, except Tuesdays.

VICTORIA THEATRE - Movies twice nightly, at 1900 & 2100, except Mondays. Matinees on Saturday and Sunday at 1400.

TENNIS COURTS - Tennis rackets and balls as well as Badminton rackets and shuttlecocks and shoes are available at the check room of the Tennis Courts. Reservations must be made one day in advance by phoning 2173. Experienced instructors on duty. Open from 1000 to 2000 daily.

GOLF COURSE - There are 9 holes to the course and a club house. Reservations may be made in advance by dialing 2578. Sets of clubs and balls may be obtained at the club house. Open daily from 1000 to 2000.

SHOOTING RANGE - Persons desirous of using the facilities presented there may do so without making previous reservations. There are pistol and rifle ranges and a skeet range, as well as archery equipment. This installation is open from 1000 to 2000.

RIDING STABLES - There are 18 horses at the Special Service Stables. Competent riding instructors are on duty at all times. Reservations may be made by telephone, the number is 2037 or 2737. There is no riding on Mondays. Tuesday through Friday the riders leave the stables at 0900, 1000, 1400, 1500 and 1800; on Saturday, Sunday and Holidays rides are scheduled for 0900, 1000, 1400 and 1500. Rides are limited to one hour.

BASEBALL FIELD - About the 21st of April there will be regular games scheduled for the various playing fields located in and around Bad Nauheim. There will be bulletins distributed from this office giving names of teams, starting time of games and location of diamond.

SWIMMING POOL - Use of the Swimming Pool will be made available on 15 May. There will be competent swimming instructors and efficient life-guards on duty at all times. The pool will be open from 0900 to 2100 hours.

A.R.C.
CONTINENTAL CLUB

SERVICES
Check desk
Package wrapping
Films developed
Cable daily 1330-1430
1900-2030
Library
Donut bar,
Coffee,
Cokes
Papers: "Tribune"
"Stars and Stripes"
Sketch artist afternoon and night
Tailor shop
Craft shop
Games

MISCELLANEOUS
Piano lessons
Shoe repair
Watch repair
Swap shop
Letter head writing papers
Envelopes
Air mail stamps
Lighter fluid
Daily orchestra music (Lounge)
German classes
Dancing class, Wed & Sat 1830-1930
Bingo, Thurs & Sun 2000-2130
Dance Fri 1930-2200
Tea Dance from 1430-1700
Bus tours Sun 1315
Carriage tour (Bad Nauheim) Sat 1315

PLEASE

The earnest co-operation of all military personnel is requested to assist us in maintaining our present high standard of military courtesy and discipline.

Bad Nauheim

SPECIAL SERVICE ACTIVITIES
IN BAD NAUHEIM

A brochure listing Special Service activities in Bad Nauheim, Germany; author's personal collection.

Bad Nauheim, Germany
Monday, 7 January 1946

Dearest Liz: Today was another busy one. I got up about eight, made arrangements for unloading our stuff from the trucks & putting it under lock & key, got my hair cut & shoes shined, checked over the 15th Army Dispensary, & saw Col.

White, the Continental Base Section Surgeon ["Surgeon" was the title for the head of all the medical personnel in the Section] about how & where they want the Dispensary set up. I'm probably going to have to get another building. . . .

In the afternoon I went down to Frankfurt to the 97th General Hospital. It is located just outside of the city in an ex-Luftwaffe Hospital. After dropping off 5 patients for consultation I went on into Frankfurt to see it & to try to locate Frau Sauer & Fritz & Ruth Weispfenning, with whom I lived while there 11 years ago. None of them were registered & the houses where both had lived were bombed out. An Emilie Weispfenning, whom I believe to be Fritz's kid sister was registered, so when I get time I'll look her up to see if she can give me any further information. She lives in a small town outside of Frankfurt toward the town of Hochst. . . .

In 1935, Frieda Sauer was Jim's landlady for the four months he spent in Frankfurt, and he became good friends with the family, especially Frieda's daughter, Ruth, and her husband, Fritz Weispfenning. Jim was an usher at Fritz and Ruth's wedding in January of 1935. Like many Germans, Frieda, Ruth, and Fritz lost their homes to air raids by Allied forces. Jim eventually discovered that Frau Sauer had moved to her hometown, Darmstadt, on the Rhine 10 kilometers south of Frankfurt. Jim stayed in contact with the family after the war and sent them care packages with food for years. Forty-four surviving letters from the Weispfenning family to the McKay family paint a grim picture of life for ordinary Germans after the war. (See Appendix, "The Sauer/Weispfenning Family Letters: 1946-1954.") The McKay family had dinner with Fritz and his wife at their apartment in Frankfurt in 1960, but that was the last contact until I met Fritz's surviving sons in 2014.

Bad Nauheim, Germany
Tuesday, 8 January 1946

Dearest Liz: . . . .

After lunch I reported to (Lt) Col. Boshoff, the Headquarters Commandant & arranged for storage space for our four truckloads of junk. After that I had an all afternoon conference with the two sergeants on the organization & administration of the new dispensary. . . .

Tonight I had dinner with the Continental Base Section Chief Chaplain, a Jesuit priest. We had a 2 hour argument about religion & Catholicism over a bottle of wine. We agreed fairly well basically, I think, but couldn't get together because the vantage point of his thinking was that Catholicism is the ONLY true religion. He said my beliefs were all right so far as they go, but that they constitute a "natural" religion, & a "supernatural" religion is better.

Liz, I wish I could drink my wine & discuss the problems of the world with you instead of with a priest. . . .

Bad Nauheim, Germany
Wednesday, 9 January 1946

Dearest Liz: . . . .

This slowdown in redeployment is not surprizing—first because we were told it would occur and second because to my mind the fact still remains that the only way we'll be able to fill our occupational needs is by universal service. All this talk about a large enough volunteer army is a lot of bologney. The large number of men now volunteering don't mean a thing. They are <u>at</u> <u>least</u> 75% men with such low points that they figured they were stuck for the period of their reenlistment anyway. . . . Quite frankly I consider Universal Service a <u>far</u> lesser evil than reduction of our occupying & garrison forces.

This afternoon was spent in making arrangements for the arrival & billeting of a dentist arriving in the dispensary, & in studying. The dentist, Capt. Eagle, is now here. . . .

Captain Eagle turned out to be less than congenial and a thorn in Jim's side. As an unabashed communist, Eagle brought out Jim's own strongly held opposing beliefs.

Bad Nauheim, Germany
10 January 1946

Dearest Liz: This will have to be short as it is after 12:30. Since 6:30 I have been arguing about Russian and the Communist Parties of various countries with Eagle, the new dentist. As usual in such an argument I came out second best because arguing with a man who believes in Communism is like arguing with a Catholic—he's right & you're wrong from the start. Communism is right because it's communism & everyone who opposes it is a Fascist in greater or less degree. All dictatorships are Fascist—except a communist dictatorship, which is OK because it is communist. Communist violence & change of direction & failure to cooperate etc. etc. are all OK because they have nothing but the highest motives. . . . The motives of anyone who opposes any part of communist procedure or practice are low, subversive, criminal & "Fascist" of necessity. <u>Only</u> a Communist can have decent thoughts & purposes. BAH! It's like reading PM [*PM* magazine was a competitor to *Life* magazine]. I should just quit trying to discuss politics &

religion. If you try to be fair you're sunk. No one is interested in that.

. . . I spent the whole day sitting around the dispensary doing nothing (Study is impossible because of noise & interruptions) because Col. Boshoff told me I was to be there during duty hours. I did get in a few good games of ping-pong on a table they have upstairs. So "good" is my physical condition that my legs are sore after that mild exercise.

. . . I had to sign a questionnaire today as to whether I wanted to volunteer for varying periods. I signed the Category V statement "I wish to be released from the service at the earliest possible date." Do you agree? . . .

Jim described how German POWs filtered back into the country as they were released. When he first arrived in Bad Nauheim, Jim was living in a house with six other officers, four of whom had German mistresses living with them. Jim thought the German women were there as a means of getting good food and decent living conditions. When Jim moved in, another officer had moved out, and his German mistress proposed an arrangement to Jim, which he refused. She was married to a German soldier who had gone missing early in the war. Not long after he refused her, her husband appeared. The husband later came to see Jim and thanked him for not taking her in (apparently unaware of her previous entanglements).

Bad Nauheim, Germany
Friday, 11 January 1946

Dearest Liz: . . .

So far I have not even seen Capt. Kill, the nurse I wrote about, & have been getting along fine with Col. Boshoff, C.O. of Hq Battalion and OK with Col White, the CBS (Continental Base Section) Surgeon. At first they kept telling me what to do, but they didn't tell me to do a single thing I wasn't able to report as already done. This afternoon Col. Boshoff told me when I asked him about leaves for a couple of the men that I was running the dispensary and could give my men furloughs & run things as I pleased as long as they went well—that it was my job and he didn't intend to interfere with it. I think he meant it. If so, it is a great advantage to start with because several of my predecessors complained bitterly about interference from him. Another bit of news was a rumor from 15th Army sources that one of their major generals was going to take over command of CBS. That would probably break the stranglehold of the present political clique.

Tonight Eagle & I went to see the much advertised "True Glory" documentary war picture. It may be good documentation, but it doesn't give a picture of what it's like to fight a war because it hits only the high spots & you don't see the dirty dog-tired eternal struggle to just exist which is the way it is when you're fighting it.

I just sorted out all the pictures of you among those you've sent in the 14 months (today) we've been apart. The similarities between little 10 year old Lizzie in her old sweater & cut foot on the coast of Maine had a striking similarity to those of her in her husband's old green cashmere sweater 15 years later. I love them both. . . .

Bad Nauheim, Germany
Saturday, 12 January 1946

Dearest Liz: . . .

This afternoon I was on duty & saw patients off & on all day. At lunch I saw Steinbring & Reed [Milton Steinbring and Charles Reed, fellow officers from the 275th Engineers], who arrived last night. I didn't have a chance to talk to them. I had another argument with Eagle, who apparently is an out & out dictatorship communist of the worst type. . . . One minute later he was praising the wholesale & universal killing (he brought the subject up—I hadn't know it before) of all Polish Officers by the Russians. He praised it because it was the way to rid the world of a bad anti-communist element, "ALL Polish officers being feudal aristocrats." He then started saying that all the "Fascists" in America should be handled the same way. He defined "Fascists" as those who want the people to work for the government, not the government for the people. He identified the "Fascists" as the "aristocracy" & bourgeoisie, whom he further identified as "those making over $5,000 a year." All such people are "Fascists" according to him & should be killed. FDR doesn't count as a Fascist, tho, nor does Marshall Field, because he owns PM. . . . He admits that the Russians use the same methods as the Nazis, but that is different, because they are communists. That is the thinking which to my mind makes communism such a menace. They appeal, as did the Nazis, to the consciences of the other side, but have no conscience themselves, but are utterly ruthless. How can ends gained by such means & with such principles be good? He scares me more than any amount of anti communist propaganda, because I honestly believe that he would feel the world would be a better place without any "Princeton aristocrats" & would slit my throat with as much compunction as I would kill a fly when the "revolution" comes. If Russia thinks the way he thinks, we are the next victims on her list and any stab in the back will be justified because we are a nation of capitalists. Eagle is a Jewish boy from the Bronx. His father is a tailor, apparently not a well off one. Why he thinks arousing prejudice & persecution of "capitalists," "fascists," & "aristocrats" is going to limit, instead of spread, prejudice against other groups such as the Jews is beyond me. As soon as that sort of thinking is thru with one victim, it looks around for another. . . .

As the occupation units became established, officers could apply to bring their families to Europe. Career officers received first priority. Jim and Liz considered it, but Jim never applied. Having told the army that he wanted to be discharged at the earliest opportunity, he was unlikely to be approved anyway. In addition, Liz had a good job and an apartment in New York. They were living month to month in the expectation of Jim's return home. Meanwhile, Jim settled into Bad Nauheim, a place that suited him well. There was good fishing nearby, excellent food, and increasing contact with the intellectually stimulating people that Jim craved.

A map of Bad Nauheim, Germany, with Jim's annotations for Liz.

The map of the town that he sent to Liz, annotated with the important buildings in his life, was a great help to me in 2014 as I searched for the places that my father frequented. I found the town little changed. As I walked south from his second dispensary location off Bode Strasse, crossing the Usa

River below the bath houses and through the park to the red clay tennis courts, I had no trouble imagining my father taking the same walk.

Bad Nauheim, Germany
Sunday, 13 January 1946

Dearest Liz: . . .

I had lunch with Charles & Milton, played ping-pong with them for a while and took a two hour nap. They said that present plans are for the establishment of 137 G-I communities here, one of which will be Bad Nauheim. The first wives are supposed to arrive about April 1st. . . . I imagine that Category V officers like me (who requested release from the Army at the earliest opportunity) will be at the bottom of the list. However, if it looks like you might get here 1 or 2 months before I leave, what do you want to do? I am pretty darn sure now that I'll get home by the end of June. . . .

Jim's letters always began with a report on what letters he had received from Liz. All his mail was addressed to him at the APO (Army Post Office) in New York, and then sent on to wherever his unit might be. His transfer to Bad Nauheim, and the snafus of the army trying to get mail to the millions of men who were being assigned to new units, caused the longest stretch of "no mail" that Jim and Liz endured. It was now over two weeks since her last letters had found Jim.

Bad Nauheim, Germany
Wednesday, 16 January 1946

Dearest Liz: . . .

This afternoon I checked supplies, fought with the postal officer over the mail service, worked on straightening out our tangled orders in the dispensary, & had an hour's talk with Capt. Kill. She is no lioness, but just a rather faded & self-important nurse, less bad on first impression than some others I've had to handle. . . .

My pay has been sort of mixed up lately with the frequent changes in station. Let me know just what war bonds & allotment checks you get starting Oct 1st & running thru to the present. I've been deducting the bond & allotment regularly, but am not sure the bond, especially, is coming thru. . . .

Bad Nauheim, Germany
Thursday, 17 January 1946

Dearest Liz: . . .

This afternoon saw my first brush with General Thrasher on the subject of sleeping pills. He sent his sergeant-major-domo over to get some. I gave him three with a label on the box that they are habit-forming. Eventually we'll clash on the subject and I suppose I'll go out on my ear with a low efficiency rating. I hope he'll take the hint, but doubt if he will. I feel very low about my job again tonight with the appearance of a mountain of administrative work & pressure from above to do things I consider poor medical practice, waste of personnel, & ordinary inefficiency. Tonight is one of those times when I need you. I'm writhing physically & mentally in a hollow tube leading to nowhere, while outside the tube at the very spot where I am, useful work could be done, were I not encased in the tube. If you were here you could at least calm me down to the point of sleeping. . . .

I just finished reading over the last of your letters I hadn't already re-read in the past 3 days. Now there's just GOTTA be mail tomorrow. Today was 2 weeks since the last letter.

Bad Nauheim, Germany
Friday, 18 January 1946

My darling Sweetie: After 15 days today was finally a good day with the arrival of your letters of January 3rd & 4th. . . .

[T]he redeployment news today was bad. It said that Congressional sentiment was strongly against continuation of the draft, but that they <u>were</u> considering [a] universal service bill instead. The hitch in that universal service bill being considered is that it stipulates that none of the training period be outside the continental limits of the U.S. . . .

This morning we moved our equipment from a storeroom to a storage place in the hotel where the dispensary is to be set up. The labor we secured was ten middle-aged well-dressed men. The system here in Germany is that no Nazis who held any sort of party office can do anything but manual labor—and that only the forced labor kind of stuff we had them doing today. So all these guys were Nazi smalltime bigwigs. One had been a regimental surgeon in the German Army. He is not allowed to practice because of his political affiliations. It both amused me & made me a little ashamed to see them working. They certainly deserve it, yet it goes a little against the grain to see elderly men taking a physical beating while young able-bodied men tell them what to do. The men (U.S. soldiers) felt the same way. I couldn't help but wonder what had made those individuals a part of the Nazi group. From looking at them I would guess they were just men who got caught in the general mob psychology but who, because of superior ability, fell into the responsible positions—for which they now have to take the responsibility. From their attitudes & types & my previous knowledge of Germany I would guess that about half of them were true dyed in the wool Nazis. The others didn't care much & let the wrong current catch them.

This afternoon I worked on my history of the 277th Medical Detachment. [This "history" was a factual report documenting where the 277th had been, which Jim was required to submit at this time. As the commanding officer of the 277th, he was responsible, even though he had only been assigned to the 277th for three weeks!] I hope to finish it tomorrow. Tonight Eagle & I had dinner with Col. Boshoff and a friend of his. Boshoff is sure a typical Regular Army sergeant. We cannot eat at the Grand Hotel any more. 15th Army eats only there now. I'm eating at the Kaiserhof, which is good but not as good.

Sweetie, if you want a lobster dinner, get it even tho it does cost $2.50 or $3.50. After all, your husband is spending the dough like water & he doesn't believe in the double standard. . . .

Jim's discussion of well-dressed Nazis doing manual labor is interesting given the situation of his friend from 1935, Fritz Weispfenning, whose family Jim was soon to find. Fritz's experience fit Jim's description very well.

Bad Nauheim, Germany
Saturday, 19 January 1946

Dearest Liz: It's twelve o'clock. Steinbring & Reed have just left after shooting the bull since quarter of ten. We were bad boys and had six(!) drinks of rye—good rye—at the Kaiserhof Bar before supper after which we went to the movies. . . . Afterward we walked back here & talked about our wives & the time at POE & the war till just now. . . .

Bad Nauheim, Germany
Monday, 21 January 1946

Dearest Liz: . . .

The rest of the afternoon was occupied with trying to get penicillin for a German woman who is dying of peritonitis & whom there is a 50-50 chance it would pull thru. She is 36 & the mother of 5 children. I was unable to get it for her, however—Military Government gives it out only for use in VD cases! Of all the God Damn things I ever heard. Here is a case of life & death and we save it for a bunch of G-I bastards & German bitches. Aside from the purely humanitarian aspects of the case, it seems to me it would be more practical for us to save that woman than to have the care of her 5 children after she dies. Personally, I think if the Army announced publicly that it was no longer going to use penicillin for VD it would do more than any other single thing to reduce the VD rate. The viewpoint of the average soldier is that he doesn't care if he gets VD—it just means a few shots of penicillin and a few days off from duty. . . .

Charles Reed & I played squash for 40 minutes tonight. It was fun but no competition. I wish to hell I could find someone who can play it. . . .

My father told me an amusing story about his difficult relationship with his superiors. Jim received a reprimand from General Thrasher because of the high VD rate among the troops. Jim wrote a memo in response, itemizing the steps he thought needed to be taken to reduce the VD rate. The memo criticized superior officers who openly kept mistresses and recommended punishment.

Here is the text of Jim's memo:

To Hq. Comd. Surgeon CBS, Hq. Comdt.
SUBJECT: Venereal Disease Program

In view of the continuing high venereal disease rate (460 per 1000 per year) in this command, it is felt that [a] specific and vigorous VD program should be initiated immediately. Such a program is herewith submitted. This program aims at simplicity and practicality. It is directed at the individual soldier in an attempt to persuade him to make up his own mind that the game of possible exposure to venereal disease is not worth the candle. Also embodied in it are certain points which are directed at diminishing contacts on the theory that opportunity and exposure to venereal disease are in direct proportion. It is directed at maintaining the interest of each individual soldier in venereal disease and in keeping him completely and correctly informed on the subject. A program similar to the one proposed was used in a small command in France during the summer of 1945 with excellent results.

Perhaps the most important single factor in obtaining the cooperation of soldiers in carrying through a program of sexual continence (which remains the fundamental principle of the official Army attitude toward venereal disease control) is the example set by their officers, especially those of high rank. It is exceedingly difficult for a medical officer or unit venereal disease officer of company grade to obtain the cooperation of enlisted personnel in a program encouraging continence when the individual enlisted man sees his unit commander in the company of notorious women and knows that his commanding general keeps a mistress. The frequency of such practices by officers, especially by those of high rank, is a specific detriment to the carrying through of a successful venereal disease program.

DETAILS OF PROGRAM:

Continuance of present entertainment facilities available in Bad-Nauheim. These are excellent.

Placing of official VD posters in prominent places in all billets and offices of the command. (Hq. Bn. Surgeon has already ordered 50 of these from CBS Medical Supply.)

Offering of prizes for ideas and execution of original VD posters to be used within the command. These should preferably contain an element of humour, be to the point, be executed so as to catch the eye, and have local or personal interest for the troops of the command.

A series of weekly 15 minute talks on VD by the Dispensary Surgeon to be held in Victoria Theater at 1000 and 1030 each Friday morning with ½ of command present at a time. Schedule of talks to be published as follows:

1st week: "Gonorrhea"

2nd Week: "Easy to Get"—VD Training Film (New)

3rd Week: "Syphilis"

4th Week: "Pickup"—VD Training Film.

5th Week "Non-Specific Urethritis"

6th Week: "Chandreid"

7th Week: "Lymphe granuloma Venereum"

8th Week: "Lice, Crabs, and Scabies"

Uniform dispensing of condoms and individual pro kits in all orderly rooms of the command; this to consist of an official VD poster directly under which is nailed a compartmented cigar box containing condoms and pro kits with directions pasted on the outside of the box. Condoms and pro kits may be procured through QM issue or purchase at the PX. Directions should read as follows:

RUBBERS- Use EACH and EVERY time you have intercourse.

PRO KITS- Use IMMEDIATELY after EACH and EVERY time you have intercourse.

Punishment of officers under the appropriate Article of War for "publicly consorting with notorious prostitutes."

Confinement of gonorrhea cases to quarters in the Dispensary for three days at time of treatment to prevent any possible sexual contact during this period. (This measure has already been instituted.) This should also help our percentage of cures.

Arrest of unescorted women looking for a "pickup" along Parkstrasse, in the neighborhood of the EM Clubs, and at the railroad station between the hours of 1800 and 2300. This should be carried out by means of hourly walking patrols without armbands by the auxiliary provost marshals. The enlisted MPs simply do not pick these women up, whatever their orders.

Overnight detention of above-mentioned women with an examination and smear for VD by the civilian specialist on the following morning and immediate hospitalization at the Hadamar VD hospital if they are found to have it.

Prohibition of women in Army Billets with strict enforcement. (This measure has already been initiated.)

Initiation of a VD program aimed at the civilian population. This could be done through Military Government and would consist of public posters in German based on similar posters used in England by the British for their civilian population, and by institution of a well-publicized free VD clinic for civilians.

R.J. McK.
Hq. Comd. Surgeon
12 Feb. 46
Phone 2248

When his sergeant typed up the memo, he brought it into Jim's office, saying, "Captain, you can't send this." Jim insisted he wanted to send it, no matter the consequences. The junior officers and medical staff hated Thrasher and his mistress Captain Kill. Jim's sergeant was a buddy of the sergeants at Continental Base Section (CBS) HQ and also of the chief EM in the office of the base surgeon (chief medical officer of CBS), Colonel White. It was the end of the day when the sergeant delivered the memo to CBS HQ, where the officer in charge had to sign it. After conferring with his friend there, the sergeant brought Jim's memo to the officer (who also had a mistress) with a bunch of other papers requiring his signature, and got him to sign it without reading it. The sergeant then took Jim's memo to Colonel White, who also had to sign it. Colonel White detested Thrasher. White read it, signed it, and told the sergeant to commandeer a jeep and deliver it to HQ in Frankfurt immediately. By this time the officer at CBS HQ had actually read the memo, and called Jim to tell him "you can't submit this," but Jim told him it was too late, it had already gone to Colonel White. The HQ officer then called White, but by then the memo was in Frankfurt. The next day, Jim got a call from Frankfurt HQ, informing him that Thrasher was being removed from command and would be coming to Jim for the routine medical exam required on change of duty, but that Jim was not to examine him, but rather refer the general to doctors in Frankfurt. General Thrasher was discharged after being reduced in rank from his wartime rank of general back to his regular army rank. Jim, Colonel White, the sergeants, and many others were very happy about the whole thing—and the fact that they had gotten away with it, with no consequences.

Jim's memo in response to the reprimand may have been one factor in a major shake-up among the generals in Europe. General Thrasher was one of several generals who were demoted to the rank they held when arriving in Europe. Jim remembered the whole episode with glee and considered it his biggest victory in his long resistance to inept leadership in the army.

Bad Nauheim, Germany
Tuesday, 22 January 1946

Darling: . . .

The big news today is that General Thrasher is out! Apparently they are busting or retiring between 300 & 400 generals, of whom he is one. I believe he is going to retire. That should put quite a kink in Capt. Kill. . . .

They have transferred all of us in & out of so many different units so many different times that the orders are almost hopelessly snarled up. I spend & have spent about 2 hours a day on the problem for the past 2½ weeks. What a typical Army waste of time. I'm getting now so I'm almost as eager to get out of the Army altogether as I am to get home.

Bad Nauheim, Germany
Wednesday, 23 January 1946

Dearest Liz: . . .

This afternoon I went to Frankfurt to check on some points of dispensary administration with the big dispensary there. Afterwards I went out to Hochst to look up the Emilie Weispfenning whom I thought might be Fritz's sister. It was. She and another sister, whom I remember meeting a couple of times, and the latter's little son live in a small room a few blocks from their house which is being used as US Billets. Emmi said they had often wondered if I were in Germany & that her sister had seen someone yesterday who looked like me & they had been talking about it last night. Fritz, who was in the Navy is now being held by the British in a civilian internment camp because he was a party member. He was released from being a prisoner of war, but is now being held as a party member. He held a minor government office as a lower court judge which necessitated his belonging to the party. I know he was not any more of a Nazi than I am a New

Dealer. However, he laughed at it and belittled it in the privacy of his home instead of getting out & fighting it, so that is that. Ruth & her sister Hilda (whose husband, Fritz Etzel, was a real fire-eating Nazi with whom Fritz just couldn't get along) are in a small town near Schweinfurt with their children. Frau Sauer is living in Darmstadt, so I will go to see her sometime. . . .

Bad Nauheim, Germany
Saturday, 26 January 1946

Dearest Liz: . . . I had a very busy & annoying day. I saw 45 patients (think what that would be at $2 a call) before 3 o'clock, fired a maid who had been stealing, hired another one, etc, etc. At 3:30 I played squash with the Lt. who is special service officer for CBS. That was a waste of time as he couldn't even get the ball back once most of the time. I then waited an hour to try to play with another guy who looked as if he could at least get the ball back, only to find he decided he was too tired. God, how I wish someone congenial would arrive, preferably you!

Last night I talked German for about 2 hours with the woman who managed the pension, the night clerk & another girl who works here. It comes back fairly well. We talked some about the bombings. They still talk about how terrible the ruthless bombings of civilian centers of population are, yet even when you remind them of it, they completely close their minds to the fact that they started it. That remains the weakness of our side of the question as opposed to the Nazis & the communists. We approach a subject with a more or less open mind, they with a closed mind against everything even remotely connected with the other side of the question. The only thing they object to about Hitler are the troubles he brought on the Germans, not those he brought on others. Blitzing London is OK. The converse, blitzing Berlin, is not. That kills a lot of "innocent" civilians. They make me so damn mad.

Speaking of finances, did you pay my life insurance premium? . . . Your report of finances really sounded as if we had saved a lot. It sounds as if we are going to start out with a lot of money—close to $8,000 total, which should see us thru 4 years without any trouble, especially with G-I Bill of Rights money & residency income & your income added to it. Financially, I think we will be in a position where you are not going to have to work. Even if I'm still in the Army after I get home, we should still save money on my income as a captain, which will be $342 a month gross & about $300 a month with my G-I insurance, food & war bond deducted. We should certainly be able to save at least the difference between my former 1st Lt. income & my captain's income—about $55 a month. . . .

You asked about the effectiveness of occupation. I think that it is effective in keeping the Germans down and I also honestly believe that, despite the effect

> German thinking is having on the G-Is, the G-I thinking is Americanizing Germany even more rapidly. . . . Some troops are overworked, others do nothing at all. A group of 30–40 people working 8 hours a day could have done in the same length of time what the 15th Army (1500 troops, 2000 civilian employees) did. On the other hand, they don't have sufficient troops to guard the storage depots in France, & certain QM & other outfits are working with 1 officer, 6 EM and 100–2000 POWs. The entire APO system is not only superfluous, but interfering with the delivery of our mail. . . . There are corresponding wastes in other quarters. For instance, I need a Field Lab Chest which a Field Hosp which is closing here in Bad Nauheim has. Instead of their just signing it over to me & calling up the Weinheim medical depot to say they've done it, so Weinheim could change their records accordingly, I have to make out a requisition, get it approved at CBS (Continental Base Section) Headquarters, take it to Frankfurt personally for approval there, send a vehicle to Weinheim (80 miles one way) to present the requisition & another one a week later to pick up the chest. . . . That is the way everything is being done, & is basically what ties up the extra personnel—just like my 20 bed dispensary—we have a stack of personnel to run it when a hospital with full facilities in the same town & with the personnel required to run at full capacity runs at ½–$^{2}/_{3}$ capacity. . . .

Allied planners were thinking about the fate of Germany and her people, once the Allies prevailed, as early as 1943. Drawing from the experience of WWI, when Germany had emerged from defeat quickly and vigorously, rebuilt, and prepared for another war in just 20 years, the planners knew this time must be different. As WWII wore on in Europe, Allied thinking around the treatment of a defeated Germany evolved from an attitude born of a desire for revenge to one born of a more practical, long-term view of what a future Germany should look like.

Jim's attitude also evolved. As a result of his time in Germany before the war, Jim knew firsthand the military, cultural, and professional sophistication of the Germans when his 75th Division hit the front lines of the Battle of the Bulge in December of 1944. His exposure to the horrors of war was rapid and lasting. He knew all about the Malmedy Massacre of 80 American POWs that occurred on December 17, just north of the 75th Division sector, which strengthened the desire for vengeance among the American soldiers. His own experiences as a doctor on the front lines could not help but influence his attitude toward Germans. He told in later years of the profound effect of his experience of walking through a snowy field in Belgium, confirming the identities of three dead soldiers and tagging them for the Graves Registration

Unit that would pick them up. He undoubtedly saw horrific wounds. He saw Belgian, French, and Dutch villages utterly destroyed. In several of his letters to Liz, Jim was unforgiving in regard to how Germans should be treated in defeat. By 1946, however, eight months after the end of hostilities, his attitude was softening as he dealt with the everyday Germans around him, and learned of the fate of his good friend Fritz Weispfenning, who had ended the war as a German U-Boat Captain and was languishing in a POW camp.

Henry Morgenthau was Secretary of the Treasury under FDR. In 1944, he set forth an idealistic plan to render Germany "a land primarily agricultural and pastoral in its character," divided into three parts, and completely without the industrial capability ever to wage war again. He suggested that the standard of living of Germans "be held down to a subsistence level." A thirst for vengeance helped make this approach popular, and FDR supported it.

Henry Stimson was Secretary of War, 77 years old, and a realist. He argued that to attempt to economically oppress the German people, who were undeniably energetic, intelligent, and resourceful, would not prevent war, but rather breed the tensions and resentments that are the seed of war. Eliminate the Nazi philosophy, yes, but then allow the Germans to rebuild a productive economy. This approach came to be known as denazification.

The policy that emerged was somewhere between the Morgenthau Plan and the Stimson Plan. In the end, there was not a unified Allied plan, but rather a loose set of guidelines, which the Allies each interpreted and implemented in their own way in the zones they were responsible for. Jim's friend Fritz Weispfenning described his own experiences with the American policies after the war in his letters to Jim in 1947–48. (See Appendix)

Bad Nauheim, Germany
Monday, 28 January 1946

Dearest Liz: . . .

Today was another <u>very</u> busy one. I saw patients till 3 o'clock, then inspected a couple of messes, advised on disinfecting for diphtheria, etc. While at the Preventive Medicine Office looking up diphtheria prevention, I met a Captain Reagan who is the executive officer of the 4th Medical Lab, the Theater Medical Lab. He is a pathologist. They are moving up here from Darmstadt & he is picking a site. He, Capt. Sam Clemente (Prev. Med. Officer for CBS), Major Seeley (Exec. Officer of CBS Surgeon's Office) & I had supper together, then retired to Sam Clemente's room where we drank cognac & bulled chiefly on medical subjects till 11:30. It was good to talk medicine again & good to talk to someone who believes that heredity as well as environment plays a part in what an individual makes of his opportunities. I get so sick of Eagle's senseless harping on a complete environmental & leveling theory.

Bad Nauheim, Germany
Friday, 1 Feb 1946

Dearest Liz: . . .

I worked for a 9½ or 10 hour day today. This morning I saw patients til 10. Sgt. Berger & I then went thru the Alicenhof with the manager, Frau Litten, arranging the rooms & our moving in. We'll move tomorrow & open the dispensary there on Monday. Thursday we expect to have the 20 beds operating & going full speed ahead. The afternoon was spent in writing the monthly sanitary report & VD supplement.

Bad Nauheim, Germany
Saturday, 2 Feb. 1946

Dearest Liz: Tonight is one of those nights when you just wonder if it's worth the struggle. I guess it's because I haven't been getting enough sleep lately. To add to the general & usual Army annoyances, it's getting so I just can't stand the sight of Eagle. He's his own worst advertisement. At first I was interested to meet a communist. I thought I might learn something—perhaps I have: that their, or at least his, cerebral stenosis is even more marked than the peculiar loss of ability to think beyond a certain point which characterizes the Nazis, the Catholics, & (I'm now sure) the communists, each along certain lines. . . . I'm really beginning to see what a menace the communists are. Their rule & idea seems to be to run the world for the dumbest ass they can find. GAWD! . . . I'm getting awfully tired of hearing Eagle tell me who is a good dentist & who isn't. . . . He has missed two dental diagnoses in the past week which I've had to override him on & tell him what was wrong with the patient & how to treat it. I really learned quite a bit of diagnostic dentistry from Hagie [dentist for the 275th Engineers]. . . . Eagle is also becoming personally aggressive & unpleasant. . . . The less contact I have with him the better.

Bad Nauheim, Germany
Tuesday, 5 Feb 1946

Dearest Liz: . . .

Business was a lot less hectic and the dispensary really started to shape up. . . . I think it is really going to be very nice—actually a small hospital minus x-ray, operating room, & bacteriological facilities. In addition I'll have a roomy apartment right there. If only you could share it!

Bad Nauheim, Germany
Tuesday, 5 Feb 1946

Dearest Sweetie: Last night your husband was a bad boy & went out with the boys instead of staying home & writing his wife that he loves. Late yesterday afternoon who should appear but Armand d'Evry, Louis LeConte's brother in law—the one whose baby died last summer. He had come up to Wetzlar on a mission for General Mousabert, the French Zone Commander, & stopped off to say hello. It took him all afternoon to locate me, because he thought I was in Frankfurt & looked all over town there before someone finally told him CBS was in Bad Nauheim. Anyway, I asked him for supper & to spend the night, which he did. They had a banquet last night for the Headquarters Command Officers, then sat around drinking brandy & talking till 1 AM, at which point I was so tired that I started a letter to you & quit after 3 lines. We had a dandy time. After supper Armand & I called up Jeanne, his wife in Baden Baden & assured her he was out with the boys & not the frauleins. Then we sat down with Capt. Blackwell, a very nice guy from the 75th who is now Det. C.O. for Hq. Bn. of CBS. There we were joined by Maj. Smith, Deputy Commandant, & Major Seeley from the Surgeon's Office. My troubles with Smith, who is a small-time ignoramus, are greatly lightened after last night. He worked for the Army as a civilian before the war, holds an infantry Commission & has no battle stars. He was very impressed with Armand, who is a hell of a nice guy, & even more so with the fact that Armand is very close to General de Mousabert. He was likewise impressed with what good friends we are, so I am now the recipient of his kow-towing to twice-reflected glory. . . .

General Bresnahan, our new general looks OK to me. He inspected the dispensary yesterday & chewed me up & down for some things which were wrong & got me on the ball about them, but the thing he really sat on was too many men employed for the number of troops we serve. Of course, he's absolutely right. He ordered Col. Boshoff to cut down to bed rock, so I sloughed off 7 of my 16 men—most of those leaving being pretty much dead weights. He also came out in officers' call this morning & bluntly said he disapproved of "fraternizing" especially by his officers & especially by married men. I like his attitude. If he practices what he preaches he'll be OK. He must be pretty good because he is said to be the only BG (brigadier general) in the ETO who wasn't busted down to his permanent rank or retired last month.

Today I worked till 2:15, slept till 3, then played squash with Major Kirsh (Head of the Operations Division of the CBS surgeon's office), took a bath, went up to Seeley's room for a drink, had supper with him, Kirsh, & a gang from the Surgeon's Office, then Kirsh & I went to see John Wayne in "Dakota" and played ping-pong for 2¼ hours afterward. I'm ready to drop again. . . .

Bad Nauheim, Germany
Monday, 11 Feb 1946

Dearest Sweetie: . . .

This morning I saw 29 patients. The afternoon was spent signing papers, reading circulars & writing up a VD program which I finally finished. I'll send you a copy after it is typed up. Tonight I went to the Red Cross with Berger, Barraco, & Strickland, 3 of my men, where we played in the "Major League" ping-pong tournament. I met the best player in the first round & he whipped me. We then came back to the dispensary & have been playing here.

Your diabetic boy sounds like the sort of problem that's in my "neglected age group."

Stalin's speech before the Soviet "election" sure sounded like Hitler stuff to me. He sure has us over a barrel. If we wait war is inevitable. If we hop in now we're in a war & we don't want war. I don't believe the Russian people want war either, but their leaders do & they have the say. In our country the leaders still have to do by & large what the people want. . . . I'm so discouraged at the outlook of things I don't know which way to turn. . . .

Jim spent a lot of time on Venereal Disease. The VD rate among the soldiers in Bad Nauheim was as high as 46% at one point. He experienced huge frustration in trying to educate the troops because of the behavior of the officers, as noted earlier.

Bad Nauheim, Germany
Tuesday, 12 Feb 1946

Dear Sweetie: . . .

The Sgt. Major at Hq called me up late this afternoon to tell me he thought my VD program was damn good & to compliment me on coming right out about the behavior of high-ranking officers & its effect on EM morale. . . .

During this period it was difficult for Liz to keep up with what unit Jim was actually a part of. He periodically wrote it out and told her who his co-workers were.

Bad Nauheim, Germany
Wednesday, 13 Feb 1946

Dearest Liz: . . .

The 277th Medical Detachment is the medical unit attached to CBS to run the dispensary. It consists of a doctor, a dentist & 8 EM. I'm the doctor & CO.

Hence my responsibility for the 1945 history. The personnel, beside me are:

Capt. Emmanuel Eagle—dentist

T/Sgt Edward Berger—pharmacist & 1st Sgt. (Philadelphia)

S/Sgt Joe Possert—chief clerk & 2nd ranking NCO. He's from N.J.

T/4 Tony Barraco—a very good surgical technician

T/5 Warren Hency—" " " medical " (Vincennes, Ind)

T/5 Mike Serlucco—Med. Technician & physiotherapist.

T/5 Dick Strickland—Surg. technician

T/5 Delles—Med technician

T/5 Cooksey—Driver

T/5 Stewart—Clerk

They are a pretty good bunch. We are one over strength, but are due to lose both Berger & Cooksey because they have 3 years service. . . .

Jim had pushed for the dispensary to be a "community" dispensary, open to the Allied forces and their families, which were starting to arrive to join the regular army officers who would be staying for the occupation. In addition there were a lot of Allied civilians working for the army. German residents used their own doctors and the German hospital in town.

By this time Jim had abundant experience with the full range of medical problems afflicting young men in the army, but only a smattering of experience with a more general population. The following letter reveals Jim's inexperience as well as his early dilemma over abortion.

Bad Nauheim, Germany
Thursday, 14 Feb 1946

Dearest Liz: . . .

Today I had a woman come in complaining of nervousness. It was apparent something was in back of it & I guessed she was afraid she was pregnant, which turned out to be the case. She is a British civilian secretary here. It put me in quite a spot because she wanted me to give her something. I finally gave her some phenobarbital, pretty much under false pretenses that it was an abortefacient. I figured it might calm her down for a few days till she could get hold of herself or her period came around anyway. I tried to get her to resign herself to either being pregnant or not. However, she says her father is a straight-laced religious fanatic & it would kill him & she'd rather do away with herself. She apparently felt there was no hope of support or even understanding from her parents. She is also engaged & is really a pretty nice girl in spite of a rather poor background. I think that an abortion in this instance is undoubtedly the thing to do. She is going to

Paris to meet her fiancée this weekend & I told her to go see the doctor there, get an A-2 test & find out if she really is pregnant, then perhaps he'd recommend a fairly reputable abortionist. It put me in a hell of a quandary & I feel the case as a dismal failure because I did not face the issue, but passed the buck. What do you think? To give her anything to even try to abort her is malpractice. I never have been able to make my own mind up, either, as to whether abortion or going thru with an illegitimate pregnancy was better under our present "code of morals."

. . . You are right that the last 3½ years have been wonderful even tho we've been apart so much. Having you has given me something to hang on to and all my memories of you & dreams of you are pleasant & wonderful with no regrets or fears or forebodings. That is something not many people have. The vivid memory I have of the morning I left Boston for Miami [a visit to Uncle Jack McKay during medical school] is the blue of the full-packed car as I got in & the blue of your bathrobe as we said good-bye & you shivered in the spring air. . . .

Jim and Liz were obviously dreaming of their future and exchanged ideas on their future family, house, and work.

Bad Nauheim, Germany
Friday, 15 Feb 1946

Dearest Liz: . . .

I agree with you on the building of a house—build a small central section, then add wings as we can afford them. That will also spread out the cost. The group clinic sounds like a good idea. It will be interesting to see how it works out. It doesn't work out in the Army because the patients only have time to wait for one clinic during an afternoon —tho I guess that's really the same set up as now—NOT group practice.

Bad Nauheim, Germany
Monday, 18 Feb 1946

Dearest Liz: . . .

As always Monday was a busy day but was distinguished today by no case of gonorhea!!!!! The rate is falling rapidly & I hope it keeps on falling. . . .

If, as you say, the bigwigs say they can't get men overseas during 1 year of universal service, then I don't see how selective service & volunteer service are the answer either. . . .This business of keeping universal service draftees home for a year is ridiculous. After 6 weeks of basic they could go overseas & complete their training there. The Army would get its occupation troops & the kids would get a trip to Europe.

That G-D bastard Eagle is in here puffing & blowing like a hippopotamus

& stinking the room up with the cigarette smoke he's blowing in my face, while he puts out his old cigarettes on my floor. I've really gotten so I actively dislike cigarettes. Eagle is a communist, tho it is a secret from the Army. . . .

Was Jim sending a not-so-subtle message to Liz, who was a smoker at the time?

Bad Nauheim, Germany
Saturday, 23 Feb 1946

Dearest Liz: . . .

Today I had a patient, a nurse, from Billings, Montana. She described it in glowing terms. Population is 28,000 in a rich agricultural area, surrounded by mountains & good fishing etc etc—& no pediatricians plus a population which likes to go to a specialist. . . .

Bad Nauheim, Germany
Monday, 25 Feb 1946

Darling: . . .

My gross income is $4344 in answer to your question, so you see that you still contribute a hell of a lot to our income. I wonder if I'll ever support you?

Bad Nauheim, Germany
Thursday, 28 Feb 1946

Dearest Liz: . . .

In the middle of the afternoon a guy arrived who told me a 7th Army inspection team would inspect us tomorrow. They actually have no jurisdiction over us, but apparently part of the mixup on our orders has given them that idea. It is unfortunate as our property book is not yet set up & that is one of the things they are sure to want to check. Ho-hum. There goes a good rating right there. . . .

I think you might as well stay at work till I call, even if you know I'm arriving. I think it will be better if you keep yourself occupied. If I arrive out of working hours I'll go direct to your apartment & then to 45 [Jim's parents' apartment] in case you aren't at your apartment. . . .

I'm continuing optimistic & still bucking to leave here between April 1st & 30th. I sure hope it works out that way. I would like to get home for our wedding anniversary—to please you only, of course. . . .

Goodnight, Liz. I love you more than I'll ever be able to tell you & I hope to be able to start telling you soon.

Jim

Bad Nauheim, Germany
Friday, 1 March 1946

Dearest Liz: . . . [T]his afternoon I heard via my underground that they are planning to move the dispensary someplace else & operate a 30 bed dispensary in place of the station hospital they expected to get & which apparently is not coming here. I'm scared stiff that I'll get the job. It is really discouraging to have it happen just as I'm getting this place to function right. I'm sick & tired of working my ears off organizing one new place after another. If they want to give all that work to someone, some of these Regular Army jokers should be doing it. . . .

When I think of Sundays, I think of our winter Sundays at 128 Ft. Washington Ave, & of those in Henderson. It was funny you should mention my operatic singing, because I was thinking of it only this morning.

Armand d'Evry called up this morning to ask me to come down to a party at Heidelberg Saturday. I couldn't, so he may come up here on Sunday.

Bad Nauheim, Germany
Saturday, 2 March 1946

Dearest Liz: Today was another good one. Your letter of Feb. 21st arrived. It was written on your way to Boston for Washington's Birthday weekend. I had another busy day seeing patients & writing sanitary reports plus four sick patients. Tonight there are eleven patients on the ward. The sickest is a guy who is having a reaction from a shot of diphtheria toxoid. He is one of my own men—Strickland. I sure hope he's better tomorrow. He has been sick as a dog all day. I had another interesting case—one who clinically sure looked like diphtheria, so I sent him to the hospital.

The weather continues to consist of snow squalls interspersed with warm spells so the snow does not accumulate. There is good skiing in the hills 20 miles from here, but I unfortunately cannot go, because there is no one to cover for me. . . .

Tonight I went with Sam Clemente to see "Arsenic & Old Lace" which I had never seen. It was very funny, but would have been much more so if I had been able to see it with you. Without you, everything seems a little bit flat.

My British girl has just missed her second period, so I'm quite sure that she is pregnant. The A-2 test doesn't get back till Tuesday. Sometime between now & then I have to find out what to do about her. It is very difficult here in a strange country. She looks so bad that I really am afraid of what she'll do when she finds out she is pregnant for sure. Even when you don't mess with WOMEN they cause you trouble. You're the exception, sweetie, that proves the rule. . . .

Bad Nauheim, Germany
Sunday, 3 March 1946

Dearest Liz: . . .

As you surmized [sic] from my remarks, the situation as regards women & VD is terrific. It is better now than before. Under 15th Army about 70% of the officers & men lived openly with women. Now it's down to about 10% & is not so open. I consider that chiefly a commentary on the behaviour of the Commanding General. General Bresnahan is a good strict Irish Catholic who seems determined not to play favorites with the rank or to have any "palace guards." You are right that it is going to present quite a problem when they do get wives over here.

The problem of your coming over here seems to be automatically solved, because I am still reasonably sure about getting home by July 1st.

Tonight at supper, the Hq Bn. adjutant, Lt. Cain, told me a buck slip was on its way requesting me to submit a plan for & set up medical service for the G-I community here. They figure it may number up to 5,000 people. That is going to be quite a job. . . .

I don't consider Eagle a maladjusted fool any more than I consider Stalin one. I think he's a lot more dangerous that he is maladjusted. People called Hitler a maladjusted fool, too, & didn't recognize the danger till it was almost too late. I think the US communists are a greater menace than ever, because they are consciously or unconsciously the tools of a Russia seeking world power & domination under the guise of "helping the working men of the world." . . .

Jim's attitude was getting decidedly tetchy, with the roller coaster of rumors about dates of re-deployment, and his growing unrest with the army. The lack of simpatico companions in his new location didn't help any. Descriptions of his social life are almost totally gone at this stage.

Bad Nauheim, Germany
Monday, 4 March 1946

Dearest Liz: . . .

On my way over to supper I stopped in at Hq. to sign in back from Frankfurt to find Maj. Smith & Col. Boshoff in quite a stew. I had included my VD Program in the monthly sanitary report with the crack about high officers & their mistresses. I made a direct reference to "the commanding general keeps a mistress" thinking of Thrasher. Boshoff had signed it without reading it & then Smith read the copy after the original was forwarded. Boshoff was so scared the general [now Bresnahan, not Thrasher any more] would see it & think it was aimed at him (which it wasn't) that he couldn't even bawl me out. He was tearing around trying to get back the original. I have to go up to see him in the morning by which time he will have recovered enough to give me hell. He told me tonight "My God, man! Sending that thru is like planting a bomb." I told him that's what it was meant to be & that stopped him, but probably won't for long. I'm a little worried but it was fun while it lasted. Of course, he is right about the "commanding general" part & I'll delete that but he'll never be able to get me to take back what else I said about high-ranking officers, because that is what he'll probably try to do & will be where the real trouble will start. I knew we were going to come into conflict sooner or later on that subject.

Most of the evening was spent playing in the ping-pong tournament at the Red Cross Club. . . .

Redeployment news remains at a standstill, but I'm less optimistic. The 18 months rotation deal is <u>not</u> going thru & the bringing over of families is going to mean they'll need more docs. Boy, I hope I don't get caught in that. I'll have to keep my pediatric training a secret. They do plan to rotate Docs after 30 months overseas, so I have only 20½ mos to go for that. However, I'm pretty sure I'll get home before that. . . .

Bad Nauheim, Germany
Tuesday, 5 March 1946

Dearest Liz: . . . I understand there is a blizzard going on in England which may be holding up shipping & is certainly holding up planes. Germany apparently has enjoyed the best winter in Europe this winter.

The interview with Col. Boshoff this morning turned out not to be too bad. I was helped by a very timely article on officers having frauleins to their quarters for the night, which appeared on the front page of the Stars & Stripes. It said there would be an investigation. I told Boshoff right out that he was one of the people I specifically meant when I wrote that. He took it much the same way Knute did when we had our little talk about the officers quarters at Breckinridge.

Another little item of interesting news cropped up today along the same lines. That was that Gen. Thrasher was removed because of his relationship with Capt. Kill. I hope it is true, because it is more or less a healthy sign. General Bresnahan is said to have received specific orders to be hyper-careful about anything like that. The latest is that he is planning to ban frauleins from the officers' club & dances. Today was the easiest one I've had since I took over. My ward is quite full, including a Lt. Col & a major, but no one is very sick. I had two interesting cases. One was a probably ruptured appendix, the other a Red Cross girl with probably amebic hepatitis. They went to the 97th Gen Hosp.

This afternoon I even had time to get a haircut & I also called on the General (professionally) to doctor his "runs." Tonight I'm going to see Bob Hope in "Road to Utopia."...

Bad Nauheim, Germany
Saturday, 9 March 1946

Dearest Liz: . . .

Yesterday I forgot to tell you that I had lunch with 5(!!) women in Friedberg! The head Red Cross worker came over in the morning & asked me to come over & see a couple of sick girls there. She said they were very dissatisfied with the Dr. there & would like me to come over & see the girls & stay for lunch. I did it. They live in a beautiful house. It was nice to sit down in a real dining room with some nice girls. I enjoyed it. On thinking it over I realized I'd had absolutely no social contact with any women for almost 2½ months. The trouble is that the closer I get to social AND sexual contact (aren't I ahful?) with the girl I love, the less I feel like bothering with others, tho I think it's still probably a good idea. Today I went back again for a visit to my patients & for lunch. . . .

Afterwards I went down to the Grand for a drink & a look at who was out with what Frauleins. Eagle had his dental assistant there. She looks like Dotty Lamour. Right after getting there I ran into one of the Red Cross girls who said one of my patients was a lot worse, so I drove over to Friedberg to check her. She has gone from the grippe into a strep throat. On the way back the generator burned out of the ambulance, but a German civilian picked me up. I came back with him & then went back with the German driver to pick up the ambulance. By the time I got back it was almost 11:30 & I felt too tired to return to the Grand, so popped some corn & am eating it & drinking beer while writing you.

Bad Nauheim, Germany
Monday, 11 March 1946

Darling: Tonight is exactly 16 months from the last time we were together. That is just 16 months too much time for us to be apart—at least to my way of thinking. Otherwise it was a good day because your letters of Feb 22, 23, 24, 25, & 28 arrived. . . .

The day was a busy one. I saw 50 patients, including Col. White, who has the grippe. I discussed the new dispensary setup with him for about an hour. It is due to open the 15th or 20th of April & it looks to me as if I don't have a chance of leaving until a couple of weeks after it is in operation, tho I think they will let me go early in May if all works out well. It means another terribly busy month or six weeks, tho, until it is set up & running smoothly.

This afternoon I did a monthly physical inspection on the MP Company & inspected their mess. Then I saw some patients & went over to Friedberg to see my Red Cross girl, who is better. Then I went to see Col. Numainville about getting the building for the new dispensary & Col. Collins about an errand he wants me to do for him in Heidelberg. The latter also gave me an introduction to the redeployment officer of the 7th Army—Col Angle. CBS is not going to be authorized to do any redeploying of medical officers until May, so my only chance of getting out before then will be thru 7th or 3rd Armies. Col. Collins did say he thought they would be able to redeploy me in May & he's the man who can do it.

Sweetie, your letters were so GOOD! They brought you very close. . . . I'm really getting along very well with the big shots in the medical section. The new set-up for community medical service will allow for 2 more medical officers & an American nurse & another dentist.

The wheat shortage hit us at supper tonight with an inferior type of bread & less of it. How is it affecting you?

The prospect of you cooing over our babies amused me, sweetie. It would be both so in & so out of character. I doubt if our babies will be very beautiful. Like you, I think they are all ugly till about a year old. I've often wondered, too, whether they'll be good looking or ugly when they grow up. The answer is—you never know!

I'm terribly tired tonight—a combination of a tough day & too many late hours recently. The past week I've stayed up late reading or bulling with Eagle almost every night. . . .

That broiled chicken with rice in Cambridge made my mouth water. That is one of your best dishes, Liz. . . .

Darling, I'm so dog-tired I'm going to go to bed now & answer your last two letters tomorrow. You have no idea how I long to be able to go to bed & really rest because you are beside me. The only real peace & contentment in my life past, present, and future is when I'm with you. So goodnight, my ahful sweet little wife that I love so very very very very terribly ahful MUCH!

Jim

Chapter Twelve

Postwar Germany: 1946

Jim's letters only touched on the conditions in Germany in 1946. Bad Nauheim was unscathed by the war, but surrounding cities were devastated and the German economy was non-existent. By March, hunger was pervasive in the German population, as it was all over Europe.

> It was not until late December [1945] . . . that the American Government faced the truth about Europe. . . . Food officials perceived the full consequences of drought on the Mediterranean harvest, assessed the shortage of seed, fertilizer, and manpower on the 1945 European crop, and recognized the critical shortage of transportation that threatened to keep even available supplies from the peoples of Europe. . . . Foreign governments rushed pleas to America for more food. The world wheat shortage forecast in September [1945] became a grim reality. . . . Europe would need 25 to 30 percent more wheat than could be shipped from all sources in the first six months of 1946. . . . Instead of combined exports of 6.7 million tons of wheat, poor harvests in Australia and Argentina forced those countries to scale down their commitments to 3.2 million tons. The Danube Basin, a traditional heavy supplier of Europe's wheat needs, would actually require imports. Reports drifted in from Asia that the East as well as the West faced mass starvation. China and Japan were in the clutches of drought, and a tidal wave had damaged thousands of acres of rice land in India. . . . Almost overnight, wheat had become the central concern of the world. . . . Europeans could live without the meats, sugar, and fats and oils . . . but they would die without bread.[20]

The world wheat shortage was aggravated by a shortage of rice. Famine threatened in Germany and in Asia, where Britain was responsible for the welfare of India, Burma, Ceylon, Malaya, and Singapore, all of which were part of the British Empire.

Herbert Morrison was sent to the US to try to persuade the Truman administration to adopt a more generous policy towards Great Britain, but *"cabled the Cabinet with the astonishing news that he had agreed to a further reduction in supplies of grain for this country, on the understanding that the Americans would share the burden in Germany and India."*[21]

In Germany, international aid was restricted to non-German refugees, recently released Allied POWs, and survivors of the concentration camps. Ethnic Germans were left to fend for themselves. It was a widely held belief that the German population should suffer in order to impress on them the suffering they had caused with a war they started. Throughout the German occupation of Western Europe, Germany had confiscated food from local populations and sent it to Germany, where the populace remained well fed. In the cold winter of 1944–45, 22,000 Dutch people died in a famine known as the Hongerwinter in the Netherlands.

Jim made little mention of the destruction and hunger in Frankfurt. He showed his concern for the Sauer family, with whom he had lived in 1935, and would continue to help them after the war. That family's situation was typical, but for other Germans he expressed no sympathy in his letters.

Heidelberg, about 75 miles south of Bad Nauheim, was the site of a large American hospital (where General Patton died a few months earlier after a car accident). The city had not been bombed and was a pleasant getaway.

Bad Nauheim, Germany
Thursday, 14 March 1946

Dearest Liz: It is 10:45 PM & we just got back from Heidelberg. I drove & Berger & Strickland went with me. I managed to get done all that I set out to do and in addition your letters of 6 & 7 March were here when we got back. That was the best part.

Last night I was so tense I hardly slept at all. So I'm going to slow down no matter what & stop letting people take advantage of my good nature. Fran Dietze, the Dr's wife from Dresden who takes care of us, gave me the dickens this morning when she heard I was only going to Heidelberg for a day. She is trying to get me to go off for a few days away from it all & thought the Heidelberg trip was for that purpose. She's right, tho, & I'm going to make a real effort to get away whenever possible.

Sick call was light this morning & we took off about 10 AM. We had lunch at the 4th Medical Lab at Darmstadt where I had a full hour session with their diphtheria expert & pathologist, really learning a lot. . . . Before lunch I had gotten Frau Sauer's address from the Military Government. It turned out to be on the road out of Darmstadt toward Weinheim & Heidelberg—both of which were on our itinerary. I found her living in her mother's house which is still undamaged, tho most of Darmstadt is a shambles. She was well but had lost some weight. I took her the last of the sugar & soap I had brought over plus a lot of accumulated PX supplies. She was glad to see me & we had a good ½ hour visit. She is quite upset about my friend Fritz who joined the party so he could become a judge but was never what we mean by a Nazi. He is still held prisoner in the British Zone. Her other son-in-law, who is a Nazi in spirit as well as in name does not worry her, because she feels the Allies are justified in being rough on him. She said Ruth had had a letter from Fritz written in January. She showed me a bunch of pictures, but like a fool I had forgotten to bring along any of you.

From Darmstadt we went to Weinheim & picked up our order of medical supplies, then on to 7th Army Headquarters at Heidelberg. There I finally got the worst part of the mix-up on the 277th Med. Det. straightened out, but got some bad news for me personally—the Lt. Col. in charge of redeployment said he had just gotten orders to redeploy down thru 50 points but no one below 50 points. Damn it, I knew that 1 point difference was going to hurt sometime. He held out no hope at all for my going home soon, implying that it may very well be July before I'll leave here. I can't help but think there ought to be enough ASTP students here by then, but then we've been thinking that for over 6 months now.

After finishing there we went on over to the 130th Station Hosp. where I had a good talk & a steak dinner with Don Sweeny, after which I looked over his preemie & another patient. He is getting pretty blue on prospects, too. We left there about 7:45 in the rain & had an uneventful ride back. . . .

The essence of postwar treatment of Germany was a process that came to be called denazification. Its stated purpose was to strengthen and assist the democratic elements in Germany, to provide security, and to punish the active Nazis and militarists. At the Potsdam summit in 1945, the policy was clarified:

> Nazi leaders, influential Nazi supporters and high officials of Nazi organizations and institutions and any other persons dangerous to the occupation or its objectives shall be arrested and interned. All members of the Nazi Party who have been more than nominal participants in its activities and all other persons hostile to Allied purposes shall be removed from public and semi-public office, and from positions of responsibility in important private undertakings. Such persons shall be replaced by persons, who, by their political and moral qualities, are deemed capable of assisting in developing

genuine democratic institutions in Germany.[22]

The essence was to make sure that Nazi philosophy was eliminated from German society. The policy sounded good, but consider the statistics. At the end of the war there were 8.5 million members of the Nazi party, roughly 10 percent of the population. There were 35 million members of related organizations. The spin doctors of their day, led by Herr Goebbels, had done a masterful job. The German people favored the Nazi party by a strong majority, even one year after the end of the war. All their political leaders, from the big names down to the mayors of small towns, were Nazi party members or sympathizers. Most of their economic leaders, from large corporations to local chambers of commerce, were Nazi party members or sympathizers. Young Germans had known no other political system. The fact was that denazification was not an easy policy to carry out.

Bad Nauheim, Germany
Sunday, 17 March 1946

Dearest Liz: . . .

Last night I was a bad boy & didn't get to bed till after two. After writing you, I went down to the Grand Hotel where I ran into Capt. Stromback (ex 75th Div & now S-4 of Hq Bn CBS), Maj. Willard (Head of Military Government of the Friedberg District, which we are in) & Lt. Roar of the Friedberg District Claims Office. We drank beer, ate hamburgers & talked till 12 when we discovered a mutual interest in ping-pong & repaired to Stromback's quarters where we played till 2, when I came home.

This morning I slept till 10:30, spending the last half hour pretending it was Sunday morning with you. I drank my weekly PX ration can of grapefruit juice for breakfast.

Bad Nauheim, Germany
Friday, 22 March 1946

Dearest Liz: . . .

I had a busy day today what with one thing & another. I have a number of sick patients & sent a very sick lobar pneumonia to the hospital. I have a virus pneumonia—not very sick,—in bed downstairs now. . . . I average about 2 admissions a day, which is quite a few. The turnover is high. Today I've had to admit a stack of guys for cellulitis & lymphangitis ("blood poisoning"). It is really quite a neat little general practice. I think I have learned a lot of practical medicine & independence in the Army so I would have no hesitation now about going into General Practice provided I did no surgery but minor stuff. I do at least 1 minor surgical procedure a day now, which mounts up. I'm learning quite a bit now, especially as I am trying to by going ahead with a certain amount of clinical experimentation. One conclusion I've reached is that either very sick people are more liable to have a reaction to influenzine, or that sodium bicarbonate with it cuts way down on the reactions. Anyway, for 3 weeks now I have used sulfadiazine (with bicarb) indiscriminately without any toxic reactions at all. I think now we withheld it too much at the expense of the patient's comfort at Harvard & Babies.

Redeployment news remains zero. I expect now to lose all my enlisted men but one next week & doubt that I'll get any replacements. I can't even requisition personnel for the new dispensary till I get a basis, which will be 7–10 days yet. Gawd how I hope I get redeployed soon to avoid all of that—aside from getting home to you.

Tonight I played squash with a guy who is supposed to be hot stuff around here at squash. He got 2 points a game. It wasn't even any exercise. Hell! . . .

Jim's letters usually cited what he had done medically that day, and highlighted anything interesting. He saw an impressive variety of maladies, which served as a solid basis for his lifelong skill as a diagnostician.

Bad Nauheim, Germany
25 March 1946

Dearest Liz: . . .

It was another busy day. The pathology continued to pour in. I had a case of acute nephritis, a case of scarlet fever, & 2 obscure cases I am at a loss to diagnose. Tonight I was called from the club to attend three men who had been badly hurt in a motorcycle-jeep accident.

I saw patients all morning, did physicals half the afternoon, then went to the Surgeon's Office to inspect them for diphtheria & to see the lay of the land. I found that CBS has very few 3100s [Jim's job series]. Among those they have, I am about 10th in line for redeployment. Col. Collins told me again that the plan was to redeploy <u>all</u> officers (including specialists probably) down thru 50 points. He thought my redeployment would be delayed for some time. That hurt. Everyone is also scared over here that we'll soon be fighting the Russians. It is UNO's first big test, but everyone feels convinced Russia will go her own sweet way—which will be the end of UNO. God, but I wish I could be more optimistic over the situation.

This place is getting to seem like a prison. I'm really starting to get ETO-happy. I'm so fed up by the end of the day that all I want to do is escape. I'm completely unable to guide myself into physically or mentally constructive channels. I stay up too late habitually because I don't sleep if I don't. . . .

Bad Nauheim, Germany
Thursday, 28 March 1946

Dearest Liz: . . .

Things are really bad right now with 5 men leaving tomorrow. I'm also being pressed to start this new Community Dispensary. Tomorrow I have to go over with the Engineers & map out just what will be where so they can start running in appropriate electric lines. . . .

I had not thought of Billings, Montana as a possible future home until that patient brought it up one day. It is a large agricultural center apparently, with many advantages. Frankly I have just about decided that it would be foolish to settle in any industrial center. We can talk that over at length when we get back. As I've mentioned before, I come out of this war in a very pessimistic frame of mind, & the only cities which escape obliteration in a modern war are those in which there is no industry. . . .

It's now 12:30. Tonight I had the boys up for drinks & lobster & nuts & dill pickles & cheese for a farewell party. Everyone had a good time I think. Those lucky guys—leaving tomorrow. . . .

Bad Nauheim, Germany
Saturday, 30 March 1946

Dearest Liz: . . .

Frau Sauer, Ruth (Fritz's wife) & Gunther, the latter's youngest son arrived toward the end of the morning & I had about an hour & a half visit with them this afternoon. Ruth wanted me to see if I could do anything to help get Fritz a hearing. Apparently he has been held for 10 months without a hearing in the automatic arrest category. She says he didn't get his judgeship till late in 1940 after he had been in the Navy a year, & that he had never sat on a bench, having routinely gotten the position as a matter of seniority. . . .

I very much wanted to find the family of Frieda Sauer on my trip in April 2014. My father's interactions with this family, from his four-month stay with them in 1935 to his last contact in 1960, spanned a period of time that demonstrated the resiliency of German families. They had lived through the nervous prosperity of the authoritarian Third Reich and the national feeling of indestructible power, then through the horrors and devastation of total defeat. They had faced starvation and deprivation, and then gone on to rebuild their lives and establish a more lasting prosperity built on democratic principles. All this occurred in the 25 years that my father knew the Sauers and Weispfennings. I felt I could gain greater understanding of the effects of this war, and of my father, by getting to know whatever members of the

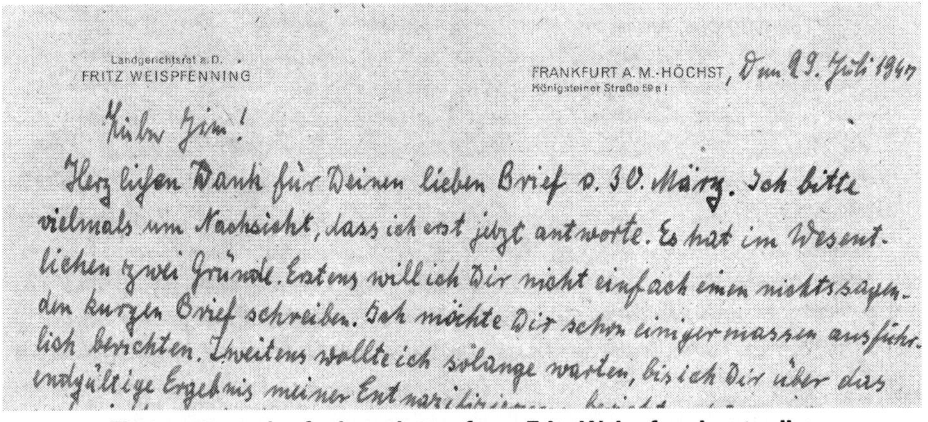
Landgerichtsrat a.D.
FRITZ WEISPFENNING

FRANKFURT A.M.-HÖCHST, Den 29. Juli 1947
Königsteiner Straße 59 a I

Lieber Jim!

Herzlichen Dank für Deinen lieben Brief v. 30. März. Ich bitte vielmals um Nachsicht, dass ich erst jetzt antworte. Es hat im Wesentlichen zwei Gründe. Erstens will ich Dir nicht einfach einen nichtssagenden kurzen Brief schreiben. Ich möchte Dir schon einigermassen ausführlich berichten. Zweitens wollte ich solange warten, bis ich Dir über das endgültige Ergebnis meiner

First paragraph of a long letter from Fritz Weispfenning to Jim written July 29, 1947; author's personal collection

family I could find.

The last known address I had was from a letter written to my father in 1947 from Fritz Weispfenning. Before my trip to Europe I spent several weeks tracking down people named Sauer and Weispfenning using internet searches, social media, the German telephone directory, and the German registry of lawyers. I sent emails and letters to likely possibilities. I concentrated on the places where I knew they had lived, namely Frankfurt, Darmstadt, and Munnerstadt. Finally, I found an obituary for a Gunther Weispfenning, who was born in 1941. That was about the right date for the youngest son of Fritz and Ruth. I emailed the author of the obituary, who forwarded the email to the family and, voila, I had found them. I exchanged emails with the two older sons, Fritz and Walter, mine in German (with the help of two native German-speaking friends who translated for me) and theirs in halting English. Fritz was born in 1935 and lives in Nurnberg, and Walter was born in 1937 and lives in Kassel. They remember well my father and the care packages from our family. I scanned the letters I had from their family and emailed them to Germany. We arranged to meet while I was in Bad Nauheim.

On April 1, 2014, I took the train from Bad Nauheim to the Frankfurt South Station, where I had arranged to meet Fritz and Walter, who were arriving from Nurnberg and Kassel. Never having met or seen photos of each other, I wondered how we would find each other on a crowded train platform. Fritz told me that he was a bald, 78-year-old man and would be carrying a newspaper so I would recognize him. As my train pulled into the station I immediately saw him on the platform, which was not crowded. My train car stopped well down the platform, and as I stepped out, I saw another man carrying a newspaper. This one had the Albert Einstein look, with wild gray hair around his bald pate. He marched up to me and with gleaming eyes introduced himself as Walter. Soon Fritz joined us and the connection between the McKays and Weispfennings was re-joined after 53 years. We walked a few blocks to their sister-in-law (Gunther's widow) Ingrid's apartment. Fritz speaks some English, Walter less, and Ingrid very little. My German is almost non-existent, so we stuck with halting English.

We slowly became acquainted over a glass of champagne. I pulled out my tablet and photos of my father, which helped get the memories flowing. I turned on my digital recorder so as not to forget the stories Fritz and Walter told.

After a time, Gunther's daughter Christiane joined us and we adjourned to the dining room for a sumptuous lunch. Christiane's excellent English facilitated the conversation and we all thoroughly enjoyed getting to know each other. Fritz remembered his mother saying that my father was very well liked by Germans, men and women alike, and that he knew how to "manage life." Grandfather Sauer died before Ruth was 20, which helped explain why Frau Sauer was taking in borders like my father in 1935. Ruth spoke little of the war to her children. Fritz told me that although he was only eight or ten years old, he had been old enough to see the "dark chapters" of the war, and they were not things you want to remember and talk about. He told me of the memorable moment sitting before the radio with his mother when the invasion of Poland was announced.

Before we knew it, the clock was about to chime three o'clock and Walter had to rush out to catch the train back to Kassel. Fritz was staying overnight, so he and I were able to sit down and talk for two more hours. Fritz told me that he is a little ashamed when reading the letters because the family was asking for help, but he says the help was greatly appreciated. The letters filled in some of the gaps in his knowledge of that time.

My father had told me what he could about his friend Fritz and his family during and after the war, but he didn't know much. Fritz Jr. and Walter described what they knew of their father's military years. His U-boat training was long and included considerable medical training so that he could handle medical emergencies at sea. Fritz remembers his father studying at home when he was on leave. When he was captured by the British and held in a POW camp in northwestern Germany he had two strikes against him. He had joined the Nazi Party to become a judge in Frankfurt in 1940, and then had been a U-boat captain, a position of responsibility in the German military. The denazification process agreed on by the Allies emphasized the need to concentrate on Nazi party members and those in positions of responsibility, since it was assumed they would have had strong Nazi sympathies to be appointed to those positions.

The British (along with the rest of Europe) suffered a severe food shortage after the war, and their POWs were fed sparingly. By the time Fritz was released in the summer of 1946, he was too weak to travel across Germany to join his family. He said the British had released him because they did not want him to die in their camp. He spent time in a hospital near the POW camp until he gained enough strength for the journey. At last he was able to travel east. His train arrived in Bad Kissingen, 12 kilometers from where his family was living in Munnerstadt. Ruth and the children rode their bicycles to Bad Kissingen to meet him. Fritz was too weak to ride a bicycle, so they helped him walk back to Munnerstadt, stopping to rest frequently. His convalescence progressed, and when he finally cleared the denazification process on November 9, 1946, he was ready to begin his 10 months of manual labor as mandated by the military court, before he could resume the practice of law.

Fritz was a bitter man after the war. According to his sons, his bitterness was not really against Americans, but rather against war and the unfairness of his life. He was a competent attorney, but was withdrawn and unhappy in his personal life.

A few months after my trip to Europe, I discovered a packet of letters that my mother had tucked away with the label "post-war letters." It contained 39 more letters from the Sauer/Weispfenning family to my parents, written between 1946 and 1954 (see Appendix). All the letters were in German, so I hired a local German friend to translate them for me. What they reveal is a story little known to Americans, told as it happened by a mother, father, and grandmother who were fighting to survive and keep their family together. I have shared the letters with Walter, Fritz, and their families. They report that much was revealed in the letters that they were never told.

On their return to Frankfurt in 1948, food was more available for the Weispfennings, and Germany overall. The German economy began to recover quickly when the new currency, the Deutsche Mark, was established in 1948. The black market had thrived under the worthless Reichsmark, and merchants had withheld food and other goods from those unable to pay exorbitant prices. When the new currency was established, the black market collapsed and food suddenly appeared on shelves again for ordinary Germans. In addition to the Germans' own food production, Americans were supplying food to a program whereby the schools and other institutions provided nutrition. The McKay family sent care packages, containing special treats including chocolate, milk powder, and cigarettes. Milk was scarce for several years as dairy herds were re-built. Ruth Weispfenning was especially thankful for the nutrition that the care packages brought.

The Marshall Plan was providing the resources to re-establish all aspects of a working society. The German people were very industrious, there were no strikes, and new technology was put to use as all the factories and infrastructure that had been destroyed was rebuilt. In a few years, the German economy surpassed those of the victorious Allies in France and England. The city of Frankfurt had a population of about 450,000 before the war. After the war there were few buildings left and the population was small. People began to rebuild immediately and soon the population grew back to, and beyond, prewar levels.

Why did my father lose contact with the Sauers and Weispfennings? Perhaps it was because my father and his friend Fritz both preferred to concentrate on their work. Fritz Jr. said his father worked with blinders on, and had very little contact with anyone. My father was single minded in his devotion to medicine, and the 1960s were the years when he built his reputation as a leader in American pediatrics. Perhaps it was also a result of their mutual desire to forget a difficult period in both their lives. And finally there was the difference in their respective lives, which reflected the result of the war. Like his country, Fritz emerged from WWII defeated and wondering what the future would hold. Unlike his country, which went on to become strong and successful, Fritz harbored the bitterness of defeat and the ruin of what had promised to be a happy and successful life. By contrast, my father came home victorious, unscathed physically and minimally scarred mentally. Living in a booming postwar period, he picked up his promising career and marriage, put the war behind him, and built a rewarding career and family life. Perhaps this contrast made it too difficult for them to maintain a friendship. Whatever the reasons, I am glad to have made contact with the next generation, and to find them happy and successful.

Chapter Thirteen
Springtime in Germany: 1946

Bad Nauheim, Germany
Sunday Night, 31 March 1946

Dearest Liz: For some reason I'm about as discouraged tonight as I've been in a long time. I feel like I did at Breckinridge when I was bucking my head against the brick wall of one batch of physically unsatisfactory replacements after another, only now I never have the consolation of being with you.

Last night I went to bed at 10:30 but couldn't sleep this morning, so got up at 7AM. It was a really beautiful warm day which seemed more typical of May than of March. Everyone was out enjoying it except me. I did intend to spend the afternoon in it, but that was spoiled by Major Smith, the deputy Hq Commandant (who is leaving Tuesday, thank God) who ran into me right after lunch & insisted on me going out to the pistol range with him. He's about the last person I'd choose to spend an afternoon with. Fortunately I got a call at 3:30 & was busy the rest of the day. . . .

To cap the climax, tonight I was called to go down to the MP station to pull one of my new replacements out of hock for impersonating an MP. Some fun. On the good side of the ledger are 3 volunteers I've had for the medics, which will enable me to release some men who don't want to be in them. One of them seemed like a good man.

Liz, today was a day when I not only needed you, but wanted you even more than usual. It was a day when it would have been a pleasure to be alive with you, but as it is, it was just a pain in the neck to watch the people enjoying the day go by while I had to work. Darling I love & miss you so much that it hurts. Things are so bad that I'm again thinking of redeployment in terms of next August or September. I'm really getting now to the point of being "ETO-happy," a psychotic condition where everything seems so bad one ceases to give a good God-Damn about anything & hates everybody & everything.

Sweetie, I apologize for this letter. I'm really low. But high or low

I LOVE YOU, DARLING!

Jim

Knowing the drive and determination my father exhibited in later life, I can well imagine the frustrations he was suffering in the spring of 1946. Wasting time was anathema to Jim, and it seemed that the army was determined to squander his time. He could see that a less motivated replacement doctor could easily perform the job he had in Bad Nauheim. He longed to get back to his career where he would study, work hard, seek exposure to the latest advances, consult with intelligent colleagues, and put to good use all he had learned in his medical training, including the experience of combat medicine and his newfound aptitude for leadership and administration. And then there was the life he ached to begin with Liz.

Bad Nauheim, Germany
3 April 1946

Dearest Liz: . . .

Saturday is "Army Day" & is scheduled to be a holiday. They should spend the day reorganizing it instead of throwing eulogies at it. Sunday 6 officers, one of whom is me, have been invited to go for a ride on the Rhine in Hitler's yacht as a delegation from Hq. Bn. I should stay here & get out a report which will otherwise be late, but I plan instead to go for my first real day off in almost 3 months. . . .

Hitler had a 435-foot ocean-going yacht called the *Aviso Grille*, which was too big to sail on the Rhine. Stories of Rhine cruises on "Hitler's yacht" likely involved one of three much smaller motorboats that were also built for Hitler during the war. In our conversations in 2011, Jim had no memory of this adventure.

Bad Nauheim, Germany
Thursday, 4 April 1946

Dearest Liz: . . .

Late this afternoon my new ASTP . . . help appeared. His name is James C. Byers, Jr. & he's from St. Louis, has been in the Army 17 months & has been overseas one month. He told me that all the station hospitals & separation centers at home had 2–3 times the number of doctors they actually needed & that a lot of them wanted to come overseas, but just aren't sent. That's just another proof that the fault lies right where we thought it does—with the Army Brass. . . .

Bad Nauheim, Germany
Sunday, 7 April 1946

Dearest Liz: . . . I had a long talk with Col. Collins. He said they are definitely going to stop redeploying on points at 50 and that from then on it will be on total service or overseas service. God that lowers my morale. . . . I feel like getting all the high-ranking, chair-sitting bastards in the U.S. & machine-gunning them. I don't think many mistakes would be made if that were done. . . . They're a bunch of lazy, dissipated, no-good, blood-sucking leeches & drones who are so lost in the contemplation of their own material comfort that they see the other fellow's material comfort only dimly & his mental comfort not at all. According to their view I have it made—plenty of calories to eat, good pay & security, a nice place to live, a fancy officers club, & my pick of plenty of nice frauleins to sleep with. As long as they offer me the opportunity of having a woman to sleep with, they don't see why I'm dissatisfied at not having my wife—I can have a woman to sleep with, can't I?—& what more do I want? Those G-D lousy bastards! . . .

Bad Nauheim, Germany
Tuesday, 9 April 1946

Dearest Liz: . . .
The ASTP boys are all struck with how completely out of touch with what is going on in the States we are here. It has been a long time. . . .

Bad Nauheim, Germany
10 April 1946

Dearest Liz: . . .

The whole day was again spent in administrative work. I did take half an hour off this afternoon & was a bad boy and bought a picture—a watercolor of the old city in Frankfurt, for which I paid 80 marks. I hope you like it, too, in view of the investment.

Eagle got back tonight from Switzerland, looking tanned & healthy. He went to Locarno in the south. . . . I heard that Col. Boshoff had already gone before a disposition board, so it looks like he may be retired. If so, I wonder who the new Hq. Commandant will be. . . .

German marks were worth about 10 American cents in April 1946. One of Jim's sons now owns the painting of Frankfurt.

Bad Nauheim, Germany
Thursday, 11 April 1946

Dearest Liz: . . .

We had 3 accident cases today. One was a Pole with a skull fractured in a motorcycle accident, one was a G-I whose skull was fractured when his truck turned over twice when he tried to avoid a German kid who ran out in front of him on the Autobahn, and the third was the kid who was brought in dead with 10 major injuries, any one of five of which would have been fatal.

Traffic accidents were very common among the occupation troops. Right after the war, the young combat veterans were understandably reckless. They were suddenly in a loosely controlled environment with time on their hands. Later, the replacement troops and those who had not seen combat were still young men, away from home, and presumably more reckless than they were at home. Drunkenness was common. Compounding the problem, the ubiquitous army jeep was a notoriously unsafe vehicle, easily rolled. Jim saw numerous civilian victims also, mostly children who would hear an army vehicle, run out in the road to see what it was, only to be hit by the next vehicle. The most notorious victim was General George S. Patton, who was killed in a traffic accident in December 1945.

With the opening of the new tennis courts, and the arrival of new doctors for companionship, Jim's mood rapidly improved.

Bad Nauheim, Germany
Saturday, 13 April 1946

Dearest Liz: . . .

This afternoon I played 3½ hours of tennis. Most of it was lousy, but I had one good set with the pro. I'm playing him again in the morning. Walking home from the courts I was thinking about playing tennis with you and about how one of my first memories of you is of playing tennis with you at Longwood. . . .

Byers has been assigned here for another 7 days and I am to get another one in addition to him! The reason is that the Lichfield trials are coming here from London this week and they expect a lot of extra people around.

Bad Nauheim, Germany
Sunday, 14 April 1946

Dearest Liz: . . .

This morning I played tennis for about an hour and a half, becoming very thoroughly pooped. After playing I took a bath, shaved, & went to lunch. After lunch I took a long nap, then sat out on my balcony for an hour reading & letting the sun beat down on one of my heels, which is getting some athlete's foot on it. About 5 o'clock, I took Hans, one of the civilian ambulance drivers, and went to our old apartment & got all my stuff which I had packed yesterday. I now have a 2 room suite at the southwest corner of the third floor of the new dispensary.

The new dispensary is really enormous. It has 96 large rooms. It is really a small station hospital with place for 70–100 beds, tho we only have 30. On the ground floor there is the clerk's office, my big office with examining room adjoining, pharmacy, dining room, waiting room, x-ray, surgical emergency room, sick call room, dental clinic, another Dr's office, & a children's waiting room. On the second floor is the lab, physio-therapy department (with trained German physio-therapist), supply room, night driver's room, Library, linen room, nurses' office, ward kitchen, & ward rooms (10 rooms with 2 beds in each, 6 with 1 bed in each). On the third floor are the operating room, central supply, officers' quarters, & store rooms. On the fourth floor are the EM quarters. We have lots of room for expansion. . . . We have 4 officers (including nurse) and 28 civilian employees besides 9 G-Is. The building is situated at the North end of the big Kurhaus Park and is nice and quiet, having the Park on the south and a big pond on the north. West of us is a big German Hospital, and east are the MP's quarters and the Park Sanitorium where allied women live.

The Continental Base Section (CBS) supported US occupation forces in Germany and Austria. The headquarters of CBS in Bad Nauheim was a growing concern in early 1946. Bad Nauheim was full of officers, many of whom were bringing their wives and families in anticipation of a long stay. This meant that Jim's dispensary was serving a growing population that was becoming more diverse. In addition to the army personnel and their families, there was a big Red Cross unit in Friedberg (sister city to Bad Nauheim). All employees in the US facilities, including nurses, waiters, drivers, and other service personnel, were German but were eligible for treatment at the dispensary. Medically, Jim had been disappointed at not being assigned to one of the large hospitals, but now he began to see a good variety of illnesses in what was essentially his own small hospital. He was at his happiest when he could immerse himself in medical challenges, and it was evident in his letters to Liz.

Bad Nauheim, Germany
15 April 1946

Dearest Liz: . . .

Today had the usual Monday irritations, but I got caught entirely up to date on my paperwork. The most irritating thing I had to do was reply by endorsement with a program for making my men better parade soldiers, with a lot of talk about personnel now being stabilized. I'm in no mood for any of that regular Army balogney. I'll run my installation well, but if they want to start that stuff, they better start using their regular Army men for it. . . .

Delles, one of my men was discharged today (he is going to continue working for us as a civilian so he can be with his Fraulein). We took him over to the Kaiserhof for beer and supper.

Charles Reed came up to me tonight in the dining room & said Rachel was arriving in 13 days! That hurts. I'm really caught. I can't go home & you can't come over. G - D - the Army!

Bad Nauheim, Germany
Tuesday, 16 April 1946

Dearest Liz: . . .

The day was beautiful but hectic, which was a little surprising for Tuesday, because Monday is usually our busy day. It was really hot—just like a summer day, tho not unpleasantly so. Last night I admitted 2 patients, one about 10 and the other about one. The second was very interesting. He complained of sudden abdominal pain after drinking, had definite tenderness over the duodenum. I figured it was probably all alcoholic, but was suspicious enough to do a blood count this morning. It showed a 17% Eosiniphilia (3–4% is normal), so we immediately suspected a parasitic disease. Since he is from Louisiana we made a diagnosis of hookworm, probably with accompanying Ascaris infection. Stool examination this afternoon confirmed the diagnosis. PATHOLOGY!! We'll start treating him day after tomorrow when he's all over his binge. This morning we admitted 5 patients to make 7 in 12 hours. That's a rough number of admissions for a regular hospital ward. 2 of the others are really hospital cases, as well as the worm-ridden one. One is a bad sacro-iliac sprain, the other is a guy with a gangrenous finger which your great <u>surgeon</u> husband debrided & incised & is going to treat! My little hospital is really getting to be one!

I'm sure sorry you are having so much trouble with sore throat & earache. As I said before, I'm really beginning to think tonsillectomy may be indicated in your case. . . . You'd better see a good doctor.

Last night was a beautiful one with a full moon which I looked at for a long time, communicating with my wife & sweetie that I love. . . .

Byers has turned out to be both good & congenial. . . . Eagle is opening our new mess day after tomorrow.

Sym's lack of expectations about being discharged sound as if I, too, will be in a while after getting back. I could stand it if I had you. Actually the present situation, once I get the administrative work in shape, would be ideal for the Army if you were only here. I literally have my own little hospital with all the resources of the U.S. Army at my command. I'm "Doc" for 1500–2000 people & think I have the respect & liking of most of them.

Aside from being the dentist, Eagle was in charge of the officers' mess, including procuring food. Rather than rely on Army supplies, he was very good at taking what the Army gave him and going out into the countryside to trade for fresh meat and vegetables with local farmers. The mess became well known in town and officers came from other units to eat there.

Bad Nauheim, Germany
Thursday, 18 April 1946

Dearest Liz: . . .

The day saw also a piece of good news for me here & of bad news for us—Byers has been put on DS here for the duration of the Lichfield trials—which should account for several months at the least. Col. Collins also told me definitely that they are going to disregard the point system and redeploy on overseas service starting within a week. The basis will be 21 months. It burns me up, because it gives absolutely no credit for combat time.

Bad Nauheim, Germany
Friday, 19 April 1946

Dearest Liz: Today was again a bad one with no mail from you. Otherwise it cleared off into a cool, clear day on which I got very little accomplished in the way of work. I spent the whole afternoon in Frankfurt getting the pregnant French wife of a warrant officer here examined. She just arrived yesterday & is due any time. Her husband wanted me to deliver her, but we're not yet set up for it & they only want us to do emergencies here. I did get a new pair of shoes while in Frankfurt. Both my other pairs of low shoes wore out within 5 days of each other & I haven't been able to get them resoled.

The whole place is in an uproar tonight with everyone mad & insulted (German help) because of Eagle's accusations about their pilfering food. Of course, you have to be strict, but he has gone off half-cocked I think & is getting everyone in an uncooperative mood.

Tonight after supper your husband went fishing! I went about 6 miles northwest on the Usa, the stream which flows thru Bad Nauheim. The fishing wasn't as good as last spring in the Sauerland, but I did get one nice 11 inch trout. . . .

Liz, walking around the 97th today with the pregnant French girl & having people think she was my wife made me think about how it will feel to shepherd you around when you have a big bump sticking out in front. I'll like that and I'll love you—even more than I do now, which is very very very very very MUCH! Jim

Bad Nauheim, Germany
Saturday, 20 April 1946

Dearest Liz: . . .

Today was a beautiful one marked by a series of time consuming incidents which would only happen in a headquarters. This morning the big incident was that one of the Red Cross girls from Friedberg cracked up a jeep & fractured her skull. That required a lot of telephoning to different people & talking to the head of the Red Cross about it. Then I saw two colonels etc. This afternoon I made a house call on a full colonel at the request of the Chief of Staff, had a hard time with a Rabbi (G-I Chaplain) who wanted me to give him some penicillin on the side for a local 3 weeks old Jewish baby who has pneumonia. I refused because (a) it would have been all over town tomorrow despite his protestations that it wouldn't, (b) the baby isn't so sick it has to have it (c) I think that letting penicillin out on the side like that eases the situation enough that no one raises a squawk about the fact that penicillin, a life-saving drug which should be available to all the world, is almost limited in its distribution to the US where it is sold on the open market to anyone who can get a doctor's prescription for it for any old disease. I believe that release of the drug would come a lot sooner if it weren't for these leaks, because it assuages people who otherwise would bring up with a big squawk an obviously inhuman situation.

Tonight we finally managed to get some lettuce, radishes, chives & spinach, so we'll get a decent diet for a while. We do need salad oil tho. Byers & I played tennis for about ¾ of an hour after supper.

Tomorrow is Easter. Our last Easter together was in New Orleans, wasn't it? I hope you got yourself an Easter bonnet & I wish even more that I could be with you when you wear it or a reasonable facsimile tomorrow. . . .

Bad Nauheim, Germany
Easter Sunday
21 April 1946

Dearest Liz: Today was a beautiful warm, sunny Easter & also a GOOD one, with your letters of Jan 6th (!), April 11, 12, 13, 14, & 15. I hope my letters are coming thru as well, so you too can know what I was doing on the preceding weekend. . . .

By the way, it will probably please you to hear that I'm now eating 2 fried eggs for breakfast every time they are offered to me! I doubt if that will hold true at home, tho, because both the other times I was in Germany I ate eggs with relish, too.

The party last night was a good one. It was a lot better than any officer's club party I ever attended. We really had a good time, tho I had to take Eagle home at midnight and Byers folded at 1:30. Your awful husband stayed on till 3:30! If you had been there, I expect I'd have gotten home LONG before 3:30. This morning I got up about 9:15, made ward rounds & a house call, & sat in the sun for ¾ of an hour reading the "Captain from Castile" by Samuel Shellabarger. It is good. I finished "Leave her to Heaven" yesterday. The afternoon was spent mostly in a long nap & more reading. After supper Eagle & I went fishing (Eagle chiefly as a spectator, as we have only one rod.). I caught 2 ten inch trout. We had to go about 8 miles to the stream. We dropped Wally, the original German nurse, off at her Aunt's in a village on the way & picked her up on the way back. In return she cooked the trout for us with fried potatoes & a mixed green salad. It was very good but kept me up till it's now 11:30. It is nice to have a kitchen in the house.

It's nice that Caleb is getting paroled. I guess it is probably partly due to the same reason I don't get paroled—that we are getting far enough away from the war now that they are forgetting & disregarding the combat soldier. Like you, I've been developing a numbness about the whole thing. . . .

Liz's brother Caleb was paroled from his second stay in prison in the state of Washington for being a conscientious objector. He was first denied C.O. status in 1942 and sent to prison for two years. In 1944, he was again denied and sent back to prison. He declared himself a Quak-

Entire Foote family in 1940, with Liz sitting lower left, and Caleb the tallest in the back.

er, and indeed his mother and her whole family were longtime Quakers, but Caleb's father was a Unitarian minister, a faith not recognized as having a religious objection to war. Like virtually all combat soldiers, Jim was not sympathetic to those who refused to fight.

Bad Nauheim, Germany
Wednesday, 24 April 1946

Dearest Liz: . . .

Today was terrifically busy. Our patient census has hit the all time high of 14. I hope we can get rid of a bunch of them tomorrow. The VD rate has shot up again. I spent the day half in administrative work, half in "snow" jobs—which are the cases which require tact to handle. . . .

Tonight Byers & I went to see "the House of 92nd Street," my first movie in 10–14 days. Afterwards we went over to the Kaiserhof & drank beer & ate sandwiches with Col. Collins. We also had a lot of fun with Eagle.—This afternoon Eagle ran into a guy whose facial nerve was anomalous (in the wrong place) & he injected it with novocain while trying to give dental anesthesia. It gave the patient a complete paralysis of the left side of the face which scared hell out of Eagle. Tonight we laid down a regular campaign to make him think the thing might not wear off for 6–7 months, till we had to have mercy & tip him off. . . .

Bad Nauheim, Germany
Thursday, 25 April 1946

Dearest Liz: . . .

This afternoon I got an example of the same thing that used to bother us—A young Captain & his wife, a Norwegian who was at Buchenwald for 10 months, came in because they were being moved out of their 2-room apartment into a hotel which is the usual Army whorehouse. They were there a few days before they got their apartment & the girl, who is very nice, just can't face going back there (a couple of unpleasant incidents occurred while they were there before as she is very cute). The husband wanted me to say she was so sick she needed to have a special diet & private quarters. She said she wanted nothing special—just the right to live privately & decently, which the high mucky-mucks here are trying to prevent because the guy brought his wife here. It was perfectly legal, tho, because it was a permanent change of station. At the same time I'd hate to guess how many colonels have set their German mistresses up in apartments—and there's no howl made about <u>that</u>. God, it burns me up. Anyway, she turned out to be anemic, so I said she should not live in a hotel because of her anemia and nervousness after Buchenwald. Actually she is just the way you used to get sometimes over the G-D Army (and me, too). Living in that hotel would ruin that marriage. . . .

Tonight Eagle & I went fishing, but didn't catch anything except a couple of minnows. After getting back I made rounds & then Hilde & Wally, the two nurses got started telling me of the unpleasantnesses they have been going thru because they work for the Americans. I'm very sorry about it, because they are both very nice, strictly business, girls. I suppose one thing is that so many of the girls who have been hired by the Americans are hired because of their willingness to do other things than work. . . .

Bad Nauheim, Germany
Friday, 26 April 1946

Dearest Liz: . . .

Frau Sauer came to see me to request a letter from me for her son Rolf who is working on his denazification papers. That took over an hour. This afternoon Byers & Eagle went to Frankfurt. I was busy all afternoon with one thing after another—administration, 4 discharge physicals, 6 Field grade officers connected with the Lichfield trials, including the infamous Col. Killian Himself, 5 other patients, 3 French wives & a child for shots, & 2 Polish girls for physical exam for entering the U.S. We really keep busy.

Tonight Byers & I played tennis. He is pretty good. There was a darn good player named Capt Moore out there tonight, tho, & I'm going to play him sometime next week. Will you start sending me some tennis balls—a dozen to start with, then 6 a week? Let me know how much they cost now and if they are available. I'd also like a half dozen leather grips from Montenegro at Cragen's. As you can see, I've really given up on getting home very soon. Rachel Reed is due to arrive day after tomorrow! That hurts. All the Regular Army & semi-Regular Army guys are going home of furloughs now, too. . . .

Captain R. James McKay in Bad Nauheim, Germany, spring 1946.

Bad Nauheim, Germany
Saturday, 27 April 1946

Dearest Liz: . . .

Tonight Eagle, Williams (our Pfc mess sergeant) and I went fishing with no luck at all. I think we need some rain before the fish will bite. It has really been too dry. It looks like it may rain tomorrow. It would suit me.

At the moment I'm sweating out payday, borrowing & sponging beer! As soon as I get paid I intend to buy a few more pictures, which will knock me down broke again. Incidentally, I discontinued my war bond buying as of Dec. 1st. You should get bonds thru the Nov 30th pay check. It got to be too darn much trouble to make out new applications for them every time I moved. So I get almost $20 more each month now. If I'm going to be here a long time, I think I'll take a leave some time pretty soon—probably in the next month. I haven't been able to make up my mind where I want to go. . . .

No 29

Bad Nauheim, Germany
Monday, 29 April 46

Dearest Liz! Today was a GOOD one but a blue one for me. On the good side your letters of the 20, 21, + 23 arrived. On the blue side the first G-I wives arrived from the U.S. tonight with Rachel Reed among them. Seeing her made me so doggoned home-sick for you I felt like bawling.

Last night I was wakened at 11:30 by Capt. Fitzgerald's wife (the Norwegian) calling me because her husband had fainted. I went over + found him somewhat weak but O.K. He has a mild chronic colitis which had been somewhat worse the past few days because of his upset over the housing situation. He's had colitis about a year + a half but no one ever talked to him about it before, so I sat down + told him about it and also gave him hell about getting irritated at his wife without real cause. It apparently had some effect because I saw them tonight + they seemed to be getting along better + he thanked me for talking to him. – Excuse the drop of blood, but I'm coming down with a cold + my nose is bleeding as it always does under such circumstances.

The day today was hectic as the dickens—

Jim's letter to Liz, including spot of blood, April 29, 1946.

Bad Nauheim, Germany
Monday, 29 April 1946

Dearest Liz: Today was a GOOD one but a blue one for me. On the good side, your letters of the 20, 21, & 23 arrived. On the blue side the first G-I wives arrived from the U.S. tonight with Rachel Reed among them. Seeing her made me so doggoned homesick for you I felt like bawling.

Last night I was wakened at 11:30 by Capt. Fitzgerald's wife (the Norwegian) calling me because her husband had fainted. I went over & found him somewhat weak but O.K. He has a mild chronic colitis which had been somewhat worse the past few days because of his upset over the housing situation. He's had colitis about a year & a half but no one ever talked to him about it before, so I sat down & told him about it and also gave him hell about getting irritated at his wife without real cause. It apparently had some effect because I saw them tonight & they seemed to be getting along better & he thanked me for talking to him. Excuse the drop of blood, but I'm coming down with a cold & my nose is bleeding as it always does under such circumstances.

The day today was hectic as the dickens, a true Army Monday. I spent the whole day working on a supply requisition, with interruptions to take care of a colonel with an acute nervous breakdown—he is a non-regular Army man who has just been heckled to the brink by the same stuff which drives me to the brink, too.

Tonight I went up to meet the train with the dependents. They sure looked nice. 7 wives came here. Rachel had the only baby, therefore she & Charles were photographed to death. Apparently Rachel was photographed a lot at Bramen, too. She looked very well—better looking than before, because she has matured—and the baby looked like a good one. She howled when she first was approached by Charles, but they soon made friends. . . .

Bad Nauheim, Germany
Tuesday, 30 April 1946

Dearest Liz: . . .

It was another hectic day, with administration again the focal point, tho we had a number of real cases on the ward—a Lt. Col with a nervous breakdown, a guy with otitis media & possible mastoiditis, a guy with hepatitis (liver disease) without jaundice, 2 guys with tonsillitis (one of which may by diphtheria), & a guy with recurrent malaria. All that plus my nurse with mumps, the lab technician with an axillary boil, Eagle with his aches & pains, a guy with arthritis who came in tonight, and the two house calls I had tonight—one a woman with migraine, the other a woman with salpingitis & possible ectopic pregnancy—gives quite a bit of variety in practice.

I'm glad you liked your Easter flowers. You should blame them on Ma. She wrote that she would get them several weeks before Easter, & being your lazy husband I never wrote her to tell her to go ahead, but just let her go ahead.

One of the things I did today was to get paid. I haven't been paid since November, so it was quite a bit. I drew $436. I sent $300 of it to you, so let me know as soon as you get it. Then I can destroy the receipt. As I said before, I've discontinued the war bonds. If you want to get some, go ahead. Stocks don't look like a very good investment right now. I'm keeping so much money in case I get a leave.

I wish I had you here to talk to the Norwegian girl (Mrs. Fizgerald) I've told you about. She is the one with salpingitis (inflammation of the fallopian tubes usually due to gonorrhea) & possible ectopic pregnancy. The following is her story & problem: she was brought up in a family where the mother was married off to the father & considered her wifely duties purely in the nature of unpleasant duty. She never, until I talked to her tonight, has ever received any instruction on sex or pregnancy. Last year she was experimented on at Buchenwald by being raped every night for 3 weeks, then operated on to see if she was pregnant, plus some electrical shock treatment of her uterus, followed by 2 weeks more raping. Either from the raping (gonorrhea) or the operation (streptococcus) she developed salpingitis & has been sick with it ever since. She doesn't know if she had gonorrhea as they never told her, tho she was eventually hospitalized outside of Buchenwald. She now has terrible pain & no pleasure on intercourse, even tho she wants to have it with her husband. It is partly physical & partly mental, but all I could do was tell her how it took even people like us a long time to get used to each other & reassure her that she would stop having trouble in time. I hope she does. . . .

Often, after receiving several of Liz's letters, Jim would write a paragraph apparently answering questions from her letters. The following is a good example.

Bad Nauheim, Germany
Wednesday, May 1, 1946

Dearest Liz: Today was a GOOD one with your letters of the 24th, 25th, & 26th. In yours of the 25th you replied to mine of the 22nd which is really good service, isn't it?

You sounded as if you had quite a strenuous Easter. I find it hard to understand why services are still so lousy. Is it because the returning G-Is are unwilling to work? I imagine many of them are. The Army is poor training for work.

. . . Your evening with the Montgomery girls [Liz's mother-in-law and her sisters] amused me. They are sure terrific talkers. As you know, that's one thing

I like about you, you are able to shut your mouth once in a while. Re your Ma's letter over your mental state: I don't believe that quitting your job now is the answer, and I rather doubt that it would be even this summer when you could be in Maine. I'm convinced that it's a good idea for you to keep busy. If you are like me, it isn't the job that's bothering you. I do think you should get away for a little while, tho. I do feel the surge of warmth & love you spoke of sometimes while reading your letters.

Today was a beautiful May Day, but hectic & I felt like hell with a semi-sore throat, sinus, & just general all-round exhaustion. Tonight I went to bed at 7:30 & slept till 10, took a sinus treatment, popped some corn, bulled with Byers till it is now quarter of one again. I've got to change my habits. . . .

Col. Boshoff came in late this afternoon to say good-bye & said he wanted to write me a letter, a copy of which I enclose. It was certainly nice of him. He is going home, having been sent back for Buerger's Disease on a railroad job because they wanted to get him out as Hq. Commandant.

This whole place is getting more & more hectic. I have had a number of people lately with nervous breakdowns of greater or less degree and there are a lot more close to it.—And what is doing it is all so ridiculous & just a lot of artificial "made" work with no significance whatsoever.

Rachel and Charles are still being heckled by photographers. They were picked as a couple to be followed for a story for Life Magazine, so they may appear in it soon. . . .

The article "Wives in Germany" appeared in the May 27, 1946, issue of *Life*, but did not include Charles and Rachel Reed. The commendation memo from Lt. Col. Boshoff read as follows.

HEADQUARTERS COMMAND.
CONTINENTAL BASE SECTION. APO 807
U.S. ARMY

1 May 1946
MEMO to: Captain R. J. McKay Jr. 277 Medical Detachment, APO 807.

1. From January 10, 1946 to this date you have served under me as my Post Surgeon. I want to go on record that I consider you an outstanding officer and medical man, who has always been on the job, regardless of your own interests. I think you have done a marvelous job here in Bad Nauheim; I consider you to be one of the loyalist [sic] officers I have ever met in the Army and you are to be commended for the fine set-up of your hospital and

dispensary that you have done in this community.

2. I wish you the best of luck for the future and feel proud that I had an officer of your caliber under me.

W.H. BOSHOFF, Lt. Col. G. S. C. 0-466828.,
Headquarters Commandant.

Bad Nauheim, Germany
Thursday, 2 May 1946

Dearest Liz: . . .

Tonight I played bridge with Lts Rader & Reek of the Surgeon's office & Miss Johannsen of the A-G Civilian Personnel. We had a good game at the Grand Hotel with beer & hamburgers & a thunderstorm outside. . . .

I believe penicillin is available in England, but not to the extent that it is in the U.S. In France it is almost unavailable. In Germany it is freely available for VD but nothing else. It isn't the Army this time, but its availability for any old thing at home.

. . . My throat is getting rawer & rawer—I think chiefly due to a recurrent sinus. I'll have to work on it.

Bad Nauheim, Germany
Friday, 3 May 1946

Dearest Liz: . . .

There is a manpower board over here now which is demanding big cuts in German civilians employed by the Army, but says or investigates nothing to do with use of G-Is for jobs civilians could do. The idea seems to be to substitute G-Is for civilians. The fact that the whole of CBS Headquarters is a completely useless outfit, set up to provide jobs for a stack of high officers means nothing. That's not wasting manpower.

Work wasn't too bad today, tho it continues busy. Our ward has been very busy this week. Tonight I played 9 holes of golf, then went fishing with Lt. Reek. We didn't catch a thing. . . .

Tomorrow morning, by order of CBS Hq we start 7 AM reveille. It may be a good idea, but not at 7, since work doesn't start till 8:30. What they should do is to start work at 8:00 & quit at 5. As it is, the men will just sit around waiting till work time. Of course, none of the Hq officers get up for reveille, but all the Hq Bn officers have to get up to take it.

Bad Nauheim, Germany
Monday, 6 May 1946

Dearest Liz: . . .

The morning was spent in disposing of one request after another. That's one of the troubles with this job. It is the only medical installation in town, & it looks like a big one, so I'm flooded with requests for everything from penicillin to lunch. I literally have 5–6 people a day coming in with one sort of time-consuming request or another. Every bad luck story in town ends up here sooner or later. For the first time I'm able to sympathize with the wealthy. Their requests for things must be terrific—and granting one means being flooded with other requests.

This afternoon I went over to a civilian dentist here whom Eagle knows. He is going to fix me up with a new front tooth to replace the one put in by the British dentist at Weert, Holland last spring. Then I saw several officer patients, following which I made a house call on Mrs. (Col) Mathias of the Engineers. She is very nice but neurotic & talkative as hell. She has the grippe but it took me an hour & 20 minutes to get out. I'm really in general practice now. Byers doesn't want to mess with the community practice, so I really get the gravy. I do the ward cases, all house call & dependents, most officers, plus anything which puzzles him. He isn't a bad doctor, but I think I'm better, which is boosting to my professional morale, at least. . . .

Bad Nauheim, Germany
Tuesday, 7 May 1946

Dearest Liz: . . .

This morning I was awakened by the sound of sirens as they brought in a guy who had attempted suicide. He was a polish UNRRA guy who we believe took 10 grains of phenobarbital he got yesterday at the dispensary. It taught Byers a lesson, anyway, I never give out over 6 grains total. . . .

It has been a very unpleasant day here because it looks like the night German aid man has been sneaking penicillin in small quantities. I have had to try to get someone to take his place & fire him. I haven't fired him yet as I can't get anyone else till the 15th. Also Eagle has been heckling the nurses till they are ready to quit. He checks up on the food in a very minute & infinitesimal fashion which even makes me uneasy to hear about it.

This afternoon I did a number of errands, planned the weaning of a 3 month old baby from breast to bottle . . . with its French mother. Then I spent 2 hours getting my tooth worked on. Tonight I spent another hour on it. Tomorrow I go to get the shade matched, & should get the tooth on Friday. Right now I'm having a lot of pain from where he dug up in under my gum.

This evening I played tennis with a Capt. Moore of the Engineers who is pretty good. He beat me 7-5, 6-4.

Goodnight, sweetie. I love you. Tomorrow is a holiday (V-E Day), but it's no holiday for me. . . .

The United Nations Relief and Rehabilitation Administration (UNRRA) was organized in 1943 and made up of 47 member governments for the purpose of giving relief and rehabilitation to people in liberated countries in Europe and the Far East.

Bad Nauheim, Germany
Wednesday, 8 May 1946

Dearest Liz: . . .

Today . . . was a holiday. I didn't get up till 9, but was busy till noon, then did get in an hour & a half nap & an hour & a half of lousy tennis. Following that I was again busy for quite a while with a broken leg, a dog bite from a dog who probably was rabid, an epileptic, a guy with a bad sore throat which may be diphtheria, and about 6 gold-bricks. . . .

Last night just as I finished writing you I was called to see Mrs. Fitzgerald, the Norwegian girl, again. She has been worried about several things the past few days & last night went out of her head after being given a sedative & thought she was back in Buchenwald being raped. She really needs quite a less emotional & more stable person than her husband. I wish you were here to talk to her. That's all she needs—someone stable to talk to & lean on for a while till she gets back on her mental feet. It's really a very interesting problem in psychiatry & human relations to handle her. It's one of those cases where success is very probable if it is handled right and where the people concerned are nice enough that the effort required would not seem to be wasted. . . .

Bad Nauheim, Germany
Thursday, 9 May 1946

Dearest Liz: . . .

This morning I was awakened to see a patient with alleged hematemesis. At 7 we had Reveille. Just as I was getting down to work a bad burn case came in & took up enough time to make the rest of the morning a hectic one. The afternoon wasn't so bad. Tonight Byers & I played tennis for about half an hour before I went to play bridge.

. . . Today we got thru a directive from higher headquarters on VD which is almost word for word my VD program & looks like maybe they mean business on tightening up on the morals required of officers.

. . . I still haven't heard from Rusty. I'll have to write him again. The Lichfield trials probably are as bad as they sound. One thing the papers don't say is that neither the witnesses (ex-Lichfield prisoners) nor those being tried are any damn good. The tables might just as well have been turned the other way. The nearest guy to being worth a damn seems to be Judson Smith, the Sergeant who was sentenced to 3 years in the 1st trial. . . .

On December 1, 1945, the US Army convened a general court-martial in London to inquire into allegations of brutality and murder committed at the 10th Replacement Depot near Lichfield, England. The Depot included a stockade where American GIs, including those who went AWOL, were held pending court-martial. At the end of the war the commandant, Colonel James Killan, and the guards of the depot were accused of running a "concentration camp for American soldiers," which led to a succession of trials that the press on both sides of the Atlantic termed the "Lichfield trials." In May, the court-martial was moved to Bad Nauheim. The trials brought out a chilling picture of beatings and shootings of American soldiers by their guards, and prompted the revision of the military justice system after WWII. After months of testimony, Killan was reprimanded and fined $500, with other officers given similar punishments.[23]

Bad Nauheim, Germany
Friday, 10 May 1946

Dearest Liz: Today was a bad one, but I am still encouraged because I heard a rumor which, if true, is good for us. It was that the 18 months overseas deal will probably go into effect sometime in June. If true, that would probably make it mandatory for me to leave the ETO by July 1st. That's only 6 weeks ahead of the time I'd get out by present criteria, but the six weeks till then look a lot bigger than 6 weeks after then—provided I've been redeployed at the splitting point.

. . . I spent most of the evening cleaning up for Col White who is bringing over the Chief of Staff tomorrow for examination. Reeck came over in the middle of it & helped me put up a set of maps on the wall. I'm using them to locate good fishing places. Afterwards Reeck, Eagle, & I sat in my sitting room drinking beer & eating Eagle's Salami & my dill pickles. . . .

Jim did a lot of fishing in his spare time that spring, catching trout of two or three pounds. He kept a set of maps on the wall of his office with colored pins to indicate spots he had fished, rated in three categories of poor, okay, and good fishing. When a colonel from Frankfurt inspected the dispensary, he was impressed by Jim's military-looking office, with its strategic map. When Jim told him what it was for, the colonel did not ball him out, but rather wanted to know where the best spots were so he and his buddies could "fish" them. What the colonel's crowd actually did was dynamite the streams to stun the fish and pick them up.

Jim fishing just outside Schotten, north of Bad Nauheim, May 1946.

Bad Nauheim, Germany
Saturday 11 May 1946

Dearest Wife: Today is the 18th month anniversary of our separation—even to the correct day of the week. I hope it won't be much longer. At least we know I'll start home about Aug. 15th & if the 18 months thing comes thru, it should be sometime in June, which was your original guess, Sweetie.

. . . I was slowed down somewhat thru having been up from 3 till 4:30 last night removing a guy's thrombosed hemorrhoid and then being wakened at 6:30 to take Mrs. Kotnik (the pregnant girl I wrote you about shepherding around the 97th) to the 97th for her labor. She delivered a boy at 12:20 today. My stock should be high, as I predicted a boy on the basis of a very slow fetal heart rate.

This afternoon Reeck & I went fishing in the Taunus Mountains about 30 miles from here. It was beautiful country & we caught 6 trout. On getting back we had the nurse on duty fry them up for us. I also found some mint along the brook this afternoon, so we had a julep in addition. Somehow, tho, the fishing is more enjoyable with you & the julep & trout taste better with you present for DUTY! . . .

Bad Nauheim, Germany
13 May 46

Dearest Sweetie: Tonight I'm again bone-tired after a long, muggy day with no mail from you. I didn't work too hard for the simple reason that I just plain couldn't. I've just about reached the end of my rope here till I can get away & get a rest, so I requested a leave to Belgium & will write Pierre immediately to try to go there. I can get nothing in the way of encouragement on the 18 month deal in June. It certainly won't go thru without a lot more replacements.

This evening I sent Mrs. Fitzgerald to the hospital with either an abortion or an ectopic pregnancy. I don't know which. I'm really getting quite a bit of variety these days. . . .

Bad Nauheim, Germany
Tuesday, 14 May 1946

Dearest Liz: . . .

It was rainy all day, which suited me fine. It has been too dry both to my taste & the crops' taste. I was busy with arranging for a VD lecture tomorrow and for getting a new chlorination system installed here in the Bad Nauheim city water system.

Bad Nauheim, Germany
Wednesday, 15 May 46

Dearest Liz: Today was a bad day, but I still have your four letters of yesterday to read over. I again had a busy day with the usual annoyances. I had to fire my night German aid man, but have a nurse starting tonight to work in his place. Tonight we showed a VD film "Pickup." Two men passed out during it, one of them requiring some stitches over 1 eye! — Guilty consciences I guess. McNerney is finally starting to clamp down on VD as I said before, so they asked me for a VD program, I told them I'd submitted one 3 months ago. Apparently no one ever took it seriously (Col. Boshoff favoured supervised prostitution under Army control). Anyway they gave me the green light, & I've now started my lecture series.

Between November & now I was living on accumulated money which started piling up in August. I also won about $40 at poker while at the 178th. That helped out. I didn't spend my full allowance on the Swiss tour either. I have spent very little at all except for PX rations up till now. Since being in Germany we've had big PX rations, I've bought pictures, wine, & beer (In Reims the beer was free), so it goes a lot faster, but I still manage to live within my means.

For once I really have the beer situation licked. The sergeant in charge of the officers' club is my boy, so he now brings over a case of beer every now & then & hauls away the empties! Even the General has to send his own orderly after it! This guy does it voluntarily! I find I get as far & as much by just doing my job as Eagle does with all the deals he pulls. He's an "operator"! . . .

As I said in a recent letter, if you are getting too tired & jumpy, why don't you quit when your family goes to Maine & go with them. I think that will occupy you as well as your work—& also be good for you. I am really starting to take better care of myself, too, so don't worry. As a matter of fact, I weigh more than I ever did—147!

. . . Your remark about the high cost of new housing will probably continue to be true. We will probably have to buy a big old house. I don't think we'll ever have the money to build one new the size we want. I was glad to hear that you had already had the chest x-ray I wrote you to get day before yesterday.

There was a shortage of beer in postwar Germany, which pained Jim greatly. He told of helping a supply sergeant with his hemorrhoids, whereupon the sergeant was so grateful he offered Jim anything. Jim requested beer. The sergeant, who had been supplying his general with two cases of scarce bottled beer each week, told the General he could now only obtain one case. Meanwhile, the other went to Captain McKay.

The GI rations from the PX were generous with cigarettes, which were non-existent for Germans. Food rationing for Germans was very tight, and there was widespread hunger. German currency, the Reichsmark, was virtually worthless by this time. The black market thrived, and cigarettes became a common currency. As one of the few non-smokers, Jim traded cigarettes for various things, including a few small paintings.

Bad Nauheim, Germany
Thursday, 16 May 1946

Dearest Liz: . . .

A notice came out today that we would send 2 tennis players from Bad Nauheim to Frankfurt on Sunday to play in a playoff for two players to represent the American occupation zone at Wimbledon on June 6th. I don't imagine I have a chance in Hades of making it, but I figure it's worth a try. So I'm now in training. Byers & I played 3 sets tonight which I won. I shouldn't have any trouble in being one of the players to go from here (Bad Nauheim).

The theoretical function of CBS is to operate the service installations (Depots & Hospitals chiefly). Actually there is no reason why it can't all be done by the appropriate "G" sections of 3rd Army Hq. It just provides work for some more guys with rank. Incidentally, I'm beginning to get a little tired of seeing these Regular Army guys who've only been here a few months after spending the whole war in the States, have their wives roll in.

Sweetie, I can imagine the cracks the dummy sailor boy made at you at Mrs. Kneeland's party. I'm sure you were picked on because you were the prettiest. . . .

Bad Nauheim, Germany
Friday, 17 May 1946

Dearest Liz: Today was a good one. There were three letters from you, all written last weekend. One was marked "Do not open before May 30th." You must have written it Sunday, which is also when I wrote you a letter for our anniversary.

The day was busy with the usual time-consuming extras. I had to work on arrangements for transferring a negro marihuana [sic] addict Lichfield witness to the 317th in Wiesbaden. Tonight Byers & I played tennis, went to see "Letter for Evie" which only I enjoyed, then came back here. Byers went on up to bed, but I was just caught by a guy with an infected foot. As I was starting on him, they brought in a negro who had been shot (another of the Lichfield bunch) in a fight he started with one of his buddies. The net result has been that it is now almost 1:15.

They changed the tennis schedule around today. The Frankfurt playoffs aren't until May 30. A bunch of men came in here today from outlying CBS units & will play in the eliminations for the best 2 CBS players. I'm wasting my time even to mess with it. I've even gone to training—tho tonight is somewhat of a breach of it.

This afternoon I called Brussels to learn that the de Smet family is in the south of France, so that kills my trip to Brussels. I don't know whether to go to Switzerland or not. I hate to go alone without anyone I know. I called Don Sweeny, but he couldn't go. There is a hell of a lot to do around here, but I do need the rest. I sort of hate to miss the tennis, but I'm pretty darn sure I'd never make Wimbledon. Oh, hell! All I really want to do is get home to you. . . .

Bad Nauheim, Germany
Sunday, 19 May 1946

Dearest Liz: . . . Yesterday was very busy, including 5 sets of tennis. Come evening I was very tired & planned to stay home to go to bed early. Eagle had been talking a lot lately about how the food was piling up, so I thought I'd look at the head & ration counts a minute. I found the books in a mess & when I had figured them out, found we are 25% overdrawn for the month so far. They are court-martialling commanding officers for being over 4% overdrawn now and all our rations thru May 28th are already ordered, leaving no time to underdraw to make up for it. Eagle's attitude, of course, was "so what?" It doesn't affect Eagle if I get court martialled. I really lit into him about it & made him postpone his date till we got the books straight & a plan made whereby we will be able to squeeze thru without getting into trouble. That took till 10:30 by which time I was mentally as well as physically exhausted & upset with a terrible headache—all nerves, I'm sure. . . .

Fritz Weispfenning was here yesterday, asking for a statement from me that he was not an enthusiastic party member. I gave it to him as I conscientiously could.. . . This afternoon I played my first round match for the CBS championship. I won & play Byers tomorrow. The winner of that will be one of the 2 members of the CBS team. I should win. That will get me to Frankfurt where I won't make the ETO team (best 2 in ETO) which will play at Wimbledon June 6th.

I got my new tooth yesterday. It is better than the other. The color is good, but it is too big. I think it can be ground down OK, tho.

Tonight we went to the movies, but hadn't been there 10 minutes till I was called to sew up a guy who cut his wrist. I had no sooner sewed him up than they brought in 4 guys who capsized in a boat on the pond. One of them has been giving me a hard time. He is complaining of terrible pain in a "hernia" which I can't feel & putting on a big show I don't believe. I've given him a sedative finally & hope that does the trick. . . .

Bad Nauheim, Germany
Monday, 20 May 1946

Dearest Liz: . . .

It was a beautiful warm summer day, but clouded over tonight & is now blowing very hard & will probably rain. I played Byers tonight in the CVS tennis tournament & beat him 6-2, 6-2, 6-1. Tomorrow I play a guy named Bowman in the finals. He'll cream me after my late hours tonight. There will be no chance of resting tomorrow as we have an I-G inspection right after lunch.

I'm so mad tonight I could bust. I worked so hard & fast today that my stomach is tied up in knots, & tonight I have been doing a lot of unnecessary night work which annoys [the] hell out of me. I'm neither getting paid for it, learning from it, or doing the recipients any good.

In addition to my other troubles practically every other person these days asks me when I'm going home in the same tone as your "What, isn't your husband home yet?" people. Boy my stomach is really tied up in knots tonight.

Liz, I wish we were together. It makes the aggravations of life so much easier to put up with. When I can pour it all out to you and hold you close . . . it makes everything so much more stable and life worth living in spite of its aggravations. . . .

I LOVE YOU!

Jim

Bad Nauheim, Germany
Tuesday, 21 May 1946

Dearest Liz: . . .

In the afternoon it started to rain. . . . It queered the tennis match this afternoon, but that suited me fine, because of my lack of sleep last night. Also it may give my belly a chance to quiet down. We play tomorrow at 4 o'clock. . . .

Tonight I'm having dinner with Charles and Rachel. Thursday I'm going to a Hq Bn dinner on Johannisberg—the big hill behind town.

Yesterday we got in four men who are going to run two prophylactic stations in Bad Nauheim. I spent half the day working on getting them started. The VD rate is bad. We had 6 new cases yesterday alone—that was the worst day we've ever had here.

Tonight I gave two VD lectures, after which I went with Stromback to see "The Milky Way," a USO show. . . .

Bad Nauheim, Germany
Wednesday, 22 May 1946

Dearest Liz: Guess what! Your husband ate too much tonight! I couldn't help it. Rachel had an enormous & delicious meal—tomato juice, chicken, soup, almost a pound of steak (just for me), corn, string beans, potatoes, hot rolls, pudding, salad, white cake with chocolate icing, & champagne! That cake was the best since leaving home. It was really good. Rachel sent her best to you & said she would write you.

The day was relatively uneventful. It rained all day, so the CBS tennis finals were again delayed. Per usual I spent the day on administrative work. . . .

Bad Nauheim, Germany
Thursday, 23 May 46

Dearest Liz: . . . Late this afternoon we played the finals of the CBS tennis. Strangely enough, I won, but it was a terrific battle. The score was 2-6, 7-5, 2-6, 14-12, 6-2! It took 3½ hours. Every muscle I have is sore tonight, but I feel relaxed and would be happy if I only had you here. . . .

The day was not too bad, chiefly because I just plain ignored my paperwork, but tomorrow will be hell. I at last got a jeep today, so now I can ride around with my little red cross painted on the radiator grill work & "Post Surgeon" under the windshield. . . .

Bad Nauheim, Germany
Saturday, 25 May 46

Dearest Liz: This is the last Saturday night in May. I should be home by 3 months from now—and discharged. At least I hope so. They can hold a doctor for 60 days after he is eligible, however. I sure hope that doesn't happen to me.

. . . I've developed a terrible cold. This afternoon I went to Darmstadt, Weinheim, & Heidelberg on business. Prokup & Seely went along for the ride. I had supper with Don Sweeny at Heidelberg. He knew nothing new. We got back at

9 o'clock & I've been busy on emergency calls since—a pseudo heart attack & a drunk with a dislocated shoulder, both in Friedberg.

Two nice things did happen to me today. At Darmstadt, at the 4th Medical Lab, one of the guys I saw (they are all new there) asked me if I were Capt. McKay. I said yes & he said he'd heard a lot of nice things about me, then said to the CO of the place: "He's the guy they told us to give anything he wants to, because he knows what he's doing!". That was quite a compliment. The other nice thing came from a Col. Fitzpatrick, assistant G-1, who has been in the infirmary the past 2 days. He told me yesterday he thought his treatment was comparable to that in a good General Hospital in the States. This morning before he left, he showed me a draft of an official commendation he is going to write to Col. White about me, requesting that it be made a part of my official record! It was nice to hear, but doesn't mean too much, except that at least someone appreciated what I'm trying to do—run a really first class little hospital.

The news of the railroad strike hit our papers today. It sounds like more confusion than we have had in a long time. It really looks as if the days of capitalism are over, because soon there will be no such thing as return on capital investment, all profits being split among those actively engaged in the business concerned. It's probably a good thing but will change the lives of many people—your parents, for instance. It's OK when you're young. I don't know about when you're old. . . .

Bad Nauheim, Germany
Monday, 27 May 1946

Dearest Liz: . . .

Brace yourself for a little news on the redeployment front—I'm not coming home right now, but it won't be too long before you are again a wife with a husband! I was over seeing Col. Collins today about getting a nurse and he told me to plan on leaving in July. Later I saw Rader & he told me he had heard they were going to lower the overseas service to 18 months on July 1st. That means I'll probably get home about the end of July, tho it might be as early as the 15th or 20th. The sooner the better as far as I'm concerned! That is still two months off, but it is also close enough to be counted in weeks, so it isn't too bad. You might figure on asking for a leave of absence started about July 15th or whenever I get back.

From what I hear about prices at home, our money may not go so far as I had hoped. However, the G-I bill of rights should see us through. Also, I figure that by the time I get home we will have saved $5,000 dollars out of what I've made since being overseas, plus any you may have been able to put by after taxes, which is probably very little. That should still give us a good start, tho I guess we'll need everything we can rake together before we are thru.

D & A's #2 male baby sure does sound as if we'll end up with 5 girls, doesn't it? Oh well, if they're all like you, it will be OK. Your receipt of the $300 was duly noted. That really went thru in a hurry—much faster than ever before, just 3 weeks from the time I sent it.

Byers & I were just called out to see a German girl they said they couldn't get a doctor for. She has a half-American baby & puerperal sepsis. The German doctor did arrive about 10 minutes after we did, but his name was already lower than mud. It was probably sort of unfair to him because he had probably been busy all day, but he should have known she was in bad shape & come to see her earlier. That sort of thing, of course, is what gives us (the Americans) a good name. People over here are always able to get us when they can't get their own. The doctors in Europe do not go out of their way for their patients nearly as much as we do. . . .

The beer situation at home sounds bad. In answer to your question—you know I like beer best, but I think I'd come home to you anyway, even tho it meant never ever drinking any beer again. . . .

I figure I'll have about 7 weeks terminal leave with pay which will amount to about $500, so we shouldn't have any monetary worries for that period, at least. . . .

Bad Nauheim, Germany
Tuesday, 28 May 1946

Dearest Liz: Today was a bad one with no mail from you. The weather was beautiful & I spent most of my time doing a lot of back errands in the jeep. This afternoon I went out to the German Hospital & had a long talk with Dr. Cellarius, the head of it, who has just returned from being a PW. He is very intelligent & a nice guy, but—he's a German & got a little deep into telling me how tough Germany & the Germans were having it for me to swallow. Later in the afternoon I went 22 miles to Giessen where we are now to get our medical supplies, & made contact with the supply officer there.

This evening I saw an old German with a fractured skull & intracranial hemorrhage. He ran out in front of a jeep without looking to see if anything was coming. Then I wrote up an accident report on that in 6 copies, then finally got a letter written to Dr. McIntosh, from whom I've never heard. I go to Frankfurt Saturday for the tennis tryouts for Wimbledon. . . .

Bad Nauheim, Germany
Wednesday, 29 May 1946

Dearest Lizzie: 3 years ago now I was sound asleep after spending an exciting afternoon & evening with my bride to be. If it must be confessed, I was excited over the events of the day to come, even in my sleep—and nervous! Wasn't that dumb? —to be nervous, I mean.

Today was a good one with your letter of the 22nd. Bad Nauheim is a town of about 5,000 population in normal times and 10–15 thousand now. As for distance, it is probably about a mile square.

. . . Tonight Byers & I played tennis for about an hour. I was hitting them pretty well. It was the first tennis since the CBS finals last week. . . . Then Col. Numainville called up & wanted me to go see Lt. Smith [pseudonym], an engineer Wac Lt. whom Byers designates as "that old whore," Lt. Smith had been sick since 6 AM, but since she is in the Commanding General's Section, they called Numainville instead of me earlier in the day. Another reason was probably because I bawled hell out of her about 3–4 weeks ago for walking into the dispensary after sick call hours & demanding to be seen ahead of a patient I was seeing because she was in the CG Section & had important work to do. She is the wife of a Regular Army Officer who died about 5 years ago & was an enlisted Wac till commissioned directly by Eisenhower. She is the first Wac Officer I've ever seen who is definitely not a lady. . . . I should have been writing you & then was kept waiting 45 minutes while she dressed because her boyfriend, who is the assistant I-G didn't want her carried out on a litter—because she was coming from his room, I imagine. . . .

The 97th General Hospital in Frankfurt was located in the triangle formed by Giessener Strasse, Friedberger Landstrasse, and Homburger Landstrasse, near exit 9 of Route 661. It was the hub of a network of clinics in the surrounding area, designed to provide medical care to the occupying troops.

Bad Nauheim, Germany
Thursday, 30 May 1946

Dearest Liz: . . . In celebration of the great anniversary, I did take most of the day off. This morning I drove down to Frankfurt, spent all morning trying to find out about the tennis tournament. This afternoon I played 2 sets with a nice kid named Schreiber who is in the tournament. He beat me thoroughly, but I wasn't playing well. He's better, tho, than I. Afterward we went to the Frankfurt Red Cross in the Palmengarten & had 2 chocolate malted milks apiece! I had supper at the 97th, looked for Lt. Beeman, who was on the 16th Corps team last year, for a while & came back, bringing Capt. Pieper, whom I had taken to the 97th this morning to visit a sick friend in the 97th. Like a damn fool when we got back I took her to see "The Lost Weekend" which I wanted to see & hadn't. Of course, just as I got back to the dispensary at 10:20, there was a call on a pediatrics case—the baby hadn't had a BM for 2 days & was grunting about it. It took half an hour to calm the parents & convince them that the reason he was crying his little head off was because he hadn't yet had his 10 PM feeding & it was now 11.

I have to be in Frankfurt at 10 tomorrow morning for the draw & will probably play the 1st round in the afternoon. The courts there are lousy.

Darling, I know that you are thinking of me tonight just as I am thinking of you & loving you, my bride & wife & sweetie. I had hoped so much that we would be together tonight, but it just doesn't seem to be our luck. Here's hoping that the 30th of July will see us together. . . .

Bad Nauheim, Germany
Friday, 31 May 1946

Dearest Liz: Today was a bad one, but I still had your anniversary letter to read over again. The lily of the valley sprig still smelled sweet. I read it over last night after I got into bed & then spent a very pleasant night dreaming of you. . . .

Today I went to Frankfurt again, but again did not play. I'm scheduled to play at 10 tomorrow morning & again in the afternoon if I win. If I win both matches I'll have a very good chance of going to Wimbledon, tho I'm not sure I will if they tell me I'll possibly be redeployed before. I'm using a racket strung with some of the gut you sent.

Coming back tonight I was scared I might have that jeep accident you've been so worried about. The fluid all leaked out of my brakes & coming back I had no brakes at all. It was a harrowing ride at a snail's pace. . . .

Jim at work at his desk in Bad Nauheim, June 1946.

They do have lilacs in Germany. . . . Wally, the chief nurse always puts a fresh bouquet on my desk each day & Annelore, the lab girl has been getting lilies of the valley now & then & putting them in front of your picture on my desk since I told her they were our wedding flowers. Yesterday they knew it was our anniversary & had a beautiful big bouquet of mixed flowers on the desk & Annelore got 3 beautiful white roses which she put in front of your picture. They are really very nice girls, both of them—neither of them the "frauleins" you hear about. . . .

There is a gap of two weeks in Jim's letters. He did not win the tennis tournament and go to Wimbledon again. Given the news in his next letter, that doesn't seem to have bothered him a bit.

Bad Nauheim, Germany
Tuesday, 18 June 1946

Dearest Sweetie: Today was a GOOD day. They called up from the Surgeon's office & said I could leave as soon as I could get ready & Headquarters Battalion would release me! Since I still have to inventory all the property, make a report of survey on what's missing, & turn the rest over to Reeck, & pack, we figured the earliest I could leave is Saturday—So, sweetie, you will have a husband again, and sooner than you expected. They told me I'd probably get to New York about July 6th or 7th! That's only 3 weeks off! I'll cable you tomorrow (I heard about it too late to cable tonight). When I get to Le Havre and find out what ship I go on, I'll try to cable you again & let you know.

In view of today's news, you had better figure on quitting your job either July 6th or June 29th. You probably won't have enough notice to quit on the latter date. I think your idea of going to the Farm & waiting there for me to call is a good one. Then you can drive down to Dix & pick me up when I'm discharged. If you haven't received my cable, stop writing when you get this.

. . . You had better get my summer uniforms & clothes out. I hope you'll be able to resign or get your leave of absence as of July 6th instead of 20th. Of course, I still may be held up and not arrive till later, but they claim everyone (MCs) goes right thru now with only 2–3 days layover at Le Havre.

Oh, darling, it really looks as if we'll be together again in a month. If you think you were manic on getting my letters saying I'd definitely leave around the first week in July, you should see me now. I've been going around with a grin as big as a house and manic as the dickens. Liz, it's going to be SO wonderful to see you and hold you in my arms & kiss you & pat your . . . That's because you're my own darling sweetie—wife I've been waiting to see for over 19 months. Oh sweetie, I love you . . ., I LOVE YOU!

Jim

This was Jim's last surviving letter from Europe. Having expected to ship out from Le Havre, he was instead sent north to Bremen, arriving there by train on Tuesday, June 25, to await a spot on a ship. Instead of the two or three days he had been told, the wait ended up being two weeks. The troops were put in "packets," groups that would ship out together. On the twenty-ninth he watched the Bardstown Victory sail away with 1,200 troops. On

July 3, Jim's name appeared on the shipment order for packet #8560. On July 4, the Lewiston Victory and the Sheepshead Victory also sailed without him. It was very hot, and the barracks was without water because some drunken air corps officers had torn things apart. Jim kept a few notes during this time, but did not write to Liz, expecting to be with her shortly. He wrote "no sugar all day on 4 July," along with other food notes. On July 5, he notes not getting into the movie "Gilda" and cites various snafus in the overcrowded staging area. On July 6, Jim's number was finally called to sail on the seventh on the Mahoney Victory.

Jim gets the news that he is going home, June 18, 1946.

WESTERN UNION

CLASS OF SERVICE
This is a full-rate Telegram or Cablegram unless its deferred character is indicated by a suitable symbol above or preceding the address.

A. N. WILLIAMS
PRESIDENT

1201

SYMBOLS
DL = Day Letter
NL = Night Letter
LC = Deferred Cable
NLT = Cable Night Letter
Ship Radiogram

The filing time shown in the date line on telegrams and day letters is STANDARD TIME at point of origin. Time of receipt is STANDARD TIME at point of destination

C75CC 1N INTL

CD FRANKFURT VIA PREWI 26 20

NLT ELIZABETH MCKAY

58 WEST 9TH STR NY

LEAVING NAUHEIM SATURDAY JUNE 22 ARRIVING NEWYORK ANY TIME

AFTER JULY 6 ALL MY LOVE

JIM JAMES MCKAY

834A

THE COMPANY WILL APPRECIATE SUGGESTIONS FROM ITS PATRONS CONCERNING ITS SERVICE

Jim's initial cable anticipating a homecoming around July 6.

WESTERN UNION (59)

CLASS OF SERVICE
This is a full-rate Telegram or Cablegram unless its deferred character is indicated by a suitable symbol above or preceding the address.

A. N. WILLIAMS
PRESIDENT

1201

SYMBOLS
DL = Day Letter
NL = Night Letter
LC = Deferred Cable
NLT = Cable Night Letter
Ship Radiogram

The filing time shown in the date line on telegrams and day letters is STANDARD TIME at point of origin. Time of receipt is STANDARD TIME at point of destination

)NBP69 INTL=N BREMERHAVEN VIA WU CABLES 24 8 1946 JUL 8 PM 12 01

VLT ELIZABETH MCKAY=

58 WEST 9THST NYK=

SAILING SUNDAY JULY 7 ON MAHONEY VICTORY ARRIVE NEW YORK

ABOUT JULY 18 ALL MY LOVE=

JIM.

.58 9THST 7 18.

THE COMPANY WILL APPRECIATE SUGGESTIONS FROM ITS PATRONS CONCERNING ITS SERVICE

Jim's cable announcing his final departure date of July 7, 1946.

Chapter Fourteen

Homecoming and Beyond

The *Mahoney* was a cargo ship with GIs packed in like sardines. Designed for much heavier cargo as ballast, she was very tippy, so seasickness was rampant. The troops got two meals each day, consisting of army rations. They landed in Hoboken and were immediately transferred by train to Fort Dix, New Jersey. Anticipating Jim's arrival, Liz was at the farm in Basking Ridge as they had planned. Jim called her from Fort Dix, and Liz drove with Jim's parents the 70 miles south to see him, reunited for the first time in 20 months. When I asked my father what it felt like to sail into New York Harbor and see the Statue of Liberty, he said it was nothing special. He knew he wouldn't see Liz until he got to Fort Dix, and that was what he got excited about.

When I asked him if it was difficult readjusting to civilian life in the States, he simply said "no." Although we as children knew nothing about it, Jim suffered from nightmares all his life, harking back to those four months of combat. He avoided war movies, although when *Patton* came out he went to see it. In the middle of the screening, he left with chest pains and went to the emergency room, thinking he was having a heart attack. His favorite TV show, however, was *M*A*S*H*.

Shortly after Jim's reunion with Liz, they set out on a 2½-month trip to the West, with an eye toward settling in the Northwest. Driving through Pittsburg they found incredible smog, with the streetlights on in midday. They visited Billings, Montana, before spending a couple of weeks in the Tetons, Yellowstone, and Glacier National Parks. Driving on, they went south through Missoula, where Jim had his first interview, then to Salt Lake City and Boise, then north again to Couer d'Alene and Spokane on the way to Bellingham, where Jim's brother, Dan, his wife, Alice, and their young son, Mike (Reb), had recently moved. Jim interviewed in Seattle and Portland. Liz wrote her parents that they liked Seattle better and could see themselves living in Tacoma. They visited Mount Ranier, Tacoma, Olympia, and the Olympic Peninsula on the way to Portland. They stopped in the Hood River Valley, fell in love with it, and considered settling there. Jim's father and uncle had tried to start an orchard there 40 years earlier, but failed. Jim and Liz continued south, visiting all towns with a population over 10,000, which Jim felt was the minimum population to support a pediatrician. That included Corvallis, Salem, Eugene, Klamath Falls, and Medford. Looking to practice privately, Jim stopped along the way to look up contacts and investigate the medical scene. They stopped at Crater Lake, then went down the California coast on the Redwood Highway to Cobb, where Liz's brother Caleb Foote was living. They stayed in Cobb for two nights, then drove on to San Francisco. They loved San Francisco, except for the "drunken Legionnaires strewn around," who were in town for a convention. In Monterey, they stopped to see Colonel Knute Hanstton, who was the commanding officer of the 275th from Camp Breckinridge until the end of hostilities. After a night at Big Sur, they drove to Pasadena, where they stayed with Liz's great aunt. From Los Angeles they headed back east, with a stop at the Grand Canyon. They stayed at a motel on a beach on Lake Mead behind Hoover Dam on a gorgeous moonlit night with no one around. One can only imagine what a wonderful trip it must have been for a couple newly reunited, with a long bright future full of possibilities in front of them.

That fall, Jim and Liz lived at the farm in Basking Ridge and Jim worked for Dr. Tesky, the family doctor in Bernardsville, while waiting to resume his pediatric training. They drove a new two-door Chevy, which Jim had bullied out of a dealer near Basking Ridge. It was hard to get cars then, but the dealer gave Jim priority because he had to have a car for the house calls that were part of his job with Dr. Tesky.

Jim returned to New York as assistant resident at Babies Hospital in January 1947. He and Liz lived for a while in Liz's one-room apartment in Greenwich Village. Liz became pregnant in the fall of 1946, but had a miscarriage, which was devastating to her. In March 1947, she realized she was pregnant again, and this time had no problems. In the fall, they needed to move before the baby was born. They took an apartment at 325 West 22nd Street. The cost of housing was still under wartime rent control, and they paid $56/month for a four-room apartment. Liz was making about $2,500/year. They had managed to save $5,000 while Jim was overseas, and Liz had about $1,000/year from a family trust. Jim was making little or nothing as assistant resident, but they felt like they were rolling in dough and were able to go to shows and do the things they wanted. The apartment was only half a block from the campus of Columbia Presbyterian Medical Center where Jim worked. On November 18, Liz gave birth to their first son, Robert James McKay III, whom they called Robbie.

Jim was doing well when he received a call from Charlie Janeway at

Harvard, who was in his third year as chairman of pediatrics. Janeway offered Jim the chief residency at Boston Children's Hospital, which was the "top plum" in pediatrics in the country. Jim had already committed to a fellowship in endocrinology at Mass General, but they let him out of it.

Jim and Liz moved to Cambridge in January of 1948, in the immediate aftermath of an enormous snowstorm. The new family lived in the apartment upstairs at Liz's parents' house at 22 Highland Street in Cambridge. Robbie was six weeks old. Jim was paid only $1,000/year to be chief resident, but their housing was free. Liz did not work during their time in Cambridge. The young couple had a lot of interaction with the Footes and other local relatives such as the Merrimans on Brattle Street (Dorothea Merriman was Liz's "Aunt Doro"). Jim's Aunt Ruth and Uncle Hoey (Sexton) and their family were also living in Cambridge at the time.

There were about 16 residents under Jim at Boston Children's Hospital. Jim found his experience commanding men in the army was enormously useful. He was always ready and able to take over difficult situations, as he had been forced to do during the war.

Jim later described his pride that he had gotten the job on his own merits, without "pull," until one day dining with his in-laws. Liz's mother said, "Jim, isn't your boss Charlie Janeway? His mother and I were best friends when we were 16." Despite Jim's lifelong battle with surgeons and "their propensity for cutting people open without looking at the whole patient," one of his biggest supporters at Harvard was Dr. Robert E. Gross, the chief of cardiac surgery at Boston Children's Hospital, who became a very good friend and advocate of Jim's. The chief got in the habit of consulting Jim on medical matters instead of the senior pediatricians, which was not popular. Bill Waters (who later ended up in Syracuse) was a good friend, as was a French resident who ended up in Montreal as chief of pediatrics at the children's hospital. He provided Jim with lots of contacts north of the border, which was helpful during Jim's career in Burlington, Vermont.

Jim described how he and Liz considered Burlington a nice small city and talked of going into practice there. Jim had become interested in teaching through his work as chief resident. His friend Bob Smith told him to talk to Bill Brown at Mary Fletcher Hospital, dean of the University of Vermont College of Medicine. There was a provisionally approved pediatric residency program at Mary Fletcher, established in 1946 with a single resident. Brown called Jim back to ask him to come to UVM to start a full-time academic Department of Pediatrics. It turns out that Bill Brown had two people he relied on for advice; Russell MacIntosh (Jim's boss in New York) and Charlie Janeway in Boston.

Each independently recommended Jim for the job. Looking for a spot where he could mix practice and teaching, Jim saw UVM and Burlington as the ideal opportunity.

In January of 1950, Jim and his growing family (son David was born in 1949) moved to Burlington to become assistant professor (salary $6,600) at the UVM Medical School. In 1949, there were 13 pediatric beds at Mary Fletcher Hospital and 20 at Bishop DeGoesbriand Hospital, just a block down Pearl Street. Both were staffed by the four practicing pediatricians located in Burlington. There was some resistance to the new structure among the independent practitioners, because they were afraid Jim would be taking away their pediatric cases. Ralph Sussman, a local pediatrician, was a great help to Jim in gaining acceptance. Even so, it was two years before any of the other pediatricians referred a patient to Jim. Meanwhile, he and Sussman ran a free clinic every week in Burlington to improve delivery to the poorer population. Vermont was well behind in pediatrics and Jim was quite isolated in his field, finding himself the only pediatrician consulting to general practitioners. He made frequent trips to Boston for professional contacts and to keep up with the latest developments. One Boston friend was Alex Nadas, the father of pediatric cardiology.

Full approval for the UVM pediatric residency program was obtained in 1952, and formal conversion from a division of the Department of Medicine to independent departmental status was achieved in 1955. Jim was the first chairman of the UVM Department of Pediatrics. In 1956, Dr. Gerald Lucey was recruited as chief of pediatrics at Bishop DeGoesbriand but resigned in 1960 in favor of Dr. McKay, in order to establish a more formally coordinated pediatric service and residency program. The two men were close friends and collaborated in the department for many years. Jim had a special interest in genetics and did some early research involving chromosomal abnormalities. After his death, I discovered among his papers a file full of job offers from medical schools all over the country. He chose to stay in Vermont for his entire career. I think it was another lesson from his army days, that a stable home for his wife and children was paramount.

Jim was active in seemingly every national and regional organization of pediatrics. He was unhappy with the petty competitions between some of the organizations, and worked to bridge those gaps. In 1970, Jim became co-editor of *Pediatrics*, the premier textbook of the discipline. The American Academy of Pediatrics elected Jim president in 1971, which meant a busy year of travel all over the country, and a three-week trip to Denmark, Sweden, Russia, and Austria with his wife and two younger sons.

Always ready to travel, especially if it involved medicine, Jim attended between 10 and 20 medical conferences every year, all over North America. Internationally, he made two trips to China with Liz as part of medical tours, and others to Western Europe. After his retirement from UVM, Jim and Liz took several long trips in their VW Vanagon, including three trips to Alaska and two to Newfoundland.

Jim retired as chairman of the department in 1980. He stayed heavily involved at the hospital and the UVM Medical School, and attended weekly pediatric grand rounds until shortly before his death. In the 1990s, he and Liz were instrumental in establishing Wake Robin, a retirement community in Shelburne, Vermont. The medical wing is named after him.

Eight months after Liz's sudden death in 1999, Jim moved to Wake Robin. He had found life without Liz to be empty, and keeping up the family home in Williston difficult. Two months later he was introduced to Martha Wellman, a neighbor down the hall. In January of 2000, they announced their intention to marry, taking their families by total surprise. On March 18, they were married at a function house across the road from Wake Robin. Martha and her first husband, Thomas, had built a camp on Lake Willoughby in the 1960s, and spent summers there from then on. The new couple settled into a pattern of summers at Willoughby and winters at Wake Robin. Martha developed a slowly progressing case of Alzheimer's in about 2005. Jim devoted himself more and more to her care as the disease worsened. He still took great pleasure in his family. October 8, 2012 was Jim's 95th birthday, and nearly all of his descendants came to Wake Robin for a celebration. He met his first great-grandchild and smiled from ear to ear. He watched in wonder as the two granddaughters who could not be there were connected by video and chatted with him over the computer. He could justifiably be very proud of a life well lived and a legacy of descendants who were carrying on his values in this rapidly evolving new world. Jim died peacefully at Wake Robin six weeks later, on November 23, 2012, the day after Thanksgiving, with me at his side.

Appendix

The Sauer/Weispfenning Family Letters: 1946–1954

In 1935, Jim McKay spent four months in Frankfurt at the age of seventeen. He had finished high school early and wanted to learn German. His landlady, Frieda Sauer, was a widow. Her daughter, Ruth, was married to Fritz Weispfenning soon after Jim's arrival. They formed a friendship that survived the war, despite the fact that Jim and Fritz had each been officers in opposing forces. I have found a total of 43 postwar letters my father received from the Sauer/ Weispfenning family spanning the period from 1946 until 1954, which paint a fascinating portrait of the German experience in the years following WWII. The letters were all in German. Excerpts from the translations of those letters follow. The first is from Fritz, dated October 16, 1946. Jim and Fritz had met twice in Bad Nauheim between the time Fritz was released from a civilian internment camp in the spring of 1946 and the time Jim had left Germany in July. By October, some six months after his release, Fritz had regained enough physical strength to return to Frankfurt to begin re-building his life.

Frankfurt/Main, Oct. 16, 1946

Dear Jim,

My denazification proceedings are behind me, at least the first stage, and it is high time that I write to you. First of all I would like to thank you again for the written statement. It did not have the desired effect, at least during the first stage, but I am hoping it will be all the more effective during my appeal.

The result of the proceedings: I have been sentenced to one year probation during which I am only allowed to work in low-level positions, plus a fine of RM 5000.

The reasoning: I had been sympathetic to the Democratic Party before 1933 and had openly acted against the Nazi ideas (student organization and legal federation where I had been nominated and elected twice by the Left). After 1933 I had not joined the national socialist mindset but had even worked against it in a small circle (my defense of non-Arians, for instance, as you know). However, with my intelligence I should have seen where National Socialism would lead and should have been working against it more actively. Therefore I have to prove myself for a year before I can be fully accepted into the democracy.

This decision looks fair at first glance, inasmuch as those people who did not actively resist during the time after 1933 should now be punished for it. That should not be used against the intelligentsia alone, though, but also against the churches and some of the unions. Nobody thinks of that, however, and the sentence against me contradicts the intention of the denazification laws.

As far as my case is concerned, the law knows 3 groups:

1) "Tainted ones"—Those in middle or lower-level leadership party positions who actively promoted and supported National Socialism. In addition to confiscation of all their possessions they can be sentenced to 5 years of labor camp and are excluded from public life, for five years altogether, later partially. For instance, they can never become civil servants, priests, teachers or lawyers.

2) "Followers"—the ones who had joined the party but did not support it actively. They only did what was demanded of them as simple members: go to meetings and pay membership fees. They have to pay a penalty of RM 2000.—but remain otherwise untouched.

3) "Those on probation" —Activists who are not hopeless cases, in the opinion of the "Spruchkammer" (trial court), and some "followers" who have a record. After a probation period and payment of a fine they fall into the category of "followers."

These legal regulations are quite clear, but the Spruchkammern (trial courts) that handle them leave much to be desired. . . . In reality not one in the whole state of Hessen is presided over by a jurist. . . . They solely judge according the "sound common sense of the people" —almost like in the days of National Socialism.

Fortunately the officials at the appeals courts have to be lawyers. So I am going to appeal, but it can take half a year before it is decided.

I definitely have to appeal, already for the fine of RM 5000.—which I do not have and will not be able to raise in the future. Even if I would sell everything I had been able to salvage it would not be enough. They sentenced me for this sum even though the law clearly states that the penalty for those in the probation group should be between 10 and 40% of their assets. . . .

There are quite a few such instances where the methods of today's leaders remind us of the ones of former leaders. It is understandable as revenge, because many of them had to suffer much; but just now, when it is important to win over all of the German people to the concept of democracy—and not just the party members—such methods are dangerous. The politically indifferent masses, in train compartments, at pubs, and workplaces are often convinced that it does not make any difference who governs, and a not insignificant number of incorrigible Nazis are using this to their advantage. You can hear about a thousand things that the Nazis were better at; that they started a war seems to be forgotten already.

One would assume that the German people were hopelessly addicted to the national socialist evil. But I do not think this is true. The average man does not think very deeply, just like in America, he only sees the hopelessness and want of today and remembers a time when he was relatively well-off; that's what he misses, not the Nazis and their madness. . . .

If we ever want to have enough to eat again we will have to be allowed to pay for the necessary imports by exporting our industrial goods. This will not be possible for years. A large portion of the industry has been destroyed; another portion has been dismantled as reparation. Some industrial products we are not allowed to pursue at all and patents for specialties (like in chemistry) have been taken away.

All this could be solved if we could rebuild energetically, but we are lacking everything. The first year after the ceasefire has passed in utter misery and need. The second year has started in the same fashion, and nowhere a sign that the future years will be any better. We cannot produce enough artificial fertilizer for our local agriculture, or cement, lime, and bricks for the building industry because we are lacking the necessary coal.

I could fill pages with details but you will believe me anyway that Germany's situation is desperate and that it is impossible to educate people to think democratically when they are drifting slowly but surely into despair and, what is worse, into stupor. The only reason we have very few communists, 10–25%, depending on the area, are the soldiers returning from Russia, where they have seen it [communism] first hand.

You will be interested to hear what people here think about another war. I still believe what I told you in April when we met again, that no German, not even the Nazis, wants it. The exceptions are the many refugees who have streamed in by the millions from the East, from the cut-off territories in Poland, Bohemia, the Balkans and Hungary. They have lost their homes and their property and are now housed in often inhuman mass quarters, undernourished and poorly dressed.

A large number of them are hoping for another war and consider a victory by the Western powers [over Russia] the only way for them to return to the countries where they and their ancestors have lived from time immemorial. They are not concerned that they would be risking life and health, which are all they have left but that have no value in their eyes. In the long run these people can only be helped through a vast emigration program, because they cannot possibly remain in what's left of Germany. . . .

At the moment I am still working as a construction helper and have to work very hard. I am trying to get away from this work and to get a job at a larger auditing and trust company. The main reason: as a laborer I do not even earn enough money to buy what the rations allow. (You can imagine what the workers as a whole, who are not much better off, think of democracy etc.) We would really be in a bad situation if Ruth's mother, my two sisters, and several fraternity brothers, especially Kurt Stein, whom you met, did not contribute constantly, and we also trade off some of Ruth's salvaged jewelry once in a while to get by. There is no longer an opportunity for Ruth to earn money in Muennerstadt; the number of people looking for work has increased too much, especially with the influx of refugees. . . .

I do not see my personal future as being too black—if there is no war and if I stay healthy. I have to wait for the outcome of my appeal. If that is successful, as I expect, and I am classified as "follower," then I am going to become a lawyer. I do not want to work for the government. I would rather reach a position where I am personally free and where I do not have to say "amen" to everything that is handed down from above. . . .

It is a blessing that Ruth is so brave and does not make matters worse by lamenting and complaining. She is developing abilities that I never knew she had; she raises rabbits and chickens, as if she had never done anything else. The children give us much joy. Fritzchen, the oldest, has skipped a grade to make up for the time lost at the end of the war when there were no teachers. . . . He has a free position at the Kloster Gymnasium (high school) even though he is protestant. He is a big help for his mother as well. He lugs wood and water, searches for food for the animals, and takes over many errands for Ruth. He is developing an amazing sense for business, something I am totally lacking. Walter, 9 years old, had been hired out to a farmer to herd cattle until last week. Ruth took him home because his health is not stable; he suffers from a lymphatic gland disorder and has to be under constant supervision. He is doing well in school; he is very conscientious and reliable. Next year he is supposed to go to the Gymnasium, I am not worried that he will pass the entrance exam, although only 30–40 % of applicants are accepted.

Günterchen, 5 years old, is cheerful and fresh. As the youngest he has not been raised as well as his brothers . . . their nutrition is probably not what it should be. A sign of it is that the two older boys constantly have boils and every wound gets infected. But they are still in far better condition than most city children.

Ruth's health is not the best; she has overdone it at times and has to be careful now. I myself am fairly well. Of course I would like to have more to eat and to drink, but I am still glad that things are going the way they are going. . . .

My main concern is that I do not have time or strength for mental activities after my physical work. This is especially bitter for me since a lot of things that we had accepted for decades have to be reexamined for their validity, and because we have to renew our contact with Western thinking—from which we had been moving away since the beginning of the 19th century. . . . I am glad that I never let the National Socialist pseudo-sciences lure me in. The small publications I was able to send off as an assistant as well as the ones by my superior Klausing are still valid today. (Klausing had taken part in the assassination attempt on Hitler on July 20, 1944, and committed suicide on July 21st).

. . . When I write to you about the conditions in Germany I do not do it to appeal to your sympathy. I am aware that we have heaped much guilt on our own heads: by complaining about National Socialism only among ourselves and by not actively fighting it, and by imagining at times that everything would settle down and reason would prevail.

Things have to change in Germany if it is not to remain a powder-keg. . . .

Please give my deepest regards to your wife.

With many greetings to yourself,

Yours, Fritz

Fritz had come from an educated and powerful family who were anti-Nazi. His father was a chemist and a director for Farbwerke Hoechst AG, a world leader in the production of coloring agents. He worked with others to form IG Farben, the largest company in Germany at the time. He was an outspoken anti-Nazi, unafraid to criticize Hitler. He called Hitler and his people criminals, but he was not prosecuted, perhaps because of his age and prominence at Hoechst. He told the story of the chief Nazi at Hoechst coming to his house to tell him his son Hans (Fritz's brother) had been killed in the war. He got very mad and blamed Hitler and his conspirators, and told the man in no uncertain terms to get out of his house. Fritz's mother died in 1935, two months before her grandson Fritz Jr.'s birth.

Fritz was caught in the middle of the Nazi machine as he sought to establish himself as a lawyer in the late 1930s. Fritz was anti-Nazi in 1935 when my father got to know him. He finished law school in 1937 and apparently joined the party as a requirement for becoming an assistant judge in Frankfurt. (In Germany, a chief judge has two assistants who write opinions and do research on his behalf.) In 1939, Fritz entered the military along with so many of his generation. He became an artillery officer and was stationed in France along the "Atlantic Wall." As the war dragged on, the German Navy needed officers for their large fleet of U-boats, and Lieutenant Wiespfenning was transferred and trained to be a U-boat captain in Danzig. He became qualified just as the war was ending, in time to take a U-boat west along the Baltic coast to avoid being captured by the dreaded Russians. He was captured by the British instead and immediately interned in a POW camp in Holstein, in northwestern Germany. After a time he was transferred to a civilian internment camp nearby.

As was common in Germany, Nazism brought political division within the family. Fritz Etzel, the brother-in-law of Fritz Weispfenning's wife, Ruth (Sauer), was a strong Nazi from the beginning. The two men were never friendly, though Hilda (Sauer) Etzel's family provided shelter to the Weispfennings at a crucial time during the war. Fritz Etzel survived the war, but returned home with mental illness, perhaps severe post-traumatic stress disorder. His wartime experiences are unknown, but he was never again the competent lawyer he had been before the war. With the help of friends, he was eventually able to perform menial tasks around the office and live independently.

The Allies began bombing Frankfurt in 1943. Fritz's wife, Ruth, and their three children moved to Ruth's grandfather Sauer's house on Heidelbergstrasse in Darmstadt, 20 miles south of Frankfurt. On the night of September 22, 1943, there was a diversionary bombing raid on Darmstadt, which was a university city of 110,000 people with no military targets. There was extensive damage and many fires. The Sauers' neighborhood was burning. Ruth organized the children with wet blankets as protection against the fire. They survived the night, and in the morning they walked to the train station to travel 60 miles east to the small town of Munnerstadt to join Ruth's sister, Hilda Etzel. Fritz Jr., seven years old at the time, remembers the walk through the bombed streets of Darmstadt, past the swollen bodies of people and horses. By leaving Darmstadt when they did, they escaped the most devastating air raid a year later, when much of the city was destroyed in a single night. By the end of the war, 78% of all the buildings in Darmstadt were destroyed, including 99% of the historic city center, and about 13,000 people had been killed in a city with no military targets.

Muennerstadt, 12/29/1946

Dear Jim,

A few weeks ago—in October—Fritz wrote you a long, detailed letter. We are not sure if you received this letter or if it got hung up at the censors. In any case we want to write you again so that you don't think we had forgotten you. How could we do that! Not only are you a dear friend from the past but we have to be especially grateful to you since you helped us so generously in these hard times.

Especially for Fritz your friendship was a great help. How sad that we could not be together more often and that we could not offer you any comfort in our own home.

The children and I are still living in Muennerstadt (in one! room) under primitive circumstances. Fritz is living with his sister [in Frankfurt] where he has a small room. We only rarely see each other, which is very hard, especially after our previous separation of 7 years. Things are not going to improve until Fritz has been denazified. . . .

At the moment Fritz works as a lawyer in an auditing office. In addition he has taken up contacts at Frankfurt University and does scientific work again.

We just have to start all over again. But we must not complain, as hard as it sometimes is, we have to be grateful that we are allowed to start over again at all. Even if we live in abject poverty right now we are grateful that the Nazi rule has been taken away from us and we can again say and think what we want without fear of being put away. We have great hope that things will get better eventually. If you and your dear wife come to Germany again sometime we hope to be able to welcome you in our own home again as our dear guests. We know it will be a long and rocky road until then, but as they say, difficulties are there to be overcome. . . .

Fritz was able to spend Christmas with us here in Muennerstadt, which was a great joy for us. A year ago we did not even have any sign of life from him; during all the war years he spent Christmas at home only once.

We would be delighted to hear from you and wish you and your dear wife all the best in the New Year!

Yours, Ruth and Fritz

Munnerstadt had about 3,500 inhabitants at the time and was in the middle of a productive agricultural area. Consequently, the Wiespfenning family was able to find food. The boys went to school at the Augustiner Kloster, where lessons were given in Latin. Hilda Etzel suffered from severe rheumatoid arthritis, and directed the household from the couch much of the time. Walter was only five or six years old, and suffered from the lack of milk, presumably a calcium deficiency from insufficient nutrition. He was sent to a dairy farm where he stayed and got the milk he needed.

At the end of the war there was only a small German garrison to defend Munnerstadt against inevitable capture by the Americans. The officer in charge was ready to follow Hitler's standing orders to defend every foot of ground to the last man. Ruth knew this would bring unnecessary destruction to the town and put her children in danger once again. When the officer left the town, she went to the doctor at the local clinic and they took all the white sheets they could find and put them on the roofs of the clinic and houses. As a result, the town was taken without being shelled. The family stayed in Munnerstadt for three more years.

Muennerstadt, 1/1/47

Dear Jim,

In the meantime the care-package has arrived that you sent to Muennerstadt; many, many thanks to you and your wife. We are humbled by your kindness!

I don't know if you can read in the newspapers what the food situation is like over here. Right now it is continuing to go downhill. For this month we are allowed 75 grams of fat and 200 grams of meat; for next month no fat at all. You are our savior in this desperate situation and we cannot thank you enough! They are hoping that soon imports of fat from abroad will be permitted, it cannot continue the way it is now. The misery is tremendous.

We feel ourselves in paradise right now, though, thanks to your help. The children are enjoying a good pudding every day and are beaming with happiness. It has been years since they had any chocolate; our youngest tasted it for the first time, since he was born during the war years. It is impossible to describe how happy you and your wife have made us. Our "Daddy" has gained two pounds already. He is 1.81 m [5 ft. 11 in.] tall and was weighing only 115 pounds, now he is up to 117!

We only have one thought: how to return the kindness you have shown us. Fritz is working very hard in order to build up a secure livelihood for us. . . . Even though the cities have become ugly due to the destruction, the countryside has remained unchanged and beautiful. You have explored many regions already with bicycle and motorcycle.

Our apartment should be finished by spring. One room and kitchen will be livable by February 1st. I am working as construction helper myself because Fritz has so little time. In the evening I do the cooking and type Fritz's material on the typewriter.

Right now I am in Muennerstadt for a few days because here I can get lumber for the floors.

And how is your dear wife? We have to think of you both very much and hope that the birth went well. We would be very happy to get good news from you soon.

Many greetings to you both,

Yours, Ruth Weispfenning

Some of the letters were from Frieda Sauer, Heidelbergerstrasse 121, Darmstadt, Germany. This was Frau Sauer, in whose house my father had stayed from January through April of 1935. She had three children, Ruth (Weispfenning), Rolf who was in Berlin, and Hilda (Etzel) in Muennerstadt.

Darmstadt, July 22, 1947

Dear Jim,

A full year has gone by since you have returned to your homeland. Exactly two days after you left I came to Nauheim with a little basket of cherries from my garden to bring you a little joy; unfortunately you had already left.

Rolf's little daughter Susi (now 2½ years old) has been staying with me for the past year; she was totally undernourished when she came. In the beginning, when we still had more to eat, she gained a little, but now with the curtailed rations I am really worried about her. Not long ago she passed a maw-worm and I asked the doctor to write me a prescription. He pointed out that it was probably impossible to get an effective worm medicine, but if I had acquaintances or friends outside of Germany I should send the prescription to them. That's why I am writing to you begging you to be so kind to get the prescribed medicine, or another one which you perhaps have already tried (for a 2½-year-old child).

Then I read in the newspaper—I am enclosing the clipping—that we can ask American friends to send a package for $6.50. I would be happy if I could ask you to make use of this offer. I would deposit the money in Reichsmark into a special account for you to use. I would keep it up-to-date according to the exchange rate. If you and your wife should come to Germany again, and our currency will have stabilized, you could be reimbursed, including interest. You would make me very happy and do me a great favor that I will never forget.

On September 11, 1946 Rolf was exonerated. I am very glad and thought it might interest you because you are familiar with his situation. Rolf and his wife will write to you as soon as he is working as an attorney again. Ruth and Fritz are diligently working to build up a home in Frankfurt again. I myself have gotten even more slim and gray (my hair) than when you saw me last.

Dear Jim, please give my best to your wife; with many greetings to you from my heart,

Yours, Frieda Sauer

The text of the ad Frieda sent was:

'Gifts of Love' Packages—Ask your friends and relatives in America to send $6.50 for the package "Ilse" to MIDLAND BROKERAGE COMPANY, 1406 West Lake Street, Minneapolis 8, Minnesota USA

It saves your friends the great trouble of packing and mailing. The package will be sent immediately after receipt of the money. It contains: 3 pounds of coffee, 2 pounds of cocoa, 2 pounds of lard, 1 pound of raisins and 1 pound of tea. All goods are of best American quality.

County Court Justice, ret.
FRANKFURT/M-HOECHST
FRITZ WEISPFENNING
Koenigsteiner Strasse 59 a I
July 29, 1947

Dear Jim,

Many thanks for your kind letter of March 30. Please forgive me for only answering now. . . .

First I want to write about the general situation. What I wrote in my first letter is still true today, nothing has changed and there are no prospects that it will get better in the foreseeable future. Perhaps the Marshall Plan will bring help one day but that will still take a while.

You (in America) are right when you say that the reason for our catastrophic situation regarding food, clothing and heating is in large part the fault of German officials. I don't think the German administrative authorities could solve this; they are too weak, spineless and corrupt. Especially corruption is rampant, something we would never have thought possible in the past. The people are hungry, and once someone has stolen a pound of butter they will take whiskey or cigarettes the next time. The only governing body that is still intact is the courts, I am convinced of that. Prosecutors and judges are totally undernourished and many of them only own the clothes they wore when they were released from prison.

I do not have much hope that the German officials will bring improvement. Only a restart of the economy from the outside would help us. This is doubly difficult now that the agreements between East and West have gotten worse and the probability that the Potsdam Agreement will be implemented is fading. It is so urgent, however, as a large part of our population is literally starving. It probably would not be bad business to help us get back on our feet through credits, because we would work and pay back. Such stimulus would be difficult to implement, though; France is resisting the rebuilding of the German steel production because she fears for her safety and views it as competition for her own heavy industry. England wants to take over the German chemical industry, especially I.G, but we cannot survive on leather goods from Offenbach, toys and musical instruments. It just has to be decided soon what we are allowed to produce and export, because we cannot continue like this; . . . every day that goes by without action increases hunger on one side, corruption and racketeering on the other.

The general mood is accordingly bad. People blame the Allies for the lack of production and export. They say: "They want to starve us to death". If the Russians should start giving out decent rations in their occupation zone West Germany would have a Russian majority, despite the experiences with Russia and the communists. Right now the Russians are just as unpopular with the working class as the Americans or British. The French are the ones that are hated most. Where shall all of this lead?

The problem is also that the intellect is silenced more and more under the influence of hunger, and with it the realization that the cause of all our problems lies with us. One can often hear comments in the overcrowded trains that only a war between East and West would save us, it could not get much worse, even total annihilation would be acceptable. Nobody talks of democracy; the little man sees it only as an institution where those people who have something are free to cheat as much as they can without repercussions.

It will interest you how I and my family are coping in this chaos. Ruth managed to enlist our two older boys who are excellent students in their school for meals at the monastery in Muennerstadt. There is some additional food available and with the ration they get at their school they have just about enough to eat. . . .

I myself am working in Frankfurt as a legal tutor and write legal advice. I really work day and night in order to earn enough money for us to purchase a few things on the black market. If we could not buy some fat (500 g for RM 300) or a loaf of bread occasionally it would look very bleak. We have nothing left to barter and have to buy extras from my income. In order to make this income stretch I am forced to hide some of it from the tax bureau. This is a misdemeanor punishable with prison but it does not burden my conscience in the least; everybody cheats on their taxes. I am satisfied that I am supporting my family through honest work and not through racketeering. . . . we constantly hope for improvement without any real foundation for this hope. If I would not have hope I would not have started to rebuild an apartment that had been damaged by bombs. I get some of the material from my fraternity brother Kurt Steim, whom you have met; whatever else I need I have to buy on the black market. Fortunately I have good connections to the building industry due to my 10 months as construction worker and know where to find material. That's where we 'Nazis' are at an advantage.

Now about my denazification: I had already told you that I had been sentenced to a penalty of 5000 RM and one year probation. You will also remember the reasoning: I could exonerate myself to a large extent but one would expect a man with my intelligence should have realized early on where it was all leading; I should have done something against it etc. During the appeal everything went smoothly. After relatively short negotiations the prosecutor asked for the verdict to be rescinded, the court agreed and I was classified into group IV ("follower") as I had asked. I thought that everything was settled now. But I had not reckoned with the Military Rulers. The Special Branch in Frankfurt and Mr. Teitelbaum in Wiesbaden apparently consider me a Nazi-activist and are attempting to rescind this verdict and start the whole process from the beginning. I don't know what it is they don't like. Perhaps it is my military rank as lieutenant, perhaps my connection with submarines, but legally that should not be a factor, only in the case of National Socialist or military activism, and that nobody has ever accused me of. I am calmly looking ahead to new negotiations. What would hit me hard, though, would be if I could not work independently in a free profession from the moment the verdict is rescinded until the new negotiations; that would destroy my livelihood which I have built up so laboriously. If I had known what difficulties Teitelbaum and consorts would cause me I would have moved to the British or French Zone a year ago and would have avoided the American denazification. . . .

When my denazification will finally be over I am going to continue to work as legal coach and also apply for admission to the bar. I am definitely not going to work for the State; I want to avoid being called a "follower" ever again. I see every day how jurists are pressured by newspapers, political parties, government offices, and unfortunately unjust laws and regulations. I want to keep my independence and my good conscience in order to fight for justice everywhere. . . .

Now I have given you a description of our situation at the moment; not a very satisfactory one right now. Maybe I portray a few details as too dark; all in all the picture is surely not too black. I am a born optimist who keeps hoping, even where there is no justification for it. If I made a mistake, it was only by not describing the reality explicitly and badly enough. . . .

Many greetings to you two from both of us,

Yours, Fritz

While Ruth and Fritz worked to rebuild an apartment in Frankfurt, their sons stayed in Munnerstadt, living at their aunt's flat and continuing in the Kloster school. Fritz Jr. remembers the considerable freedom the boys enjoyed there.

Starvation was widespread in Europe in 1947, with drought compounding the problem of a devastated agricultural system.

Muennerstadt, 9/28/47

Dear Jim,

I have hesitated for a long time wondering if I should write you this letter. . . . It is with great reluctance that I approach you with a request today, but my concern for husband and children forces me to take this step. The situation here has gotten considerably worse since our last report. Due to the severe drought the harvest has turned out to be much worse than expected.

Our boys are still eating here in Muennerstadt, but it is not enough and they have lost a lot of weight. If they did not get food rations at school it would be even worse. Our Walter has an intestinal infection and is very run-down. On top of that he is very anemic. Only children up to 3 years get milk. I myself commute between Muennerstadt and Frankfurt; I am needed at both places. Fritz is my main concern. He is totally ruining himself by working day and night in his attempt to build up an existence and to take care of his family. He has always been a hard worker, but then the nutrition was better.

There are no potatoes—our main food—and no vegetables; he is only eating dry bread. In order to make it go down easier he cooks it into a mash. With 150 grams of fat in 4 weeks you cannot do much cooking and if you spread it on bread it is gone within a few days. 400 grams of meat does not go very far either. Even the bread is not enough for a man like Fritz with his 1.80m [5 ft. 11 in.], who works mentally 18 hours a day and only gets 6, mostly only 4–5, hours of sleep. We used to barter the few items we were able to salvage after the bombing raid (totally bombed out, <u>everything</u> burned) to get some food from farmers so we would not starve, but now there is nothing left to barter with.

We could trade coffee and tobacco products but we don't have the money. One pound of coffee costs 350 RM, 1 pack of cigarettes (20 pieces) 100 RM. We can barely afford ½ pound of coffee once a month which Fritz has to drink in order to be able to work. It is not good for his health but helps him to hold out.

In order to be brief: If you are planning to send a Care package to Germany anyway we would be extremely grateful if you could direct it to our address. We will certainly reimburse you the cost as soon as there is an opportunity for it; I hope this will not be too far off. . . .

Right now Fritz lives with his sister Emmi in Frankfurt/Main-Hoechst, but

Fritz and I are fixing up an apartment in the city of Frankfurt. . . . The actual work is done by Fritz and me. It will take months until it is finished because we cannot buy anything. Everything comes only through bartering, always bartering.

Since Fritz and I are very busy we often forget our worries and our hunger. We have to hold out for our children, it has to get better some day. By the way, Fritz does not know I am writing you this letter, and he must not know about it. You know how he is; he would rather perish than beg. A wife and mother ignores much when it comes to the wellbeing of her loved ones.

Right now I am in Muennerstadt for a few days to check on the children. . . .

Please don't be angry with me.

With many greetings to you and your wife,

Yours, Ruth Weispfenning

Muennerstadt, Nov. 25, 1947

Dear Jim,

Many thanks for your kind letter! I wept with joy when I read that you are so extremely kind and want to send us Care packages. Two packages a month is almost too much. . . . I have had a very bad conscience since my last letter, because Fritz does not know I wrote to you. He is very proud and would rather perish than to complain.

The food supply in Germany has gotten worse again: 100 grams fat and 400 grams meat for 4 weeks, and no milk at all. Before the war we used that much in a day, and now it is supposed to last 28 days.

Our oldest, 12 years, is now 1.52 m [5 feet] tall and weighs only 68 pounds. The youngest, Günter, has been suffering from a purulent rash due to a protein deficiency. It is no wonder that the children will be damaged for life due to insufficient food. But the worst off is "Big Fritz." He looks so terrible that you would not recognize him. The poor man is working day and night to support his family. . . .

With many greetings to you and your wife,

Yours, Ruth Weispfenning

P.S. It will be January or even later before I can move to Frankfurt with the children. We hope to have finished at least one room and the kitchen by Christmas so that at least Fritz can move in, and the burdensome commute by bus and streetcar will have an end. It takes him over two hours a day. He will be able to use this time to rest a little at noontime. Right now he gets up at 7 and comes home around 9 in the evening or later, without dinner all day. Of course he cannot keep this up.

Once we will have the apartment plus your help through Care I am sure he will soon recover. At the moment I am really worried about him.

R.W.

Frankfurt/Main-Hoechst, January 8, 1948

Dear Jim,

What a wonderful surprise when we returned to Hoechst from Muennerstadt and found the notification from Care that we could pick up two packages! Fritz and I never carried a package so happily! We thank you and dear wife so very much for you kindness and generosity! The packages contained wonderful items that we had to do without for years. These past few days we were able to eat to our heart's content until we were full! You probably cannot imagine what a feeling that is—you feel like a new person. Now I am going to fatten up Fritz who is undernourished and weak. . . .

We are still trying to finish our new apartment but it is turning out to be more difficult than we originally thought. The biggest problem is organizing the material. If we finally find the material somewhere we don't find a car to transport it. If we have finally accomplished that, then the workers don't show up. In spite of all the difficulties we are slowly going ahead. One room will be done by the end of this month and we can move in. This way we eliminate the daily commute from Hoechst. . . .

Trusting that you and your family are well I am with many greetings to you and your wife. . . .

Yours, Ruth Weispfenning

March 12, 1948
Ruth Weispfenning
Frankfurt/Main
Hebelstr. 5, II, left

Dear Jim,

Since Fritz is working harder than ever and is actually sitting in front of his books every night till 3 o'clock—even though he has to get up at 7 o'clock in the morning—I would like to thank you in his stead for the Care package we received two days ago. . . . I don't think you can imagine <u>how much</u> you have helped us again. When one has enough to eat, without that awful feeling of hunger and weakness, one enjoys working so much more. And we do have to work in order to slowly reach a better standard of living.

Fritz has been denazified for the third time—hopefully for good now—and has been listed in group IV. All limitations have been lifted; he has immediately applied for acceptance at the bar and is hoping to be accepted within 3 months. . . .

Here in Germany you have to earn a lot in order to live. Especially people like us who have lost everything during the bombing raids and who have to buy everything piece by piece. . . . At the moment there is nothing to be had openly; everything goes through the black market, through the backdoor, at exorbitant prices. We are glad if we can get a pair of shoes for the children this way. Other things we cannot even think about; especially food prices are so high that only racketeers and black market dealers have enough to eat. . . . We have nothing to compensate, but fraternity brothers of Fritz are helping out. Especially Kurt Steim, whom you may remember, is helping with his hardware so that we can trade it in for building material for our apartment.

Meanwhile we have moved into the new apartment, but don't ask under what circumstances. We are a long way from being finished; only the kitchen and one room have been plastered. Floorboards have not been laid yet so that we are almost suffocating from the dust. . . .

In the evening I type the most necessary texts for Fritz and take care of his correspondence. Please don't be angry if Fritz has not written you in a long while; he is totally overworked, he has no diversion, like a movie or perhaps a little beer, anymore. Always work, work. But he is happy to do it and has a lot of willpower. . .

Yours, Ruth Weispfenning
and Fritz

County Court Justice, ret.
FRITZ WEISPFENNING
Frankfurt/Main
April 20, 1948
Hebelstr. 5, II

Dear Jim,

First I have to apologize for not answering your kind letter sooner, but I am so overworked with my job at the moment that I cannot get to anything else. I have to give more than 40 lessons a week. . . . Many thanks for your affidavit. Fortunately I did not need it anymore. The trial court [Spruchkammer] presiding over this matter after the repeal has confirmed the original verdict. Now I will have peace and quiet I hope. It is unfortunate that I lost a whole year over this matter and now the Bar [Anwaltschaft] is giving me a hard time regarding my admission. A year ago I would not have had a problem. It will cost me another fight, but I have learned patience and tenacity during the denazification process and my battle with the Labor Exchange; I am going to prevail.

I would like to thank you and your wife from the bottom of my heart for the Care packages. The food is such a great help for our children and for us that we cannot thank you enough. With our rations of 200 grams meat and 150 grams fat (often you cannot even get any meat), these packages mean so much to us; they lift us into another life and nourishment standard. You cannot even fathom over there what a great help this is for us. We were also very happy with the package of wool fabric. We debated back and forth and have finally decided to have a coat made for Ruth, since the fabric is best suited for it. It is a heavy, light grey fabric. This fabric shipment was an especially great gift, as our ration points for textiles expired on March 31, because there is nothing to be had in the stores. The goods that exist are only available on the black market. Material for a suit costs from 3 to 5 thousand marks, depending on quality; a pair of shoes about 1,200 marks. Of course we cannot afford this.

I want to report a little about the conditions here. Not much has changed since my last letter. Industry, including the building industry, are down because of a lack of coal, the foundation for all industry. The figures for export are slowly rising but still are frighteningly low compared to the time before the war. However, this is mainly due to a higher export of coal and wood; both are raw materials that we desperately need here. If this does not change not even a Marshall Plan can help us, because we would never be able to pay for the food we need on the world market. . . . The communists are gaining ground under these circumstances of course. Only the fact that so many Germans were in Russia and that the Russians treat their prisoners so inhumanely is the reason why Communism has remained relatively weak here; but now they are confident of victory more than ever before. Next Sunday's elections will show how strong they really are. The uncertainty in global politics has a paralyzing effect on us as well.

More and more people believe that there will be an open conflict between East and West, that it is only a matter of time. Most Germans are already wondering how they can escape any participation, because we all had enough of the previous war, except for the refugees who hope to return to their old home. We cannot imagine what the world would look like if another war with even more horrible weapons would arise, considering the insane destruction of the last war.

. . . We would never restore an apartment with our last reserves and all our strength if we were really convinced of another war. The same is happening with the economy. Every manufacturer, every tradesman is trying to rebuild his business as much as the current circumstances allow, so that they can be ready immediately when the overall situation improves. . . .

Many greetings to you and also to your wife and little son,
Yours, Fritz

Rations were creeping higher in the spring of 1948. It had been three years since Germany's surrender. The Weispfennings' problems, frustrations, hopes, and efforts were a microcosm for Germany as a whole. Things were about to change. The food supply was increasing thanks to improved crops worldwide, and in June of 1948 currency reform was instituted. The Reichsmark, which had lost nearly all its value, was replaced with the Deutsche Mark. Overnight, food and other goods appeared on shelves as shopkeepers realized they could sell goods for a currency that had value. In July, price controls were lifted. The black market that had flourished since the war collapsed, and life for the ordinary German began to improve dramatically.

Frankfurt/Main, June 20, 1948

Dear Jim,

Finally I am pulling myself together to write to you. First of all thank you for the latest two Care packages. I cannot mention it often enough but we would not know how to survive with our three growing boys. On paper I have earned a lot of money but through honest work, without dealing on the black market, you cannot make enough to feed such voracious eaters. It is supposed to get better now. In the next rationing period we are to get 700 grams fat; and horse meat is supposed to be en route from America. To compensate, the bread rations will be curtailed substantially until the next harvest. After that we should be in much better shape, I hope. Due to the drought last year and lack of animal feed a large number of German livestock had to be slaughtered, causing difficulties in the meat supply for years to come.

Everything is overshadowed by the currency reform this weekend. Everybody received 40 DM (Deutsche Mark) today against payment of 40 RM, and in July there will be an additional 20 DM. All the old money is to be deposited at the banks and will be blocked for the time being. We don't know yet how much of that we will get back. We are not affected too much because we always spend everything I make, either for the apartment construction or for our daily life.

My income will go down quite a bit, because a large number of my students, who were studying either using their own savings or that of their parents, will have to quit. . . . Everything would be easier if I had been accepted by the Bar, but that did not work out, as I had feared. . . .

The proponents of the Morgenthau Plan are still playing a major role, as you in America have heard, too. If this does not change the whole currency reform will have been for naught and the black market will dominate again before long. . . .

Now to a more pleasant subject. The children, especially the two older ones, are giving us much joy. Fritz is by far the best student at the Muennerstadt Gymnasium, and he does not even work at it. . . . Walter, the second, is a good student and has a talent for math, not so much for languages. . . . He will not be affected in today's "clean-up action" with which all average or lesser talented students will be chased away from high schools. Günter, the third, is a fresh and lazy fellow who has to be dragged to do his homework. . . .

Many greetings to you and your wife, and your little one, also from Ruth.

Yours, Fritz

The specter of Soviet domination hung heavy over Germans. Friends and family who lived in the Russian-controlled eastern zone were reporting terrible conditions. There was little reason for the average German to think that the Russians would stay where they were. Fritz could see that the Allies were not going to take up arms directly against the Soviets, and the letters make clear that he feared Soviet domination of Europe was inevitable.

Frankfurt, September 4, 1948

Dear Jim,

. . . The rations have gotten better but whatever is "freely" traded now has gone up in price to an extent that is almost unaffordable. All the more reason for us to be grateful to you—we are reminded of that every day. . . .

At least I have the prospect of increasing my income through diligence and ability; however I will not be able to carry the current workload in the long run. I would like to find some time for scientific work again but that is out of the question; I can barely keep my head above water. . . .

As far as the general situation is concerned, not much has changed, other than the present political détente which will probably not last long. One cannot see any hope for Germany in the long run. The French are in the process of turning their zone into a region of misery by dismantling [industrial sites] to an unheard of extent. It is better in the other zones, but there, too, the export industry is being dismantled. Our hopes that America would move away from the Morgenthau Plan turned out to be delusive, and we will have to pay for our food stuff with raw material for a long time to come. The workers have not realized this yet; it is being kept a secret from them. But they will feel it soon enough, not just in the French Zone.

We have no right to complain and demand better treatment. That's why I have resigned myself to it. We have to endure this fate and leave the future to God.

Continuation September 19, 1948

. . . Since political involvement is absolutely pointless I consider raising and supporting my family and keeping a certain level as my only duty. I am not particularly interested in a high standard of living. . . . But I do want to see to it that my sons will have the same educational possibilities and means that had been available to me. . . .

We know that we cannot expect anything from the Western powers but we know that conditions under the Russians would be horrible—perhaps not for the workers but to the remnants of the former middle class. We know that from the conditions in the Eastern Zone. . . .

In any case I want to thank you for the immeasurable help you have given us in these difficult times. You and a large number of other Americans have shown a private generosity that will never be forgotten in Germany.

Many greetings to you and your wife and your little son,

Yours, Fritz

Frankfurt/Main, November 2, 1948

Dear Mrs. McKay, dear Jim,

. . . Things have gotten better, as far as food is concerned—honestly—especially potatoes and vegetables are available; other items are still scarce. We had expected more from the harvest and had hoped the rations would get more generous; but if we look at it realistically, improvement can only come very slowly. The Marshall Plan has to get established first. Our industries have to produce again so that we can export in order to get foreign currency for imports.

We know that things cannot get better in such a short time after the total collapse caused by the terrible war. Three years are not enough after the long war during which everything was destroyed, through our fault. We had expected too much from the currency reform too. Now, three months later, certain items are becoming scarce again. . . .

It is wonderful how America is helping a vanquished country! And that you both are so kind to us. May God reward you! We are totally in earnest when we say that—if you and your wife agree—we would love to take your son as a guest in later years, that is if you even want him to get to know such a destroyed country, and that he can stay as long as he likes. We would treat him like our own son. We will never forget our gratitude towards you.

Thank you for writing to us in spite of all your work, and sending us such a nice picture of your dear little Robbie. We congratulate you with all our heart on your professional success and wish you the very best! To become Professor of Pediatrics at the University of the State of Vermont is a wonderful thing. How proud your wife and little son must be of you! . . .

Yours, Ruth and Fritz

As of January 1, 1949, Fritz was accredited as a lawyer again. It had taken over three years of struggle to work his way through the denazification process and prove himself worthy of resuming a professional career. This was typical of the people Fritz termed the intelligentsia in Germany. The most competent leaders at all levels of German society, as well as the military, had been excluded from helping to reorganize their country after the war. While this was incredibly frustrating to Fritz and his contemporaries, the process undeniably slowed Germany's rebound, which was one objective of American policy.

Frankfurt, February 16, 1949

Dear Mrs. McKay, dear Jim,

. . . Fritz has finally been admitted to the bar, which means quite a battle for him in the beginning. Naturally it will take a while until he can establish himself and gain a reputation. . . . Once his practice will be better established he will be able to give up the tutoring, at first in part and later altogether. . . . He gets angry when I say something and so I don't say anything anymore. The only thing I can do is to take good care of him and help with the work as much as I can as his secretary. I do enjoy it, although I also have to run the household on the side. . . . [E]very German has to pull himself together and do his utmost duty; only then will we create an acceptable standard of living again, out of our own energy and with the help of the Western powers.

We did not live in luxury before, as you dear Jim, know, but at least we lived without worry. Today we are filled with great angst. Of course there are people who are gay and go dancing etc., especially now during the carnival season, but they are a minority. . . . There is hardly any social life; we never get together with acquaintances to talk anymore. Families stay to themselves, partly out of financial reasons. Since the currency reform wine and spirits are available but very few can afford them.

By the way, we do <u>not</u> miss it at all. Our daily bread is now our main concern and we are filled with thanks at every meal. Eating one's fill is not a given anymore, like in the old days, and we always think of it as a gift of God. . . .

You may have read that we had a flu epidemic here. Our three children were seriously ill and we were worried. Now all three are up and getting slowly better. Fritz and I did not feel well either but we could not take a break of course. All that is behind us now.

We think of you three often . . .

Yours, Fritz, Ruth and children

Ffm [Frankfurt am Main], March 8, 1949

Dear Mrs. McKay and Jim,

We were speechless with joy and surprise when the notification came yesterday that we could pick up a turkey at the slaughter house! Heartfelt thanks for the wonderful holiday package that was surely supposed to reach us for Christmas. . . . It has been years since we could eat our fill on meat. The five of us have been enjoying this delectable animal for two days already and there will be another meal tomorrow.

I had written my mother in Darmstadt right away that she should come to share the meal with us but unfortunately she has a bad cold and is not feeling well. . . .

After we had all gotten over the flu our Walter (the second one) is in bed again with fever. He is quite weak, health-wise, whereas we can be satisfied with the other two. . . .

With our best wishes and heartfelt greetings from house to house,

Your grateful Ruth Weispfenning

The European flu epidemic of 1948–49 struck Germany in January and February. It was not particularly deadly, and by March life was looking up again. Talk of Easter goodies shows how much things had improved.

Darmstadt, March 18, 1949

My dear Jim, my dear Mrs. McKay,

What a surprise yesterday's mail brought me when I was told: "A turkey plus a package with precious food items had arrived in Germany and I should pick it up."

I was moved to tears by your kind, beneficent attention in our still existing time of need. . . . From the attached letter I saw that the turkey had already been ordered in the middle of November; you, dear Jim, and dear Mrs. McKay, had intended it as a Christmas surprise for us. . . . Your kind gift was doubly appreciated as I had been ill with the flu for four weeks and am having a hard time getting back my strength. The precious food items and the turkey will help me so much to get stronger sooner.

Rolf [Frieda's son, Ruth's brother] and little Susi join me in my heartfelt thanks. The little sweet-tooth is delighted with the chocolate and candy and said out of the blue: "Uncle Jim, Aunt Liz, and Robbie are getting many kisses from me because they are so kind." I had talked to her about you many times. . . . Soon the Easter Bunny will come to all the little children here in Germany. . . .

May you, dear Jim, be very happy with your wife and sweet little son, now and forever! This I wish you with all my heart,

Your always grateful, Frieda Sauer

My best wishes to your dear wife as well, and a kiss for Robbie.

Fritz Weispfenning, Frankfurt/Main
Attorney-at-Law Hebelstrasse 5, II (am Scheffeleck) Tel. 44192
Business Hours: Daily from 5–7 pm.
Except Wednesdays and Saturdays

September 18, 1949

My dear Jim,

Please consider my heavy workload and tension as an excuse for my long silence; building up my law practice has definitely added to the load. . . . The gifts which you and your compatriots are sending over here, combined with sane politics, will hopefully contribute to the goal that we will become a reliable part of the Western world and a buffer zone against the East. Only then will they really have fulfilled their purpose.

. . . It will interest you to know that I am planning to get involved in the greater problems of our torn world, in addition to my daily workload. I don't know if I ever wrote you that I had been very active politically as a student—before 1933. First I was a pure Liberal, then I slid a bit to the right until I found myself, partly with, partly without my intension, in the SA [storm troops]. That concluded my political career. I am not thinking of throwing myself into the turmoil of daily politics but I cannot shut myself off from the obligation not only to think of ourselves but to work on the realization of the greater ideas of humanity, love for one's fellow-men, and international understanding. So I have let close friends (fraternity brothers) draw me into joining the Freemasons, where I will be accepted soon. It was a weighty decision for me, a life-changing decision. Politically speaking one draws a line between oneself and any kind of exaggerated nationalism on one hand, and collective socialism on the other. But I believe that I am old enough for it now. . . .

Yours, Fritz

Fritz's revelation that he had been a member of the SA before 1933 exposed what may well have been the primary reason for his prolonged denazification process. While the SA (also known as the "Brown Shirts") was known as a paramilitary organization that used brutal tactics of intimidation, it is instructive to note that in 1933 the SA boasted two million members, fully 20% of the total German population, and well over half of the young men Fritz's age. A small percentage of the SA were actual "Storm Troopers" carrying out the brutality for which the organization was infamous.

Frankfurt/M., September 22, 1949

Dear Mrs. McKay and Jim,

. . . Our heartfelt congratulations on the birth of your second son! How proud you must be now. . . . Our boys fight and box one another a lot and yet they love each other and don't like to be without the others. That's how it will be with your boys too. . . . Perhaps you will have an opportunity to visit us before—that would be nice! Frankfurt does not look as bad anymore as after the war. A lot has been rebuilt and we hope it will get even better when the Federal Government will move here, but that has not been decided yet. . . .

It is true that we can buy most of the foodstuffs again but the prices are exorbitant. For instance one egg still costs 46–50 Pfennig; 1 pound of pork 5 marks; one orange 68 Pfennig; one loaf of bread 75 Pfennig. That means we only buy the most necessary; we also have to buy clothing and shoes for the children and have to divide the money very carefully. Everything costs more than double than before. We are also in need of the most necessary furniture. Our oldest was very happy when we bought him an American army cot that was cheap and in good condition. . . . We do not get anything from the government, of course, and have to help ourselves. . . . True friends that really want to help are rare and we will never forget your kindness. . . .

We would also be grateful for old, worn clothes that you do not want to use anymore; we could make something out of them for the children. But I must not burden you with the work of such a package—please forgive me, it was just a thought. Right now it is out of the question anyway because you have enough work with your own children. . . .

For now we are still at the beginning. . . . We just have to be patient. It took 2 to 3 years until a lawyer had established himself in normal times, so we have to be glad when we notice a slight uphill trend. Right now the tutoring is still feeding us. . . .

With the very best wishes and greetings,

Your grateful Fritz and Ruth

Frankfurt/M., March 7, 1950

Dear Mrs. McKay,

What immeasurable joy you have given us with your two packages of clothes! . . . When I had asked for used clothes in one of my letters I had a very bad conscience after the letter had been posted. . . . You are such a kindhearted person! I would be so happy if I could meet you one day and express my thanks to you personally. . . . We are going to alter the nice officer's jacket (the long one) a bit. We are going to take off the shoulder-straps and the stripes on the sleeves so nobody will think that he is trying to impersonate a member of the Armed Forces. Everything else he can wear the way it is.

Dear Mrs. McKay, you have helped us again immensely, more than you can perhaps imagine. . . .

Your grateful Ruth and Fritz

As always, Fritz's letters were few and far between, but those he sent were very detailed and thoughtful. His analysis of the situation at the end of 1950 is enlightening, and finally he announced to Jim that the Weispfennings no longer needed help from the McKays. Mention of university and sports bring home the improvement.

Frankfurt/M., December 27, 1950

My dear Jim,

. . . In November I was able to discontinue the tutoring job which had taken so much of my time. That was a great relief but meanwhile my time has been filling up with other duties. I have become active in the "Civil Liberties Union," an organization for civil rights. The work in this field has been done mostly by Americans and German emigrants with the best intensions, and it deserves the highest praise. It can only be of limited success, however, because the German people meet any foreigner and immigrant with suspicion, and because the Americans (even more so than the hated English with their still ongoing demolition) arrive with preconceived opinions. . . .

It is good that there does not seem to be any appetite for communism, contrary to expectations, in spite of the worsening economy (no coal, rising prices, growing unemployment). In that respect we are better off than the democratic France and Italy. . . .

We have been lucky with our three boys so far—knock on wood. Fritz is 15 years old now and will go to university in 2½ years. He is not studying for school all the time anymore but has interest in other things as well. Right now he and his brother Walter are outside with the skis they got for Christmas.

Walter, the second, is doing fairly well. He is not as ambitious and quick intellectually as his brother Fritz, but keeps a good average in school without having to work too much. Above all he is the kindest, most devoted, and most helpful of the three rascals. . . .

About Günter, the third, I can report that he continues to be a fresh street urchin, growing up quite wild, but able to stand his ground among his buddies. I have to point out, now that he lives closer to me again, the tenacity with which he pursues the sport of soccer. There is not a free minute in which he does not chase after the "pigskin." . . .

As to the general situation—I agree with you completely that it is very, very bad. The main topic being discussed here in the streets is rearmament. In serious political circles there are no doubts that we are tied to the West for better or for worse. Even the man in the street knows that he does not want communism. . . . [T]he man in the street says: why should I fight against the Russians? Number one: I have no mood for fighting and secondly: they will come anyway, whether I risk my life or not. So he is against rearmament of any kind as long as he sees no chance that the battle lines along the Elbe River can be held. . . . Everybody has contemplated what he will do in the case of an invasion from the East. . . . The end result will be that we, of course with extreme Allied control and help, will build up an effective defense system ourselves before it is too late. . . . .

We have attained a life again, remarkable in the current German situation, and hope that we will be even better off in the future. Therefore I would like to ask you to send your packages where there is real need. What will happen in Korea or another theater of war? Those who risk their lives or the natives who have barely saved their skins are needier than we for whom it is merely a satisfaction of comforts. We are deeply grateful to you for your help during the worst times and will always remain so. But we are not living in want anymore. . . .

[Fritz]

The resurgence of Germany was always on my father's mind. He feared the potential consequences his whole life. When Germany was finally reunified in 1990, he was mistrustful. While my father's letters to Fritz did not survive, I am sure that there was much discussion of the politics of Germany, to which Fritz responded.

Frankfurt/Main, November 10, 1951

Dear Jim,

. . . My practice has grown. . . . I represent a cosmetics company (Mouson) in their trademark and competitive cases. I hope other companies will follow, once word gets around. . . . In order to get better known I have taken up my scientific work again. . . .

More is written about Neo-Nazism than is warranted, in my opinion. When a worker who enjoyed social advantages during the Hitler regime, and which he does not enjoy anymore due to our poverty or—as he thinks, due to the rule of capitalism—says that things were better under Hitler, he does not want to identify with the idea of Nazism. He only wants what was "good under the National Socialists." . . . Here may lie a danger, but I cannot imagine that it would lead to a new Hitlerism with racial frenzy, imperialism, and all the other madness and crime. Besides, the federal government is keeping a watchful eye on these people, and the Allies hold the keys with which they can prevent the spreading of possible causes. . . .

Yours, Fritz

I have no letters from 1952 or 1953, and I doubt there were any. Both Fritz and my father were working very hard to establish careers and both had busy families.

FRITZ WEISPFENNING
Attorney-at-Law
FRANKFURT AM MAIN
Alte Gasse 27/29. Tel. 9 46 20

May 16, 1954

Dear Jim,

I have been silent for so long, it is high time that I reach for the pen again. . . . With great expense we have moved to more representative rooms in a better location. . . .

Our oldest, Fritz, has finished high school and is studying law at the Frankfurt University. So far he has taken just as many classes in philosophy as in jurisprudence, though; at least as far as I can see. He is following in my footsteps by joining [the fraternity] "Austria" as a "Fuchs" (freshman) and is taking fencing lessons.

Walter, our second, still has two years before finishing school. . . . We always have to be after Günter, our youngest. If we don't watch him constantly he does not study and brings home bad report cards from school. . . .

All in all we have to be content. We have enough to live and can only hope that it will continue in this direction. We have to ignore the fact that the political situation is, and probably will remain, uncertain and doubtful. We have to wait and see, and hope, and above all: work.

Hoping that you and your wife and children are well I remain

Yours, Fritz

The final letter was written in the spring of 1955, ten years after the fall of Germany.

FRITZ WEISPFENNING
Attorney-at-Law
Frankfurt am Main
Alte Gasse 27/29 – Tel. 9 46 20

April 14, 1955

Dear Liz, dear Jim,

Many thanks for Jim's letter announcing the birth of your fourth son! Congratulations! . . . I myself am the mother of boys and know how wonderful these little ones are. . . .

When we got Jim's letter I went right away and bought a book with children's songs with music for accompanying piano. I think it is wonderful that you sing with your children in the evening. We think of you very often and pray for God's blessings for you and your children. . . . You are such kind people and we would not want you to have any sorrows. . . .

I would have written much earlier, if we would not have had an automobile accident (we have a Volkswagen) right after we received Jim's letter. It was a miracle that Fritz was unhurt; I suffered a small concussion and bruises. Fritz lost control in a curve, the car overturned and I was thrown from the car. Just before a slope the car stopped, righted itself and Fritz was able to climb out unscathed. I do not even want to think what would have happened if he would have gotten hurt. . . .

You are right; the political world situation does not look rosy. We can only hope that peace will prevail, now and in the future. No woman and mother wants war, ever.

All the best to you and your dear children,

Yours, Ruth and Fritz Weispfenning and boys

Fritz and Ruth continued their hard work until their deaths in the 1970s. The Weispfenning boys all grew up to be successful. Now retired, Fritz Jr.

established a law practice in estate and tax law in Nurnberg, now run by his son. Also retired, Walter became an associate judge in Kassel, where he remains. Günter became a financial analyst, philanthropist, and extreme sport enthusiast. He died suddenly in 2011.

The McKays and Weispfennings met briefly in Europe in 1960, but then lost touch until my meeting with Fritz Jr. and Walter in 2014.

Acknowledgments

This is my first book and would not have been possible without a lot of help. Most important was my father's willingness to sit down with me and share his memories of a painful but meaningful time in his life. Like most other combat veterans, he had never really talked about his experiences before.

On my trip to Europe to explore the places and people my father knew there, I was assisted greatly by a number of individuals: Markus Schmellenkamp, Rolf Wilmark, and Horst Hassel in Plettenberg, Germany; my B&B host Peter Geis in Bad Nauheim, Germany; Dennis and Karin Thalmann in Husseren les Chateaux, France, who provided wonderful hospitality to my whole family and facilitated our spending a day with Lise Pommois, who appears to know everything about American WWII participation in Alsace and Lorraine; Musee Memorial des Combats de la Poche de Colmar in Turkheim, who opened for us on their day off; Pascaline Watier of the Bibliothèque Georges Pompidou in Chalons-en-Champagne, France; Francois Dutroux, who facilitated everything around Vielsalm, Belgium; Odon Jeunejean, Bertrand and Jean Pierre Goosse, Francois Franck and his family, and all the people I met in Vielsalm who were so welcoming and helpful; my B&B hosts Samia and Pietro in Salmchateau; and my B&B host Sophie Alexis and local expat WWII historian Michael Bart in Fanzel, Belgium.

I feel privileged to have met the family of Fritz and Ruth Weispfenning, and thank them for their openness in sharing a painful chapter in their family's history. May the friendship of our families continue into the future.

Two friends and writers, Alan Boye and Ellen Bartlett, helped me navigate the tortured paths leading to a finished book and along with Lynne Lawson gave me helpful feedback on the manuscript. Hertha Forrai, Jutta Scott, and Barbara Hegenbart all were very generous in translating letters written in German.

Finally, I offer my thanks to my family, both immediate and extended, for their interest and encouragement.

Endnotes

1. Aldo H. Bagnulo, *Nothing But Praise—A History of the 1321st Engineer General Service Regiment*, ed. Michael J. Brodhead (Washington, D.C.: Department of the Army, 2010), 36.

2. Extract from the "Stories" page of the website of the Centre de Recherches et d'informations sur la Bataille des Ardennes, Liege, Belgium, http://www.criba.be/fr/stories/detail/the-battle-of-grand-halleux-21---23-december-1944-42-1. Used by permission.

3. *American Experience*, season 14, episode 3: "War Letters," aired November 11, 2001, PBS.

4. Hugh M. Cole, *The Ardennes: Battle of the Bulge* (Washington, D.C.: Office of the Chief of Military History, Department of the Army, 1965), 578–95, http://www.history.army.mil/books/wwii/7-8/7-8_CONT.HTM.

5. The Green Books are available online at http://www.history.army.mil/html/bookshelves/collect/ww2-eto.html.

6. Excerpted from *The 75th Infantry Division in Combat*, a division history published by the US Army in January 1946. From the author's personal collection.

7. *The 75th Infantry Division in Combat*, 4.

8. To watch a wartime film showing the construction of temporary bridges, including the Bailey Bridge, see http://www.liveleak.com/view?i=721_1298657407.

9. *The 75th Infantry Division in Combat*, 19–20.

10. 275th Battalion Monthly Action Report for February, March 1, 1945. Records of the 75th Infantry Division, National Archives, College Park, Maryland.

11. *The 75th Infantry Division in Combat* (Washington, D.C.: US Department of the Army, 1945), 18. Author's personal collection.

12. Monthly Action Report for March 1945. Records of the 275th Engineer Combat Battalion, 75th Infantry Division, National Archives, College Park, Maryland.

13. Charles B. MacDonald, *US Army in World War II, ETO, The Last Offensive* (Washington, D.C.: US Department of the Army, 1973), 18.

14. Monthly Action Report for March 1945.

15. Summary of Activities of the 275th Engineer Combat Battalion from 1 April to 30 April, 1945. Records of the 75th Infantry Division, National Archives, College Park, Maryland.

16. US Army, *Pictorial History of the 75th Infantry Division, 1944–1945 Campaigns* (Baton Rouge, La.: Army & Navy Publishing Co., 1946), 34.

17. Interview with the author, recorded 2011.

18. Summary of Activities of the 275th Engineer Combat Battalion from 1 May to 31 May 1945. US Army Records of the 75th Infantry Division, National Archives, College Park, Maryland.

19. See Seymour Taffett, *Binding Up the Wounds: The Life Story of a WWII Frontline Battalion Surgeon* (Overland Park, Kans.: Leathers Publishing, 2006).

20. Allen J. Matusow, *Farm Policies and Politics in the Truman Years* (Cambridge, Mass.: Harvard University Press, 1967), 18.

21. Paul Addison, *Now the War is Over: A Social History of Britain, 1945–1951* (London: BBC/Cape, 1985), [page number].

22. *Protocol of Proceedings of the Potsdam Conference (Berlin, 1 August 1945)* (The Centre Virtuel de la Connaissance sur l'Europe [CVCE], 2004–14),

5, http://www.cvce.eu/en/obj/protocol_of_proceedings_of_the_potsdam_conference_berlin_1_august_1945-en-a602127f-c124-4053-8db6-cf62a-b16846a.html.

23. A full treatment of the trials can be found in Jack Gieck, *Lichfield (The US Army on Trial)* (Akron, Ohio: The University of Akron Press, 1997).

CPSIA information can be obtained at www.ICGtesting.com
Printed in the USA
BVOW02s0928230715

409369BV00002B/3/P

9 781634 136242